NORAGAMI
STRAY GOD

ADACHITOKA

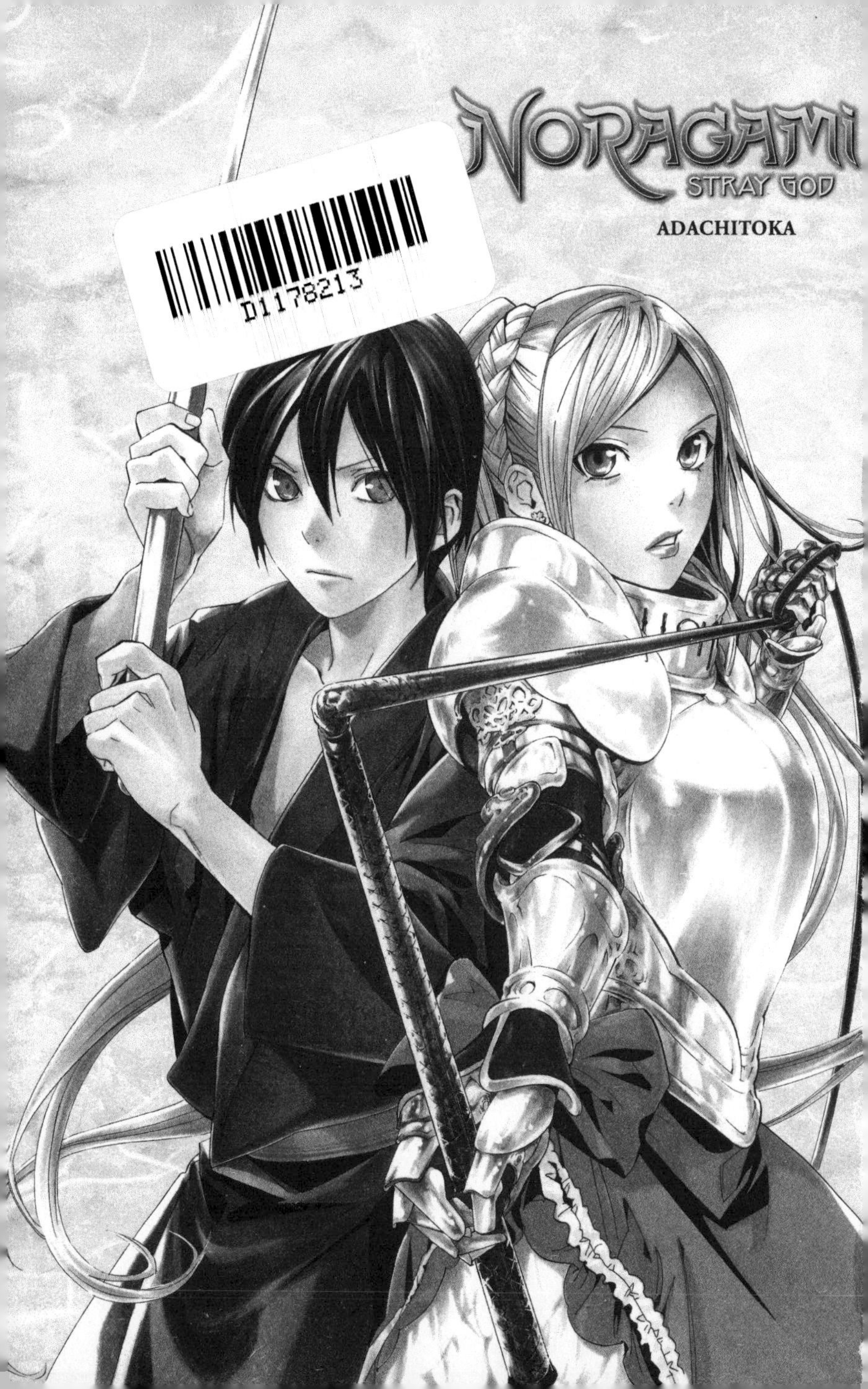

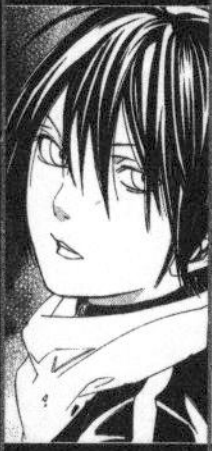

YATO

A minor deity who always wears a sweatsuit.

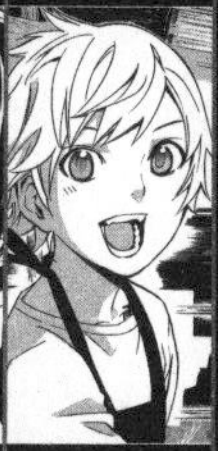

YUKINÉ

Yato's shinki who turns into swords.

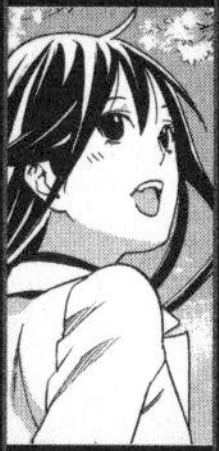

HIYORI IKI

A high school student who has become half ayakashi.

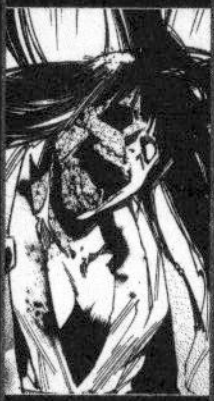

IZANAMI

The mother of the gods and the queen of Yomi.

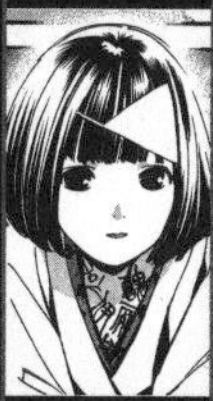

STRAY

A shinki who serves an unspecified number of deities.

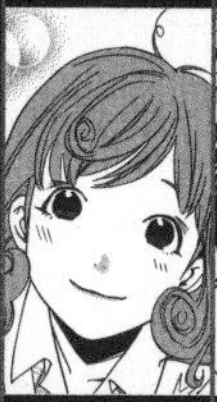

KOFUKU

A goddess of poverty who calls herself Ebisu, after the god of fortune.

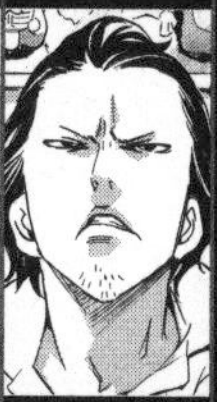

DAIKOKU

Kofuku's shinki who summons storms.

characters

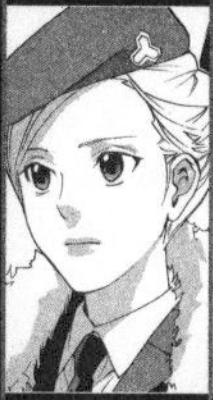

BISHAMONTEN

A powerful warrior god, one of the Seven Gods of Fortune.

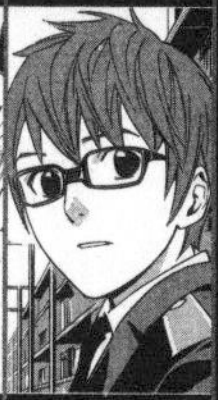

KAZUMA

A navigational shinki who serves as guide to Bishamon.

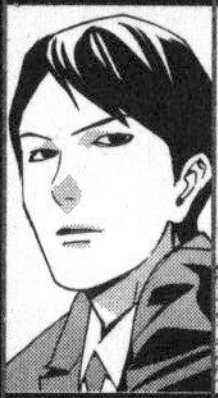

EBISU

A no-nonsense business-god, one of the Seven Gods of Fortune.

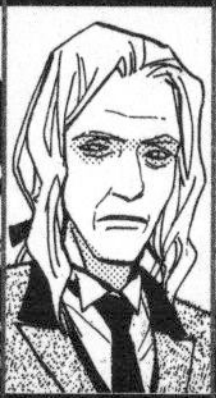

IWAMI

Ebisu's shinki and guide.

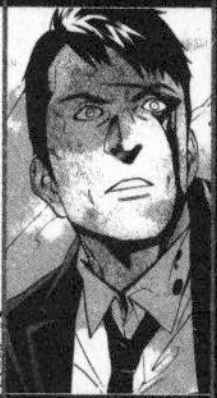

KUNIMI

Ebisu's shinki who enhances his motor skills.

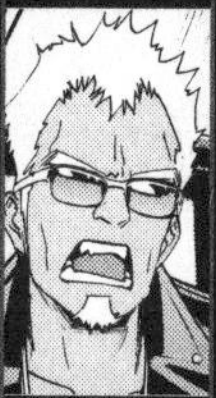

ÔKUNINUSHI (DAIKOKUTEN)

Number one of the Seven Gods of Fortune.

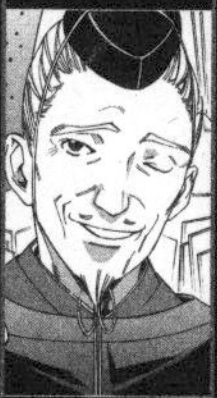

TENJIN

The god of learning, Sugawara no Michizane.

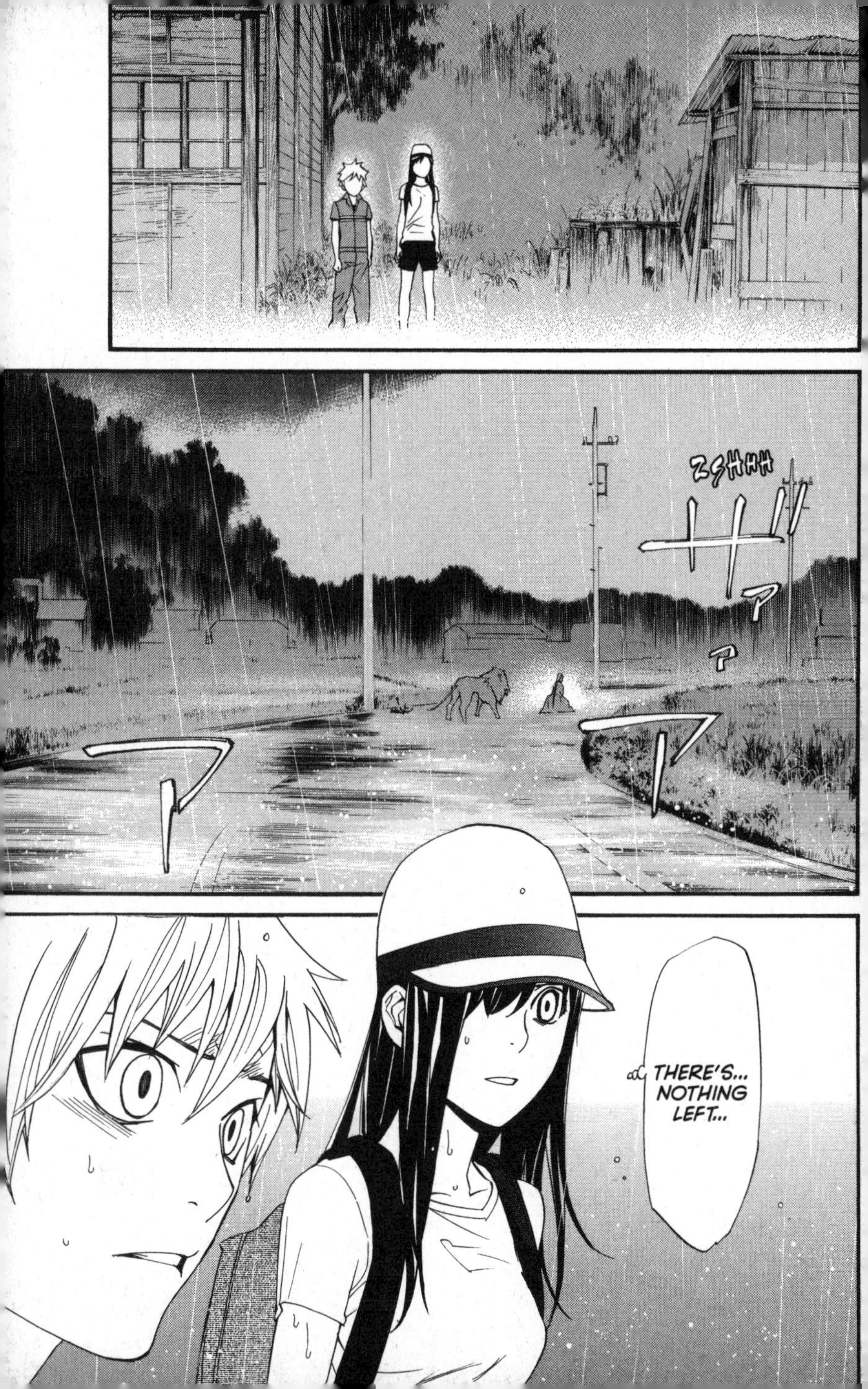
ZSHHH
THERE'S... NOTHING LEFT...

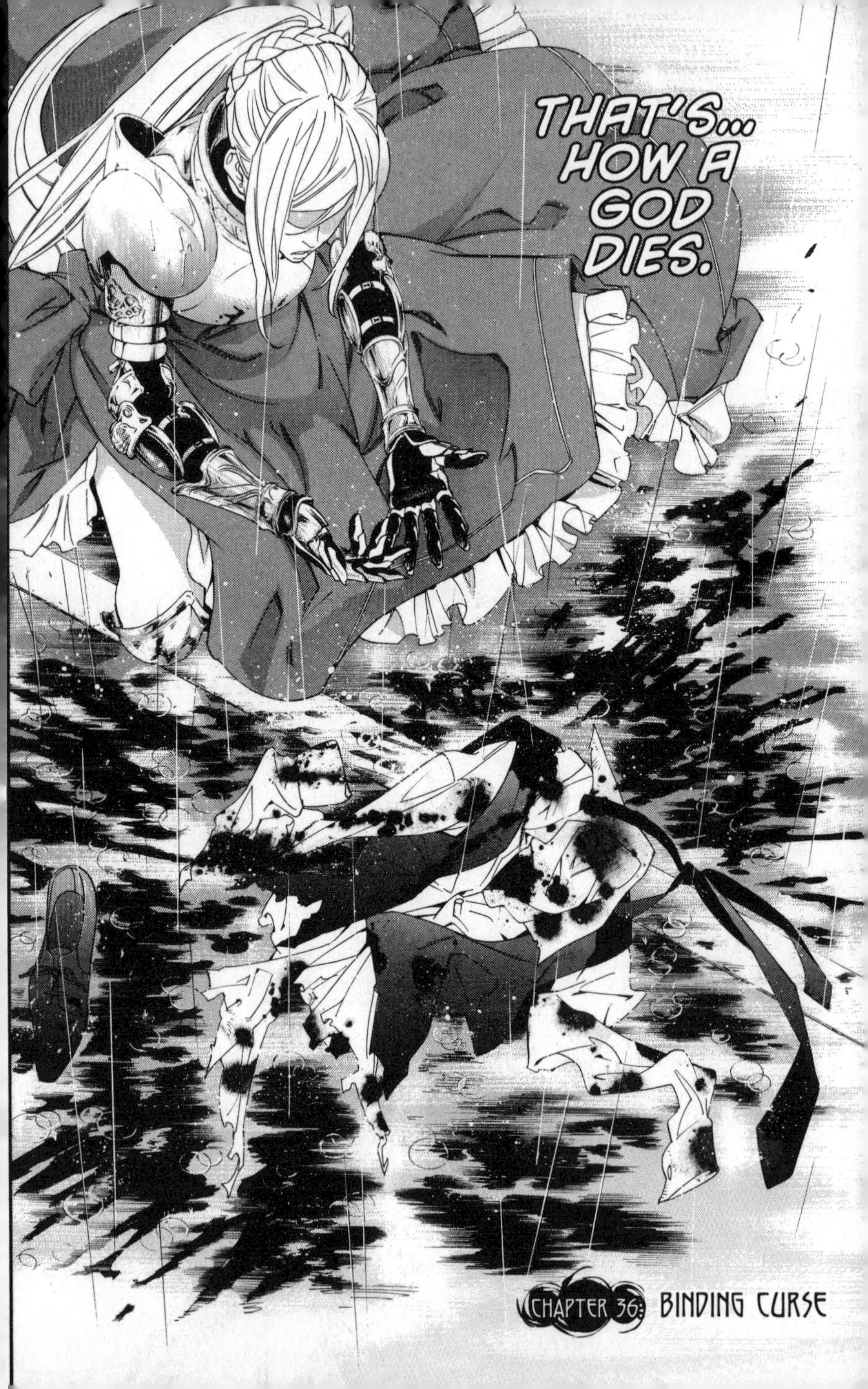
THAT'S... HOW A GOD DIES.
CHAPTER 36: BINDING CURSE

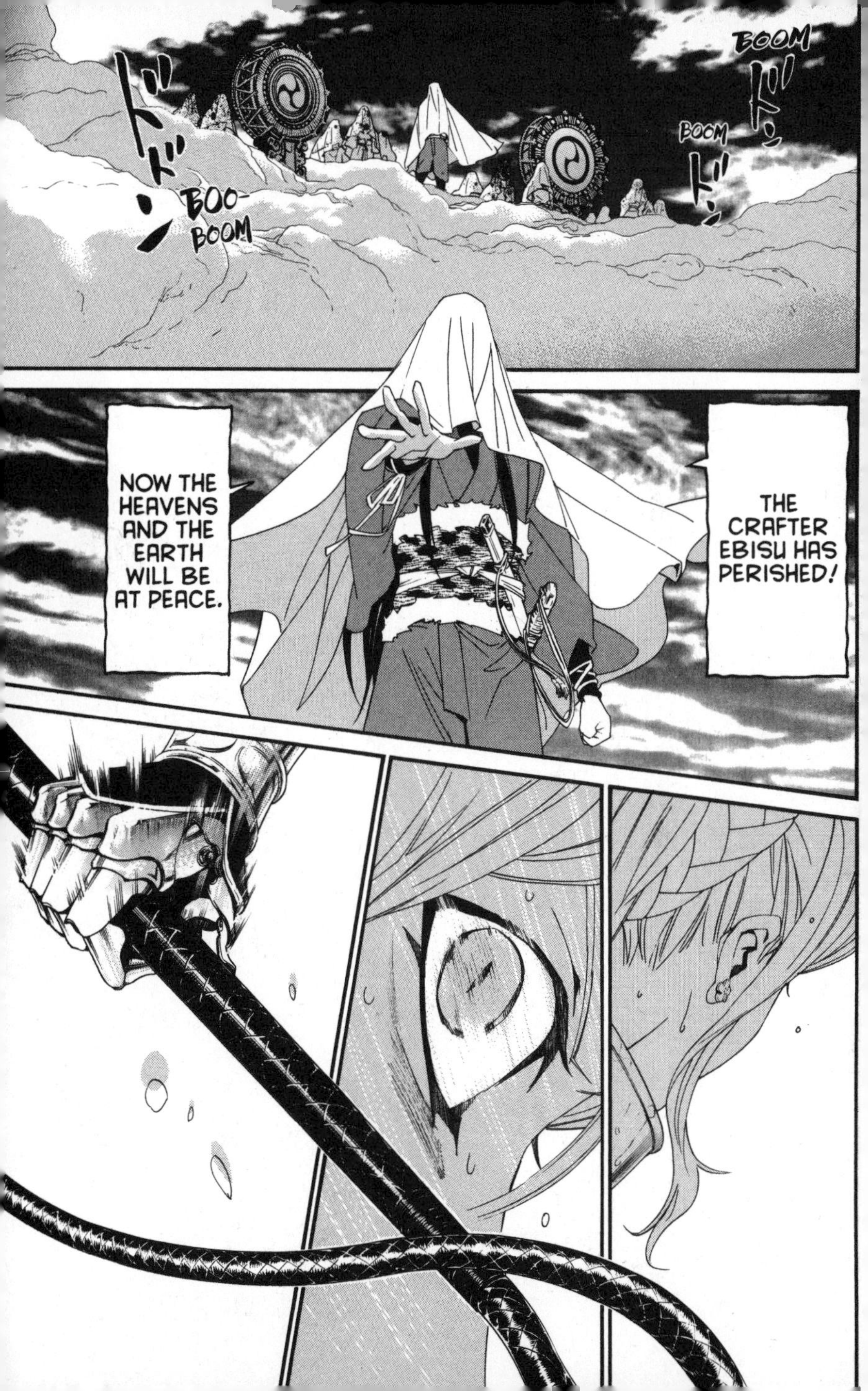
BOOM
BOOM
BOO-BOOM
THE CRAFTER EBISU HAS PERISHED!
NOW THE HEAVENS AND THE EARTH WILL BE AT PEACE.

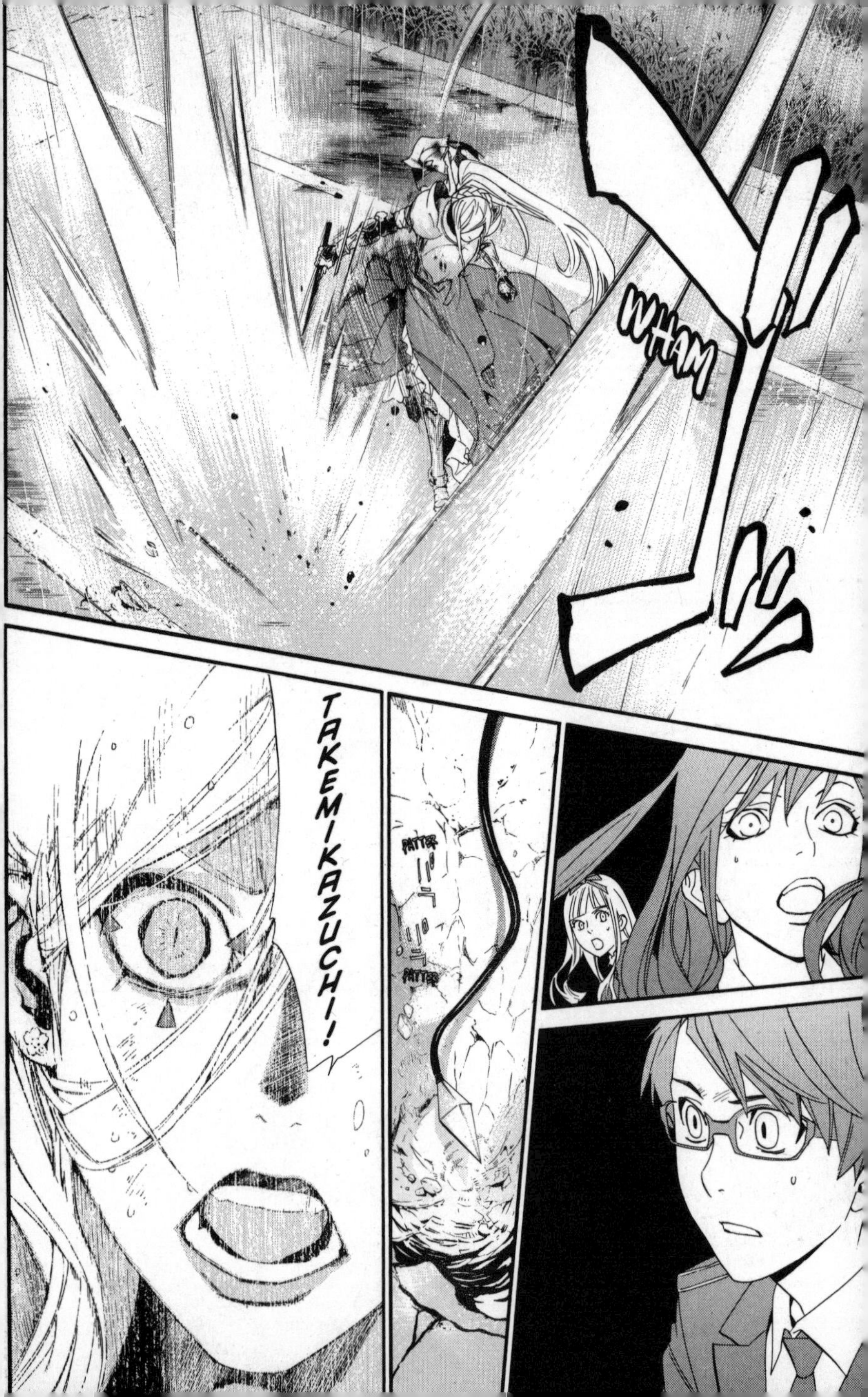
WHAM
PATTER
PATTER
TAKEMIKAZUCHI!!

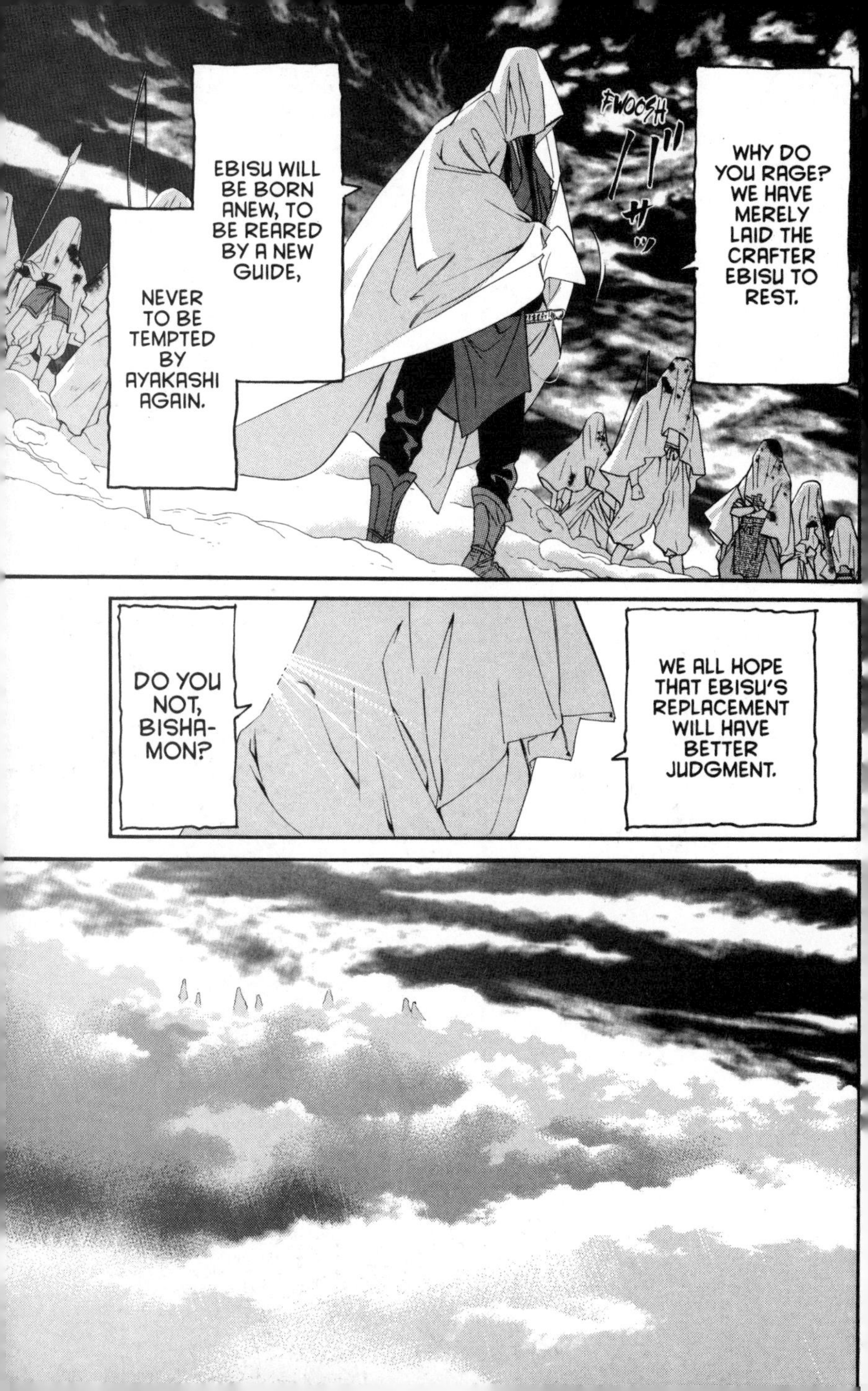
FWOOSH
WHY DO YOU RAGE? WE HAVE MERELY LAID THE CRAFTER EBISU TO REST.
EBISU WILL BE BORN ANEW, TO BE REARED BY A NEW GUIDE,
NEVER TO BE TEMPTED BY AYAKASHI AGAIN.
WE ALL HOPE THAT EBISU'S REPLACEMENT WILL HAVE BETTER JUDGMENT.
DO YOU NOT, BISHA-MON?

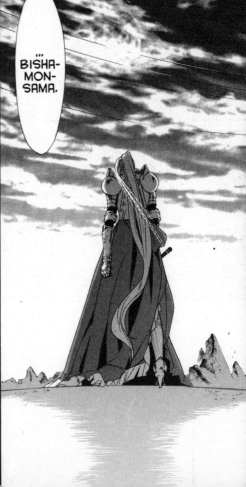

...BISHA-MON-SAMA.

...YOU.

EBISU TOLD ME...

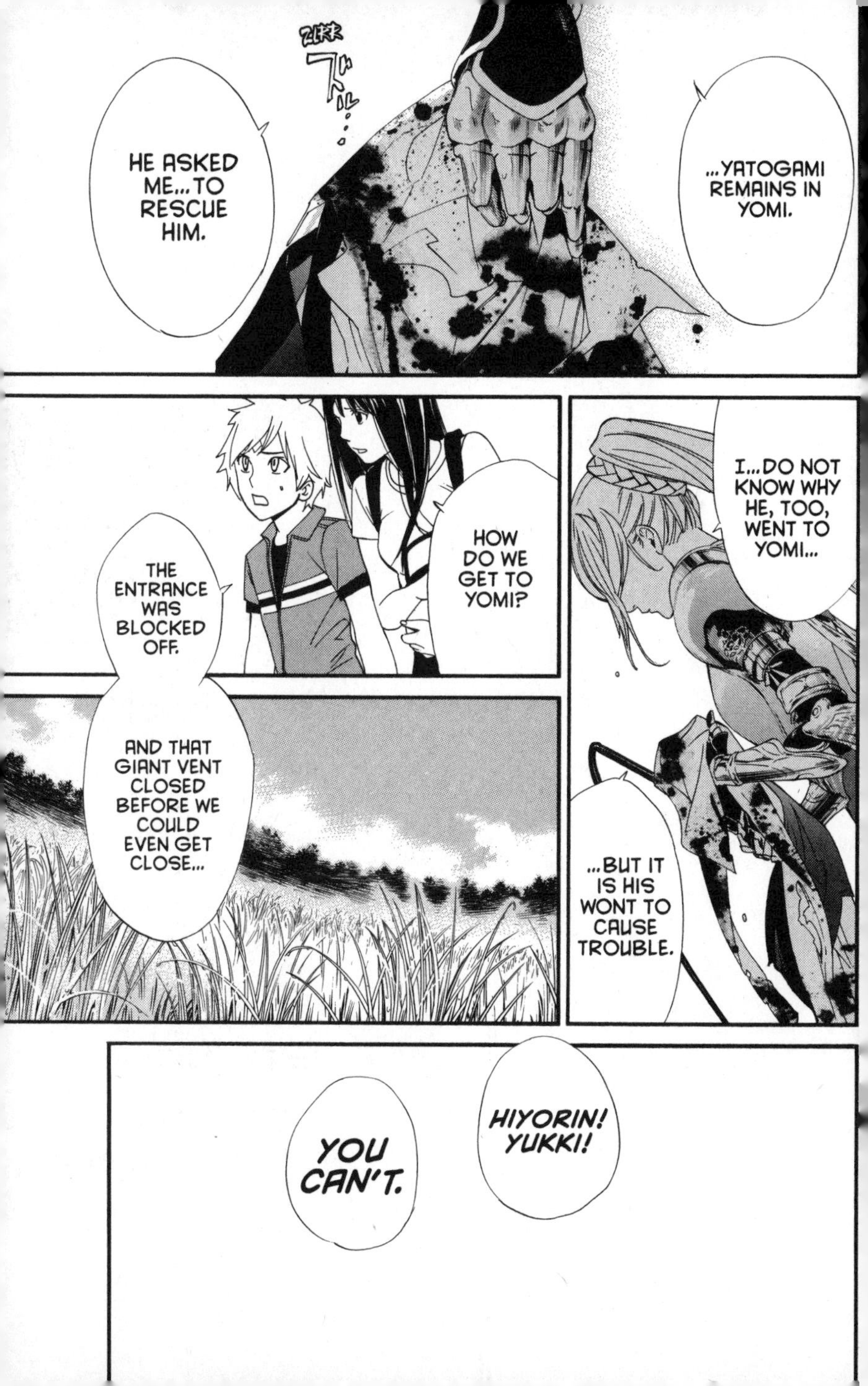
...YATOGAMI REMAINS IN YOMI.
HE ASKED ME...TO RESCUE HIM.
I...DO NOT KNOW WHY HE, TOO, WENT TO YOMI...
...BUT IT IS HIS WONT TO CAUSE TROUBLE.
HOW DO WE GET TO YOMI?
THE ENTRANCE WAS BLOCKED OFF.
AND THAT GIANT VENT CLOSED BEFORE WE COULD EVEN GET CLOSE...
HIYORIN! YUKKI!
YOU CAN'T.

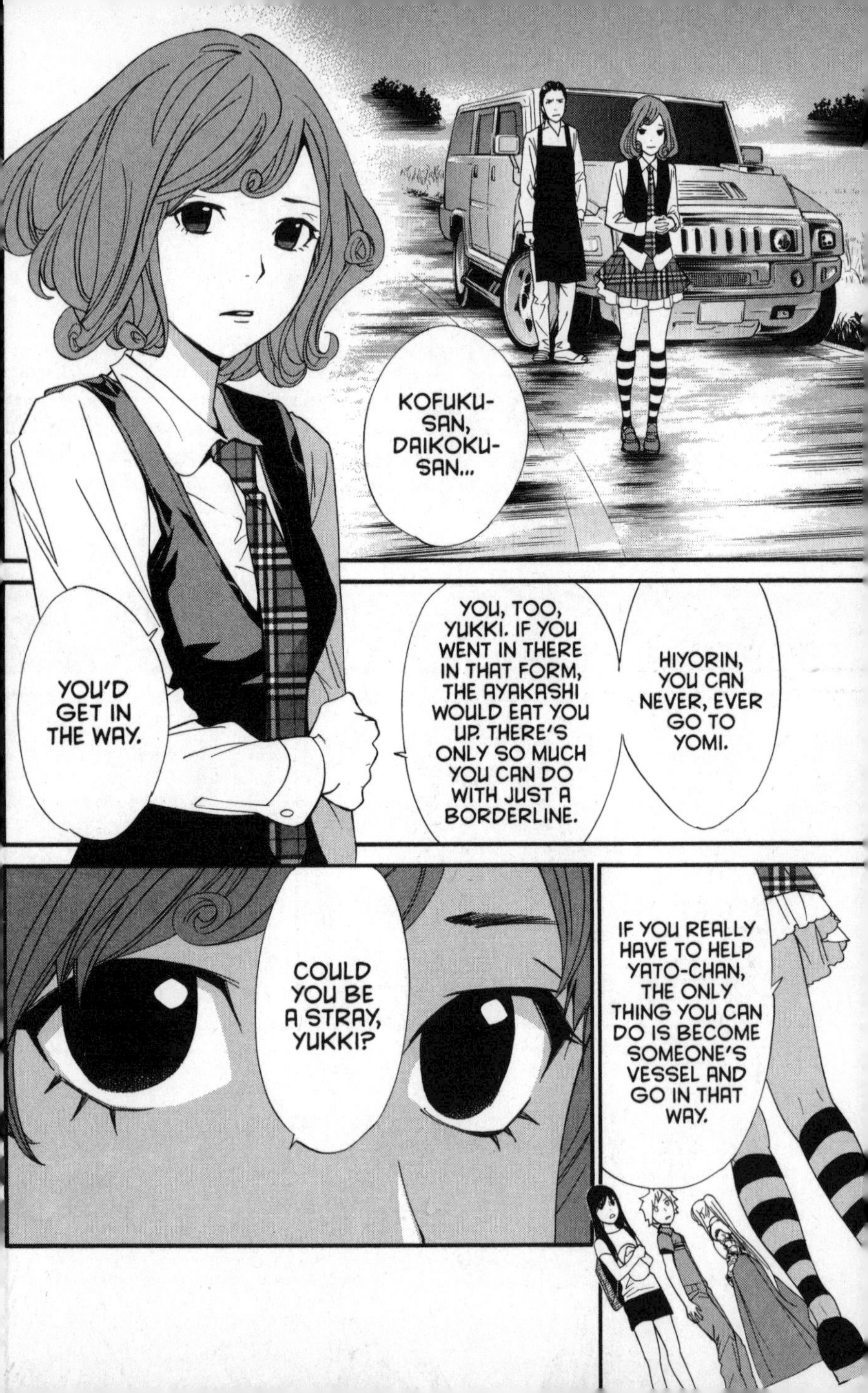
KOFUKU-SAN, DAIKOKU-SAN...
HIYORIN, YOU CAN NEVER, EVER GO TO YOMI.
YOU, TOO, YUKKI. IF YOU WENT IN THERE IN THAT FORM, THE AYAKASHI WOULD EAT YOU UP. THERE'S ONLY SO MUCH YOU CAN DO WITH JUST A BORDERLINE.
YOU'D GET IN THE WAY.
IF YOU REALLY HAVE TO HELP YATO-CHAN, THE ONLY THING YOU CAN DO IS BECOME SOMEONE'S VESSEL AND GO IN THAT WAY.
COULD YOU BE A STRAY, YUKKI?

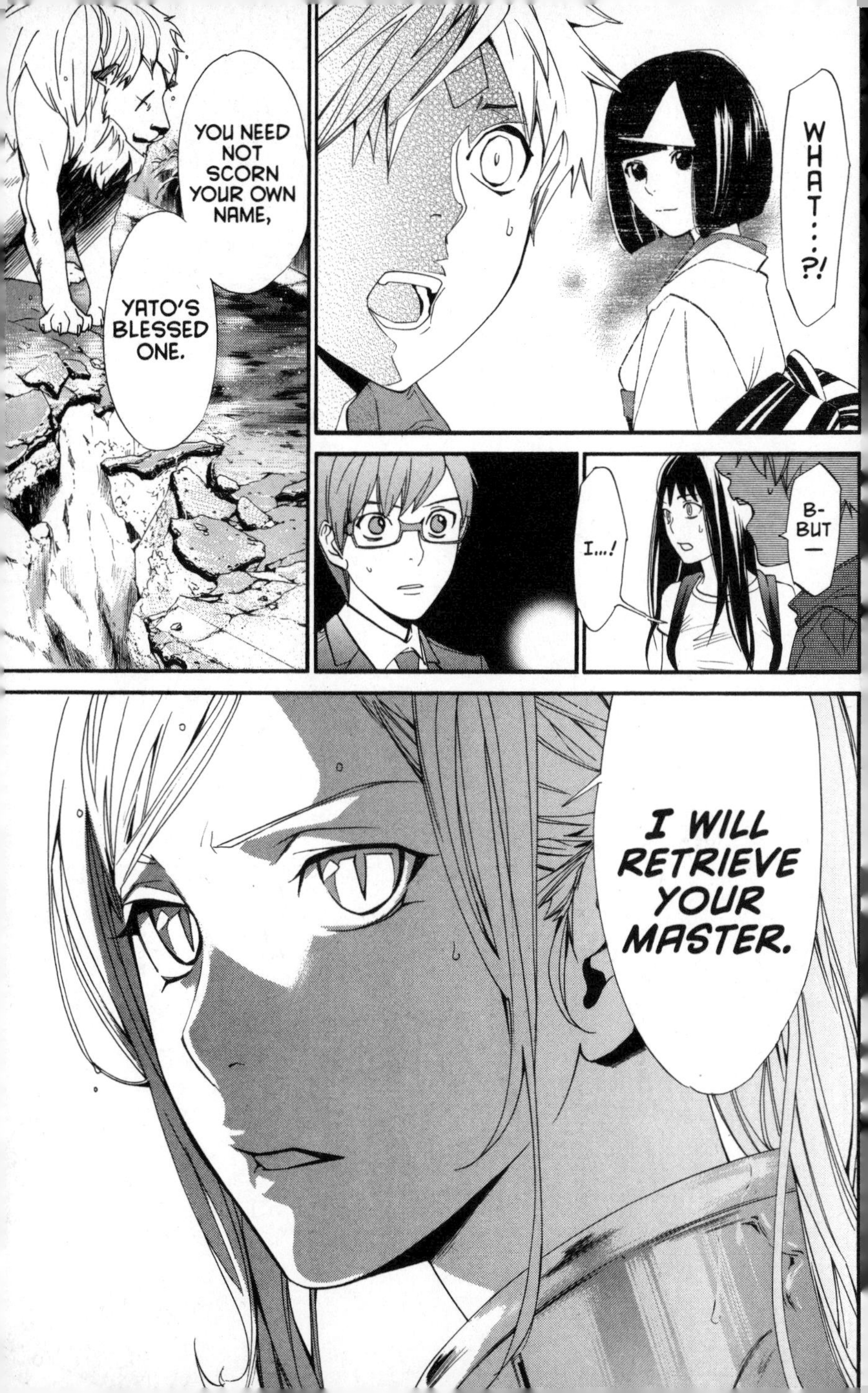
WHAT...?!
B-BUT —
I...!
YOU NEED NOT SCORN YOUR OWN NAME,
YATO'S BLESSED ONE.
I WILL RETRIEVE YOUR MASTER.

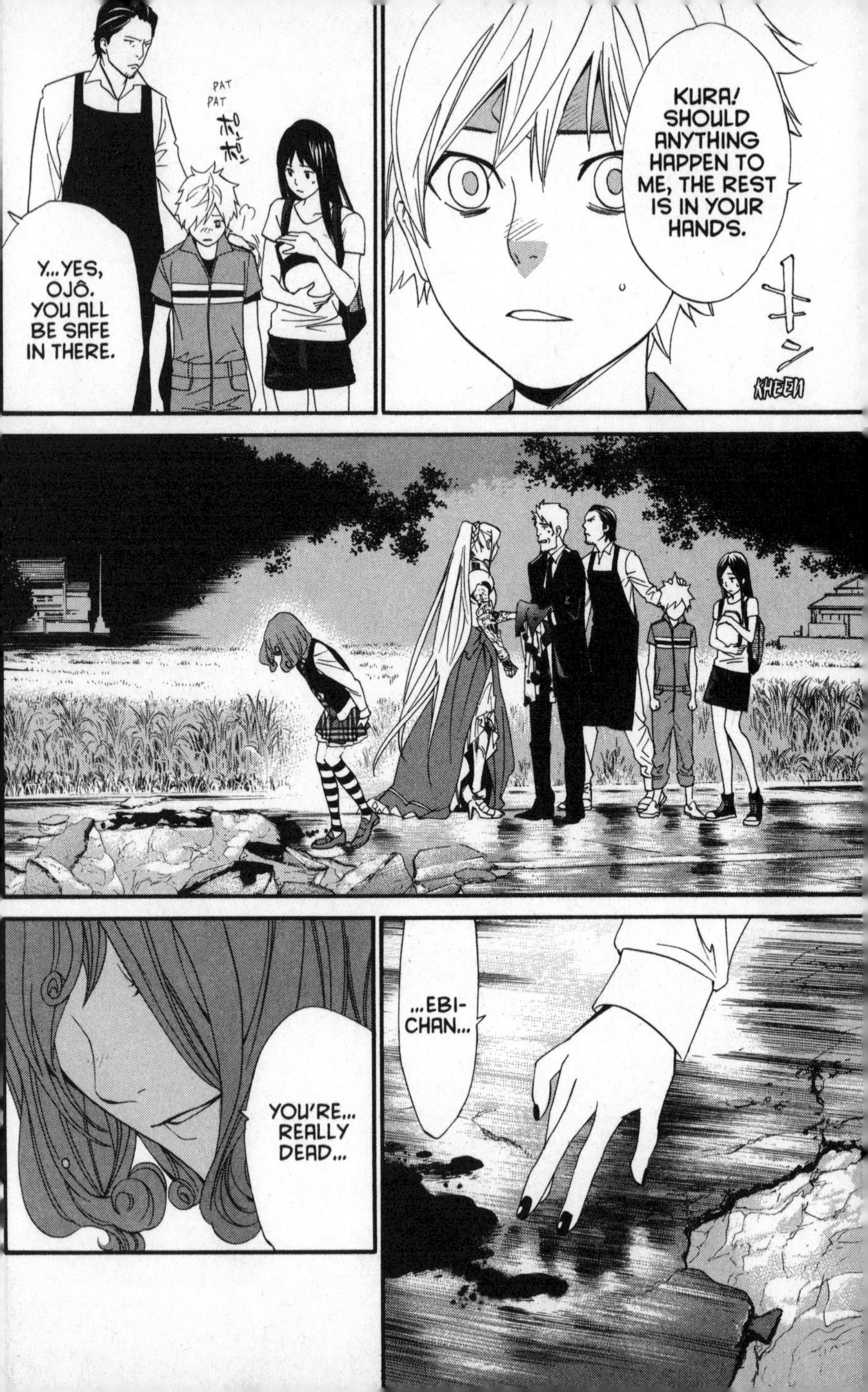
KURA! SHOULD ANYTHING HAPPEN TO ME, THE REST IS IN YOUR HANDS.
KHEEN
PAT PAT
Y...YES, OJÔ. YOU ALL BE SAFE IN THERE.
...EBI-CHAN...
YOU'RE... REALLY DEAD...

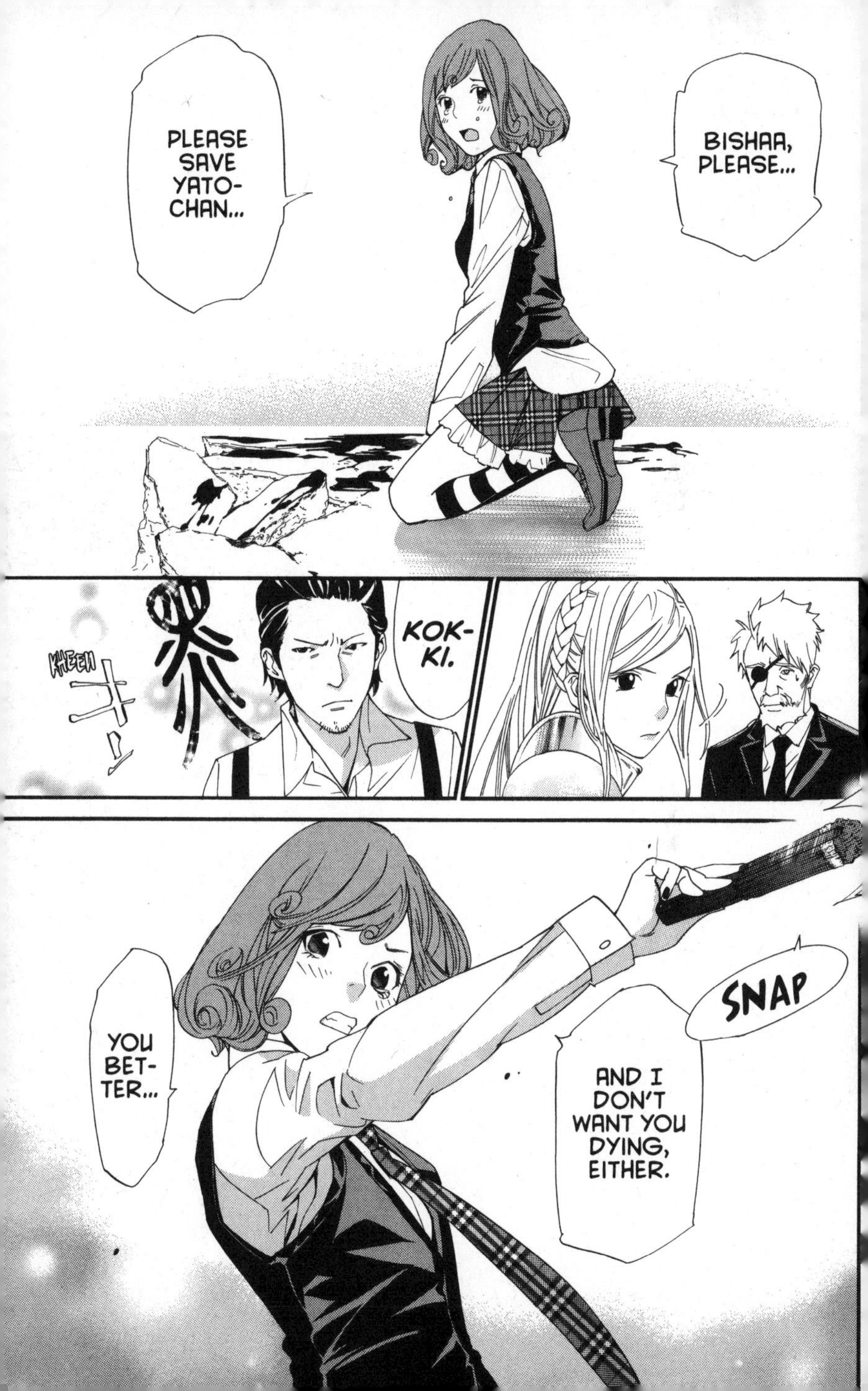
BISHAA, PLEASE...
PLEASE SAVE YATO-CHAN...
KOK-KI.
KHEEN
SNAP
AND I DON'T WANT YOU DYING, EITHER.
YOU BET-TER...

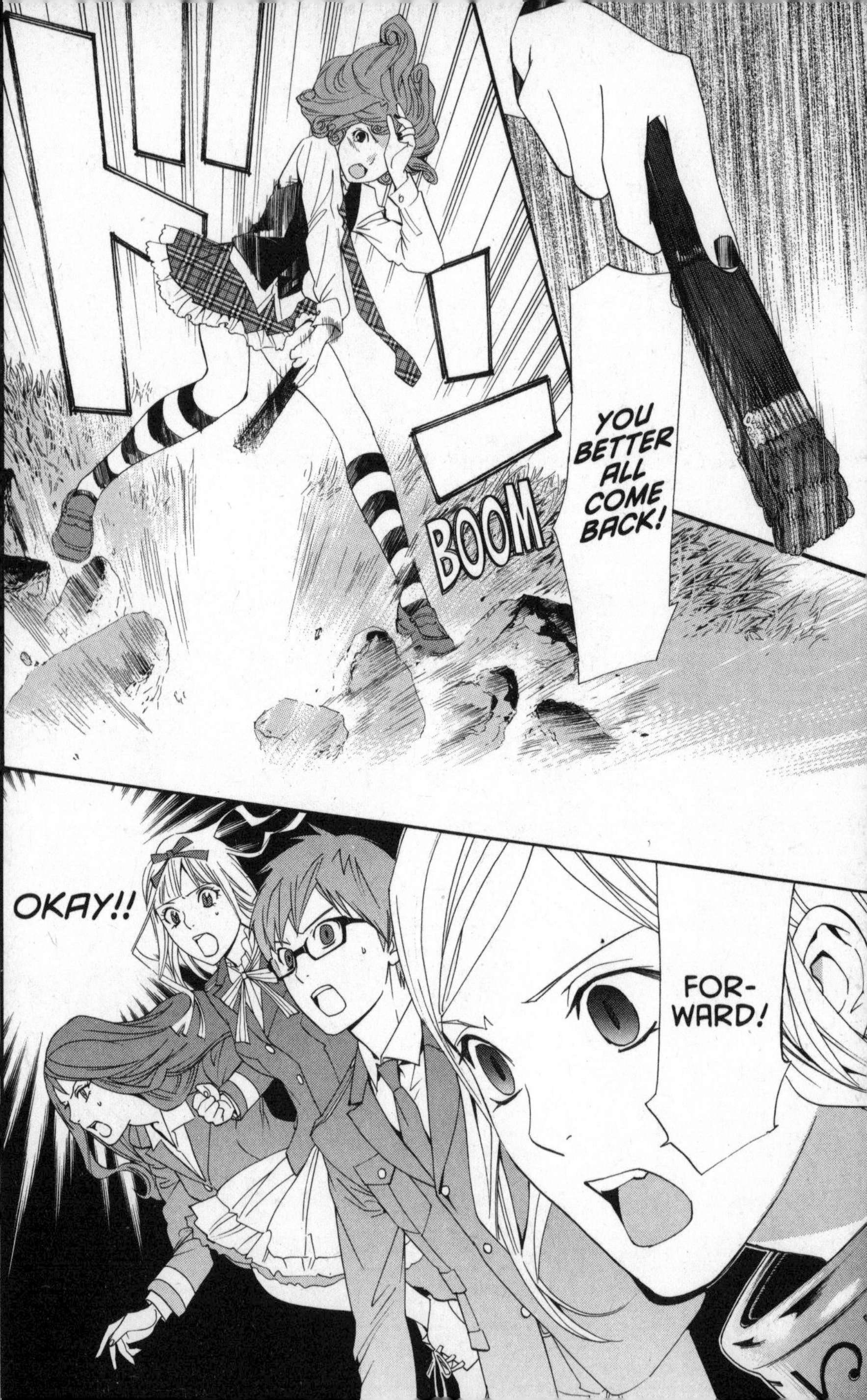
YOU BETTER ALL COME BACK!
BOOM
FOR-WARD!
OKAY!!

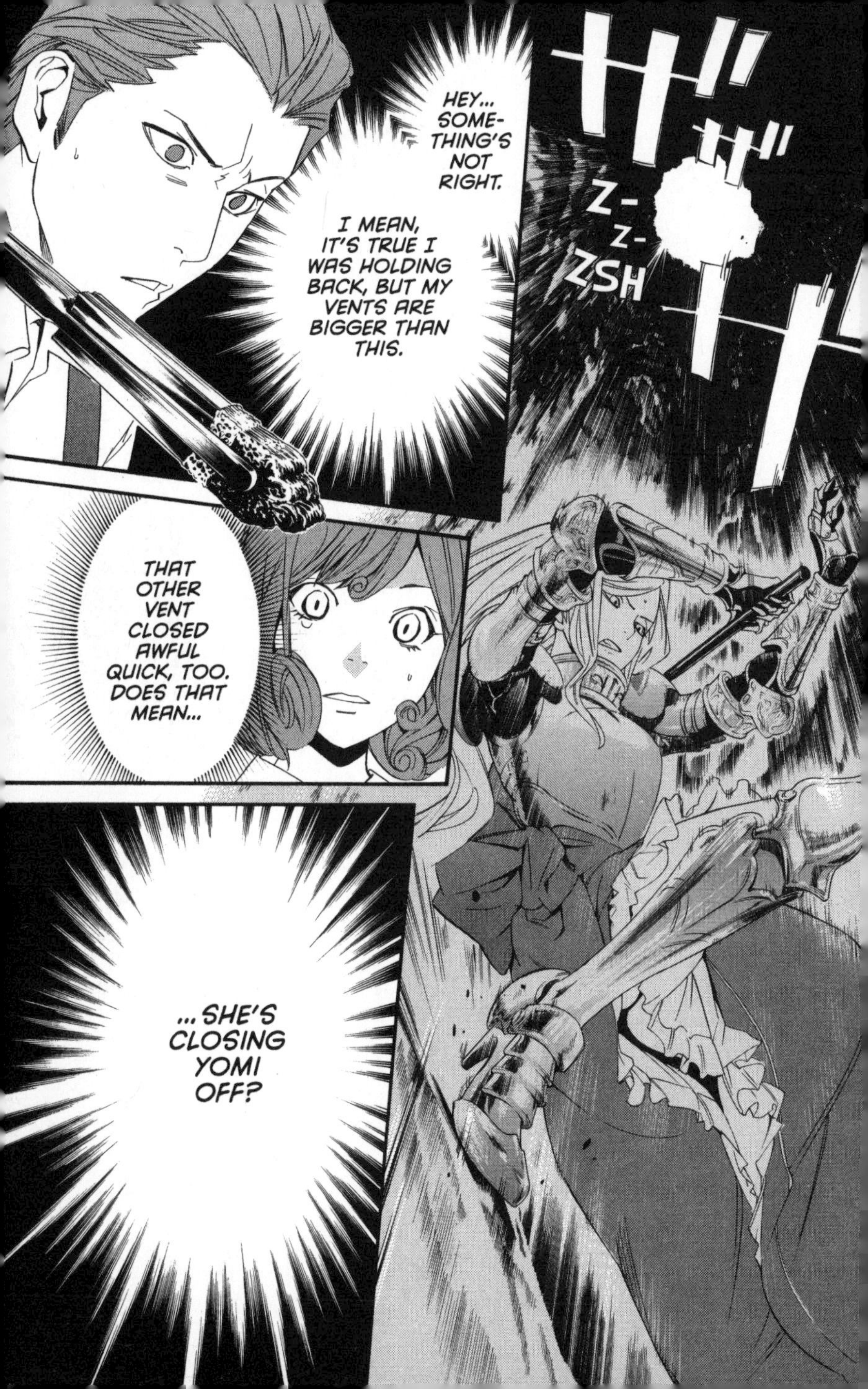
Z-Z-ZSH
HEY... SOMETHING'S NOT RIGHT.
I MEAN, IT'S TRUE I WAS HOLDING BACK, BUT MY VENTS ARE BIGGER THAN THIS.
THAT OTHER VENT CLOSED AWFUL QUICK, TOO. DOES THAT MEAN...
...SHE'S CLOSING YOMI OFF?

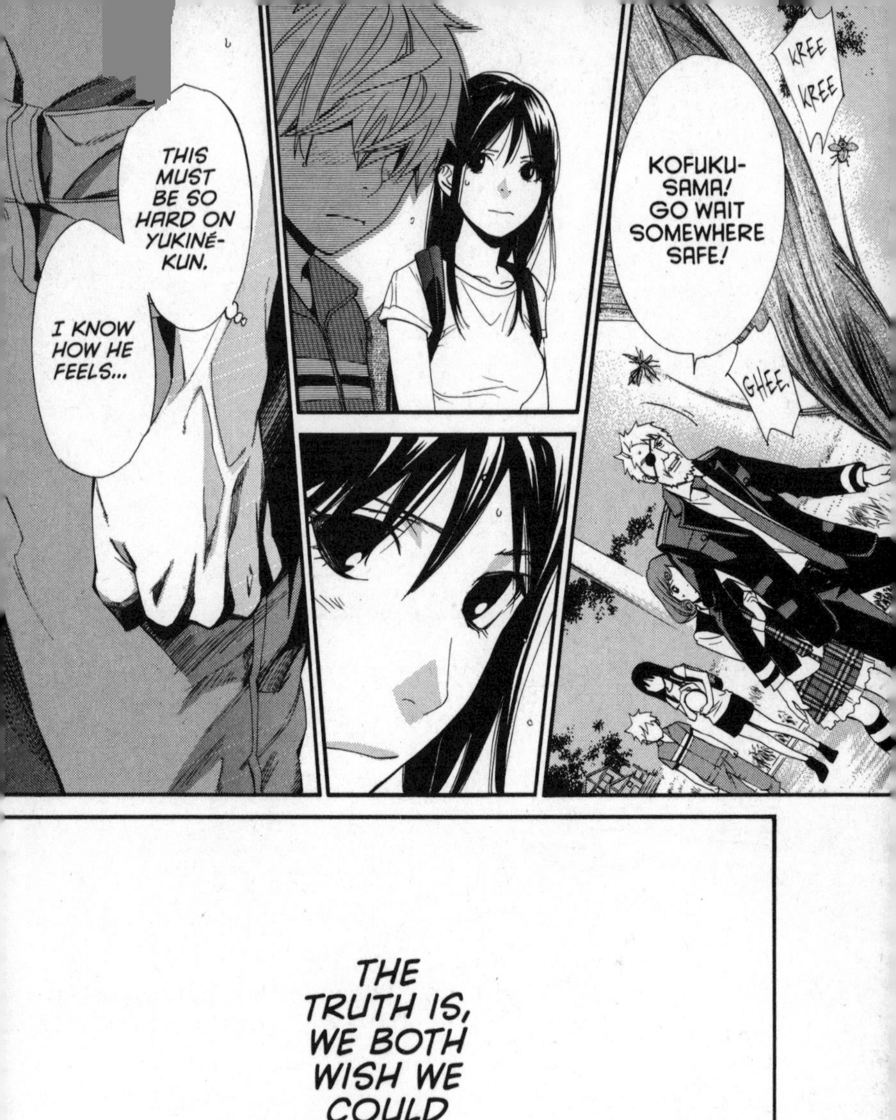
KREE KREE
KOFUKU-SAMA! GO WAIT SOMEWHERE SAFE!
GHEE.
THIS MUST BE SO HARD ON YUKINÉ-KUN.
I KNOW HOW HE FEELS...
THE TRUTH IS, WE BOTH WISH WE COULD HELP.

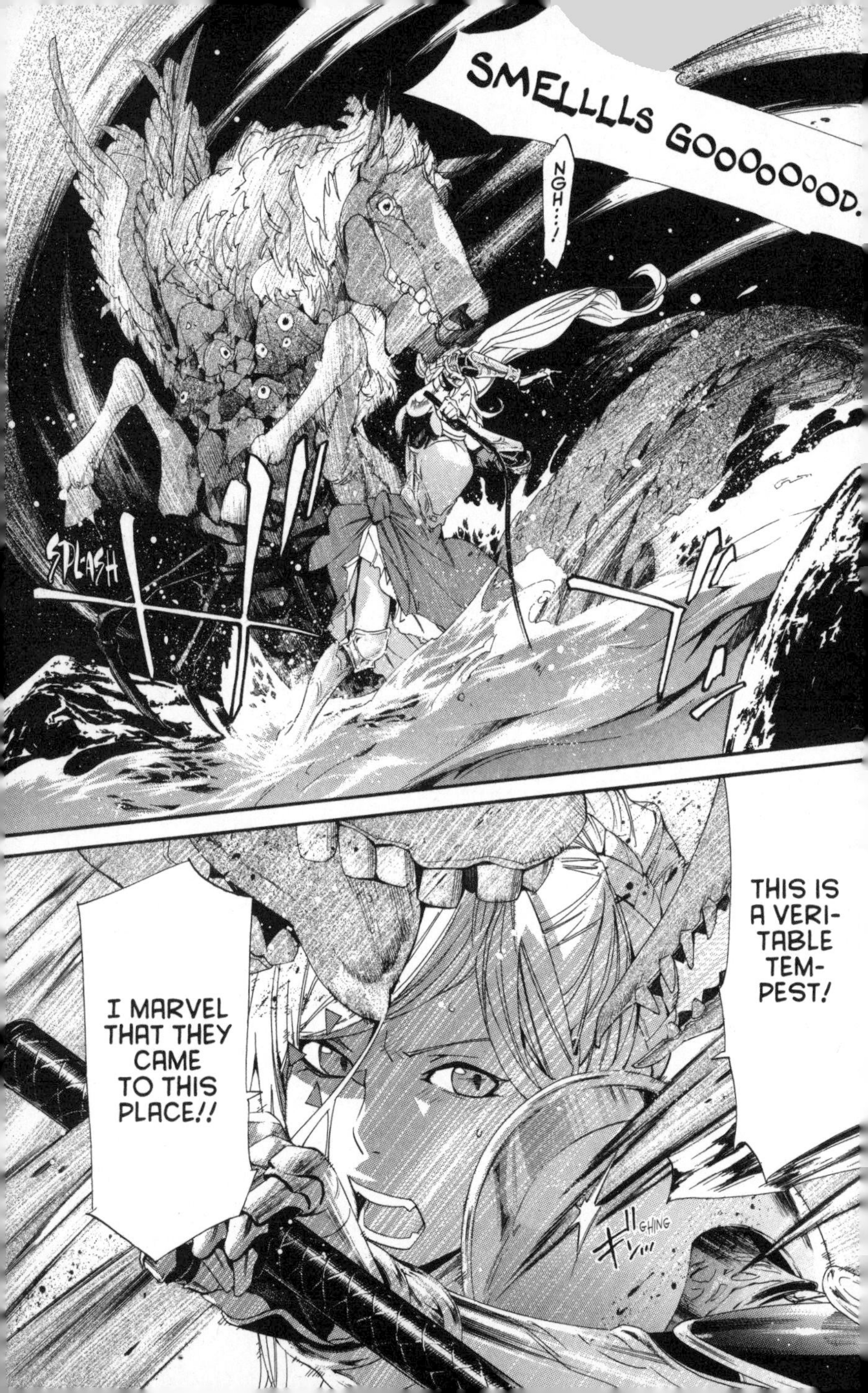
SMELLLLS GOOOOOOOD.
NGH...!
SPLASH
THIS IS A VERITABLE TEMPEST!
I MARVEL THAT THEY CAME TO THIS PLACE!!
GHING

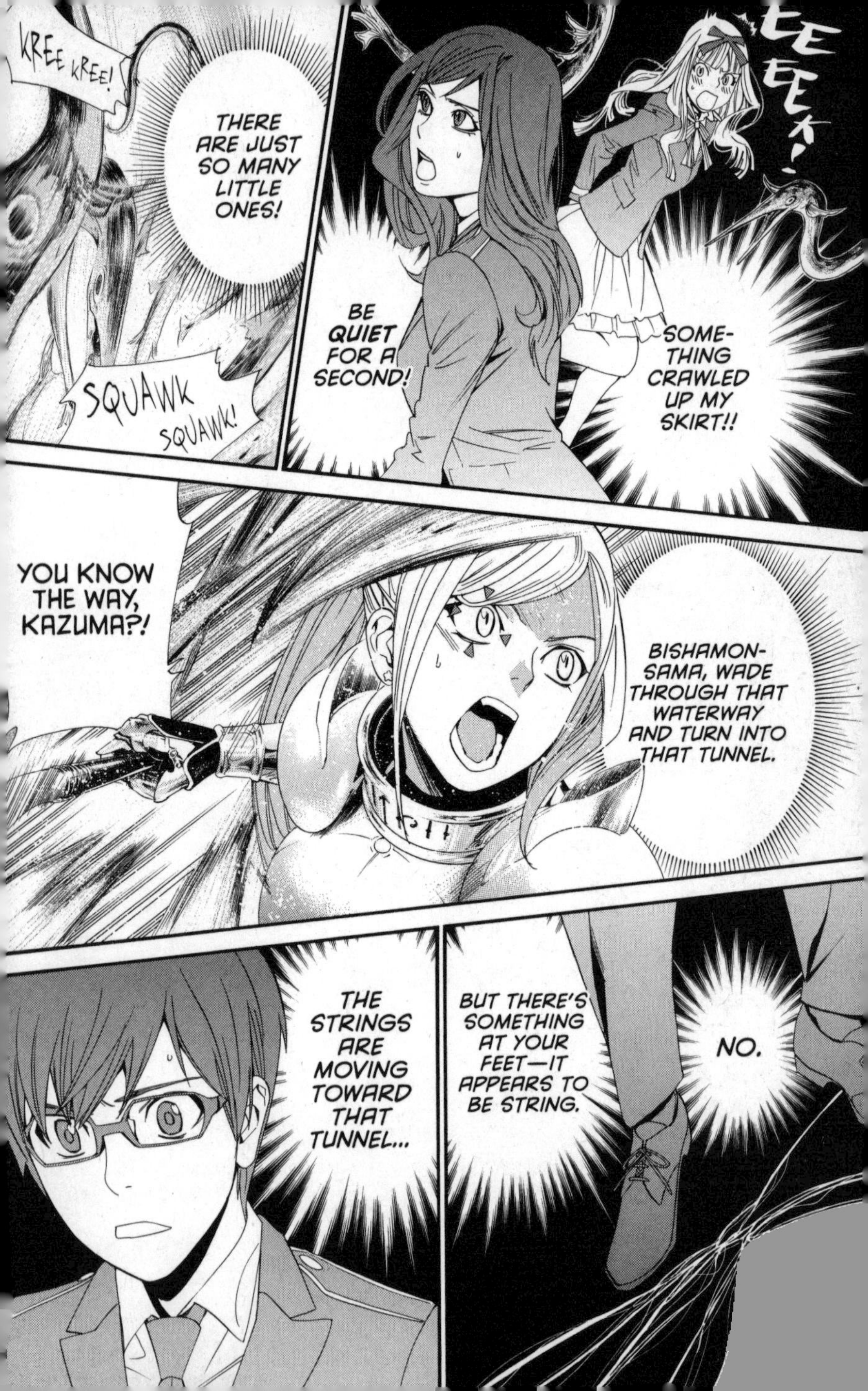
EEEEK!
SOMETHING CRAWLED UP MY SKIRT!!
BE QUIET FOR A SECOND!
KREE KREE!
THERE ARE JUST SO MANY LITTLE ONES!
SQUAWK SQUAWK!
BISHAMON-SAMA, WADE THROUGH THAT WATERWAY AND TURN INTO THAT TUNNEL.
YOU KNOW THE WAY, KAZUMA?!
NO.
BUT THERE'S SOMETHING AT YOUR FEET—IT APPEARS TO BE STRING.
THE STRINGS ARE MOVING TOWARD THAT TUNNEL...

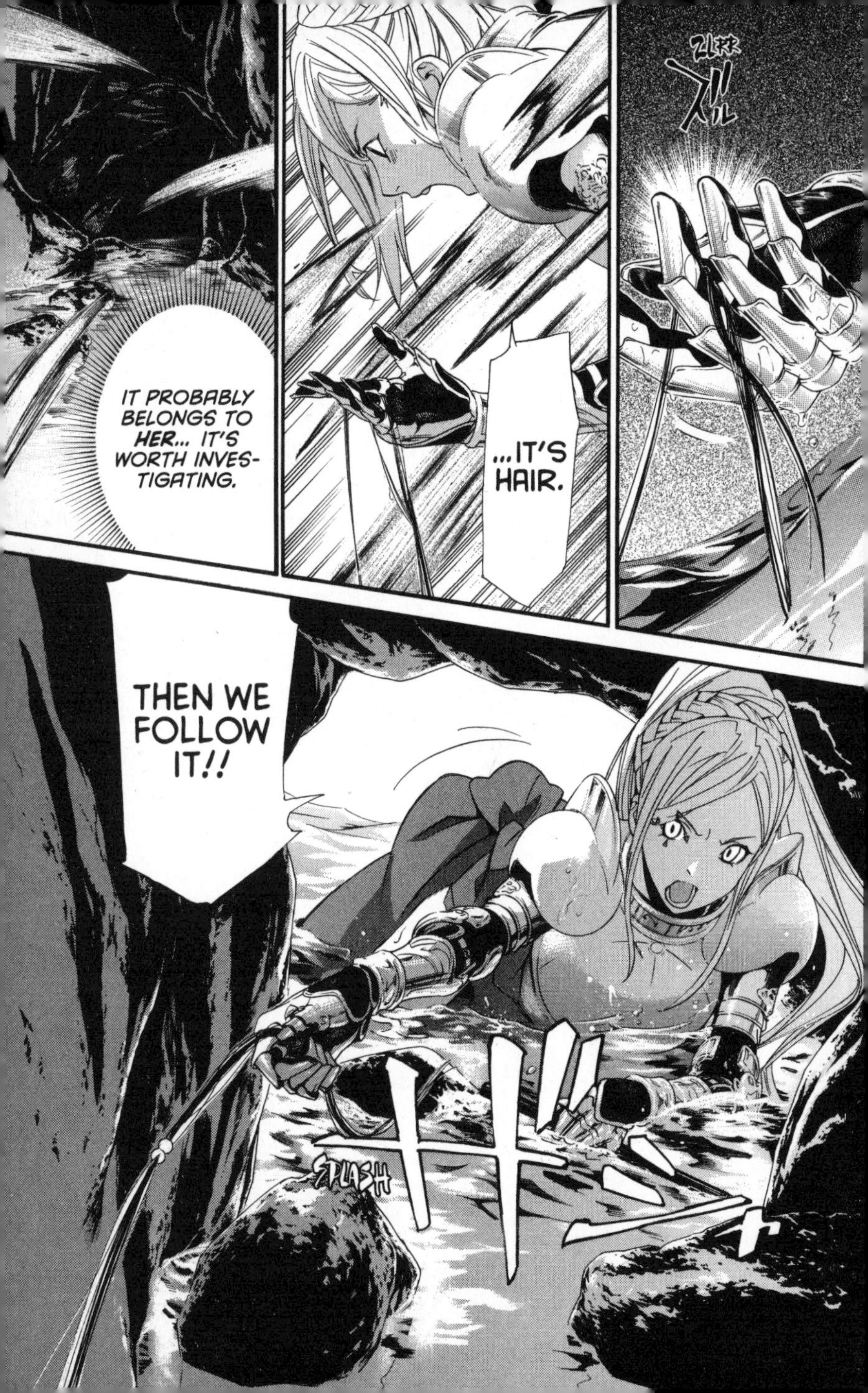
...IT'S HAIR.
IT PROBABLY BELONGS TO HER... IT'S WORTH INVES-TIGATING.
THEN WE FOLLOW IT!!
SPLASH

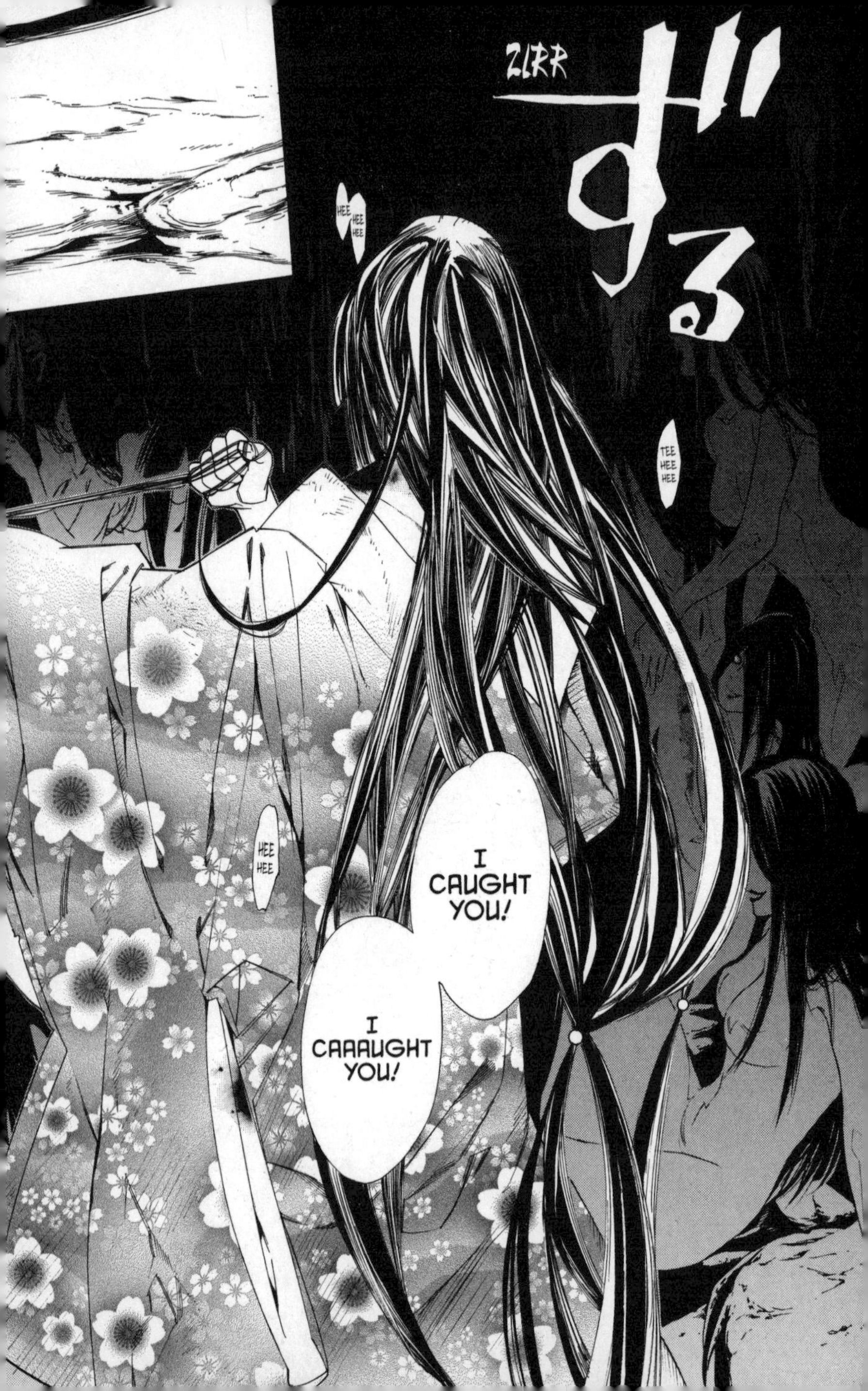
ZLRR
ずる
HEE HEE HEE
TEE HEE HEE
I CAUGHT YOU!
HEE HEE
I CAAAUGHT YOU!

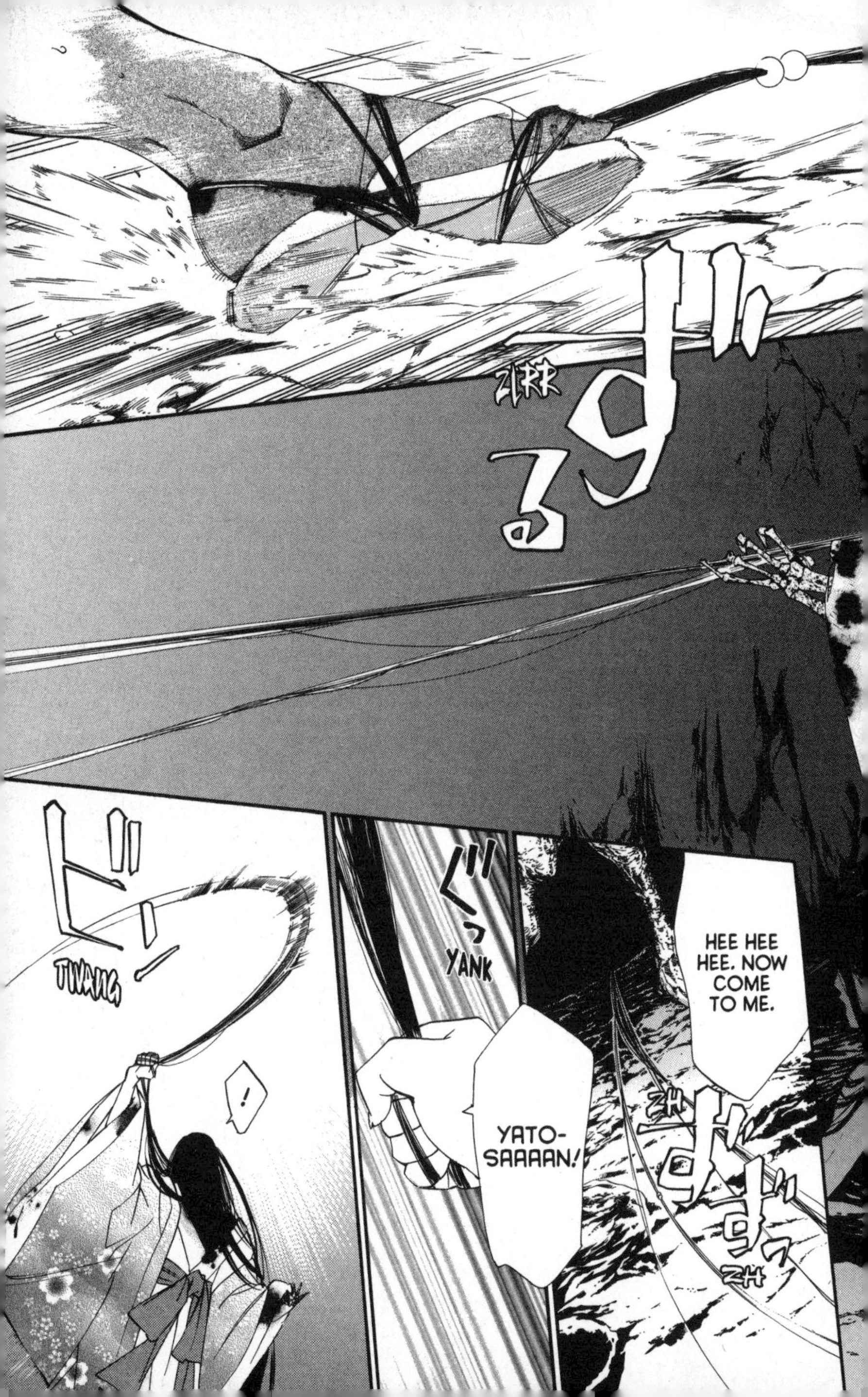
ずる
ZIRR
HEE HEE HEE. NOW COME TO ME.
ZH
ZH
ぐっ
YANK
YATO-SAAAAN!
TWANG
!

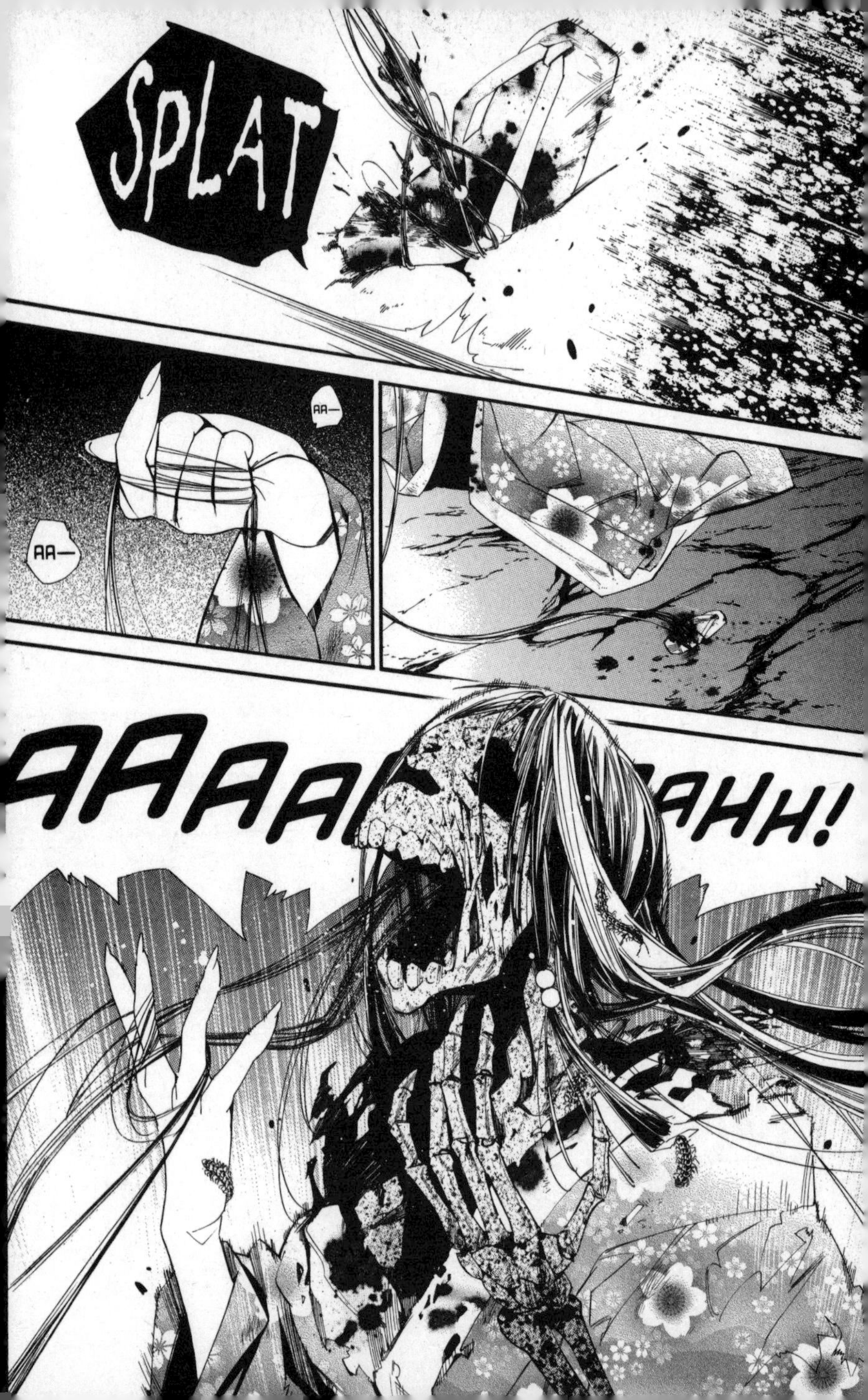
SPLAT
AA—
AA—
AAAA
AHH!

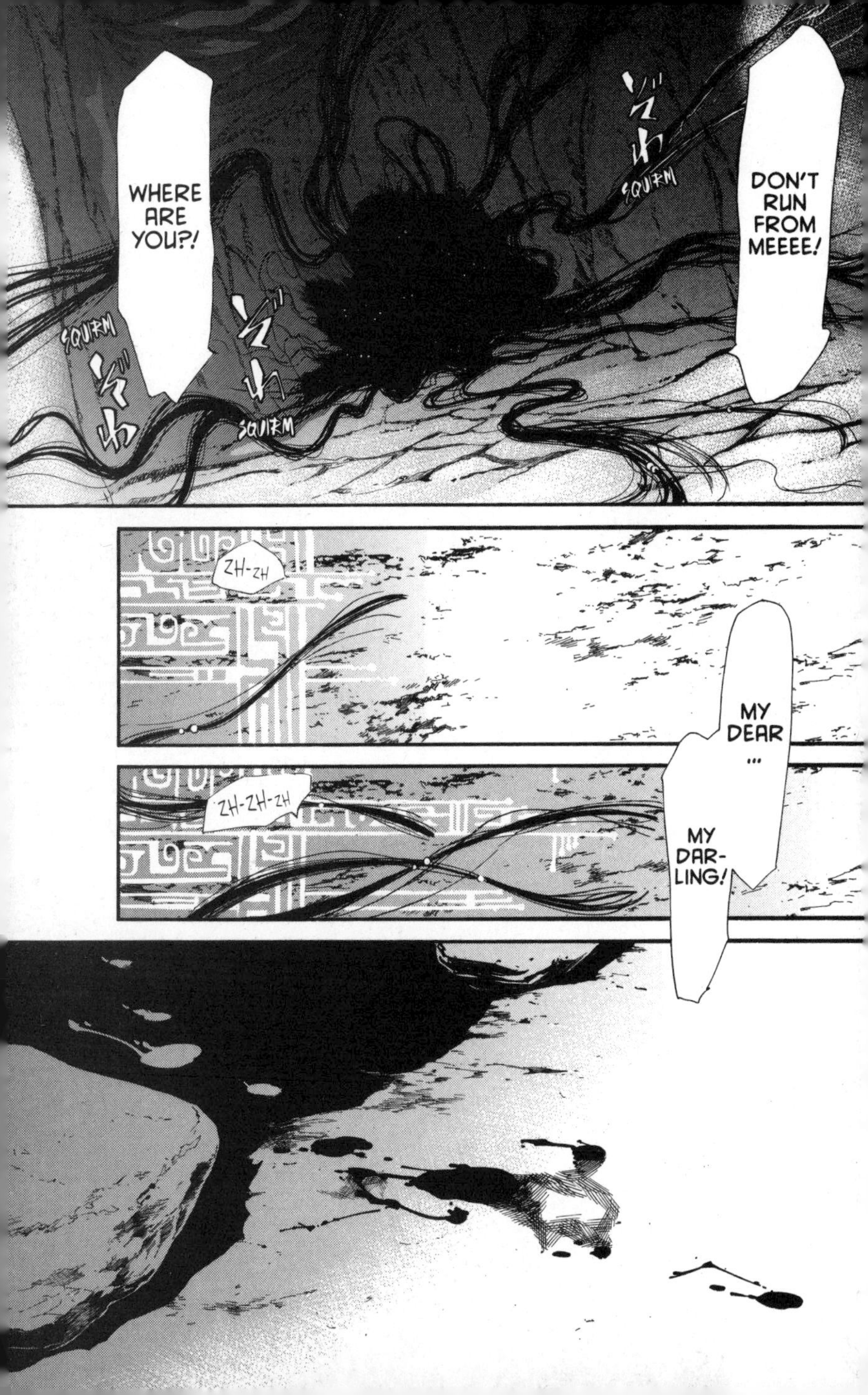
DON'T RUN FROM MEEEE!
ざわ
SQUIRM
WHERE ARE YOU?!
ざわ
SQUIRM
ざわ
SQUIRM
MY DEAR ...
ZH-ZH
MY DAR-LING!
ZH-ZH-ZH

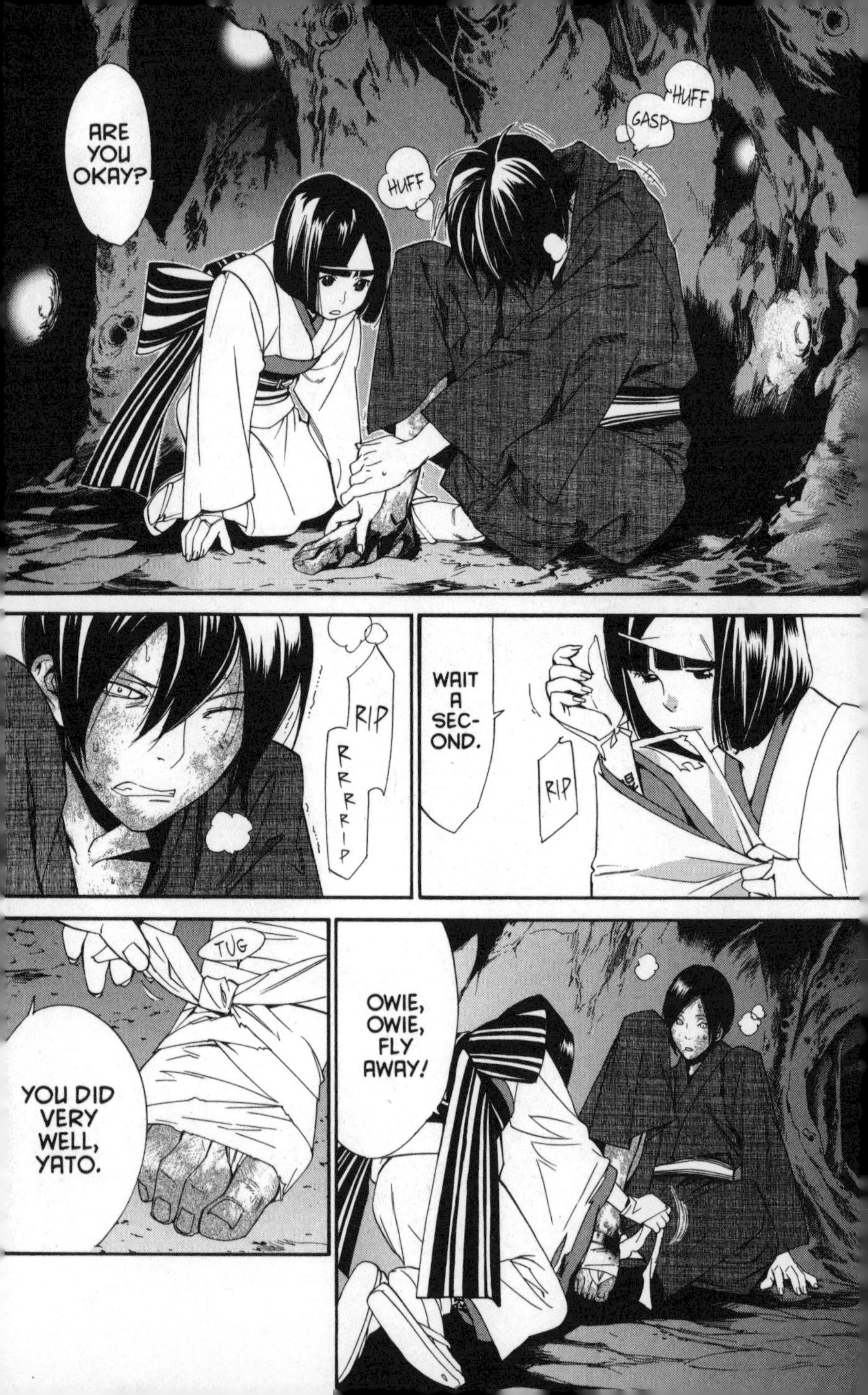
HUFF
GASP
HUFF
ARE YOU OKAY?
WAIT A SEC-OND.
RIP
RIP
RRRRRIP
OWIE, OWIE, FLY AWAY!
TUG
YOU DID VERY WELL, YATO.

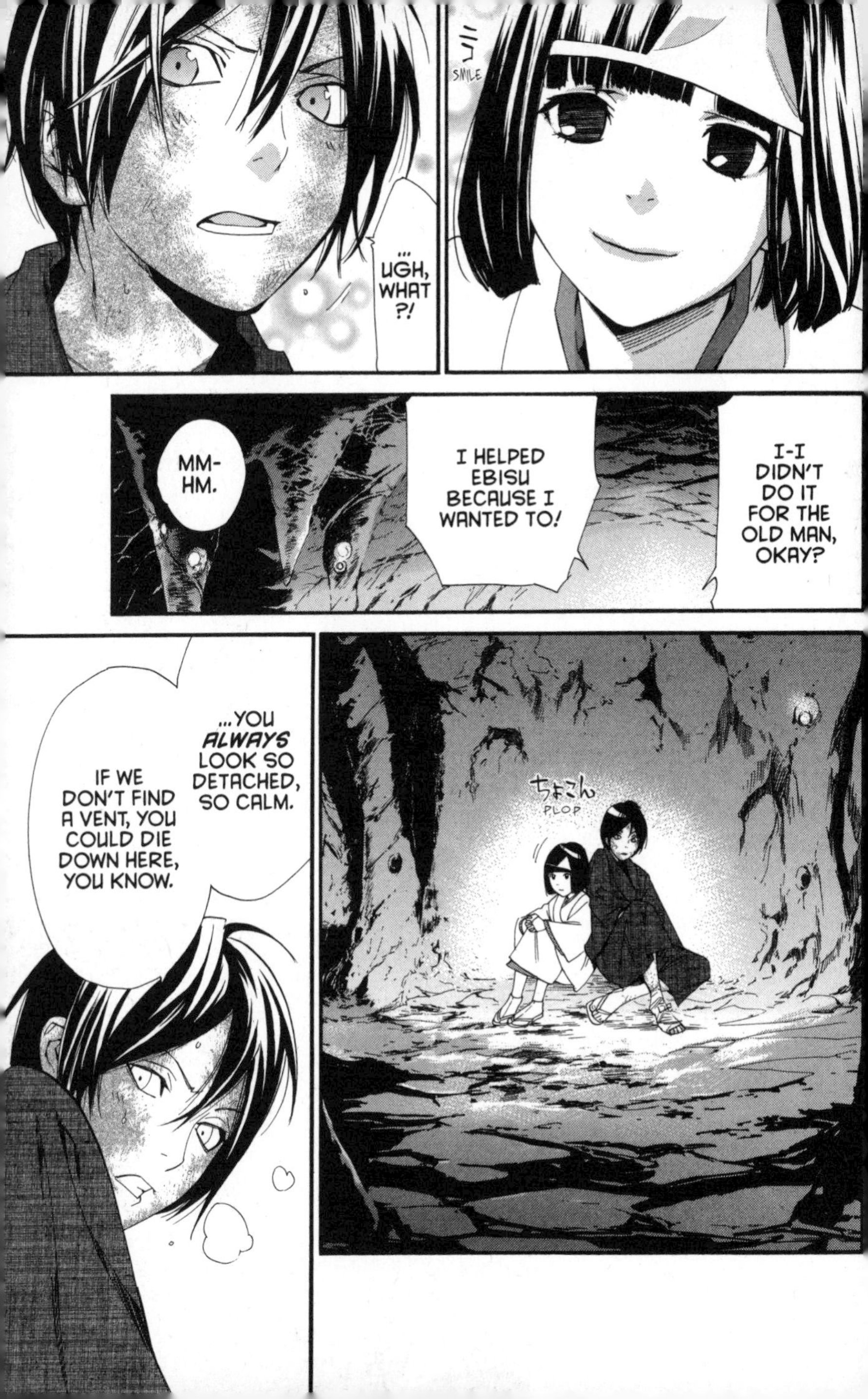
ニコ
SMILE
...UGH, WHAT?!
I-I DIDN'T DO IT FOR THE OLD MAN, OKAY?
I HELPED EBISU BECAUSE I WANTED TO!
MM-HM.
ちょこん
PLOP
...YOU *ALWAYS* LOOK SO DETACHED, SO CALM.
IF WE DON'T FIND A VENT, YOU COULD DIE DOWN HERE, YOU KNOW.

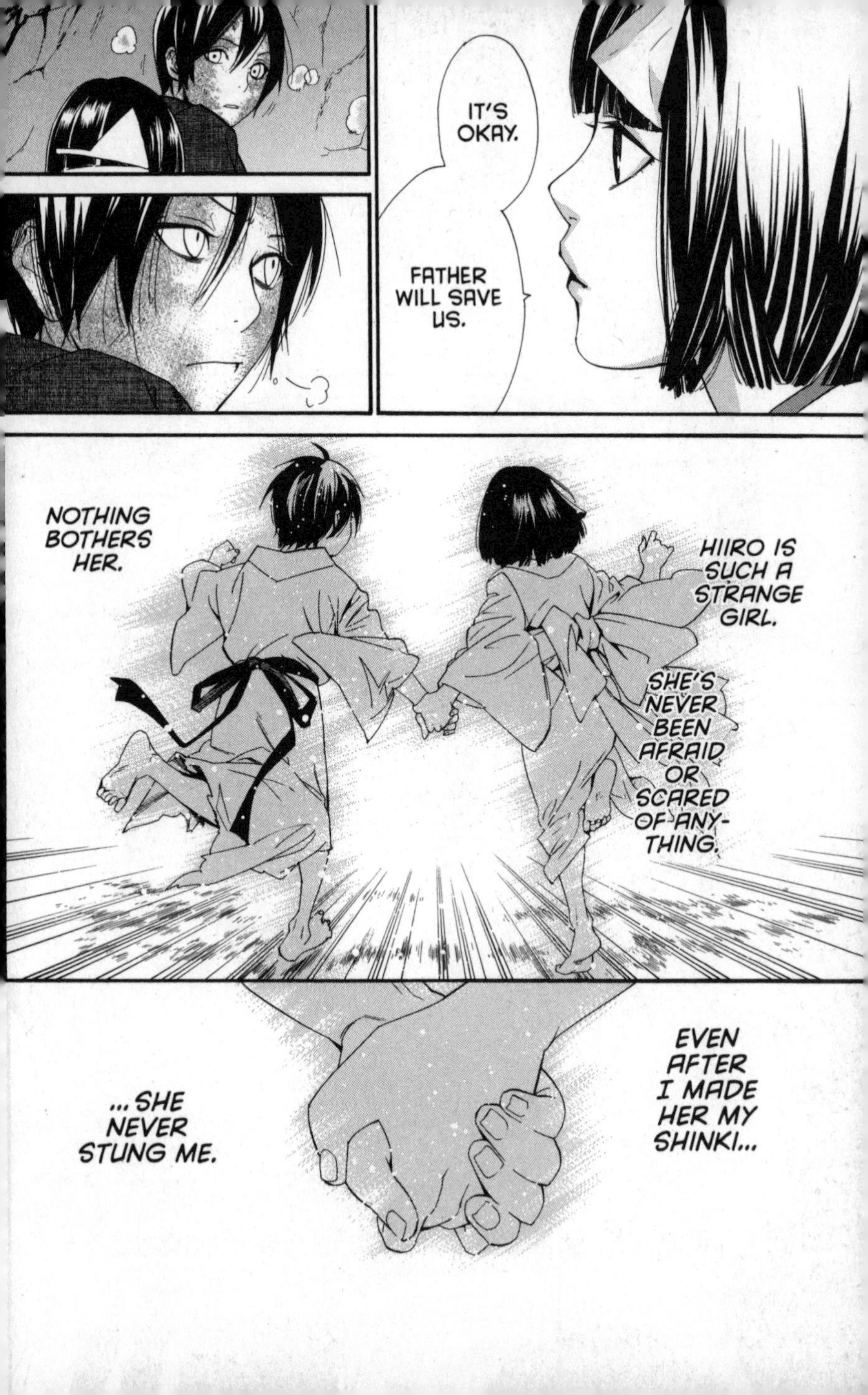
IT'S OKAY.
FATHER WILL SAVE US.
HIIRO IS SUCH A STRANGE GIRL.
SHE'S NEVER BEEN AFRAID OR SCARED OF ANY-THING.
NOTHING BOTHERS HER.
EVEN AFTER I MADE HER MY SHINKI...
...SHE NEVER STUNG ME.

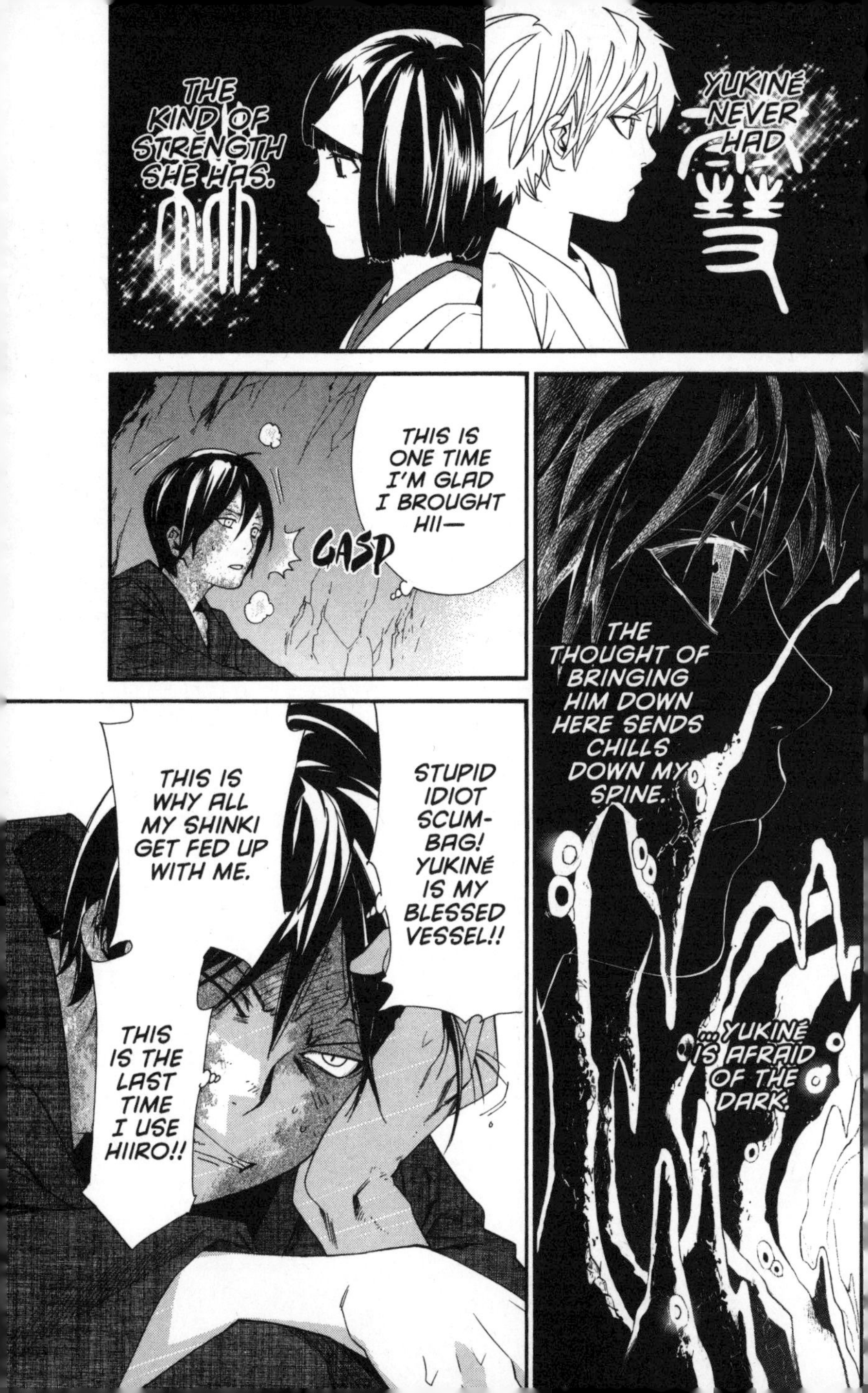
YUKINÉ NEVER HAD
THE KIND OF STRENGTH SHE HAS.
THE THOUGHT OF BRINGING HIM DOWN HERE SENDS CHILLS DOWN MY SPINE.
...YUKINÉ IS AFRAID OF THE DARK.
THIS IS ONE TIME I'M GLAD I BROUGHT HII—
GASP
STUPID IDIOT SCUM-BAG! YUKINÉ IS MY BLESSED VESSEL!!
THIS IS WHY ALL MY SHINKI GET FED UP WITH ME.
THIS IS THE LAST TIME I USE HIIRO!!

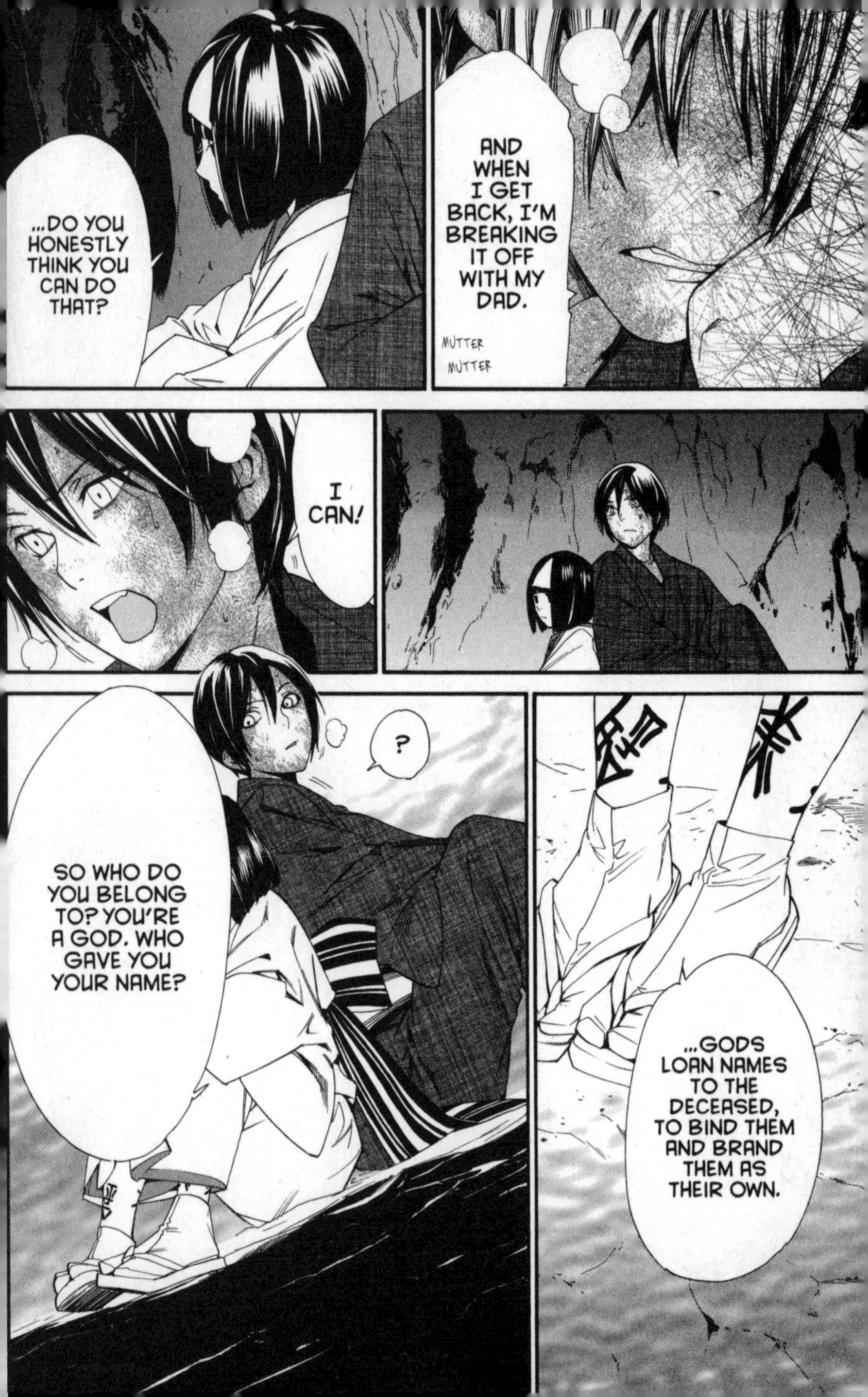
AND WHEN I GET BACK, I'M BREAKING IT OFF WITH MY DAD.
MUTTER
MUTTER
...DO YOU HONESTLY THINK YOU CAN DO THAT?
I CAN!
...GODS LOAN NAMES TO THE DECEASED, TO BIND THEM AND BRAND THEM AS THEIR OWN.
?
SO WHO DO YOU BELONG TO? YOU'RE A GOD. WHO GAVE YOU YOUR NAME?

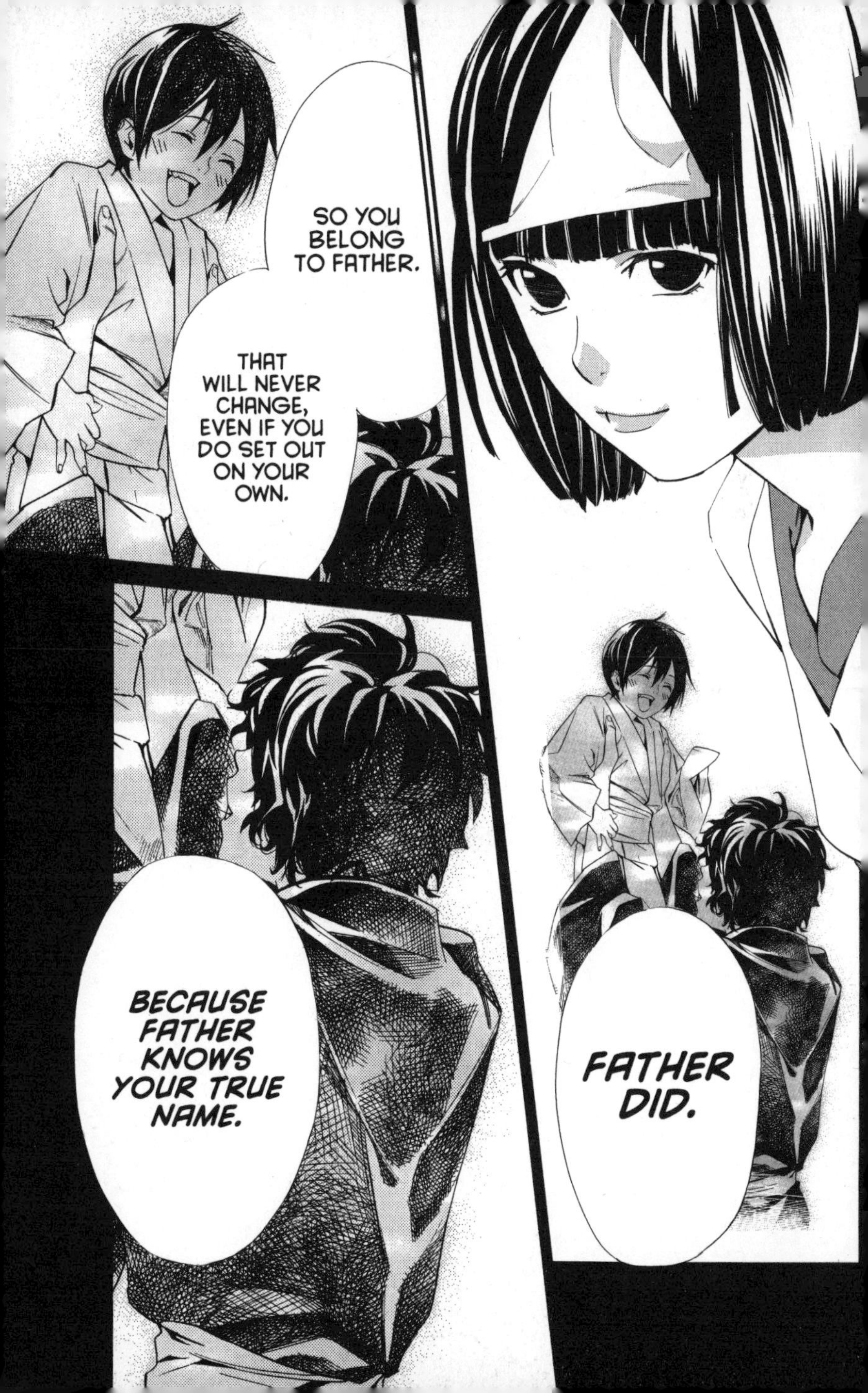
FATHER DID.
SO YOU BELONG TO FATHER.
THAT WILL NEVER CHANGE, EVEN IF YOU DO SET OUT ON YOUR OWN.
BECAUSE FATHER KNOWS YOUR TRUE NAME.

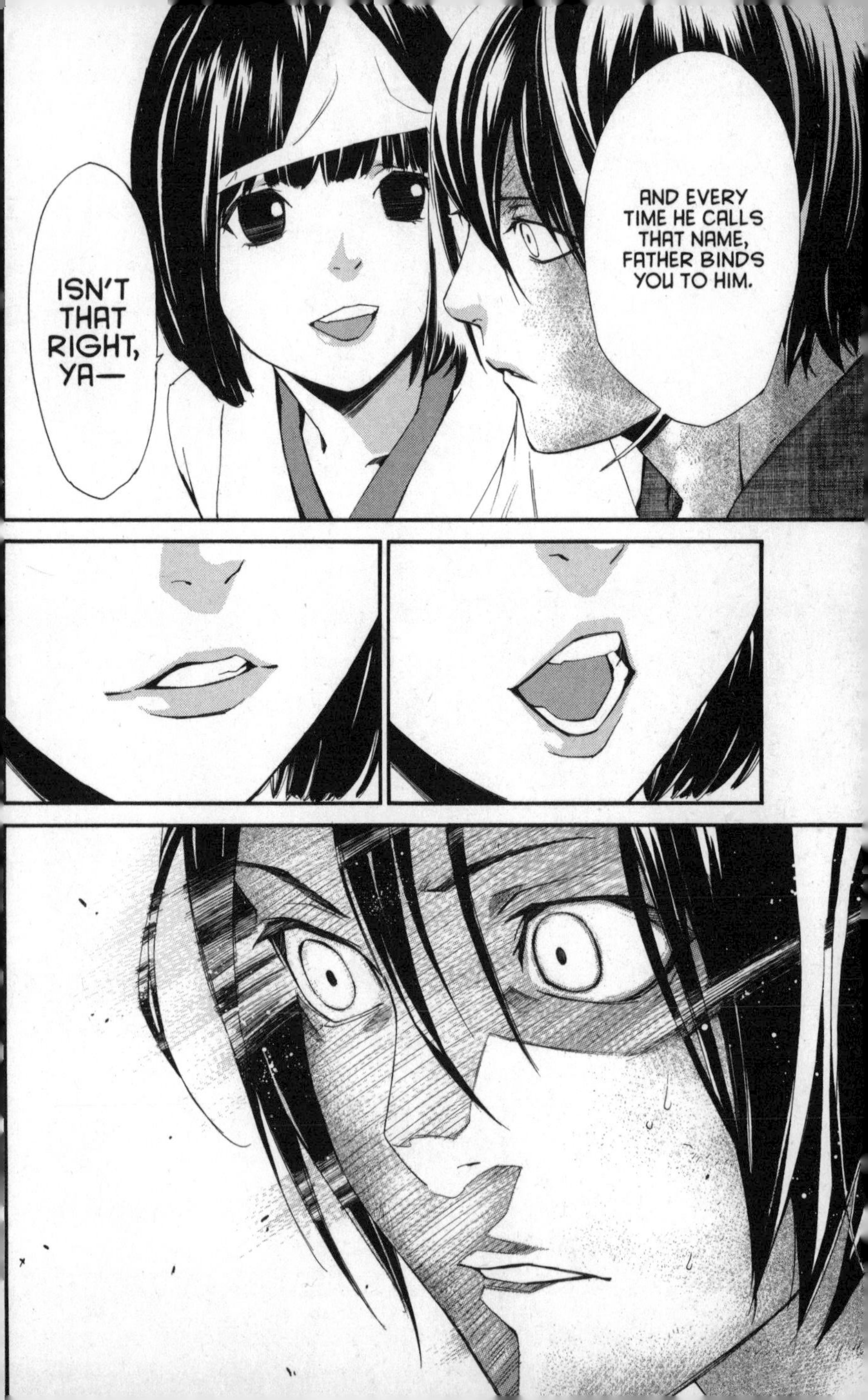
AND EVERY TIME HE CALLS THAT NAME, FATHER BINDS YOU TO HIM.
ISN'T THAT RIGHT, YA—

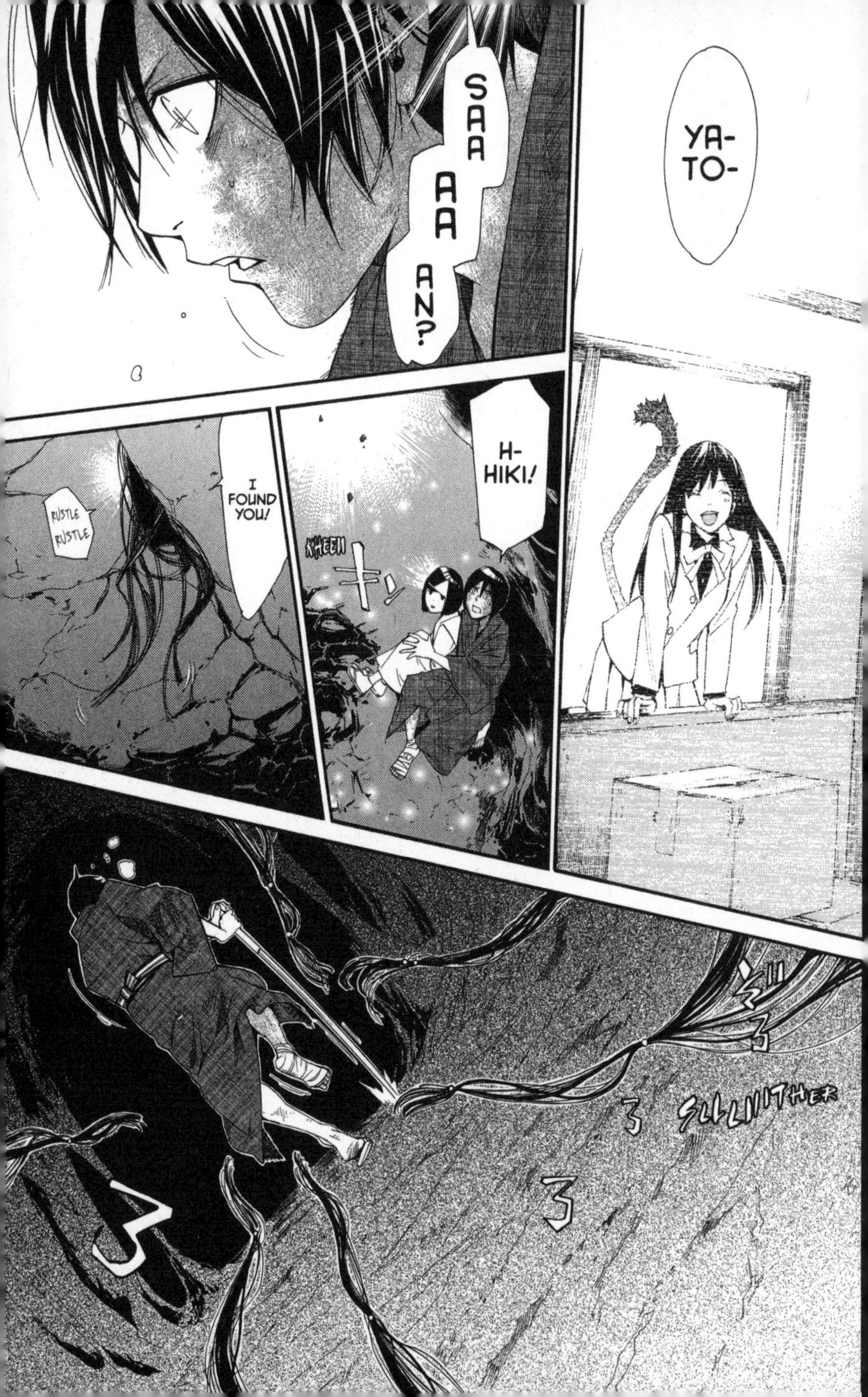
YA-TO-
SAAAAAN?
H-HIKI!
KHEEN
I FOUND YOU!
RUSTLE RUSTLE
SLLLITHER

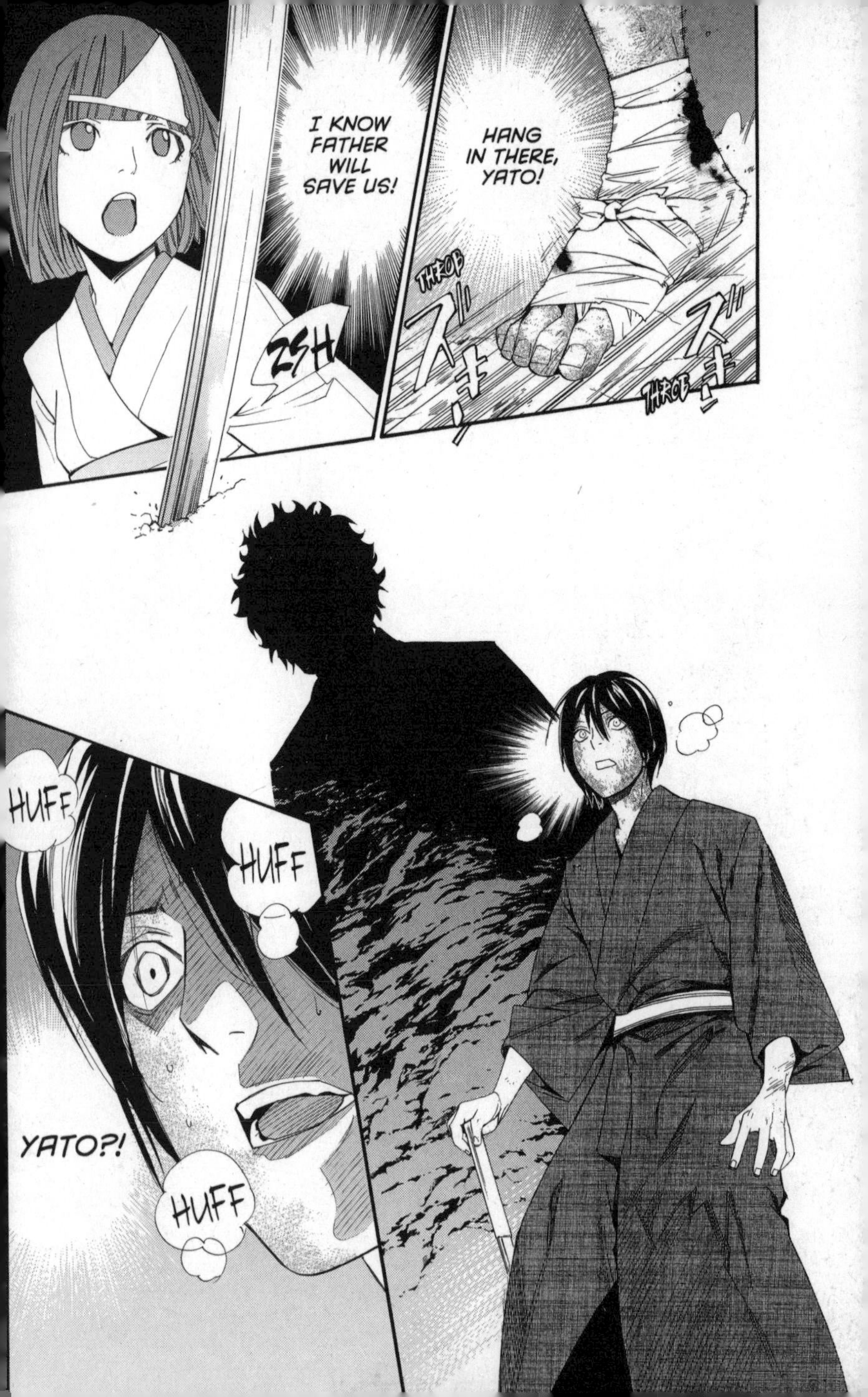
HANG IN THERE, YATO!
THROB
ズキ
THROB
ズキ
I KNOW FATHER WILL SAVE US!
ZSH
HUFF
HUFF
YATO?!
HUFF

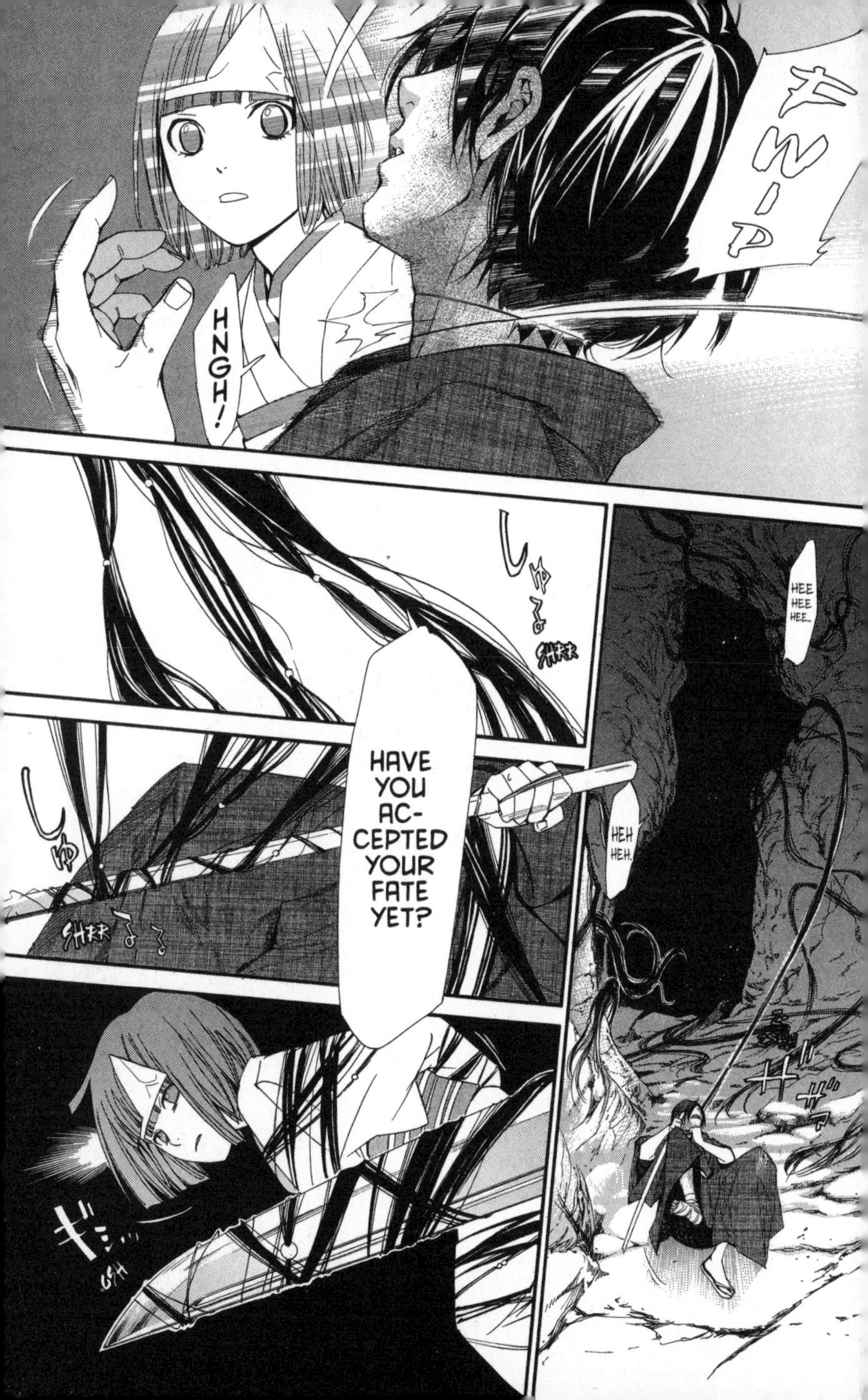
TWIP
HNGH!
HEE HEE HEE..
HEH HEH.
SHRR
HAVE YOU AC-CEPTED YOUR FATE YET?
SHRR
GSH

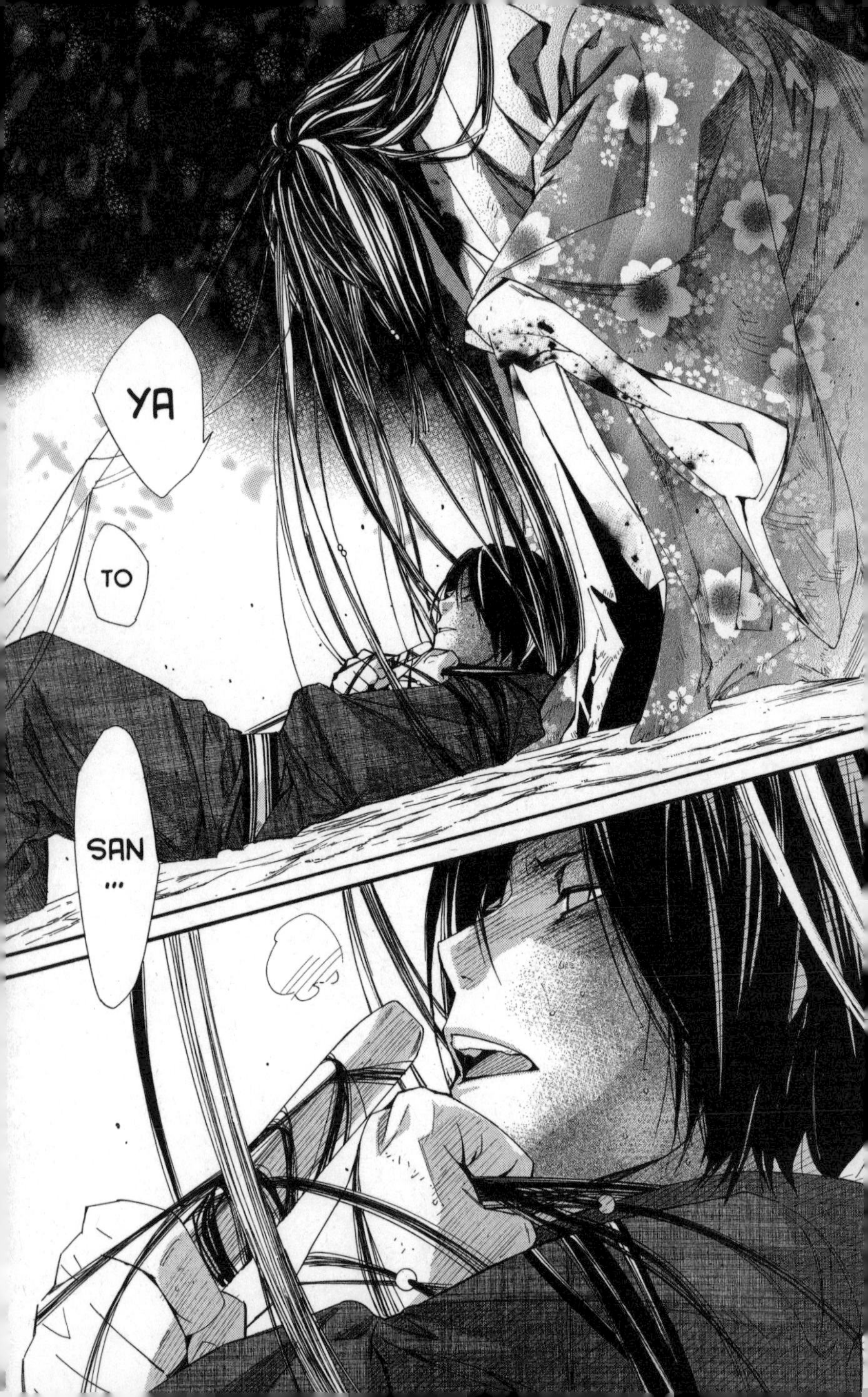
YA
TO
SAN...

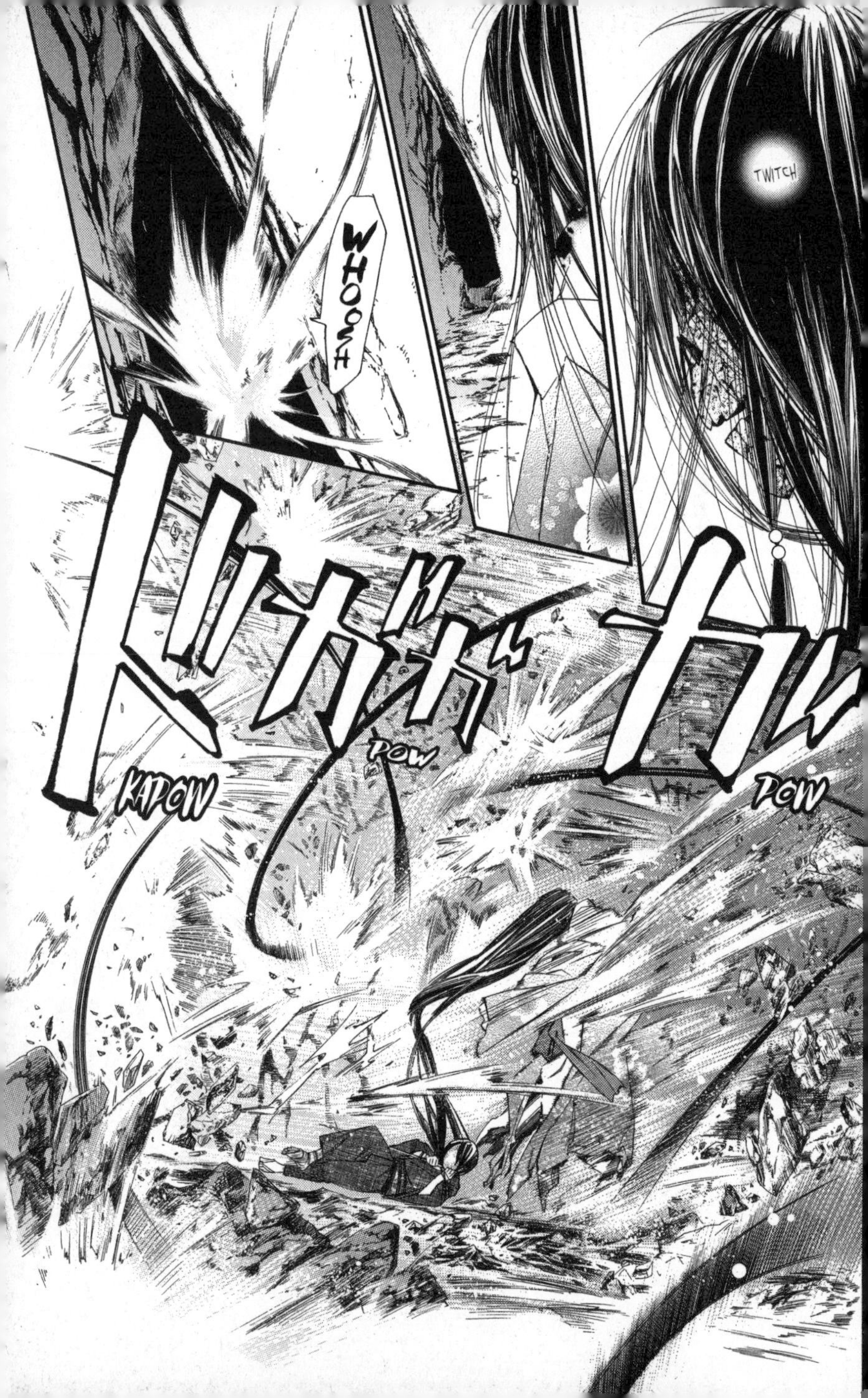
TWITCH
WHOOSH
POW
POW
KAPOW

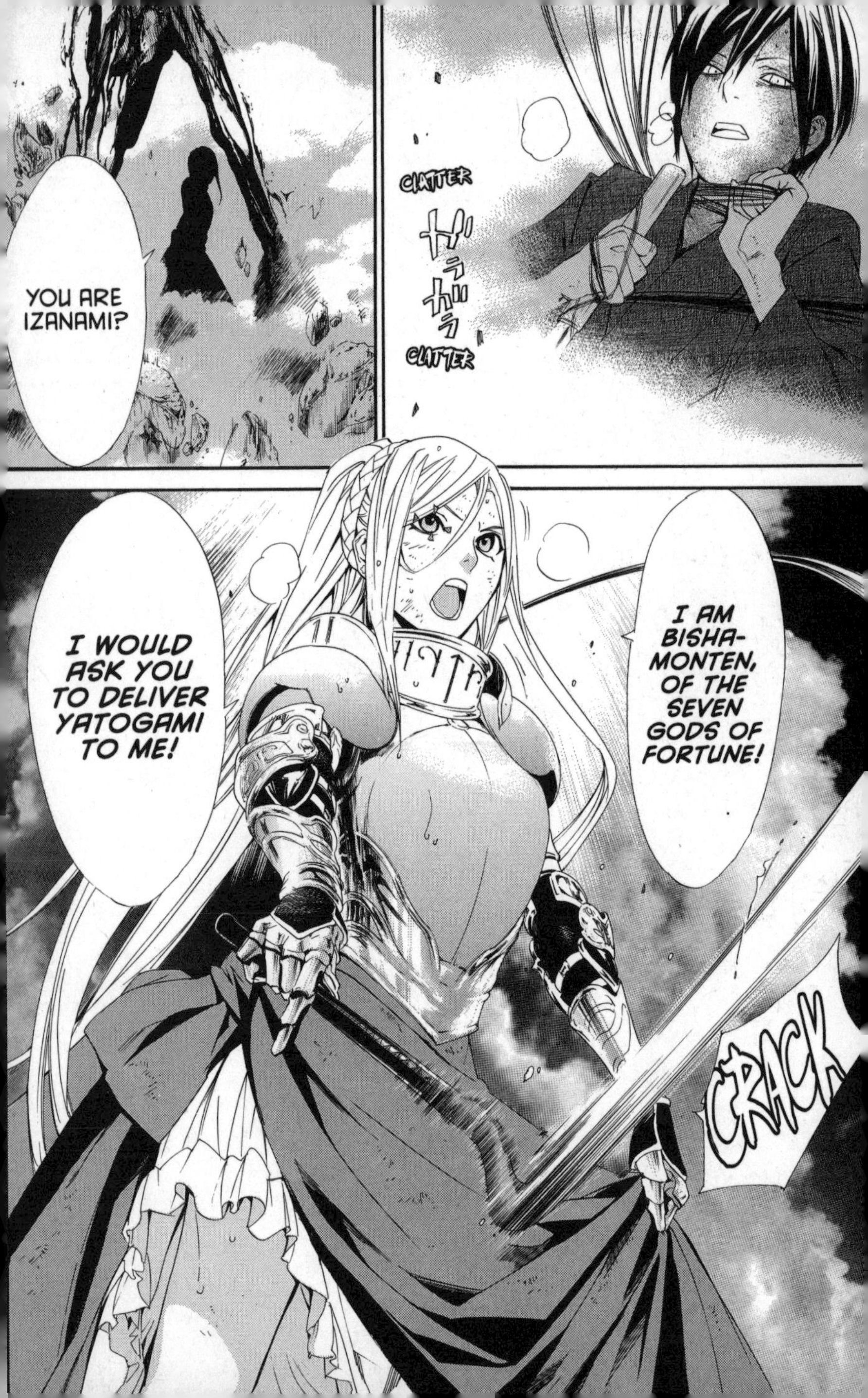
CLATTER
ガラガラ
CLATTER
YOU ARE IZANAMI?
I AM BISHAMONTEN, OF THE SEVEN GODS OF FORTUNE!
I WOULD ASK YOU TO DELIVER YATOGAMI TO ME!
CRACK

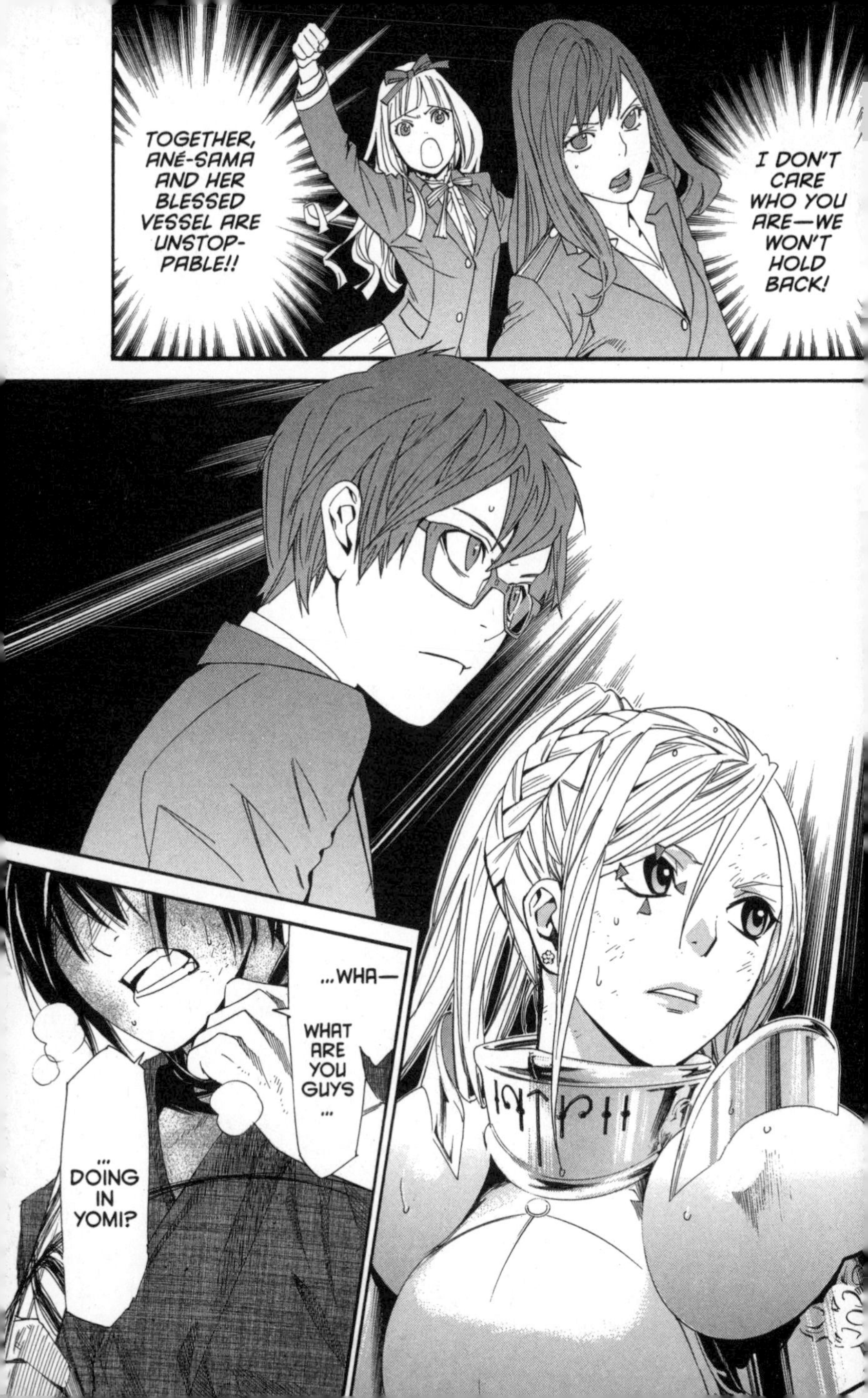
I DON'T CARE WHO YOU ARE—WE WON'T HOLD BACK!
TOGETHER, ANÉ-SAMA AND HER BLESSED VESSEL ARE UNSTOP-PABLE!!
...WHA—
WHAT ARE YOU GUYS ...
... DOING IN YOMI?

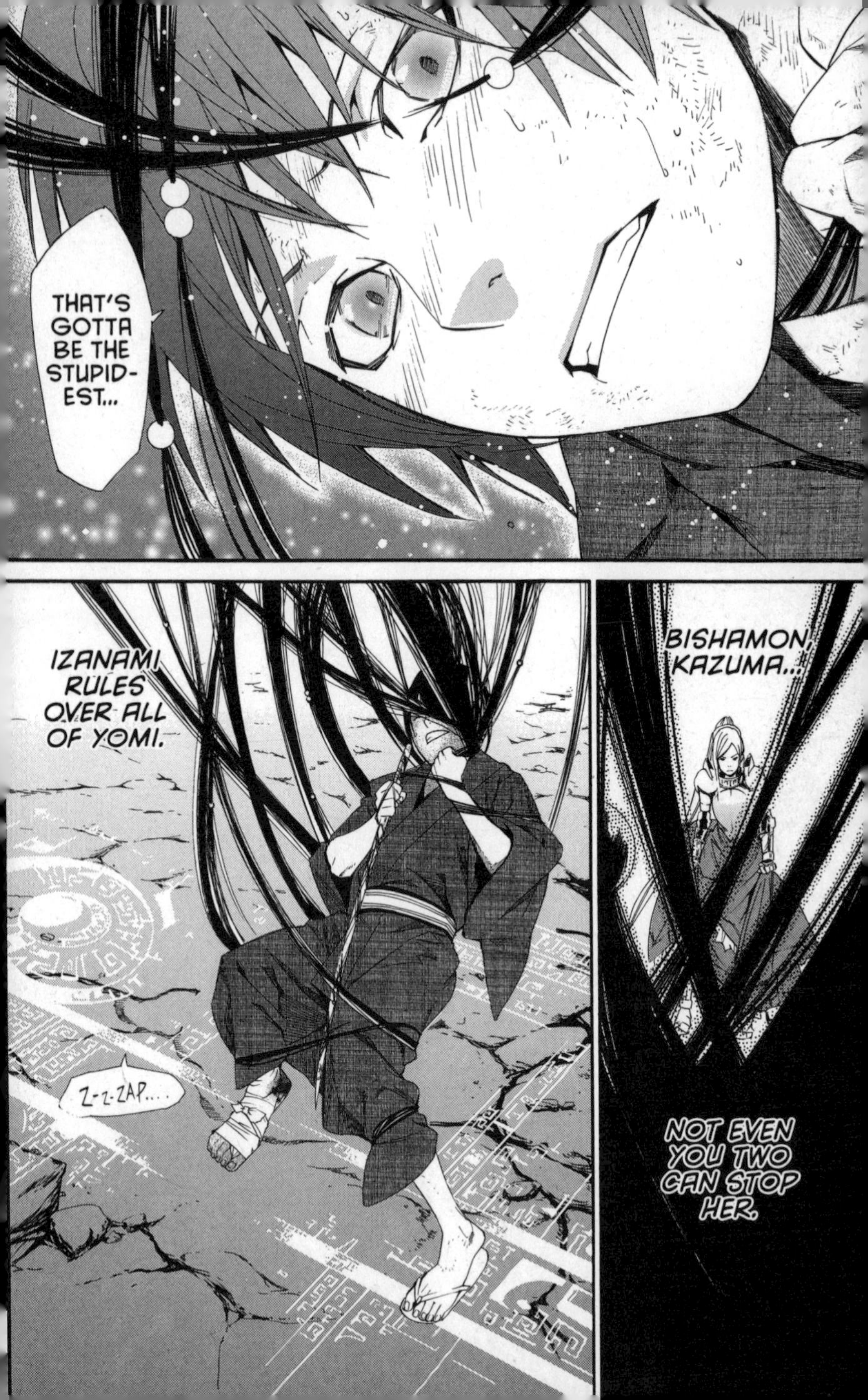
THAT'S GOTTA BE THE STUPID-EST...
BISHAMON, KAZUMA...
NOT EVEN YOU TWO CAN STOP HER.
IZANAMI RULES OVER ALL OF YOMI.
Z-Z-ZAP....

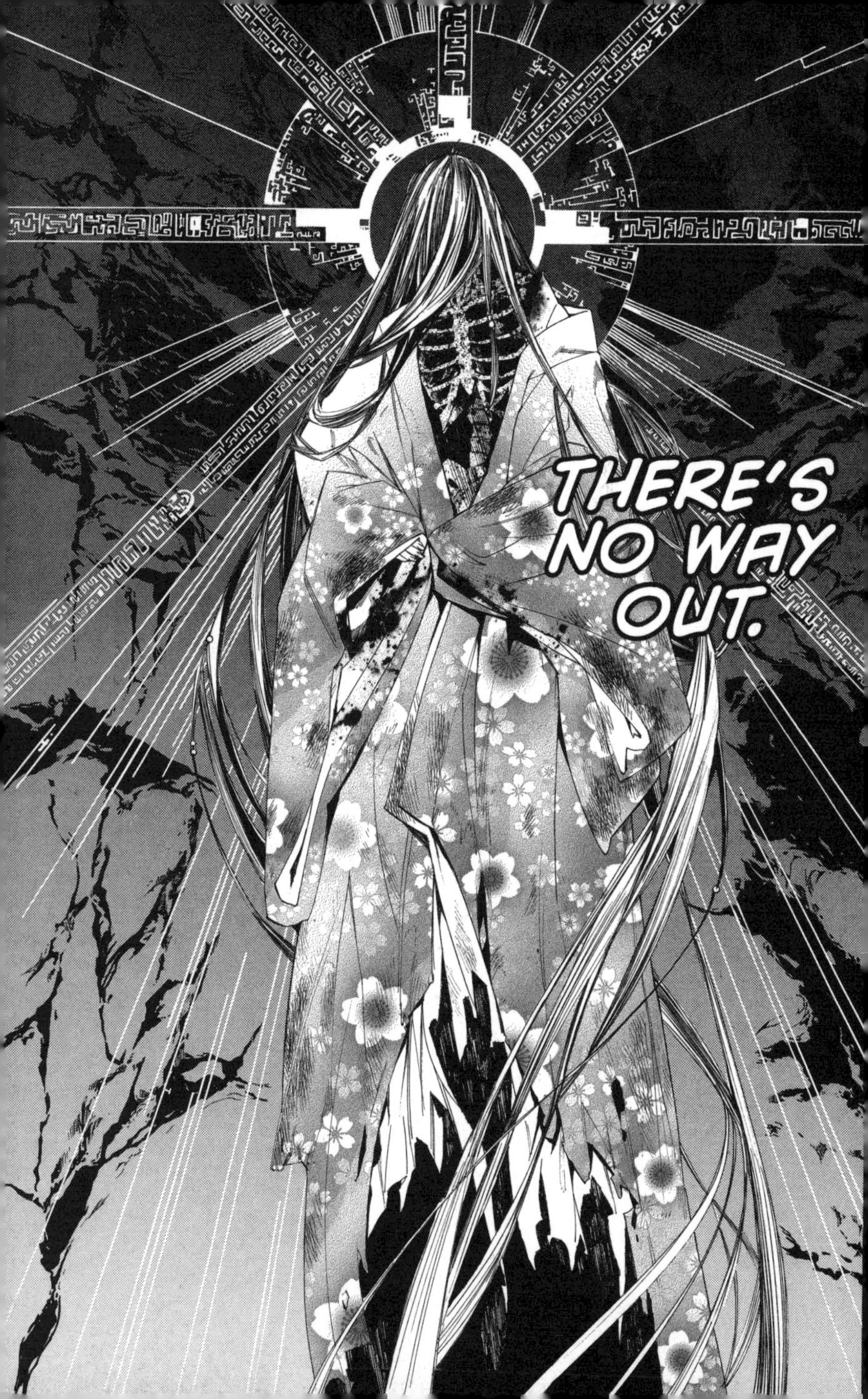
THERE'S NO WAY OUT.

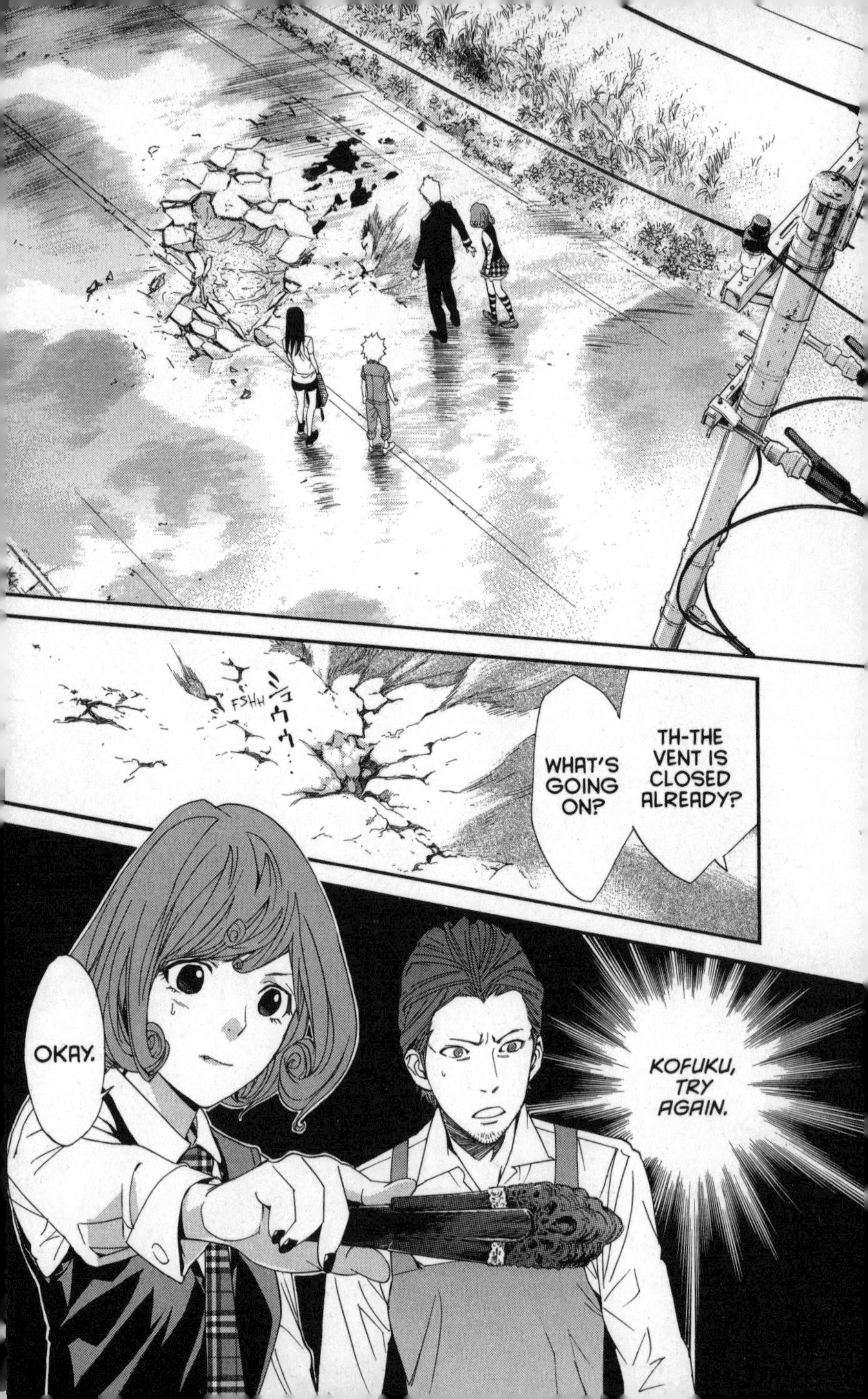
TH-THE VENT IS CLOSED ALREADY?
WHAT'S GOING ON?
FSHH
シュウウ…
KOFUKU, TRY AGAIN.
OKAY.

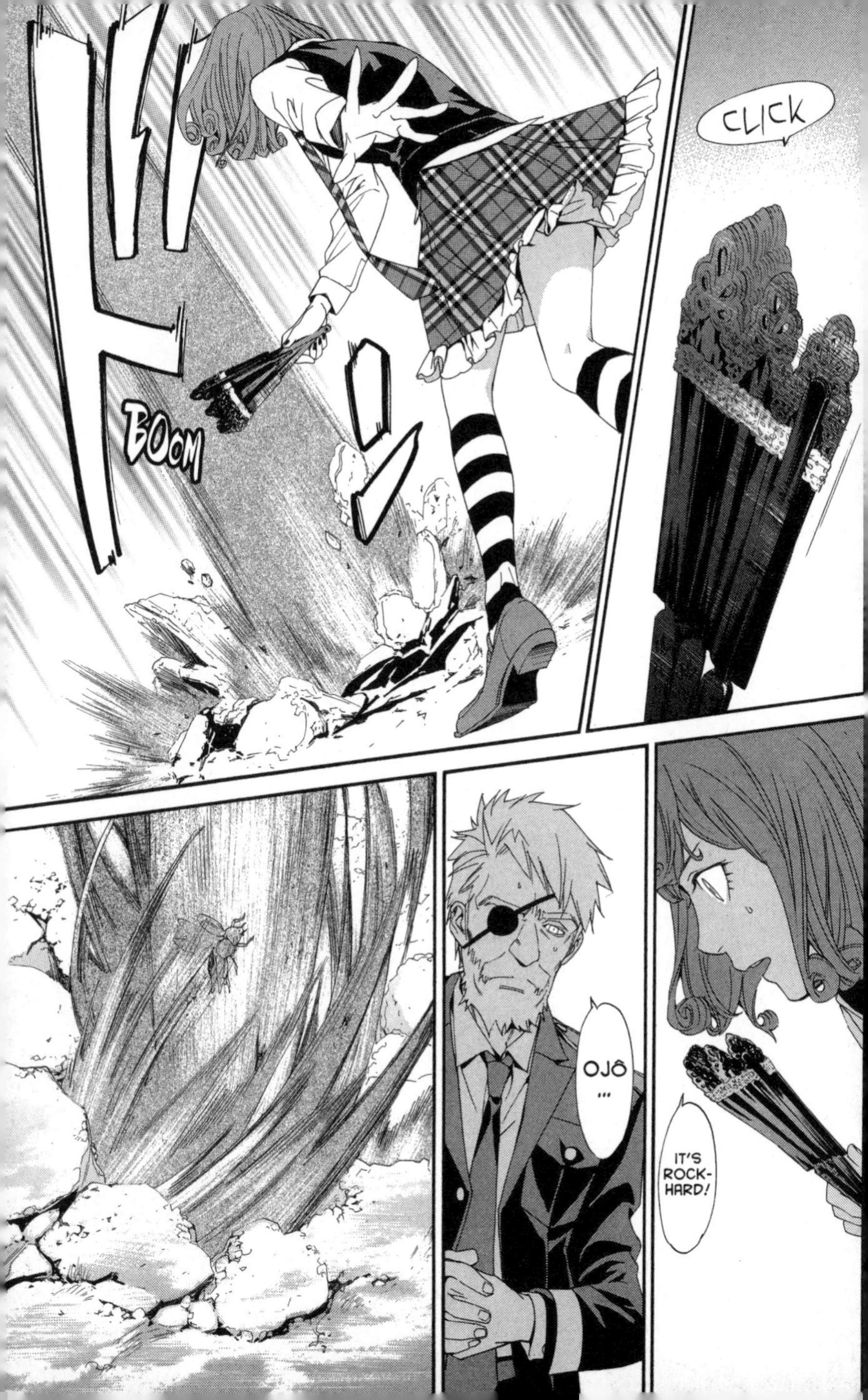
CLICK
BOOM
IT'S ROCK-HARD!
OJÔ ...

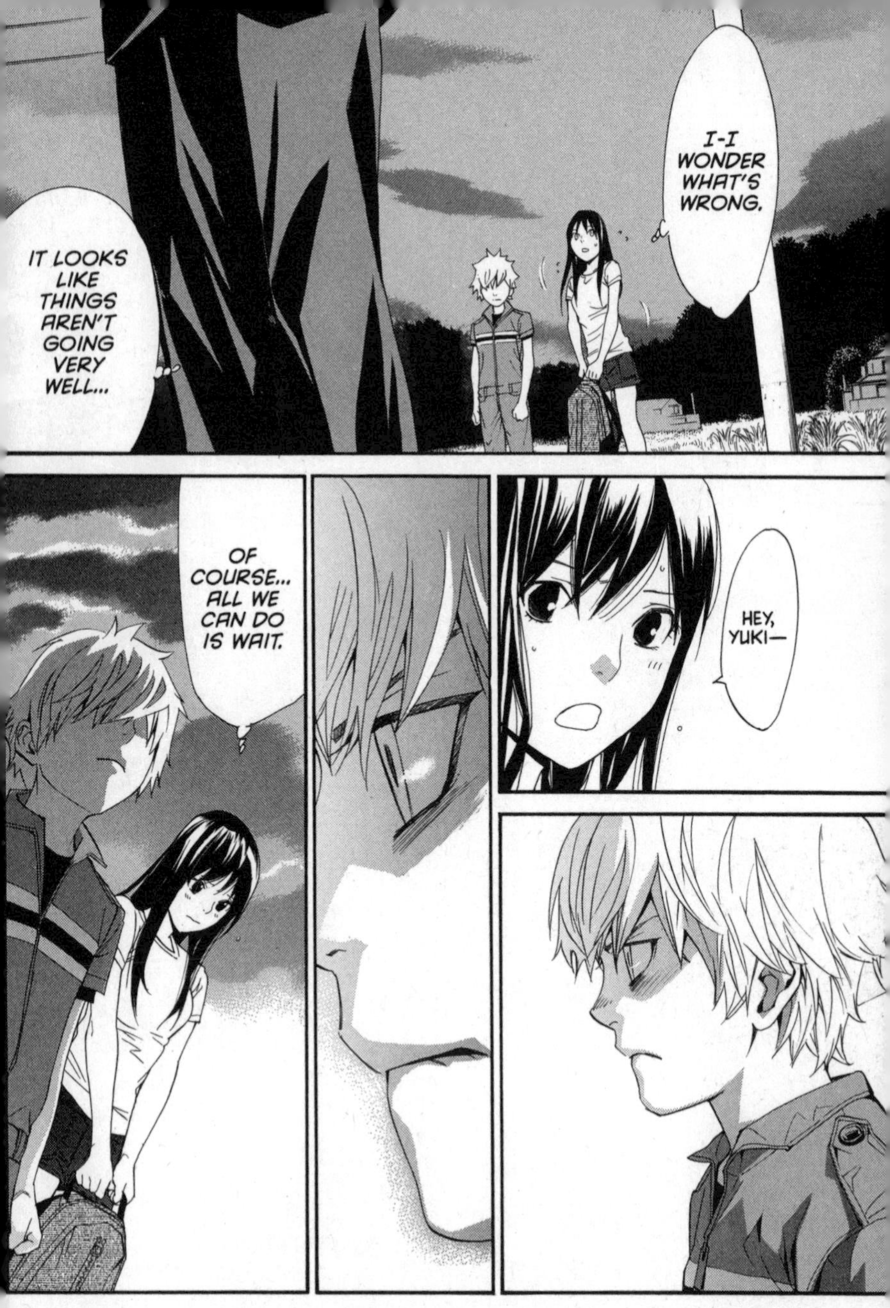
I-I WONDER WHAT'S WRONG.
IT LOOKS LIKE THINGS AREN'T GOING VERY WELL...
HEY, YUKI—
OF COURSE... ALL WE CAN DO IS WAIT.

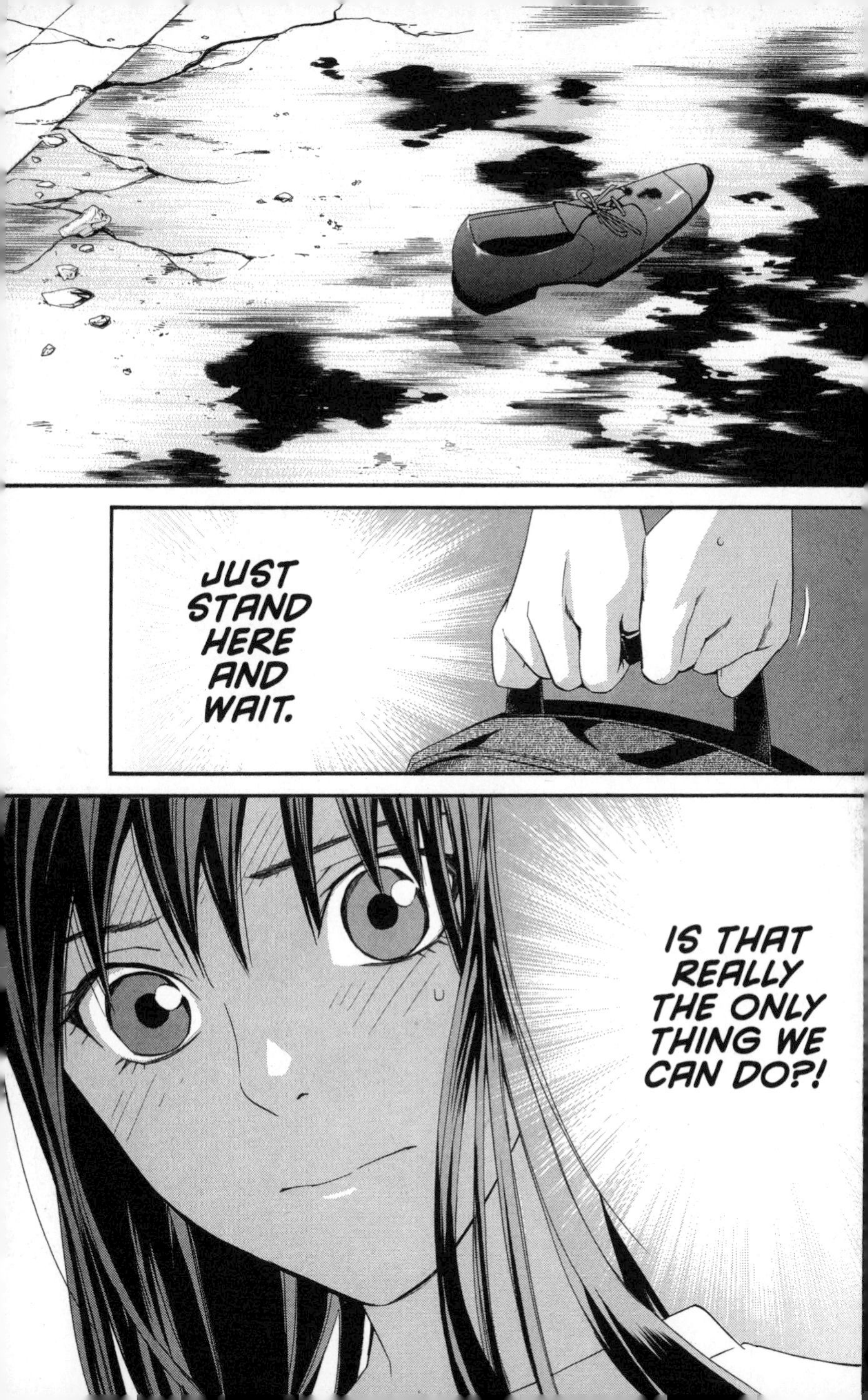
JUST STAND HERE AND WAIT.
IS THAT REALLY THE ONLY THING WE CAN DO?!

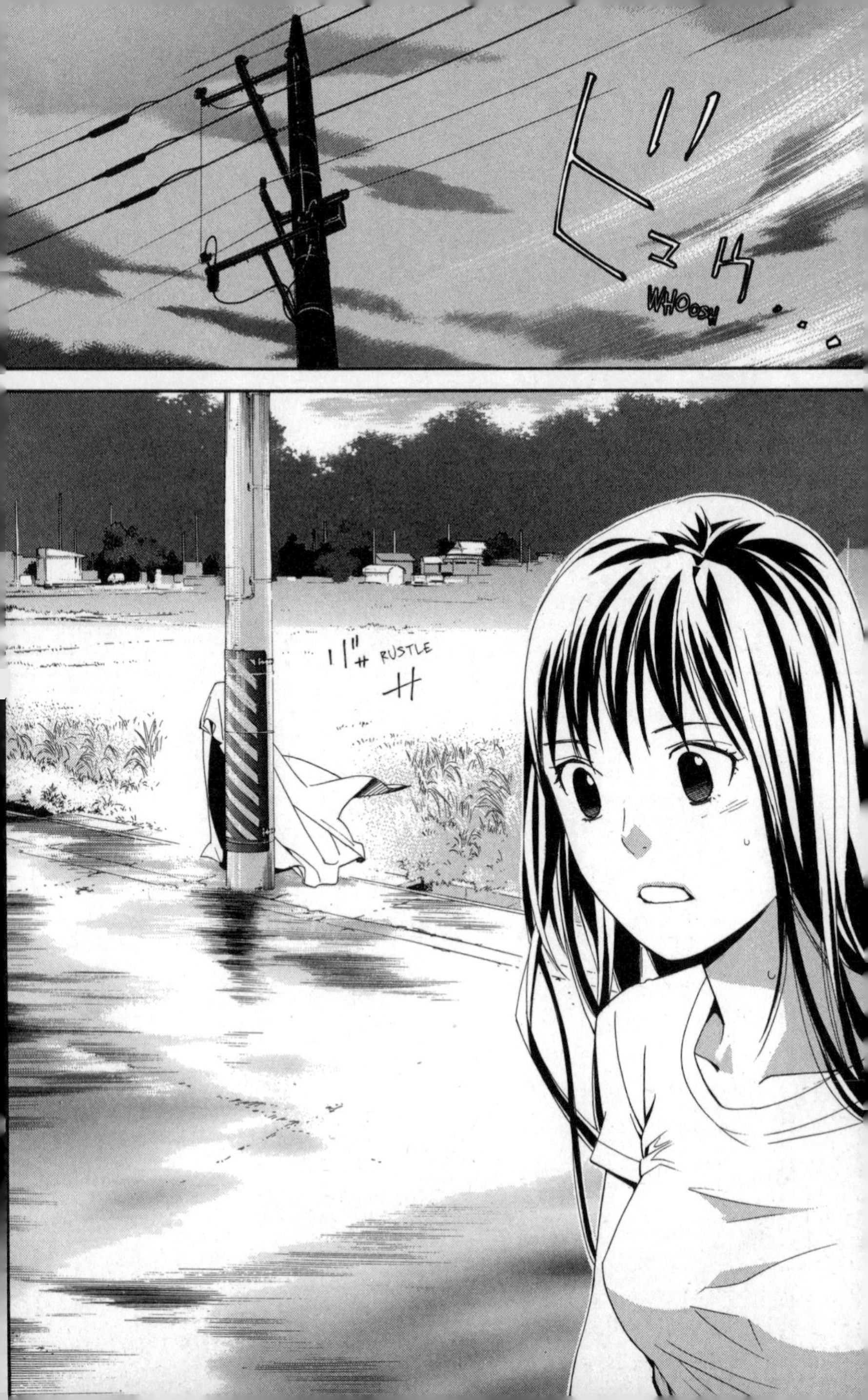
WHOOSH
RUSTLE

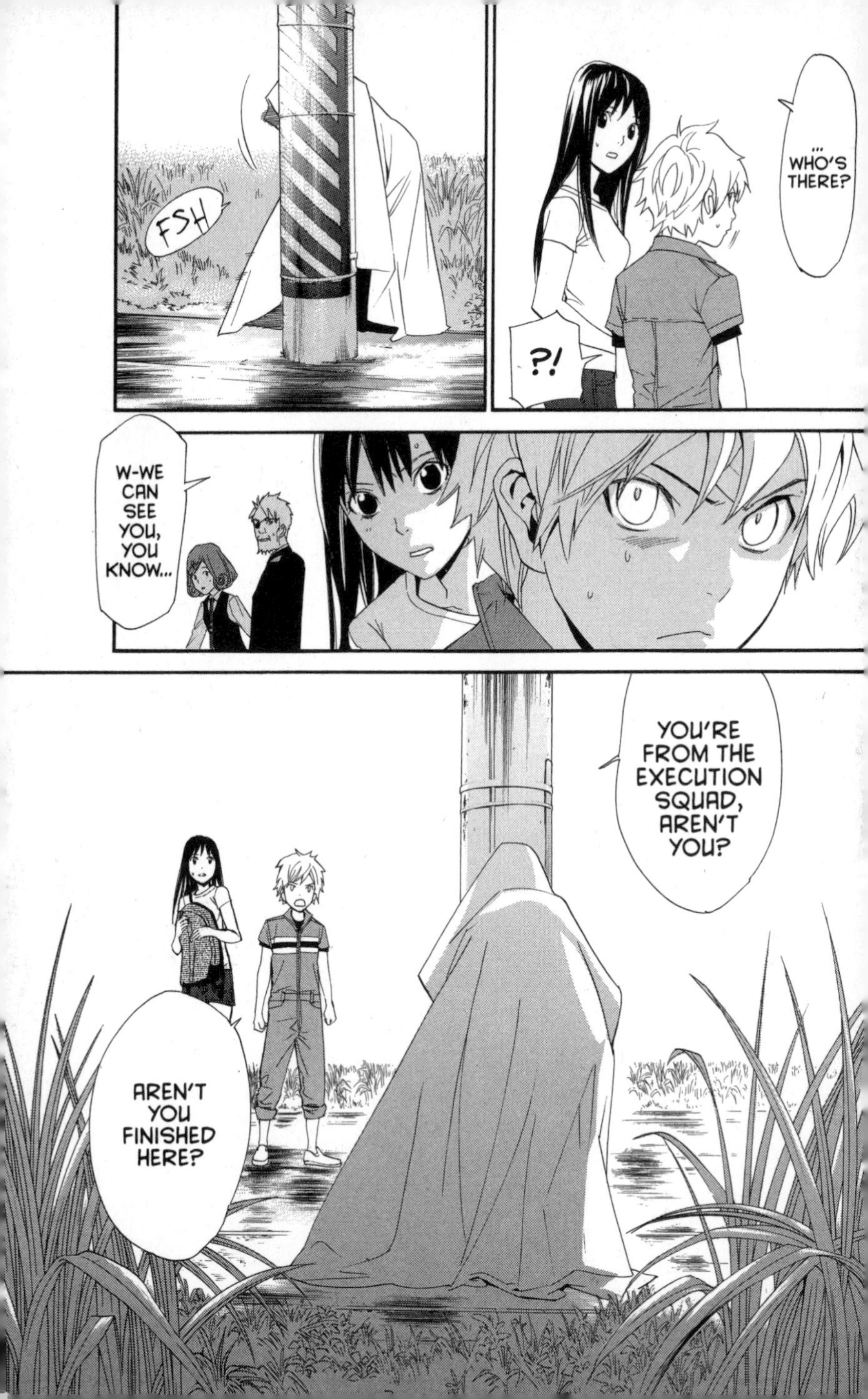
... WHO'S THERE?
?!
FSH
W-WE CAN SEE YOU, YOU KNOW...
YOU'RE FROM THE EXECUTION SQUAD, AREN'T YOU?
AREN'T YOU FINISHED HERE?

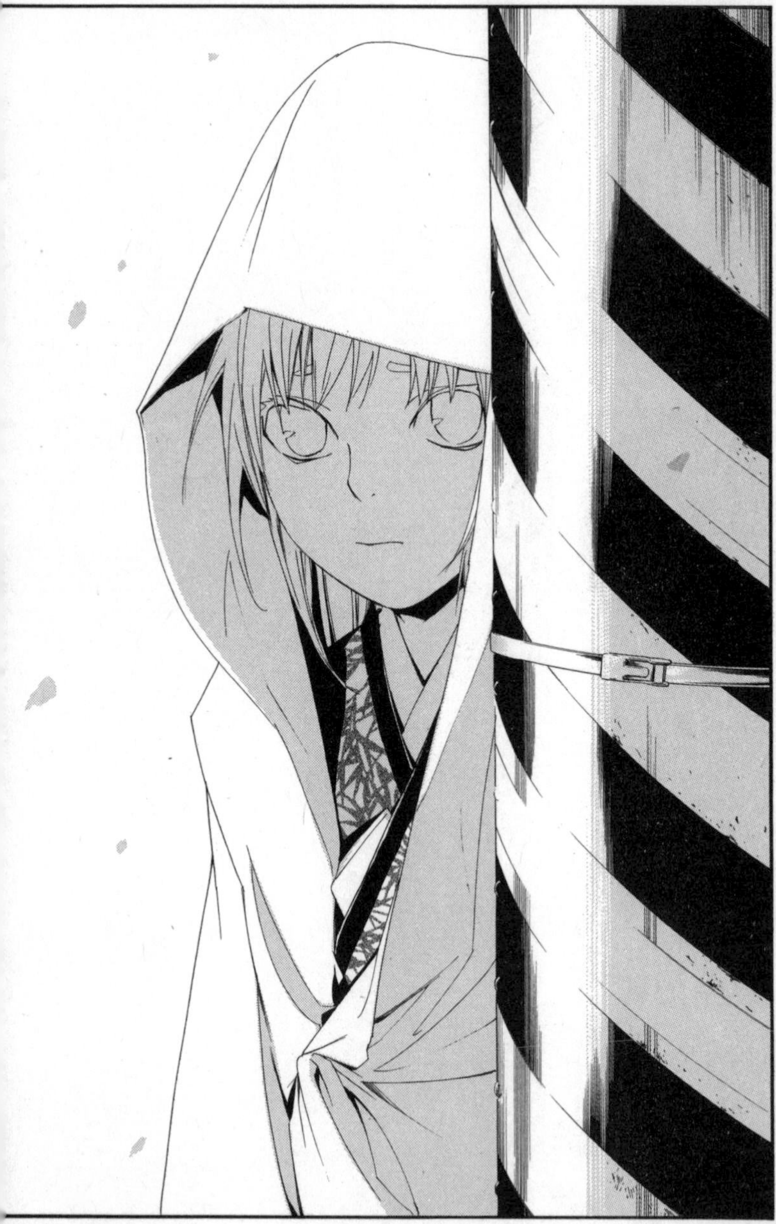

CHAPTER 36 / END

野

兑

神

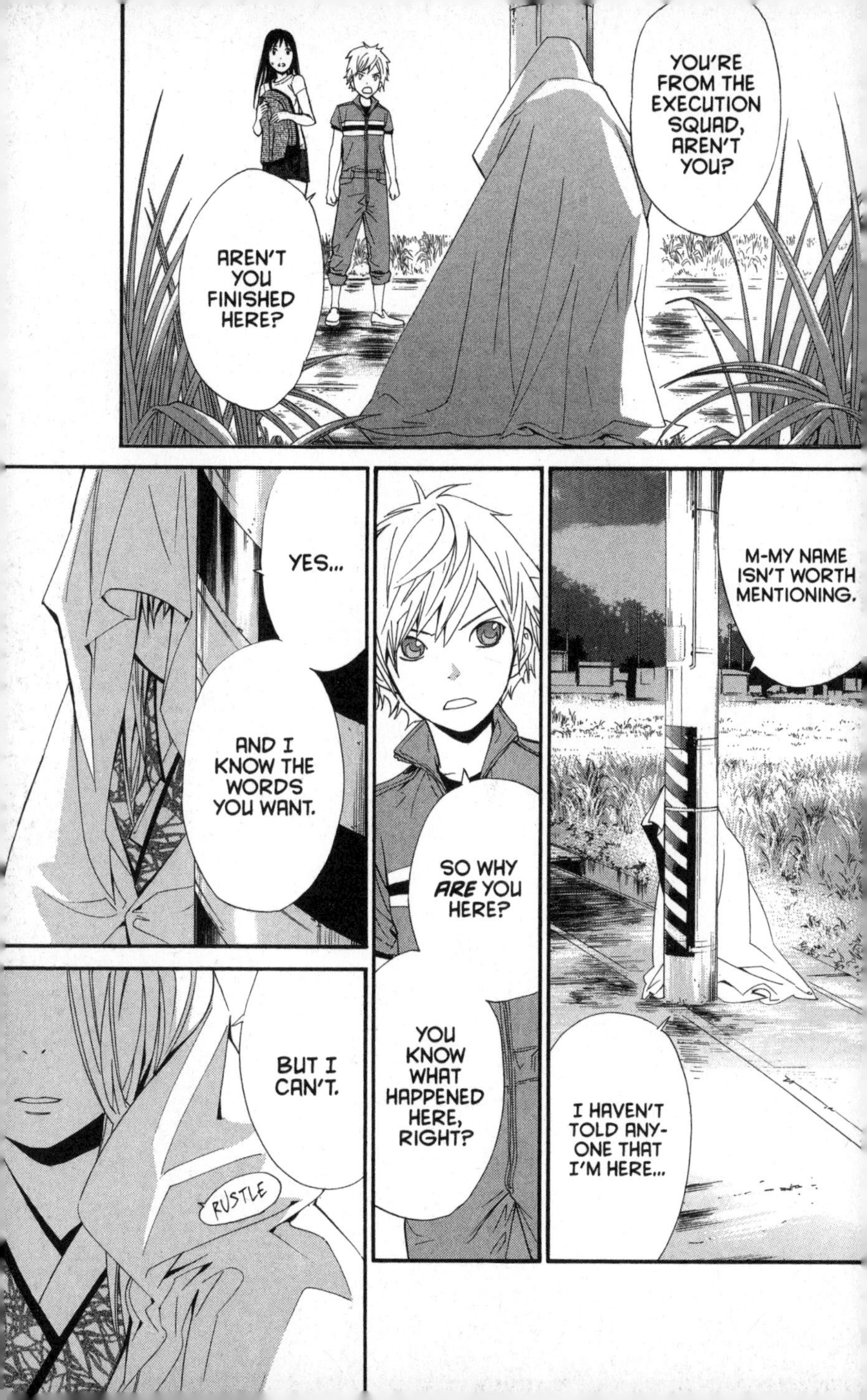
YOU'RE FROM THE EXECUTION SQUAD, AREN'T YOU?
AREN'T YOU FINISHED HERE?
M-MY NAME ISN'T WORTH MENTIONING.
I HAVEN'T TOLD ANY-ONE THAT I'M HERE...
SO WHY *ARE* YOU HERE?
YOU KNOW WHAT HAPPENED HERE, RIGHT?
YES...
AND I KNOW THE WORDS YOU WANT.
BUT I CAN'T.
RUSTLE

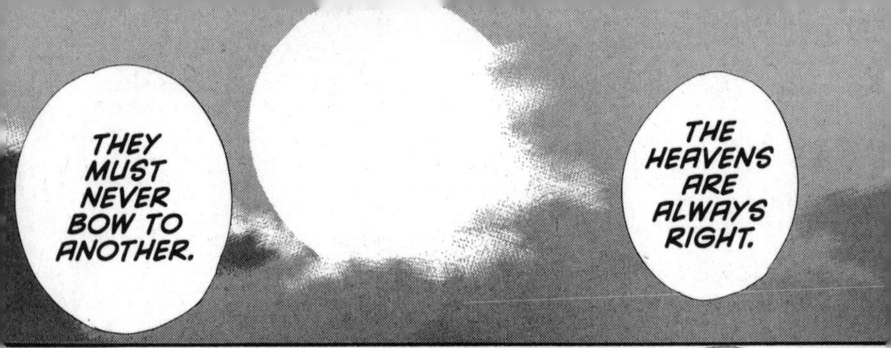
THE HEAVENS ARE ALWAYS RIGHT.
THEY MUST NEVER BOW TO ANOTHER.
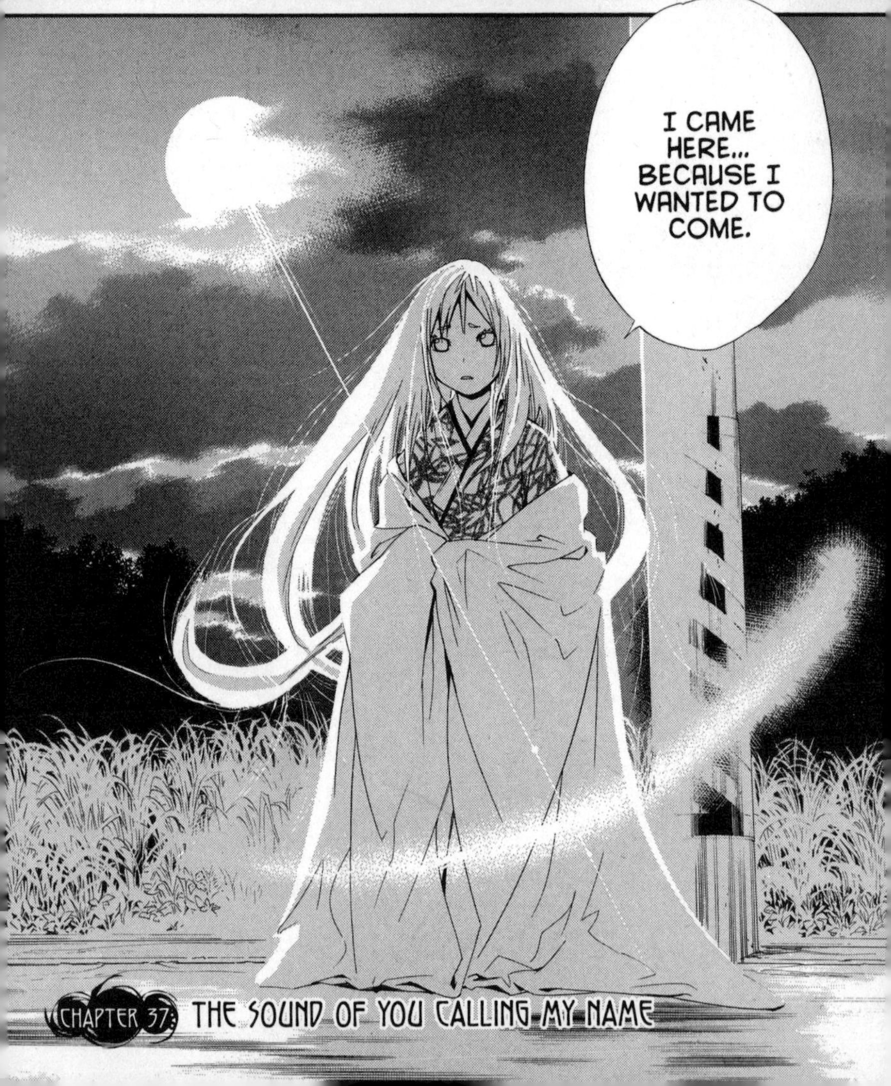
I CAME HERE... BECAUSE I WANTED TO COME.

CHAPTER 37: THE SOUND OF YOU CALLING MY NAME

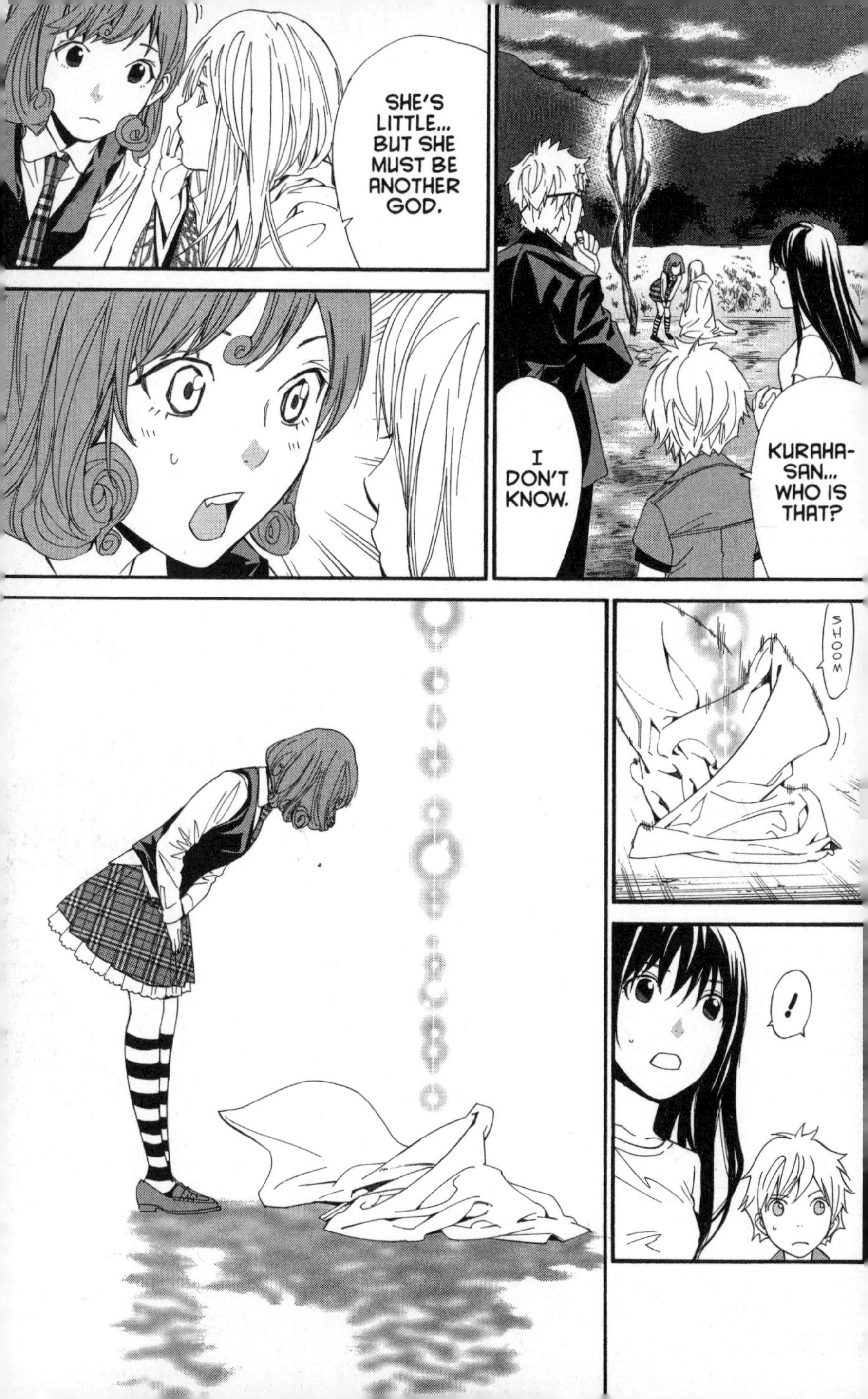
KURAHA-SAN... WHO IS THAT?
I DON'T KNOW.
SHE'S LITTLE... BUT SHE MUST BE ANOTHER GOD.
SHOOM
!

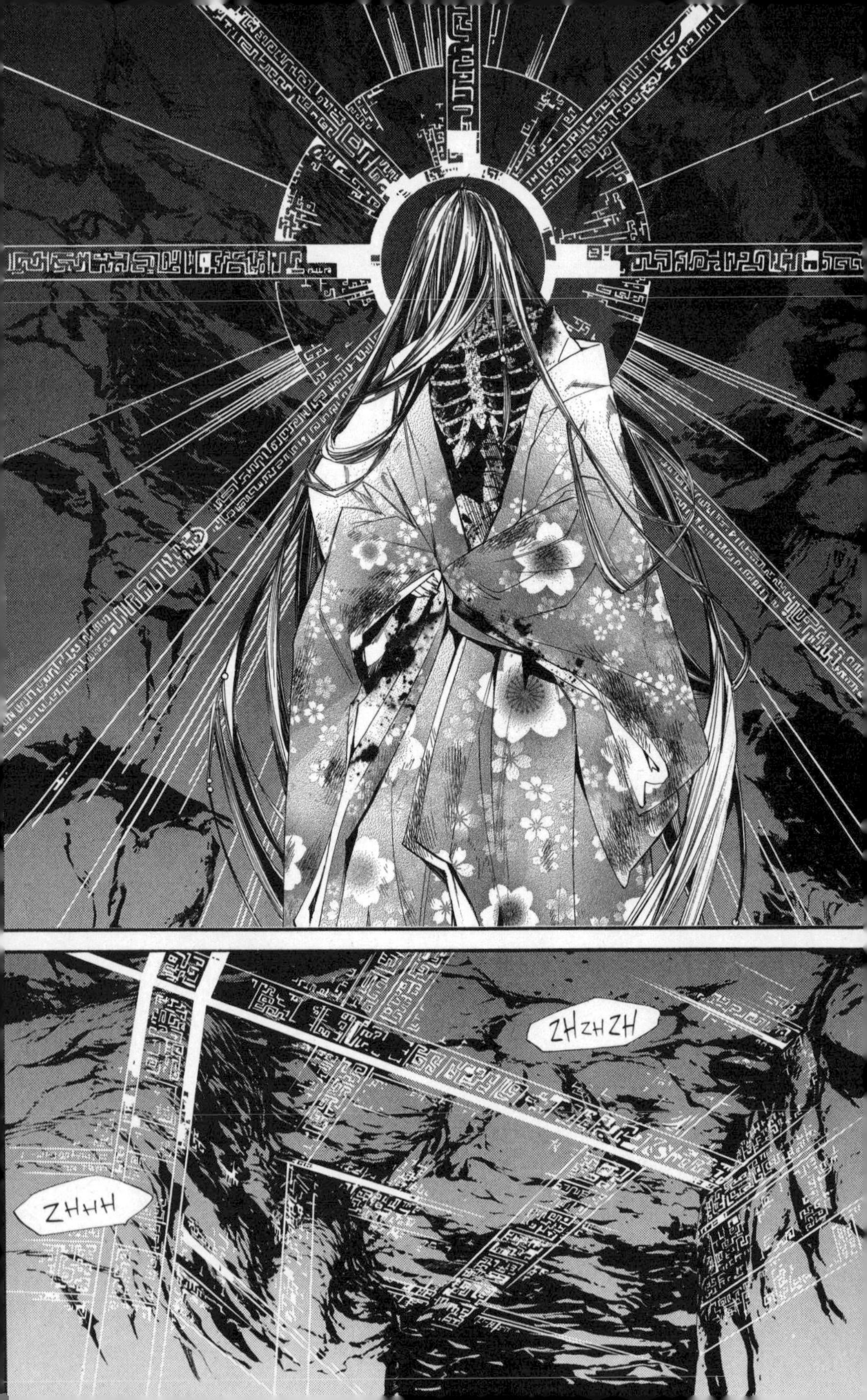
ZHZHZH
ZHHH

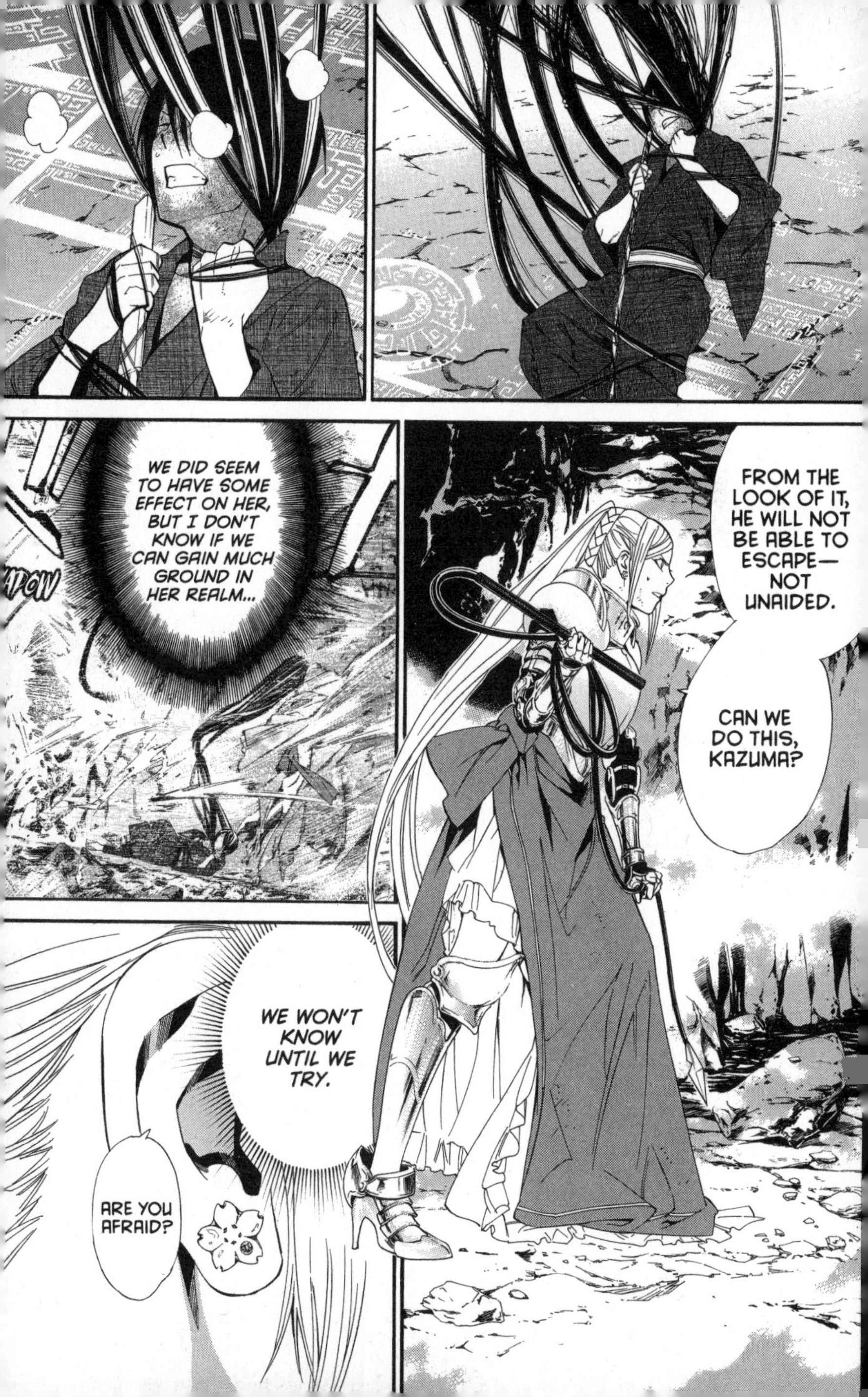
FROM THE LOOK OF IT, HE WILL NOT BE ABLE TO ESCAPE— NOT UNAIDED.
CAN WE DO THIS, KAZUMA?
WE DID SEEM TO HAVE SOME EFFECT ON HER, BUT I DON'T KNOW IF WE CAN GAIN MUCH GROUND IN HER REALM...
WE WON'T KNOW UNTIL WE TRY.
ARE YOU AFRAID?

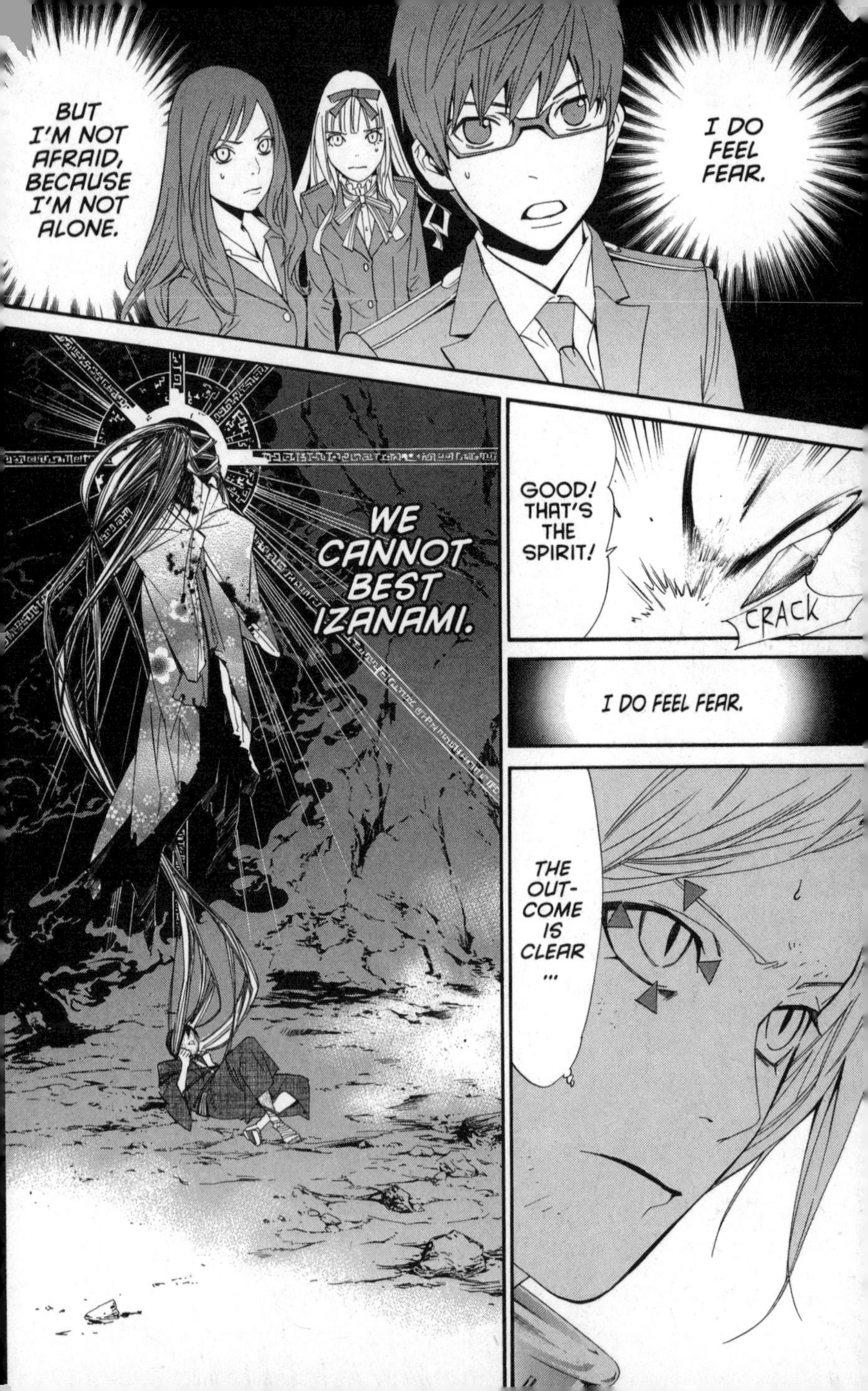
I DO FEEL FEAR.
BUT I'M NOT AFRAID, BECAUSE I'M NOT ALONE.
GOOD! THAT'S THE SPIRIT!
CRACK
WE CANNOT BEST IZANAMI.
I DO FEEL FEAR.
THE OUT-COME IS CLEAR...

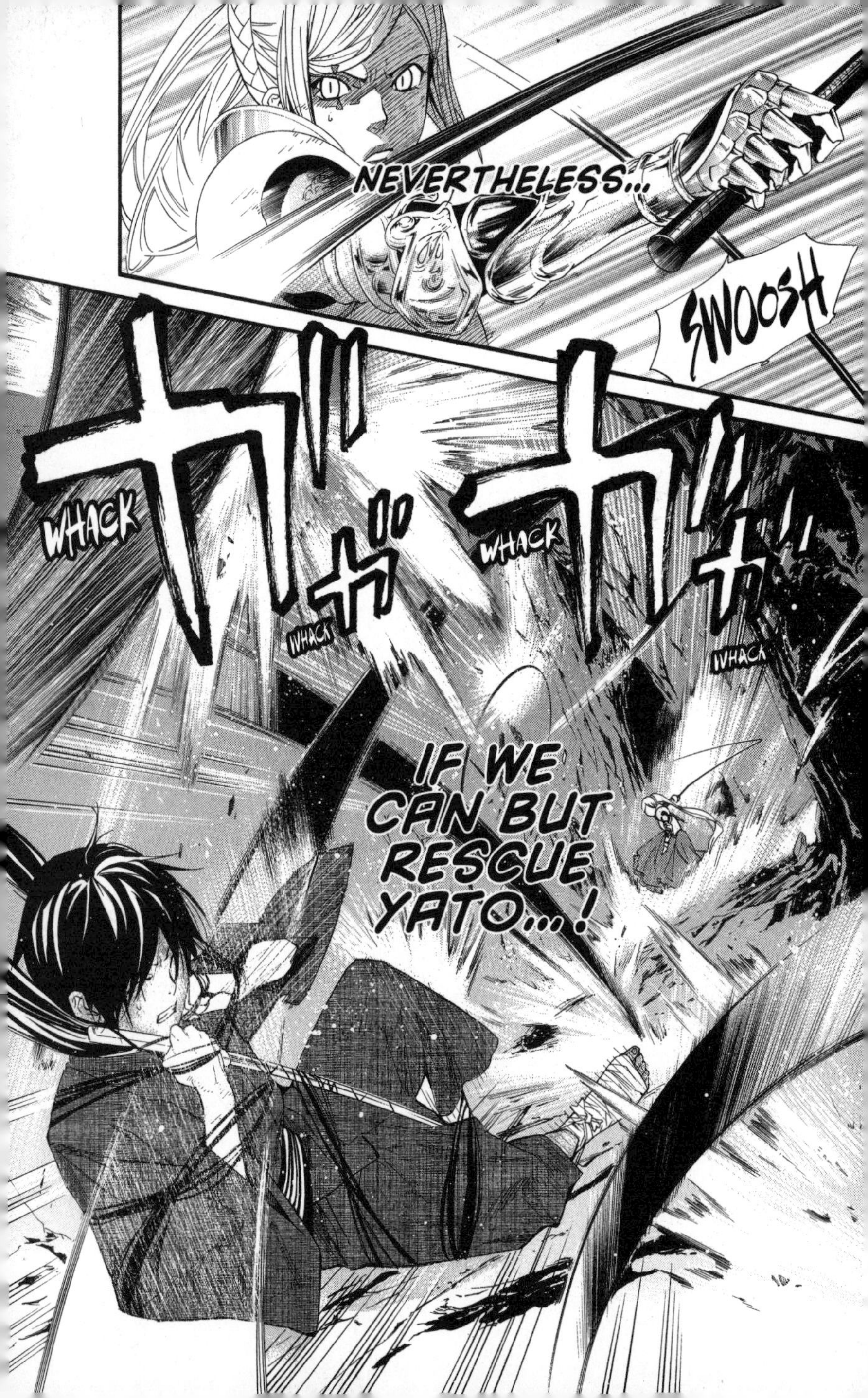
NEVERTHELESS...
SWOOSH
WHACK
WHACK
WHACK
WHACK
IF WE CAN BUT RESCUE YATO...!

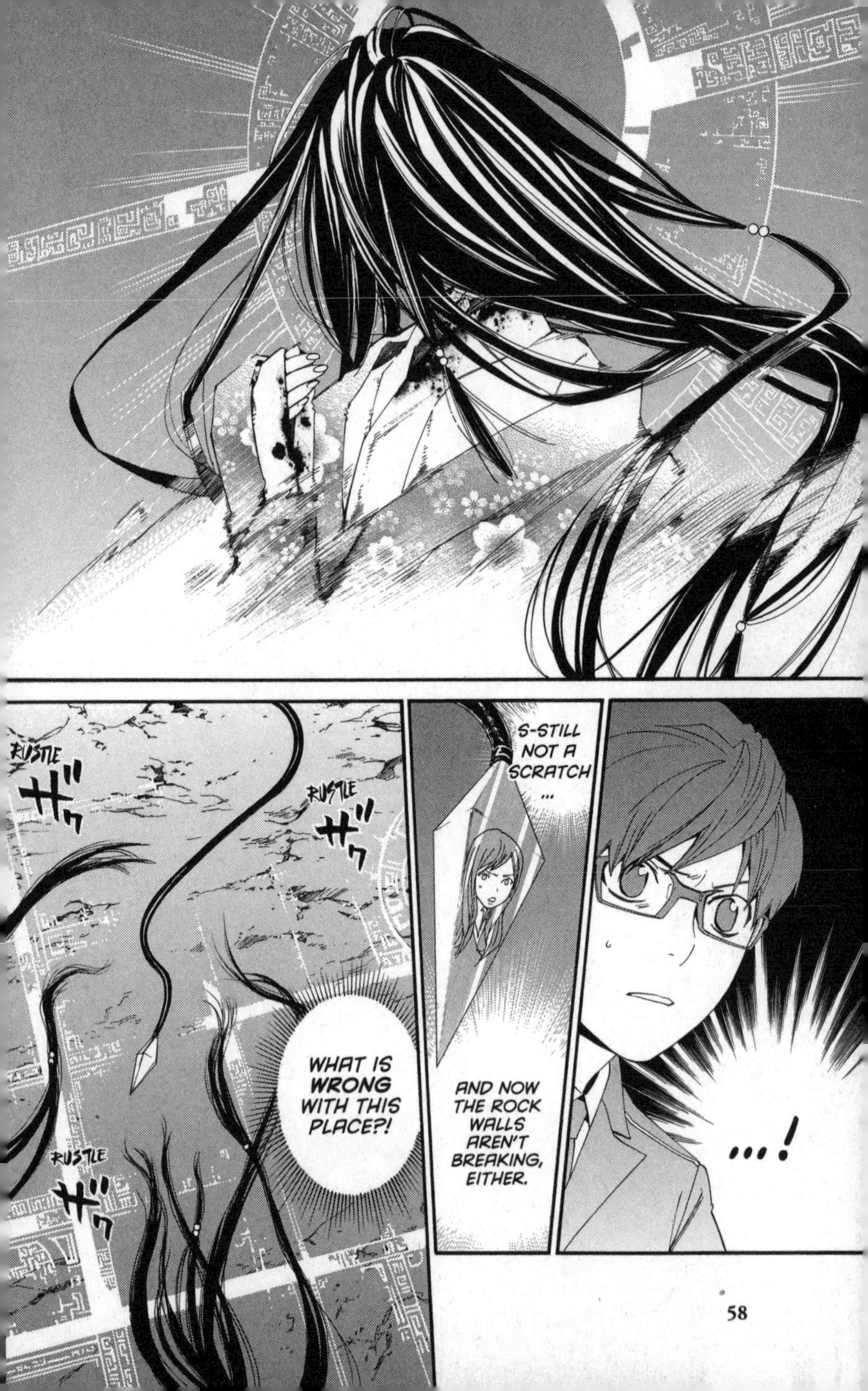
...!
S-STILL NOT A SCRATCH...
AND NOW THE ROCK WALLS AREN'T BREAKING, EITHER.
RUSTLE
ザク
RUSTLE
ザク
WHAT IS WRONG WITH THIS PLACE?!
RUSTLE
ザク

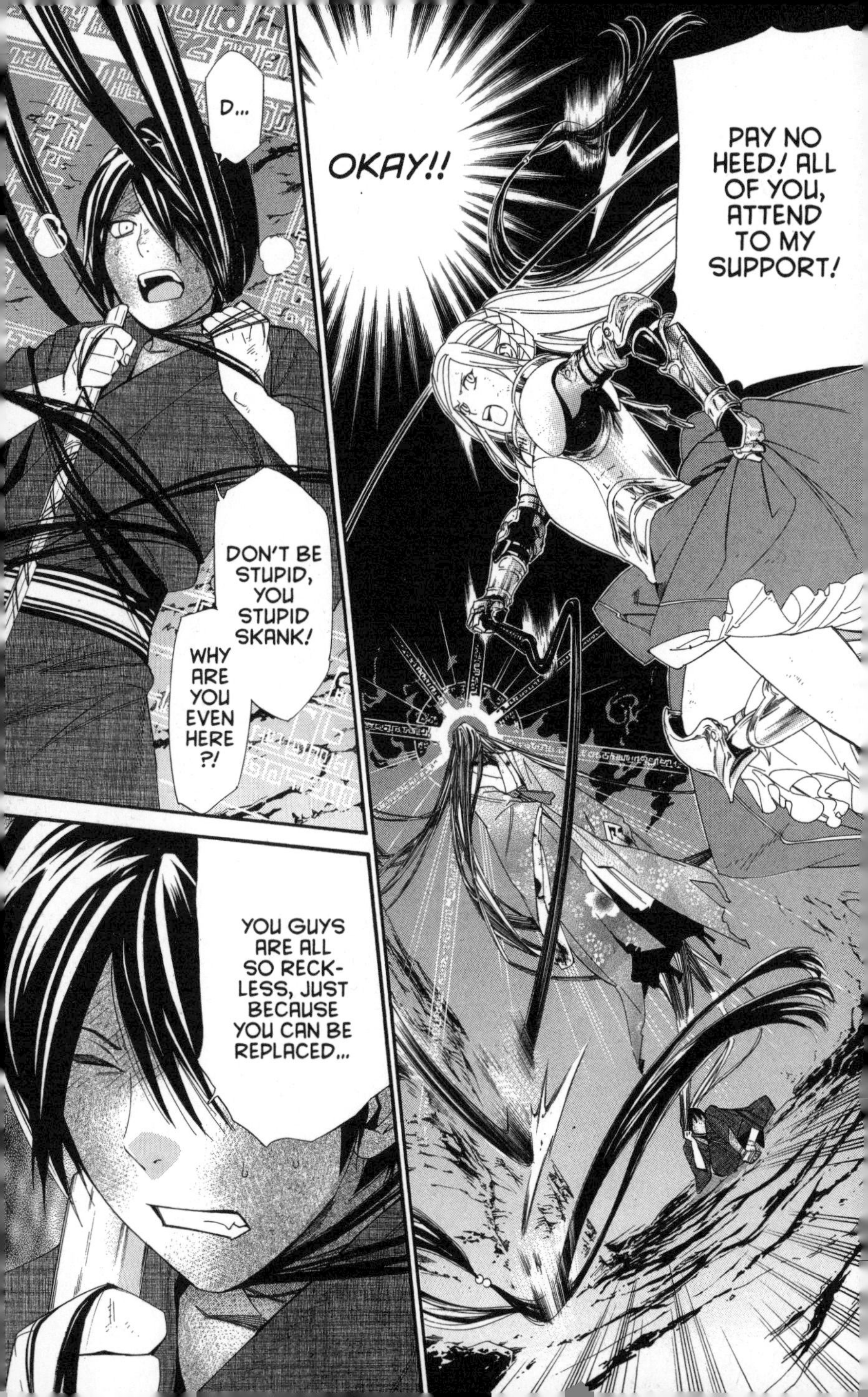
PAY NO HEED! ALL OF YOU, ATTEND TO MY SUPPORT!
OKAY!!
D...
DON'T BE STUPID, YOU STUPID SKANK!
WHY ARE YOU EVEN HERE?!
YOU GUYS ARE ALL SO RECK-LESS, JUST BECAUSE YOU CAN BE REPLACED...

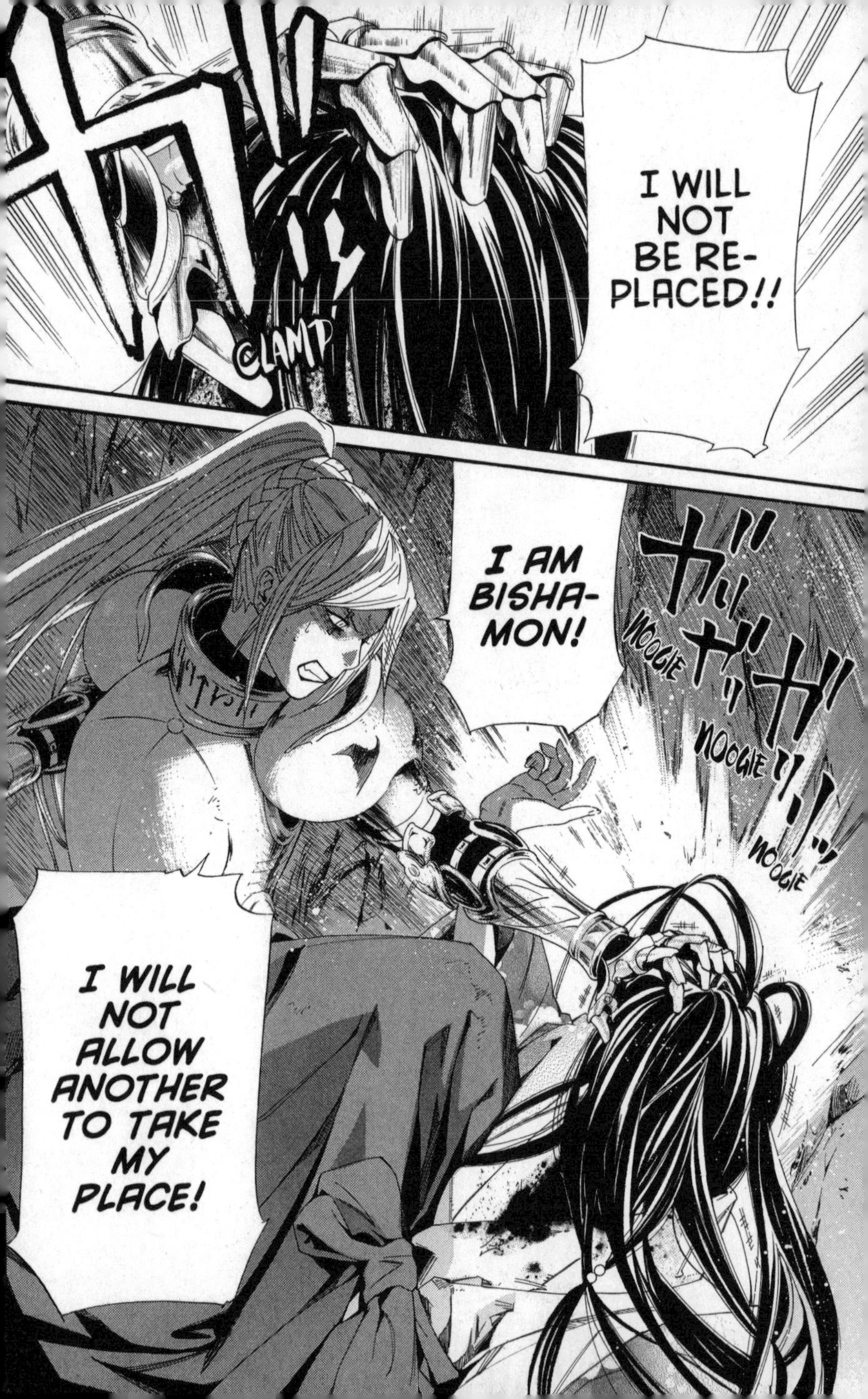
I WILL NOT BE RE-PLACED!!
CLAMP
I AM BISHA-MON!
NOOGIE
NOOGIE
NOOGIE
I WILL NOT ALLOW ANOTHER TO TAKE MY PLACE!

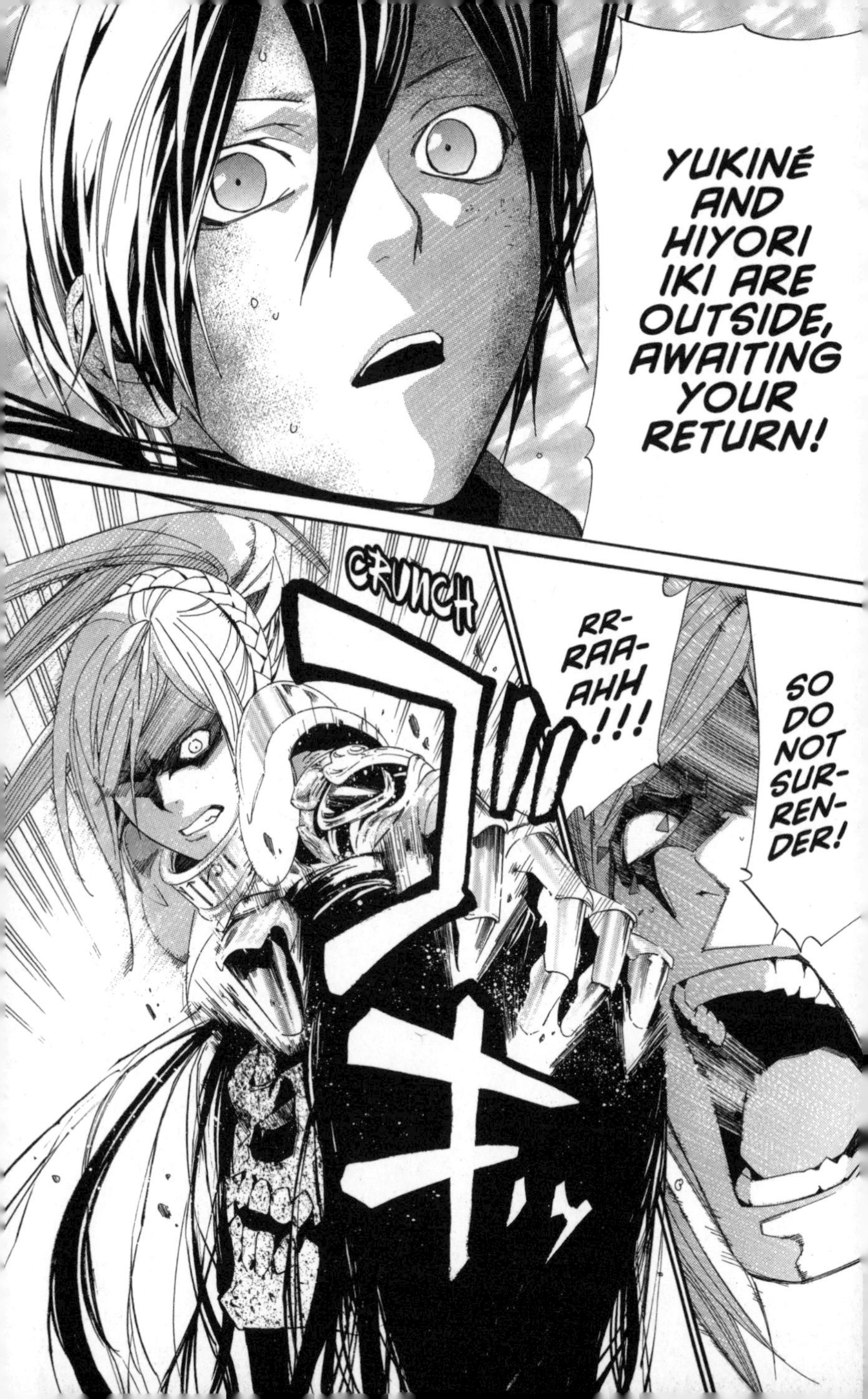
YUKINÉ AND HIYORI IKI ARE OUTSIDE, AWAITING YOUR RETURN!
SO DO NOT SURRENDER!
RR-RAA-AHH!!!
CRUNCH

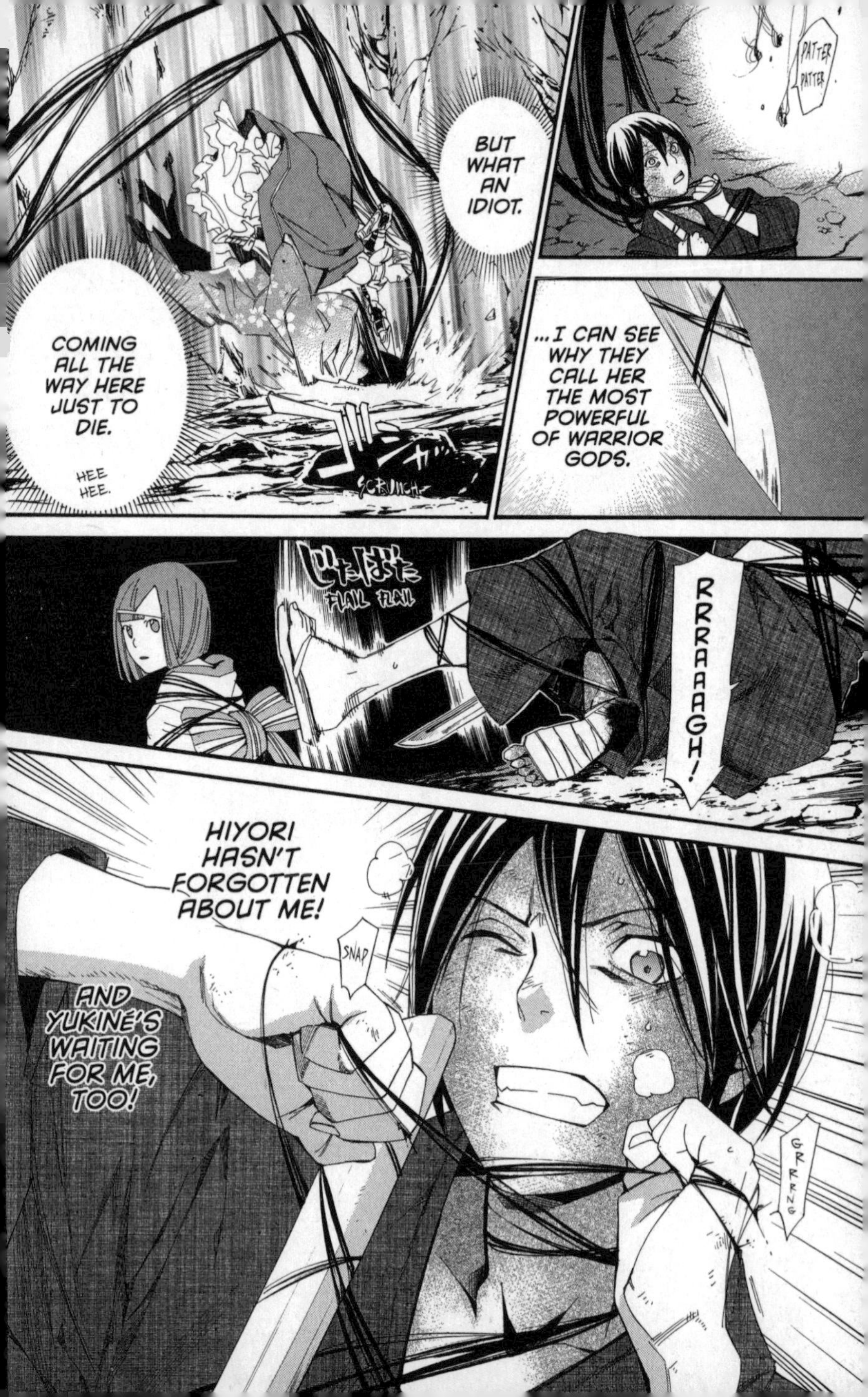
PATTER PATTER
...I CAN SEE WHY THEY CALL HER THE MOST POWERFUL OF WARRIOR GODS.
BUT WHAT AN IDIOT.
COMING ALL THE WAY HERE JUST TO DIE.
HEE HEE.
SCRUNCH
RRRAAAGH!
FLAIL FLAIL
HIYORI HASN'T FORGOTTEN ABOUT ME!
SNAP
AND YUKINÉ'S WAITING FOR ME, TOO!
GRRRNG

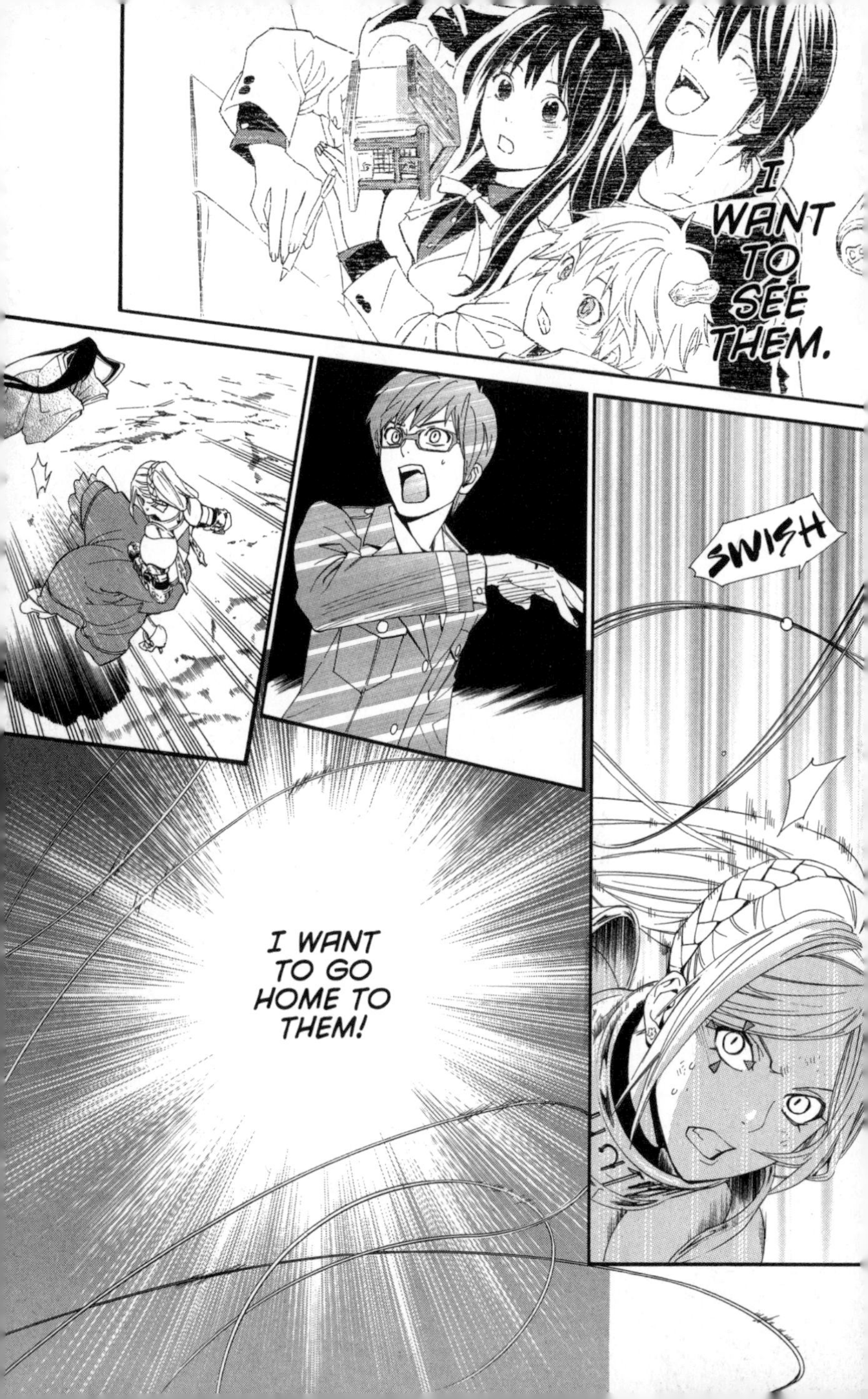
I WANT TO SEE THEM.
SWISH
I WANT TO GO HOME TO THEM!

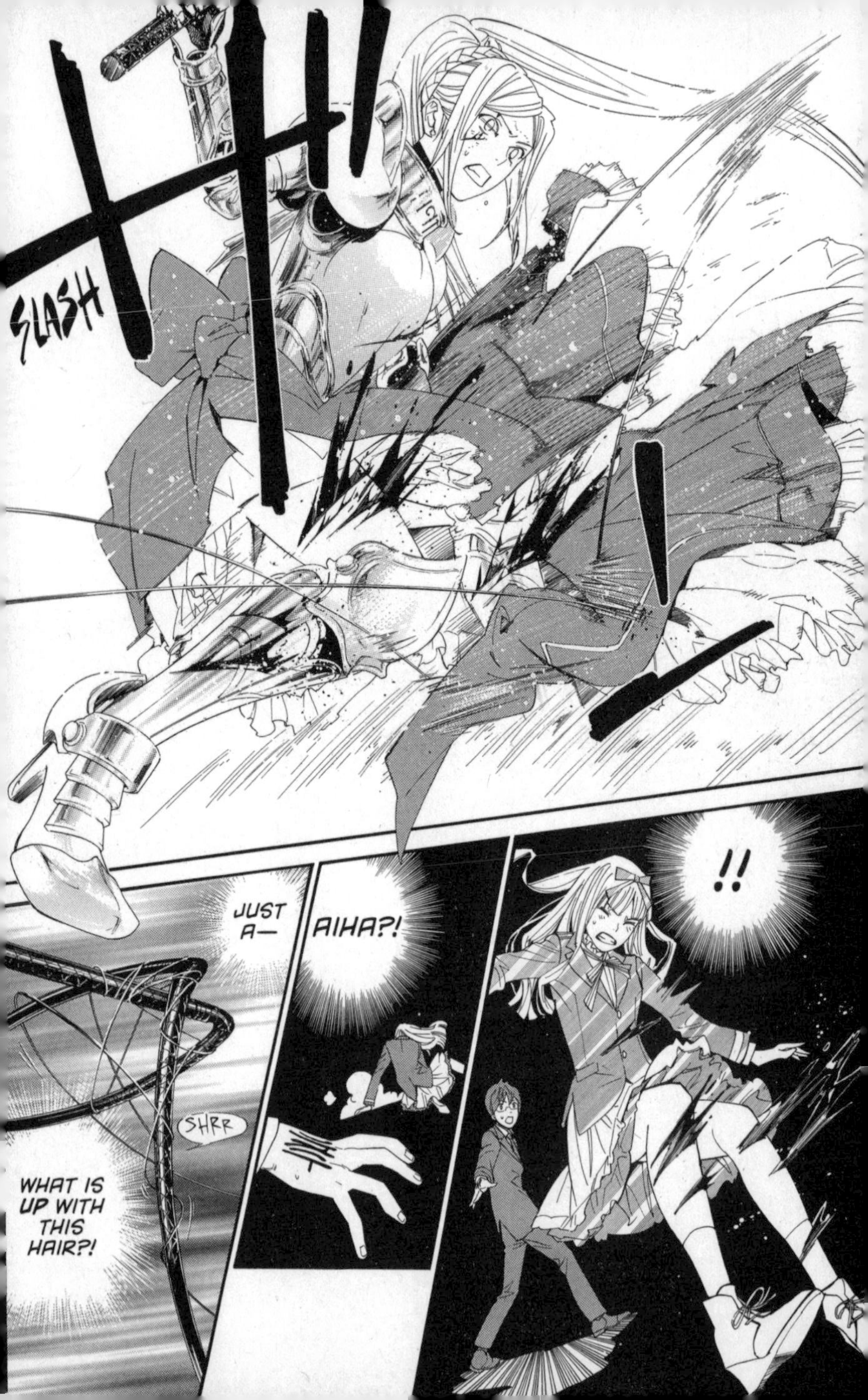
SLASH
!!
AIHA?!
JUST A—
SHRR
WHAT IS UP WITH THIS HAIR?!

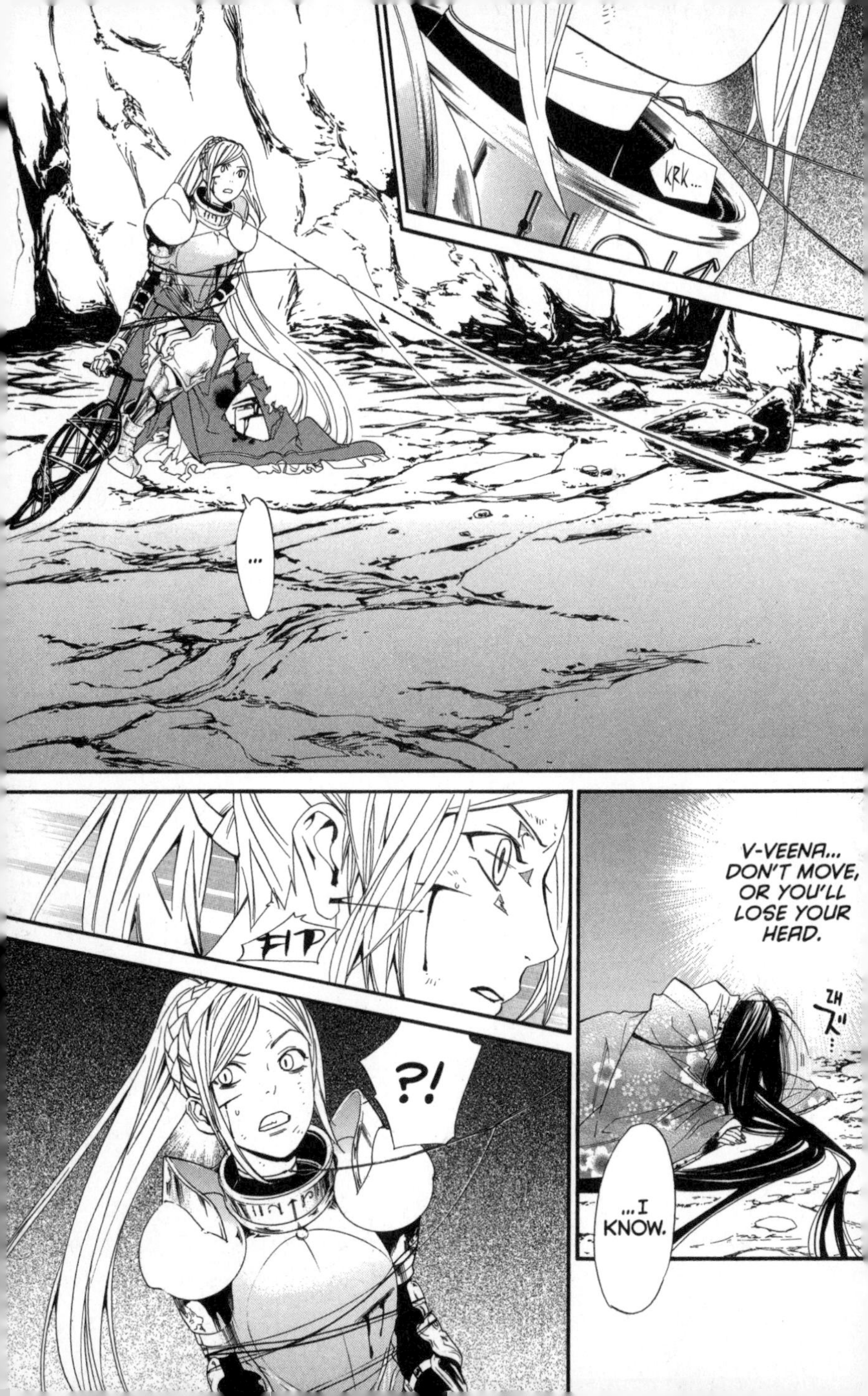
KRK...
...
V-VEENA... DON'T MOVE, OR YOU'LL LOSE YOUR HEAD.
ZUH ズ...
...I KNOW.
FIP
?!

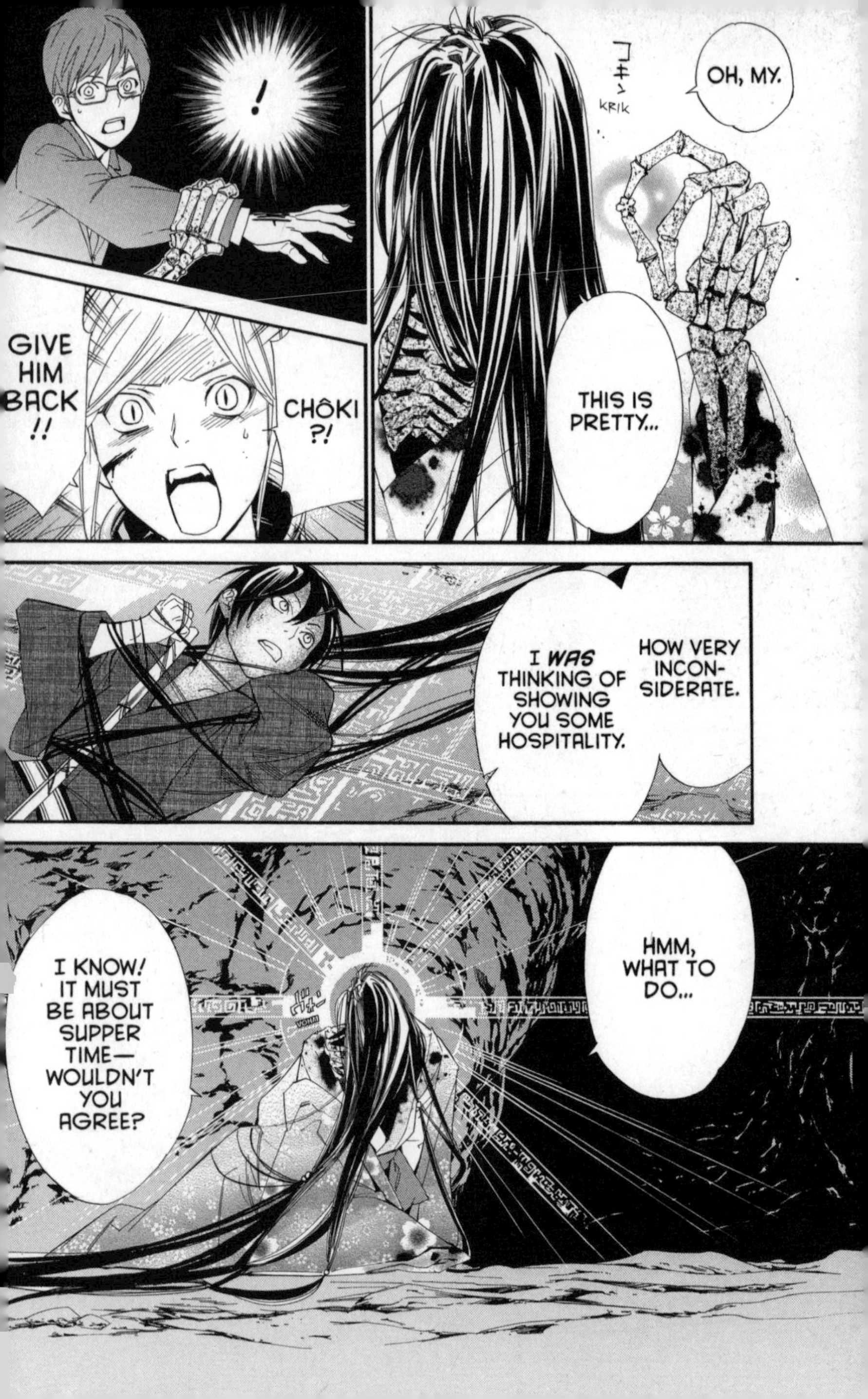

KRIK
OH, MY.
THIS IS PRETTY...
!
CHÔKI ?!
GIVE HIM BACK !!
HOW VERY INCON- SIDERATE.
I *WAS* THINKING OF SHOWING YOU SOME HOSPITALITY.
HMM, WHAT TO DO...
VOHM
I KNOW! IT MUST BE ABOUT SUPPER TIME— WOULDN'T YOU AGREE?

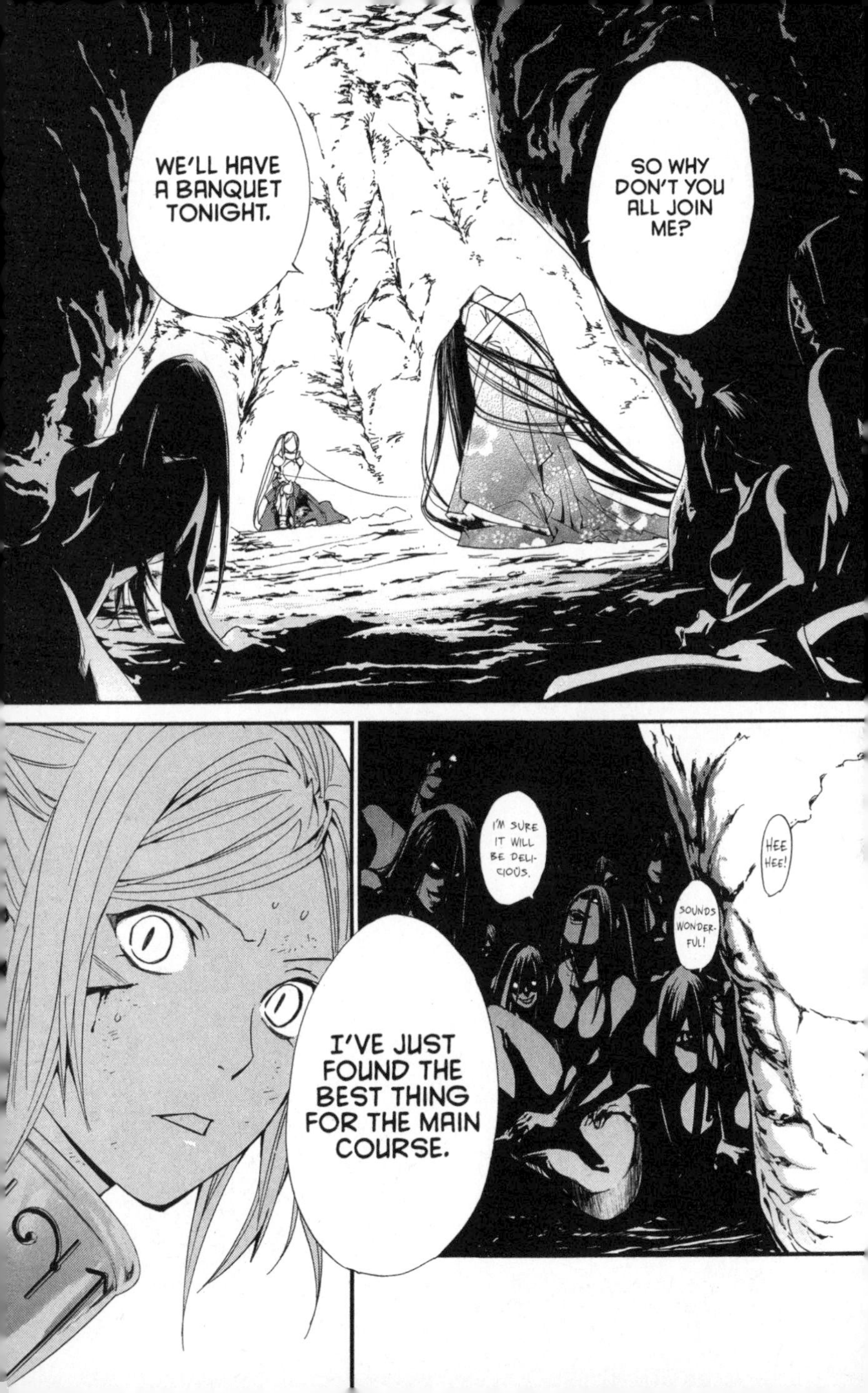
SO WHY DON'T YOU ALL JOIN ME?
WE'LL HAVE A BANQUET TONIGHT.
HEE HEE!
SOUNDS WONDER-FUL!
I'M SURE IT WILL BE DELI-CIOUS.
I'VE JUST FOUND THE BEST THING FOR THE MAIN COURSE.

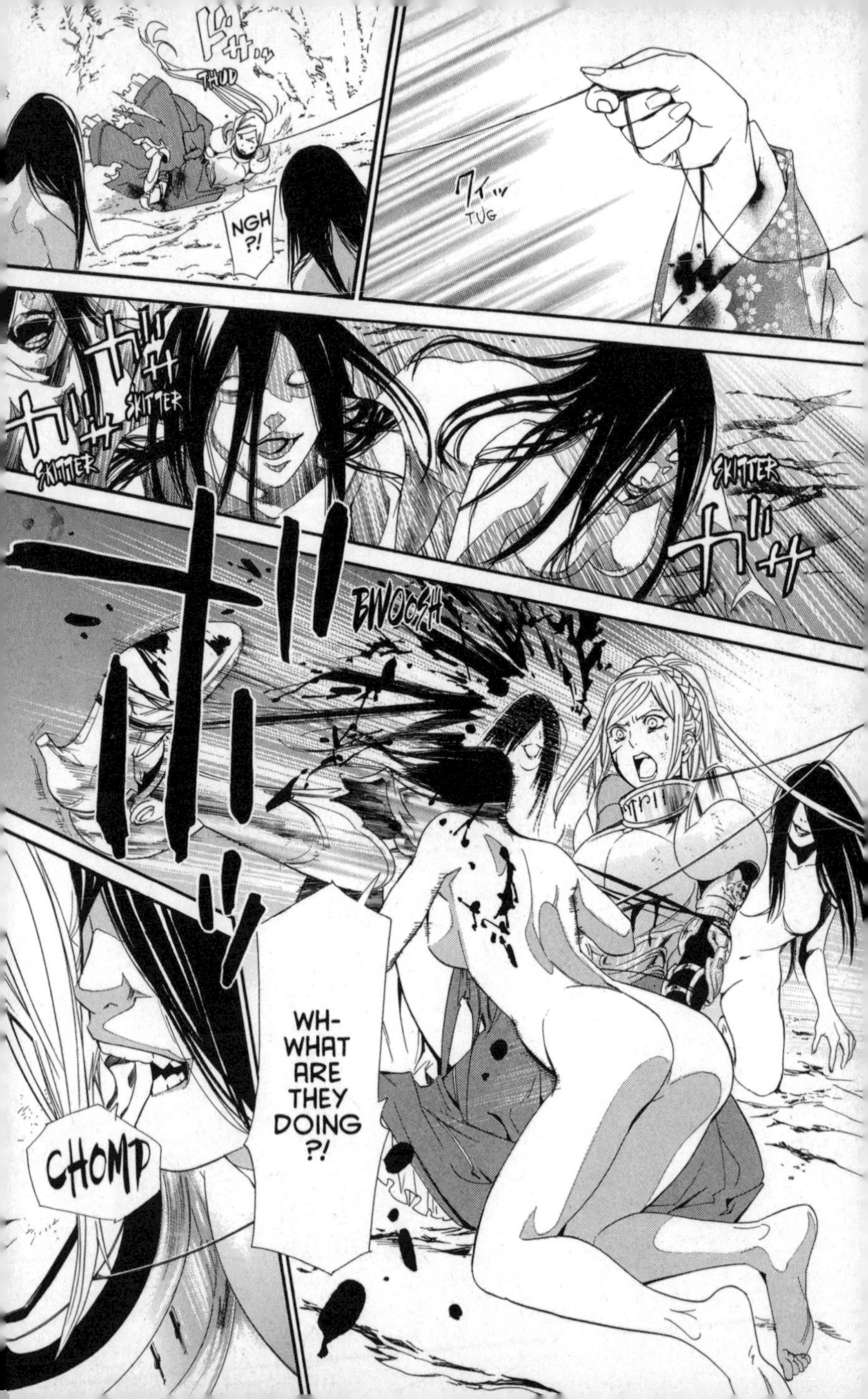
TUG
THUD
NGH?!
SKITTER
SKITTER
SKITTER
BWOOSH
WH-WHAT ARE THEY DOING?!
CHOMP

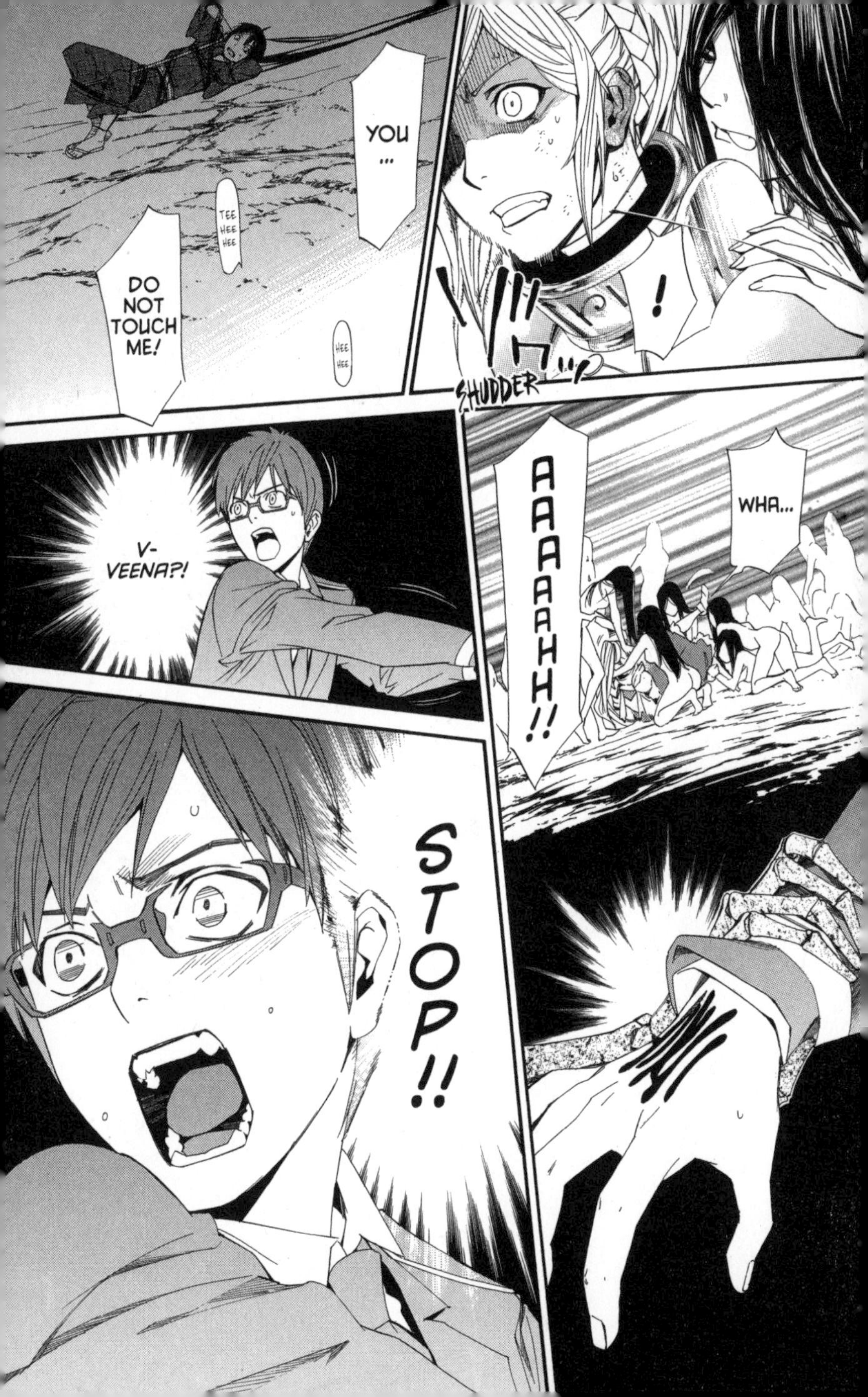
!
SHUDDER
YOU ...
TEE HEE HEE
DO NOT TOUCH ME!
HEE HEE
WHA...
AAAAAAAHH!!
V-VEENA?!
STOP!!

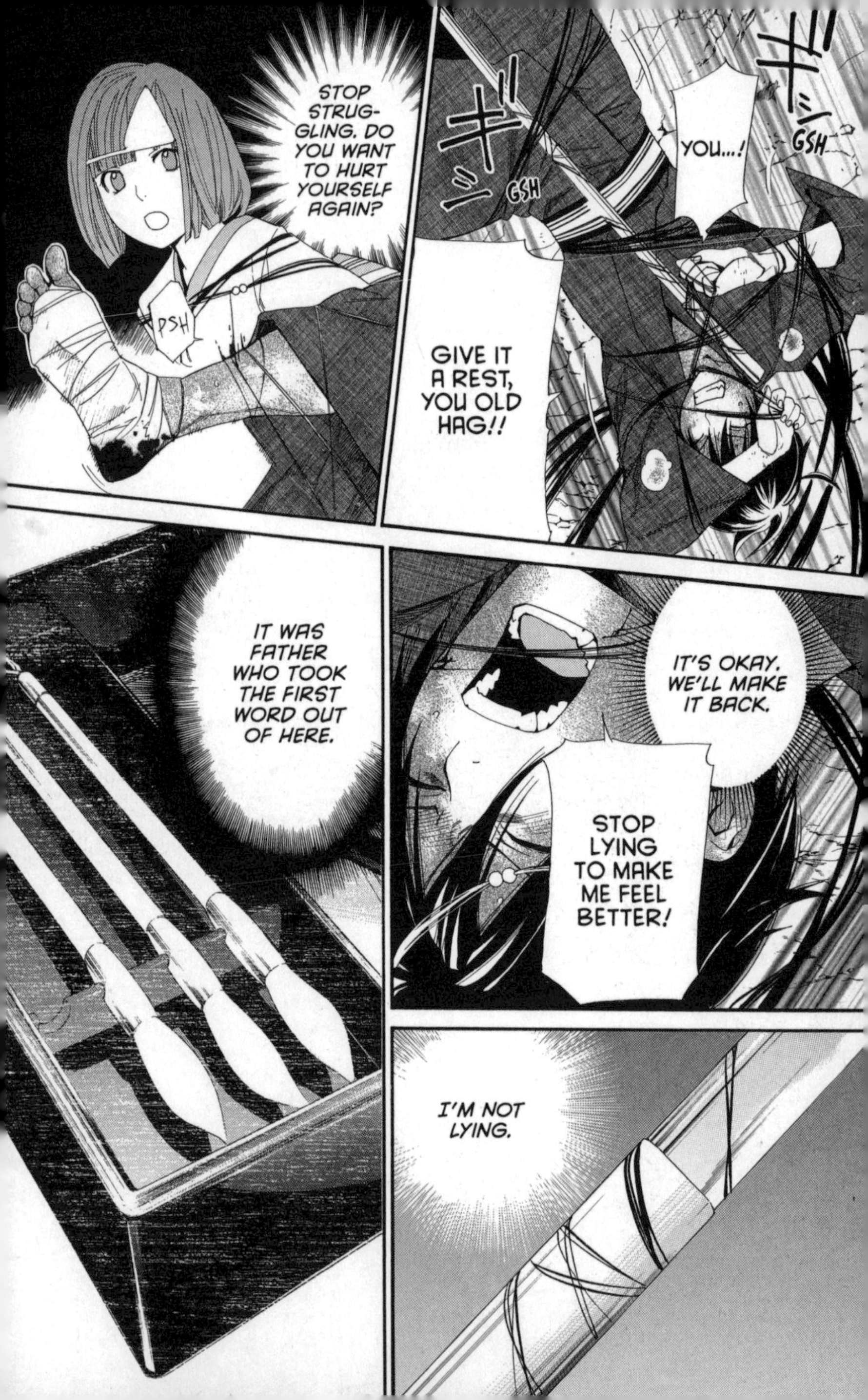
GSH
YOU...!
GSH
GIVE IT A REST, YOU OLD HAG!!
STOP STRUG-GLING. DO YOU WANT TO HURT YOURSELF AGAIN?
PSH
IT'S OKAY. WE'LL MAKE IT BACK.
STOP LYING TO MAKE ME FEEL BETTER!
I'M NOT LYING.
IT WAS FATHER WHO TOOK THE FIRST WORD OUT OF HERE.

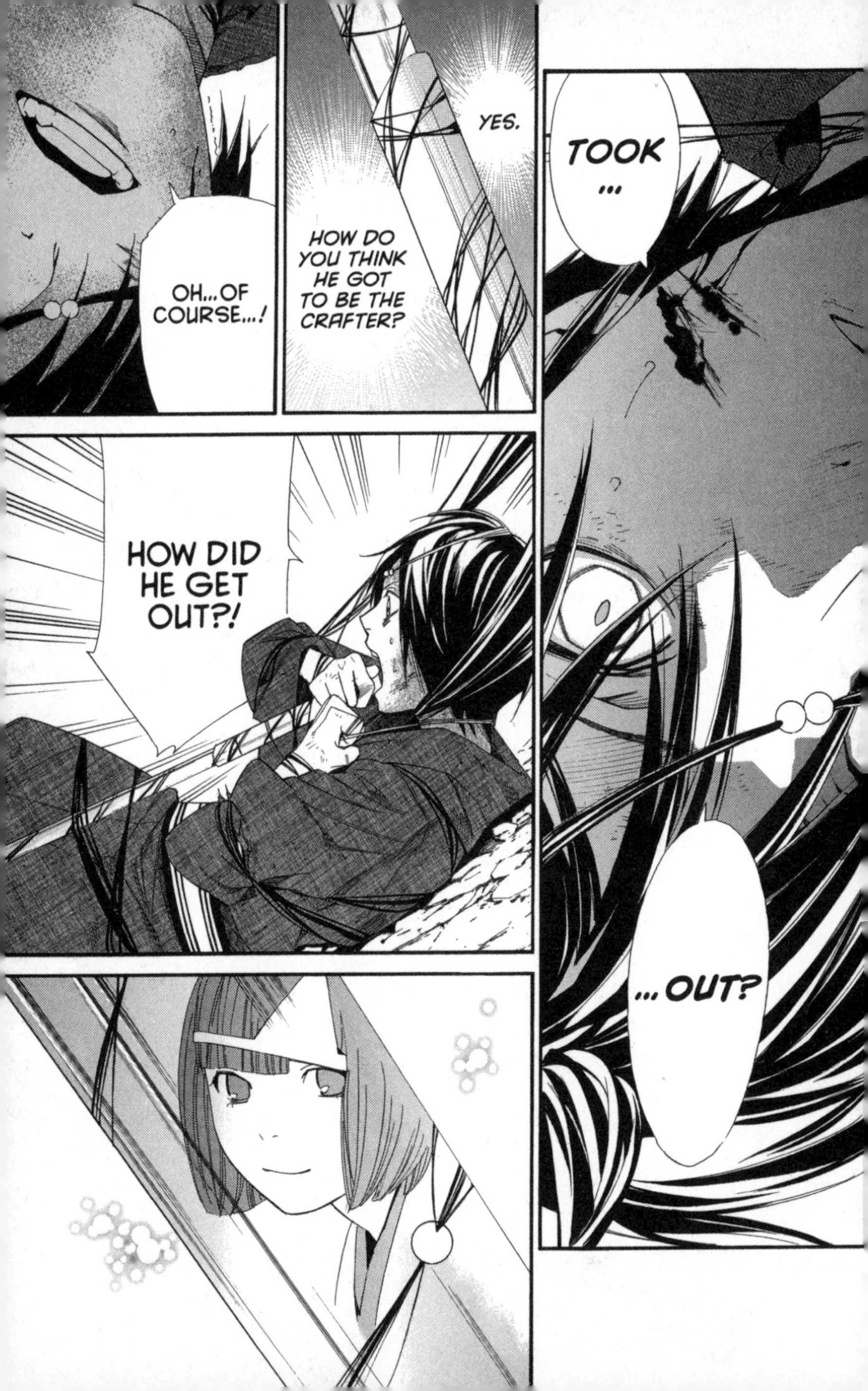
TOOK ...
...OUT?
YES.
HOW DO YOU THINK HE GOT TO BE THE CRAFTER?
OH...OF COURSE...!
HOW DID HE GET OUT?!

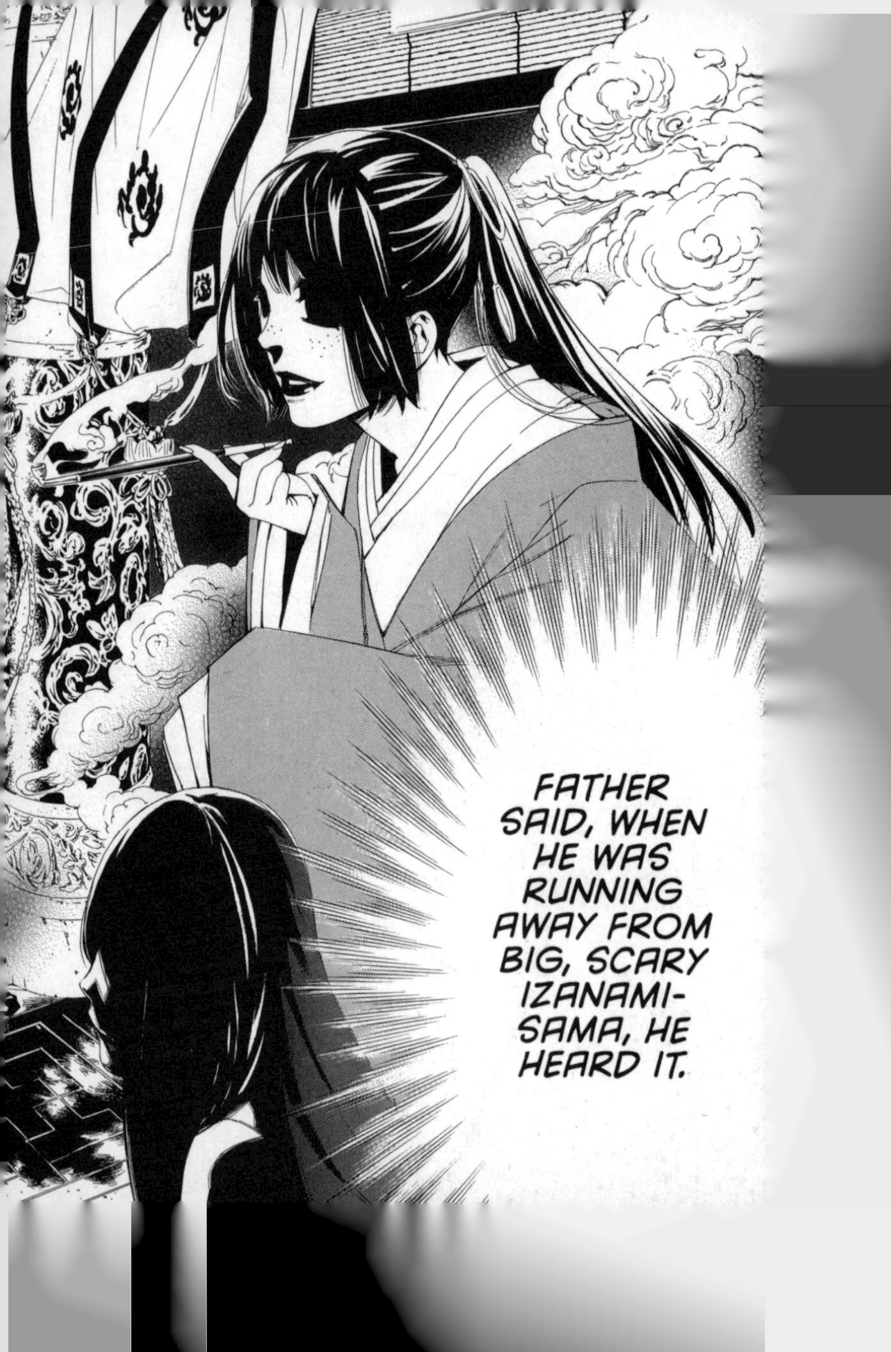
FATHER SAID, WHEN HE WAS RUNNING AWAY FROM BIG, SCARY IZANAMI-SAMA, HE HEARD IT.

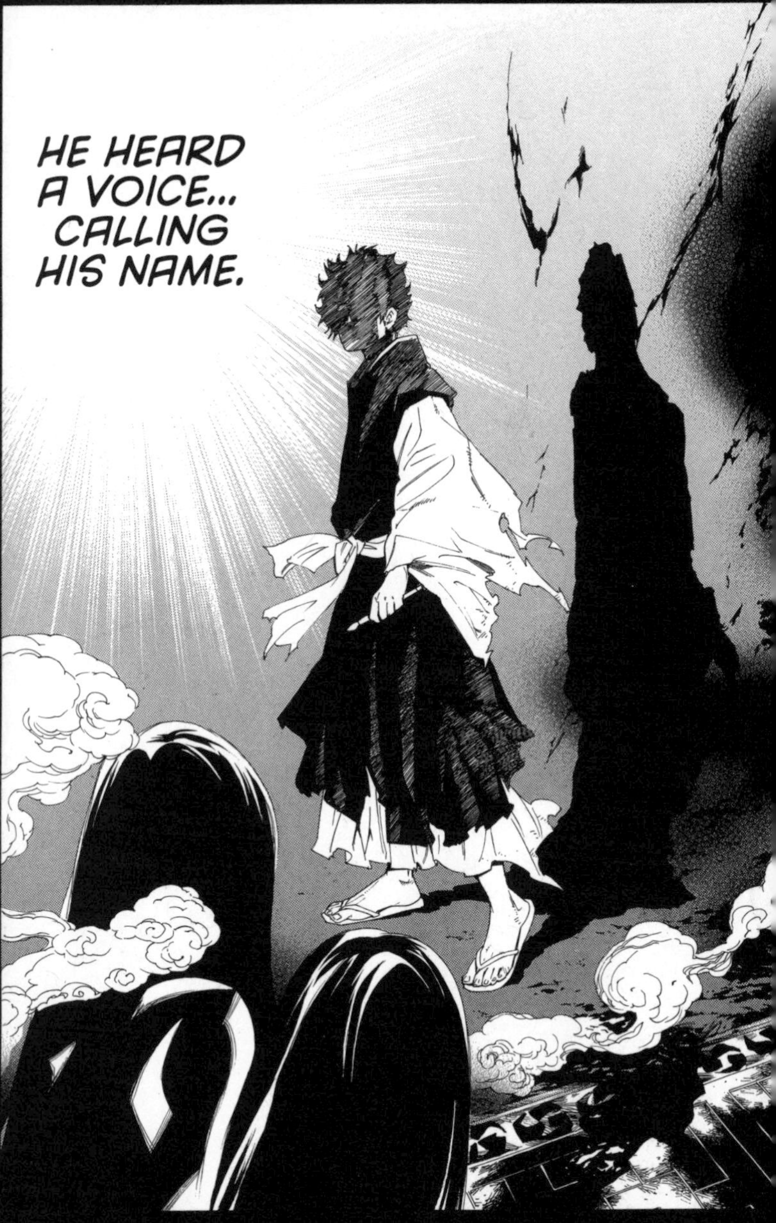
HE HEARD A VOICE... CALLING HIS NAME.

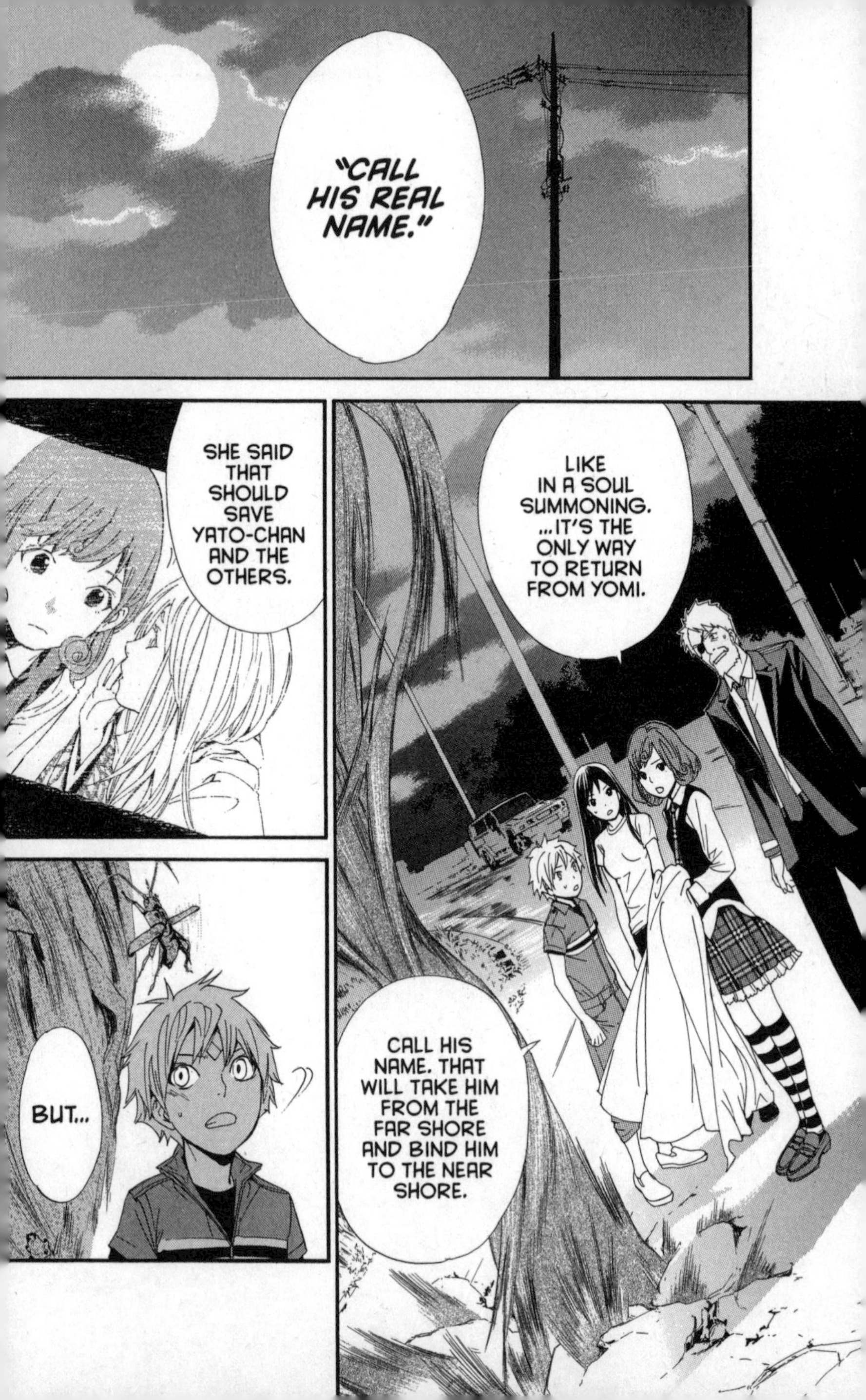
"CALL HIS REAL NAME."
LIKE IN A SOUL SUMMONING. ...IT'S THE ONLY WAY TO RETURN FROM YOMI.
CALL HIS NAME. THAT WILL TAKE HIM FROM THE FAR SHORE AND BIND HIM TO THE NEAR SHORE.
SHE SAID THAT SHOULD SAVE YATO-CHAN AND THE OTHERS.
BUT...

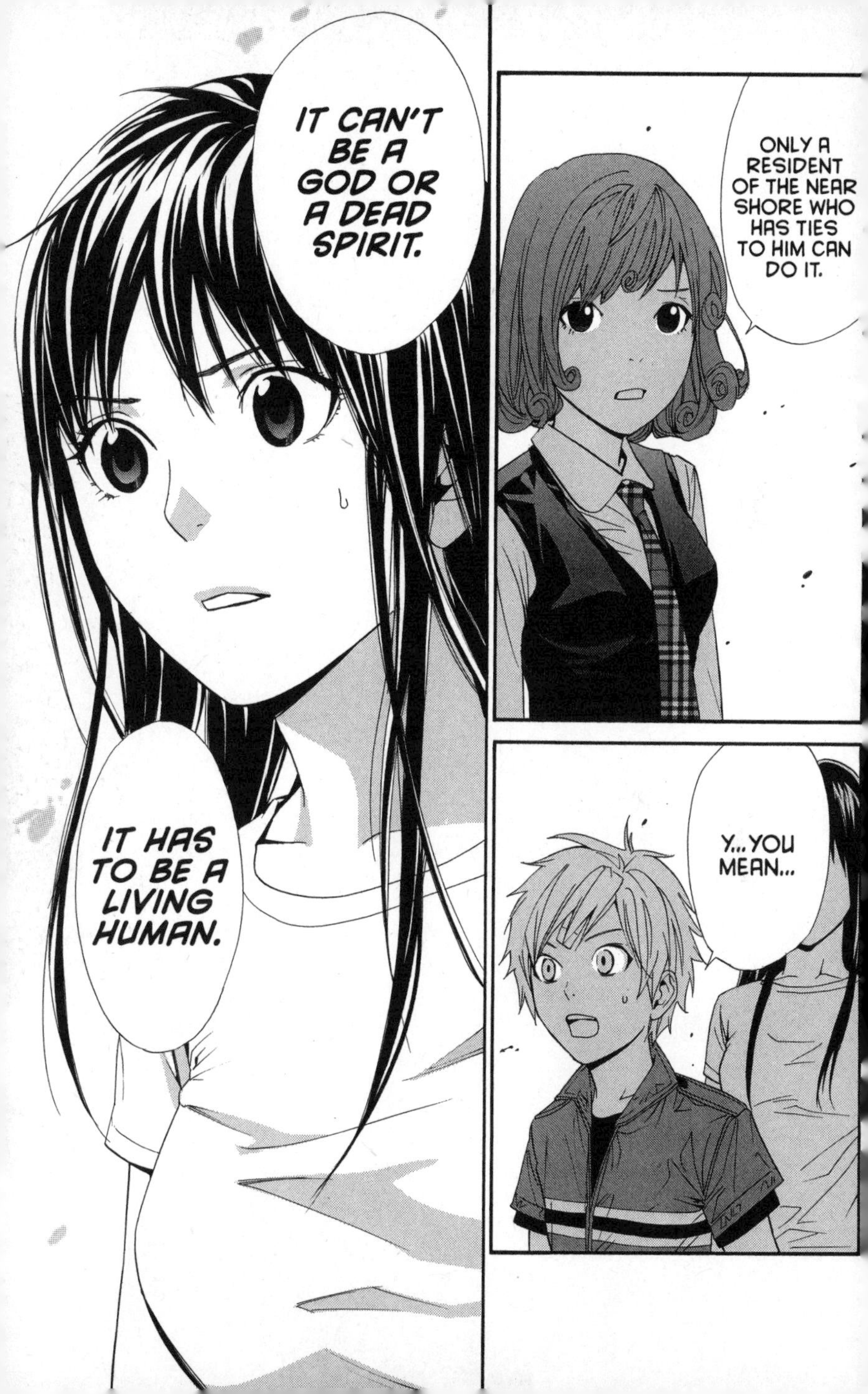
ONLY A RESIDENT OF THE NEAR SHORE WHO HAS TIES TO HIM CAN DO IT.
Y...YOU MEAN...
IT CAN'T BE A GOD OR A DEAD SPIRIT.
IT HAS TO BE A LIVING HUMAN.

YES.

IT WILL WORK.

IS THAT TRUE?!

AND THAT'S WHAT SHE TOLD YOU?!

YA—

WHO... WHO WAS SHE?

THUD

TMP

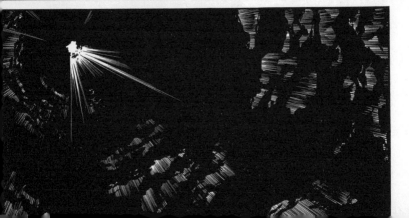

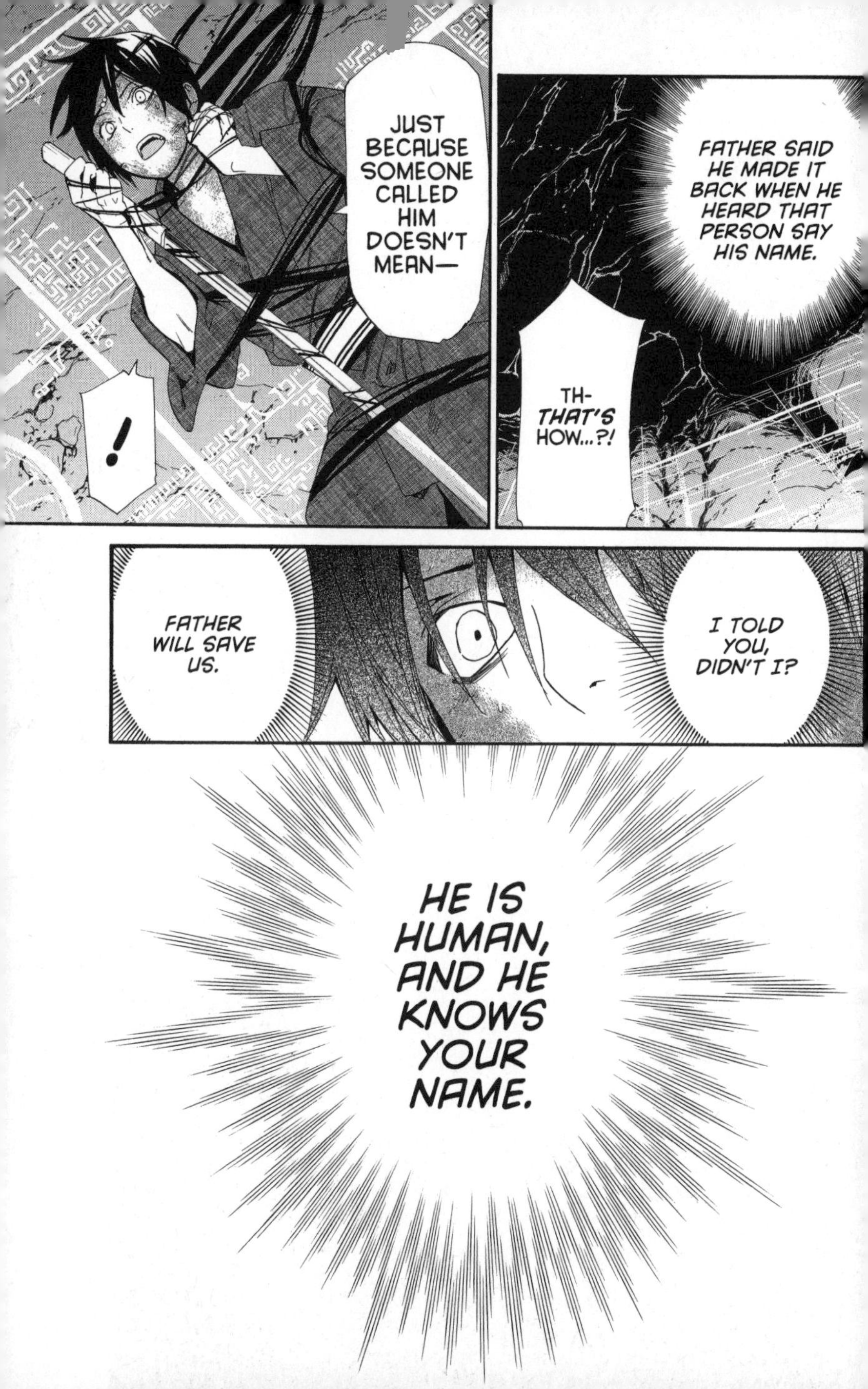
FATHER SAID HE MADE IT BACK WHEN HE HEARD THAT PERSON SAY HIS NAME.
TH- THAT'S HOW...?!
JUST BECAUSE SOMEONE CALLED HIM DOESN'T MEAN—
!
I TOLD YOU, DIDN'T I?
FATHER WILL SAVE US.
HE IS HUMAN, AND HE KNOWS YOUR NAME.

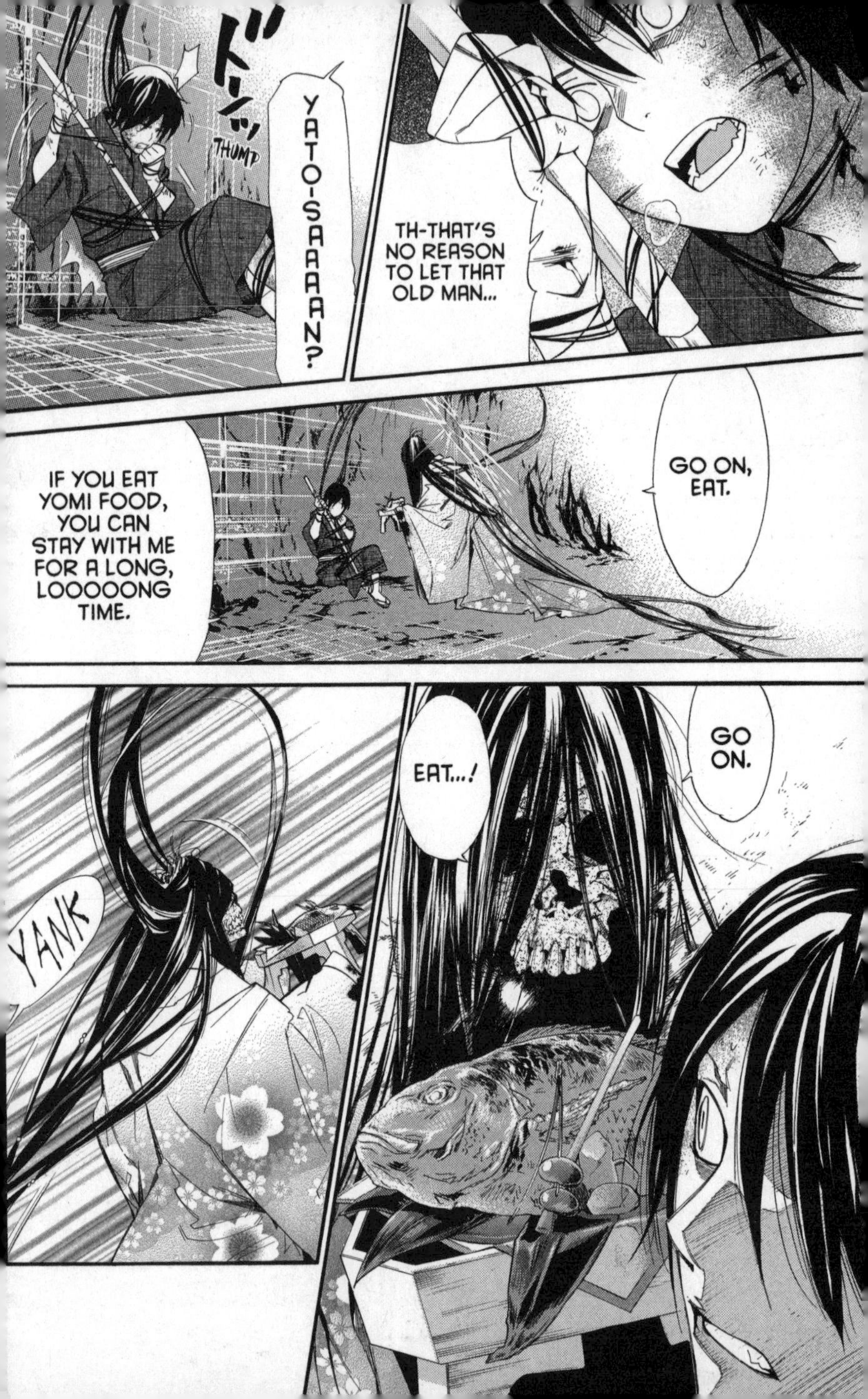
TH-THAT'S NO REASON TO LET THAT OLD MAN...
YATO-SAAAAN?
THUMP
GO ON, EAT.
IF YOU EAT YOMI FOOD, YOU CAN STAY WITH ME FOR A LONG, LOOOOONG TIME.
GO ON.
EAT...!
YANK

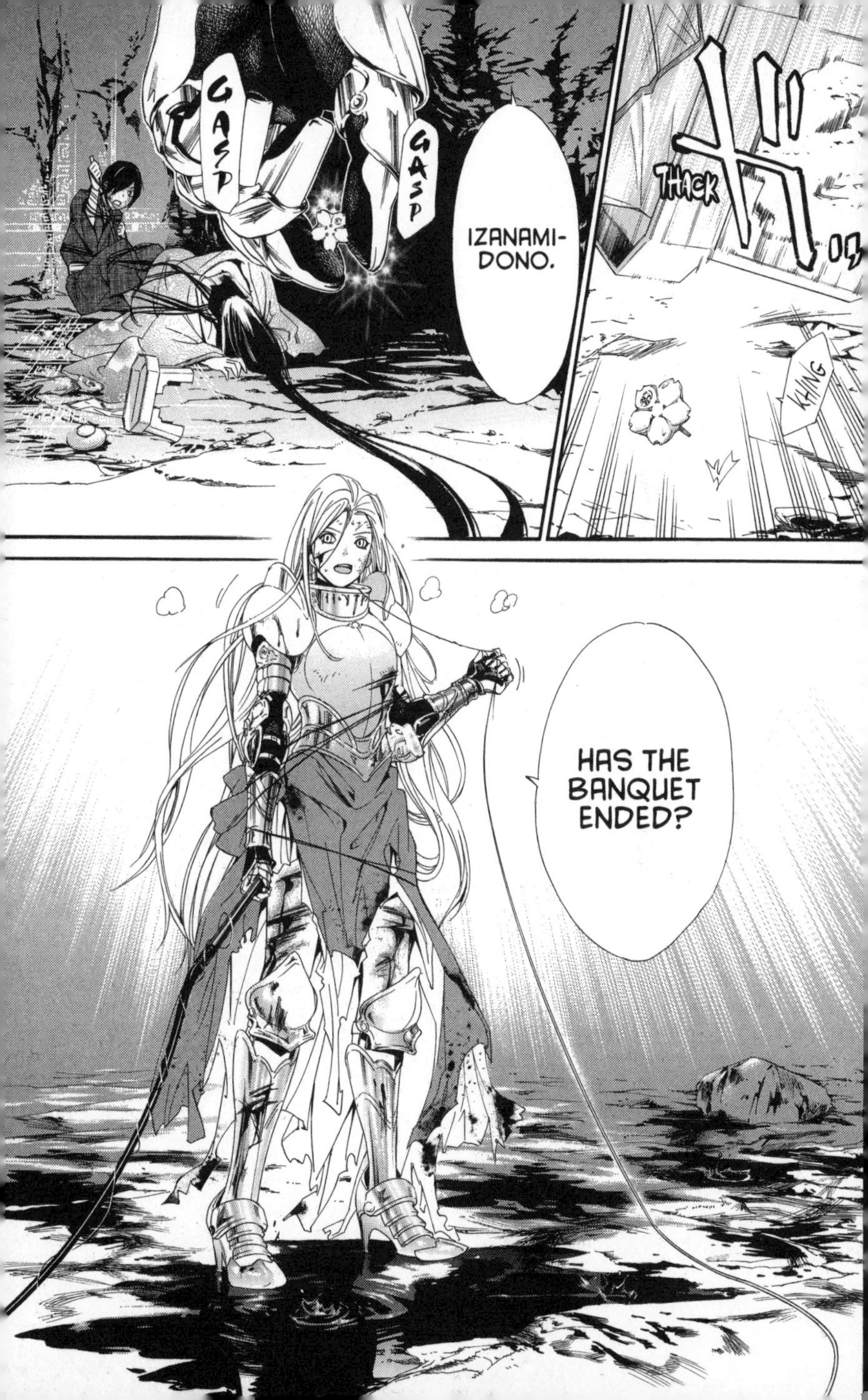
THACK
KHING
IZANAMI-DONO.
GASP
GASP
HAS THE BANQUET ENDED?

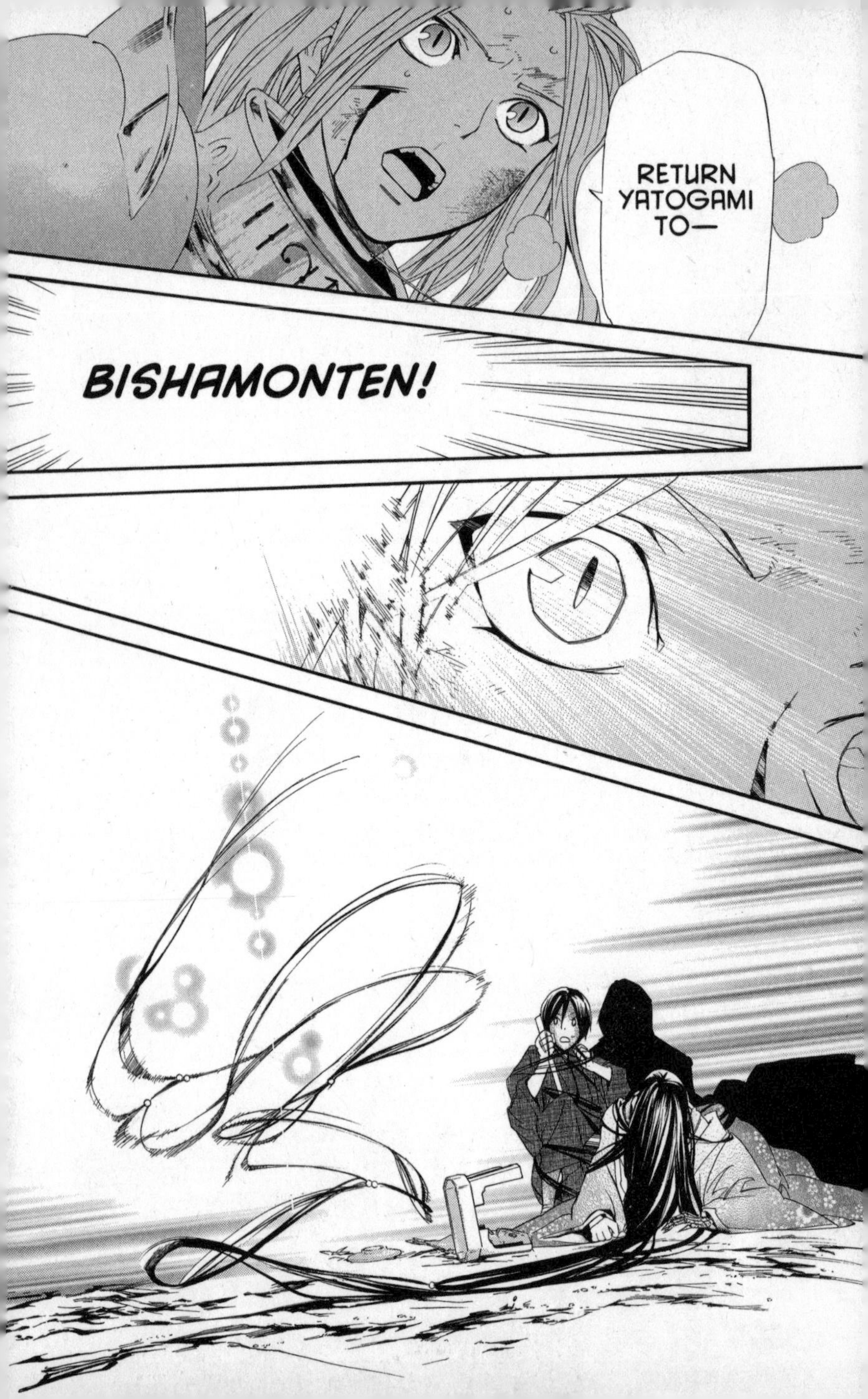
RETURN YATOGAMI TO—
BISHAMONTEN!

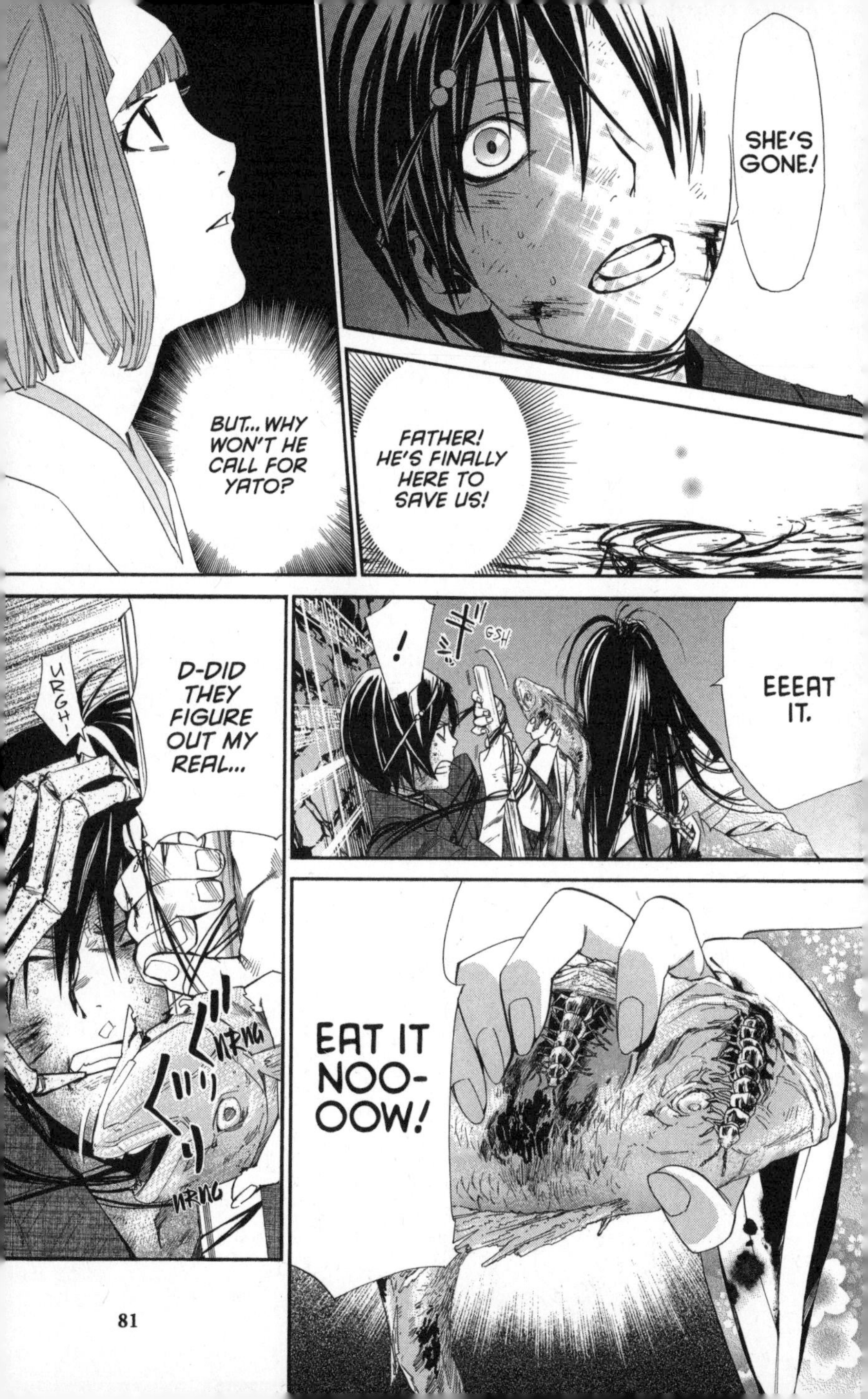
SHE'S GONE!
FATHER! HE'S FINALLY HERE TO SAVE US!
BUT... WHY WON'T HE CALL FOR YATO?
EEEAT IT.
GSH
!
EAT IT NOOO-OOW!
D-DID THEY FIGURE OUT MY REAL...
URGH!
NRNG
NRNG

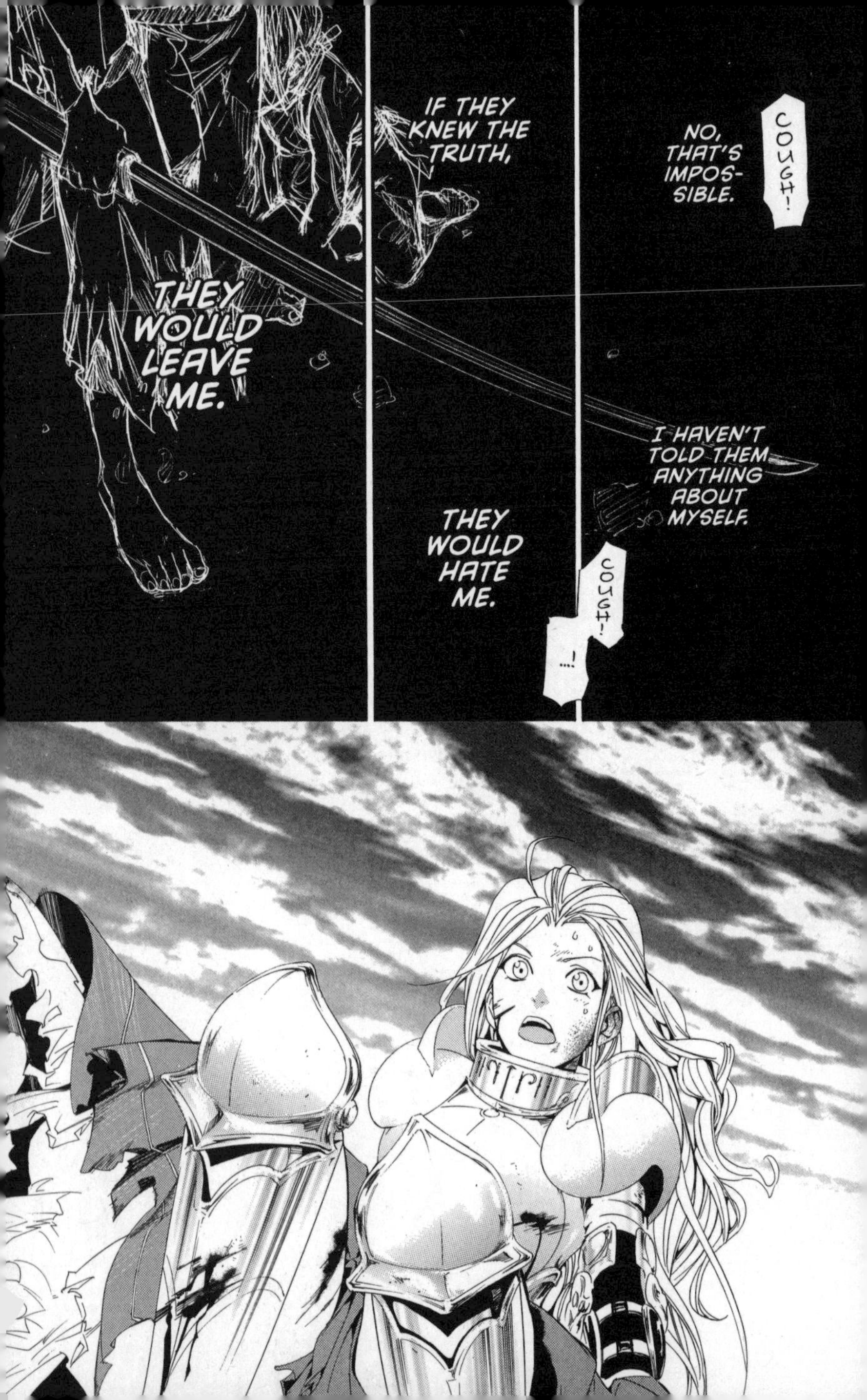
COUGH!
NO, THAT'S IMPOSSIBLE.
I HAVEN'T TOLD THEM ANYTHING ABOUT MYSELF.
COUGH!
...!
IF THEY KNEW THE TRUTH,
THEY WOULD HATE ME.
THEY WOULD LEAVE ME.

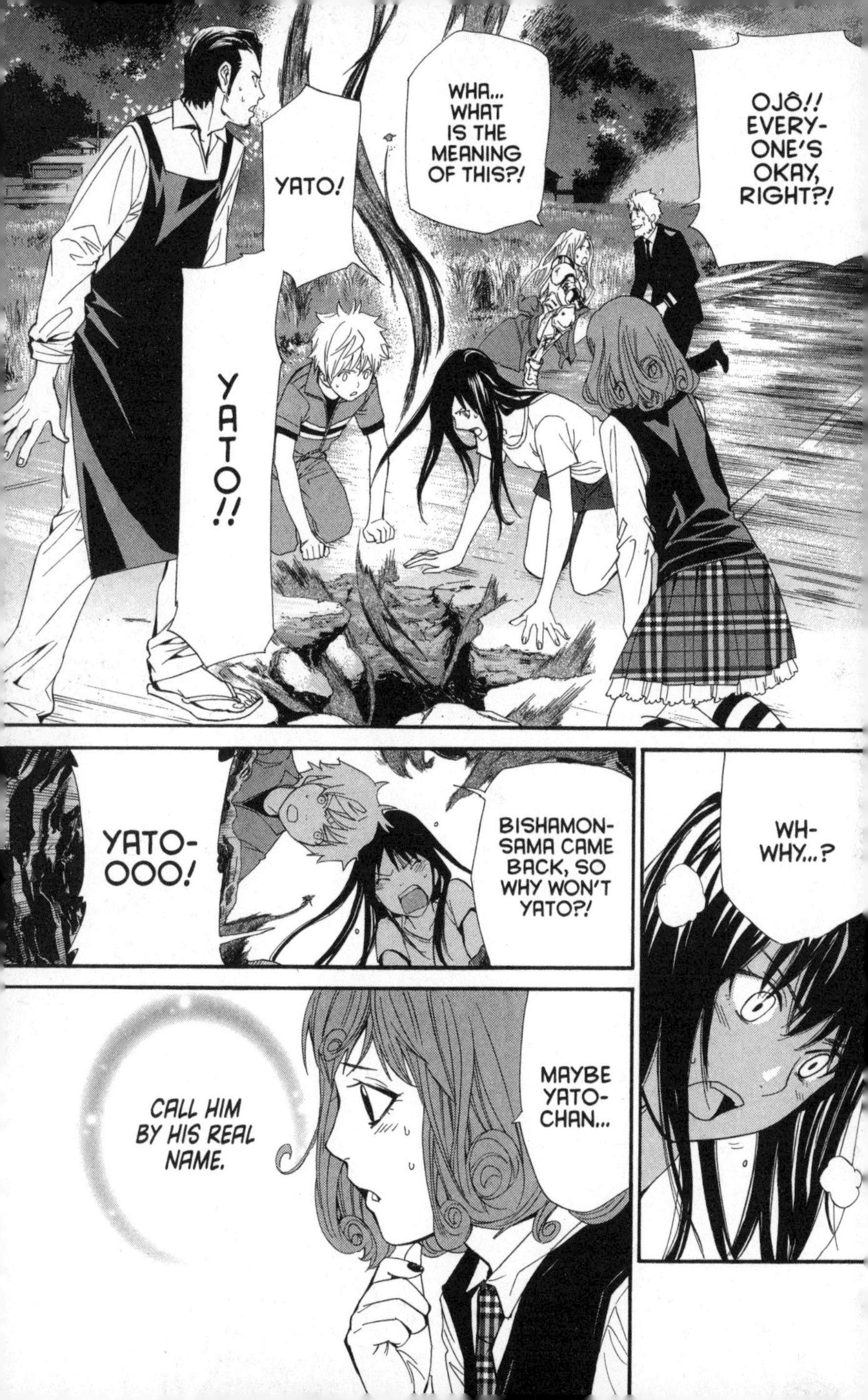
OJÔ!! EVERYONE'S OKAY, RIGHT?!
WHA... WHAT IS THE MEANING OF THIS?!
YATO!
YATO!!
WH- WHY...?
BISHAMON-SAMA CAME BACK, SO WHY WON'T YATO?!
YATO-OOO!
MAYBE YATO-CHAN...
CALL HIM BY HIS REAL NAME.

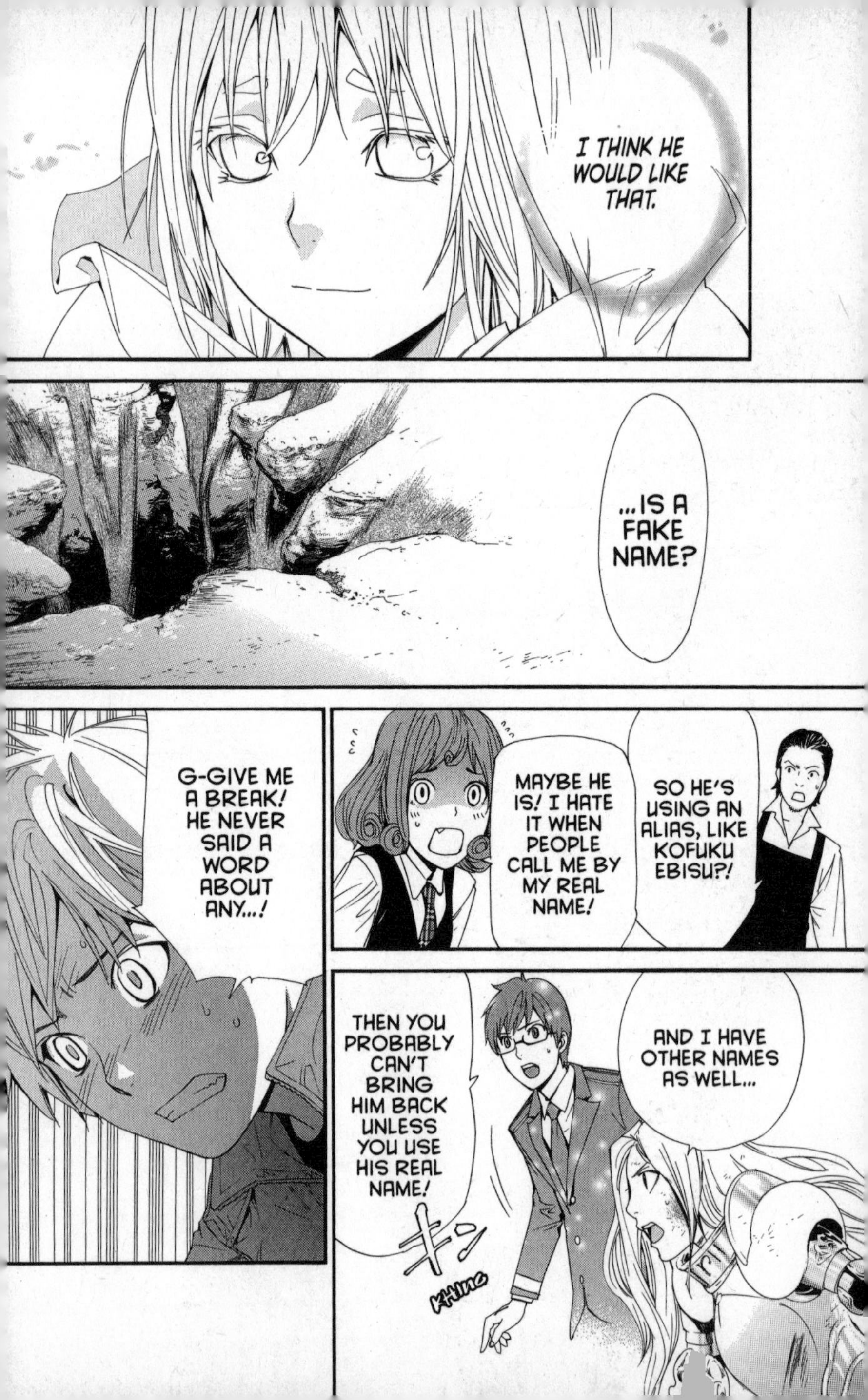
I THINK HE WOULD LIKE THAT.
...IS A FAKE NAME?
SO HE'S USING AN ALIAS, LIKE KOFUKU EBISU?!
MAYBE HE IS! I HATE IT WHEN PEOPLE CALL ME BY MY REAL NAME!
AND I HAVE OTHER NAMES AS WELL...
THEN YOU PROBABLY CAN'T BRING HIM BACK UNLESS YOU USE HIS REAL NAME!
KHING
G-GIVE ME A BREAK! HE NEVER SAID A WORD ABOUT ANY...!

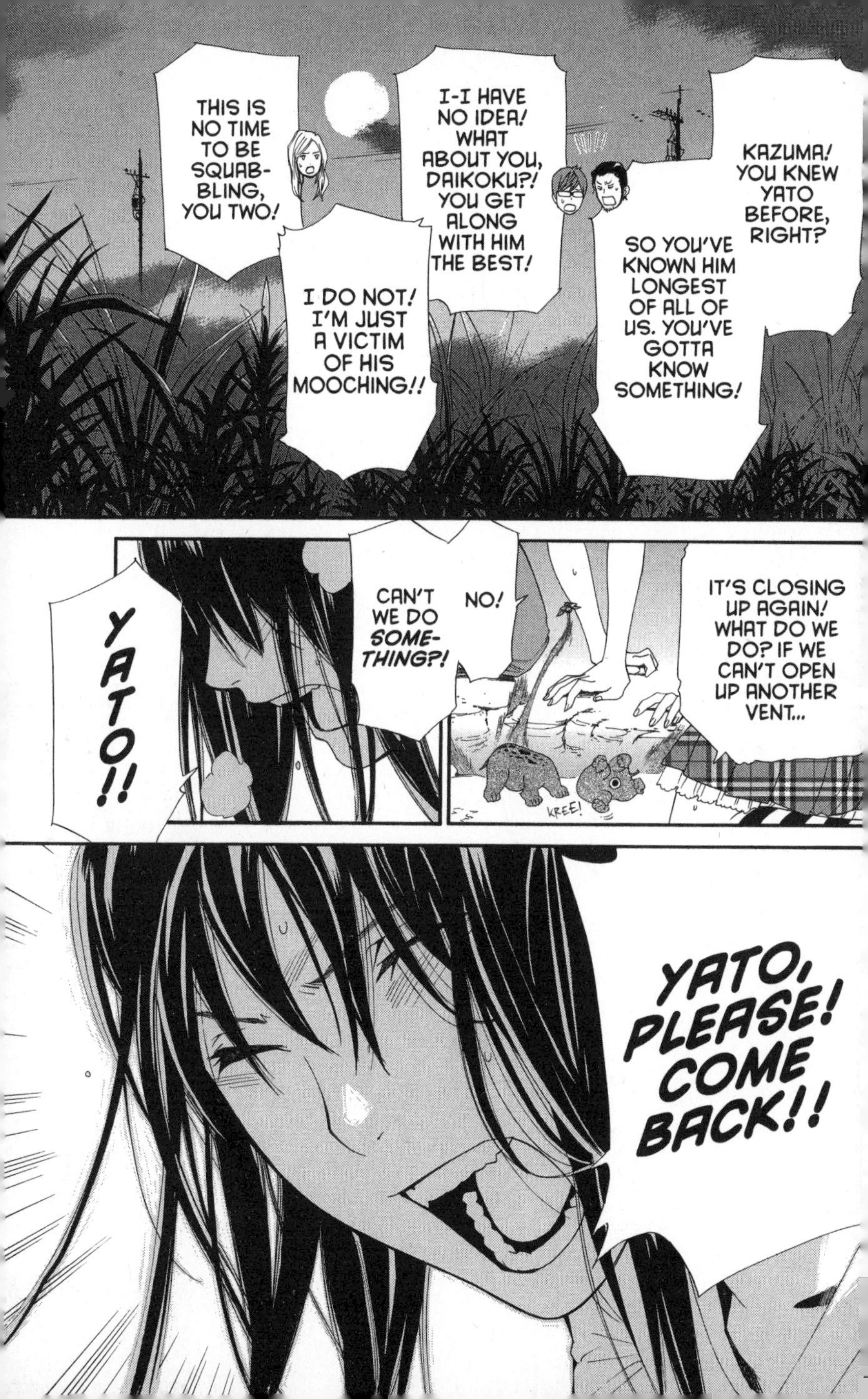
KAZUMA! YOU KNEW YATO BEFORE, RIGHT?
SO YOU'VE KNOWN HIM LONGEST OF ALL OF US. YOU'VE GOTTA KNOW SOMETHING!
I-I HAVE NO IDEA! WHAT ABOUT YOU, DAIKOKU?! YOU GET ALONG WITH HIM THE BEST!
I DO NOT! I'M JUST A VICTIM OF HIS MOOCHING!!
THIS IS NO TIME TO BE SQUAB-BLING, YOU TWO!
IT'S CLOSING UP AGAIN! WHAT DO WE DO? IF WE CAN'T OPEN UP ANOTHER VENT...
KREE!
NO!
CAN'T WE DO SOME-THING?!
YATO!!
YATO, PLEASE! COME BACK!!

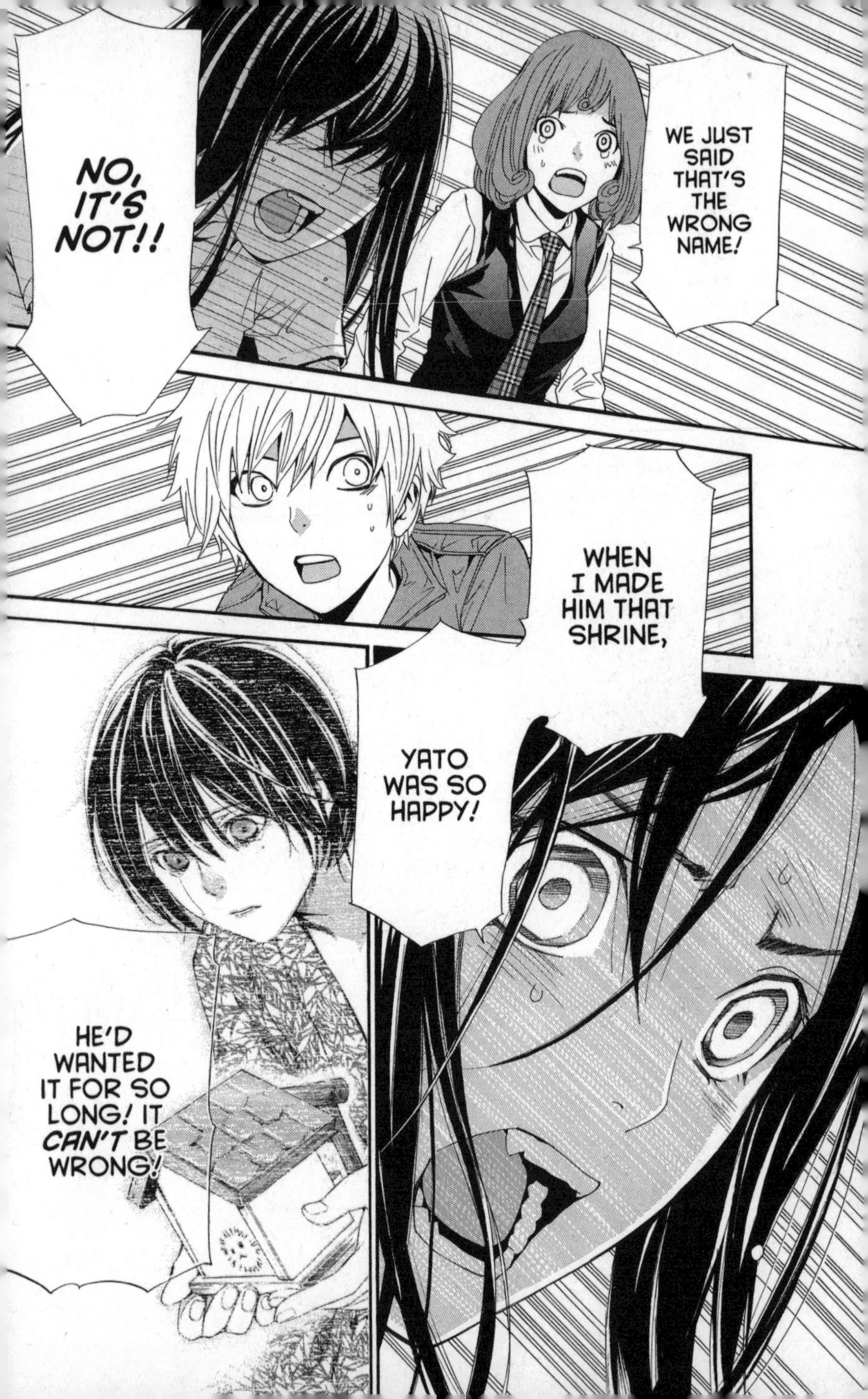
WE JUST SAID THAT'S THE WRONG NAME!
NO, IT'S NOT!!
WHEN I MADE HIM THAT SHRINE,
YATO WAS SO HAPPY!
HE'D WANTED IT FOR SO LONG! IT *CAN'T* BE WRONG!

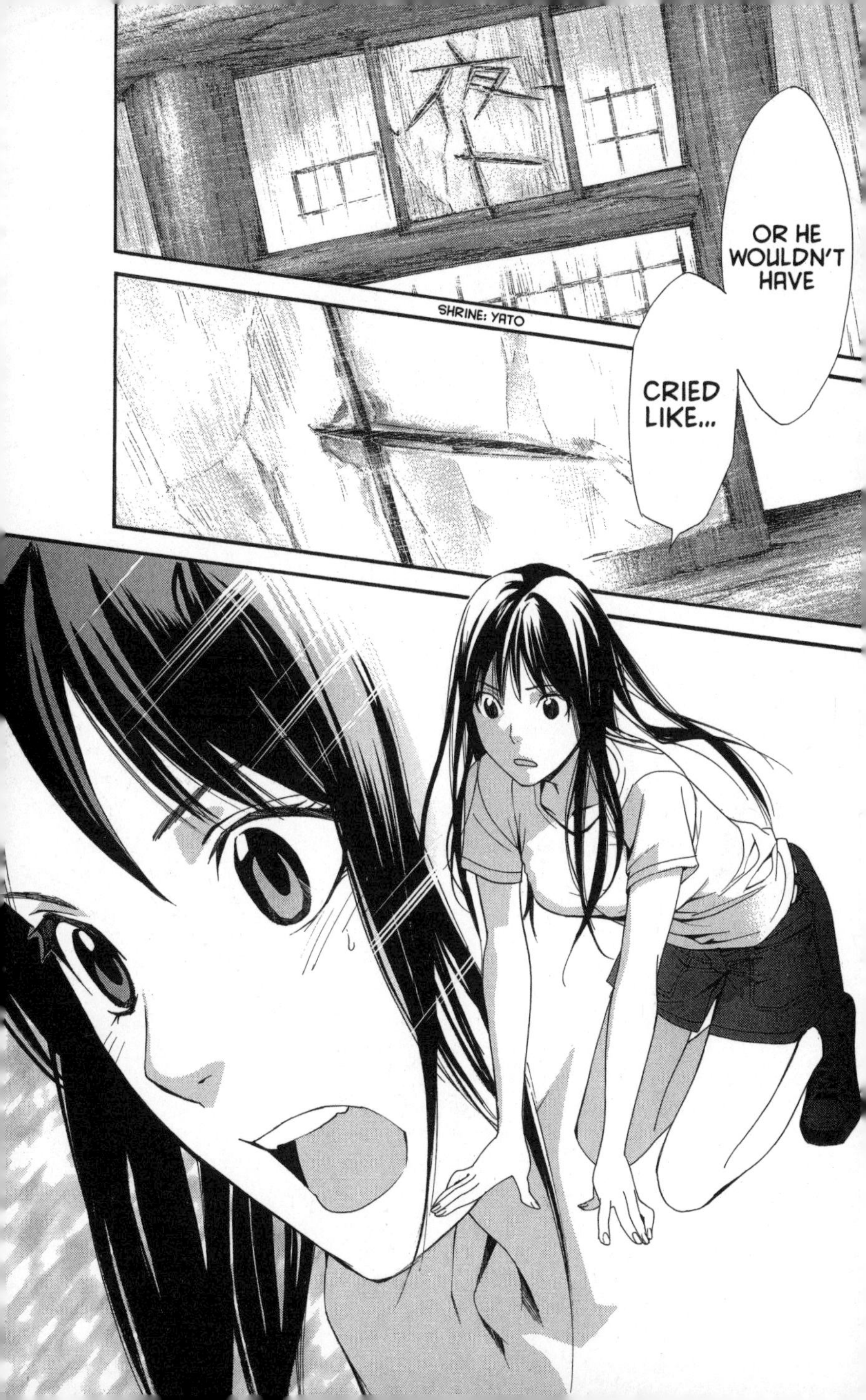
OR HE WOULDN'T HAVE
SHRINE: YATO
CRIED LIKE...

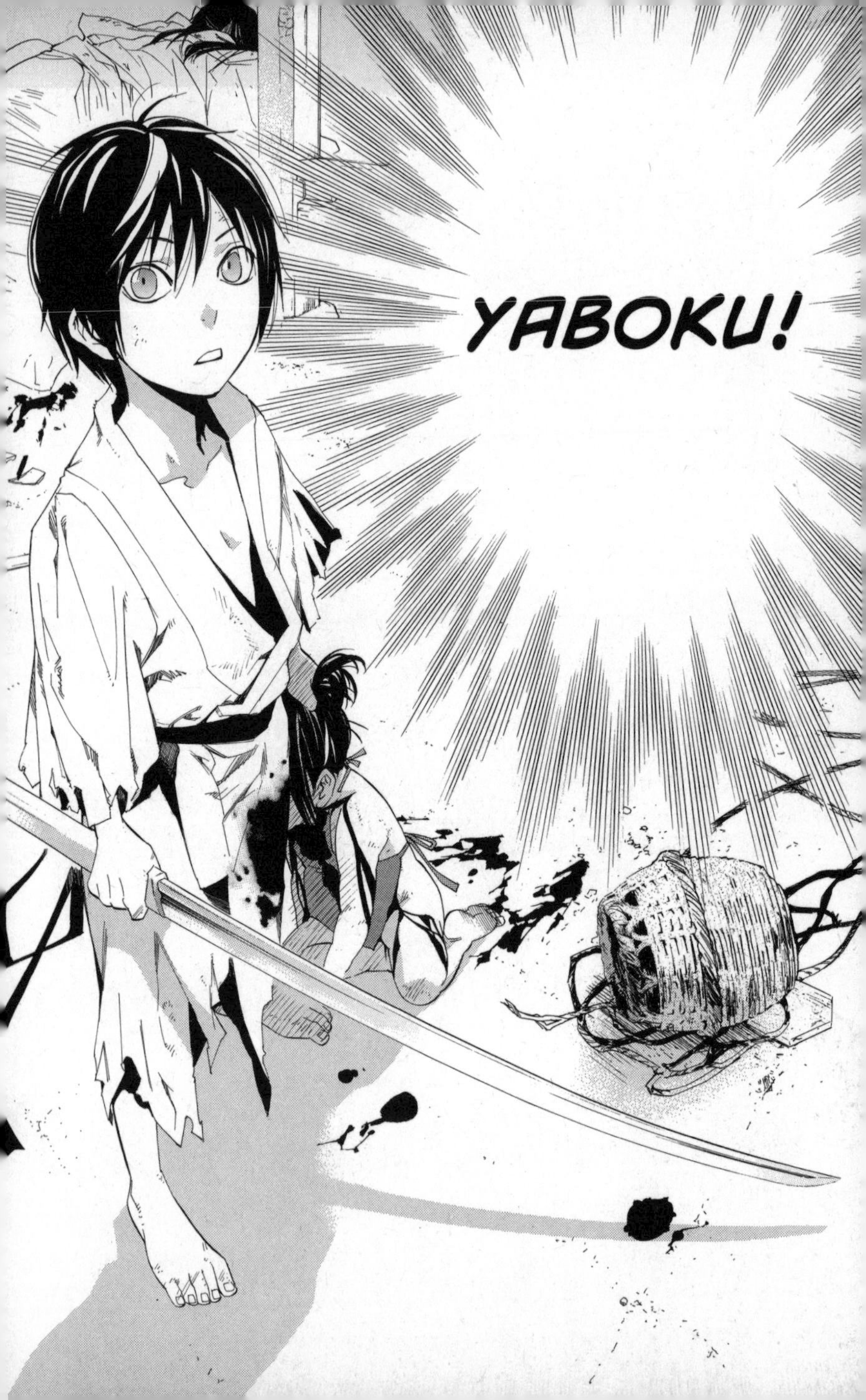
YABOKU!

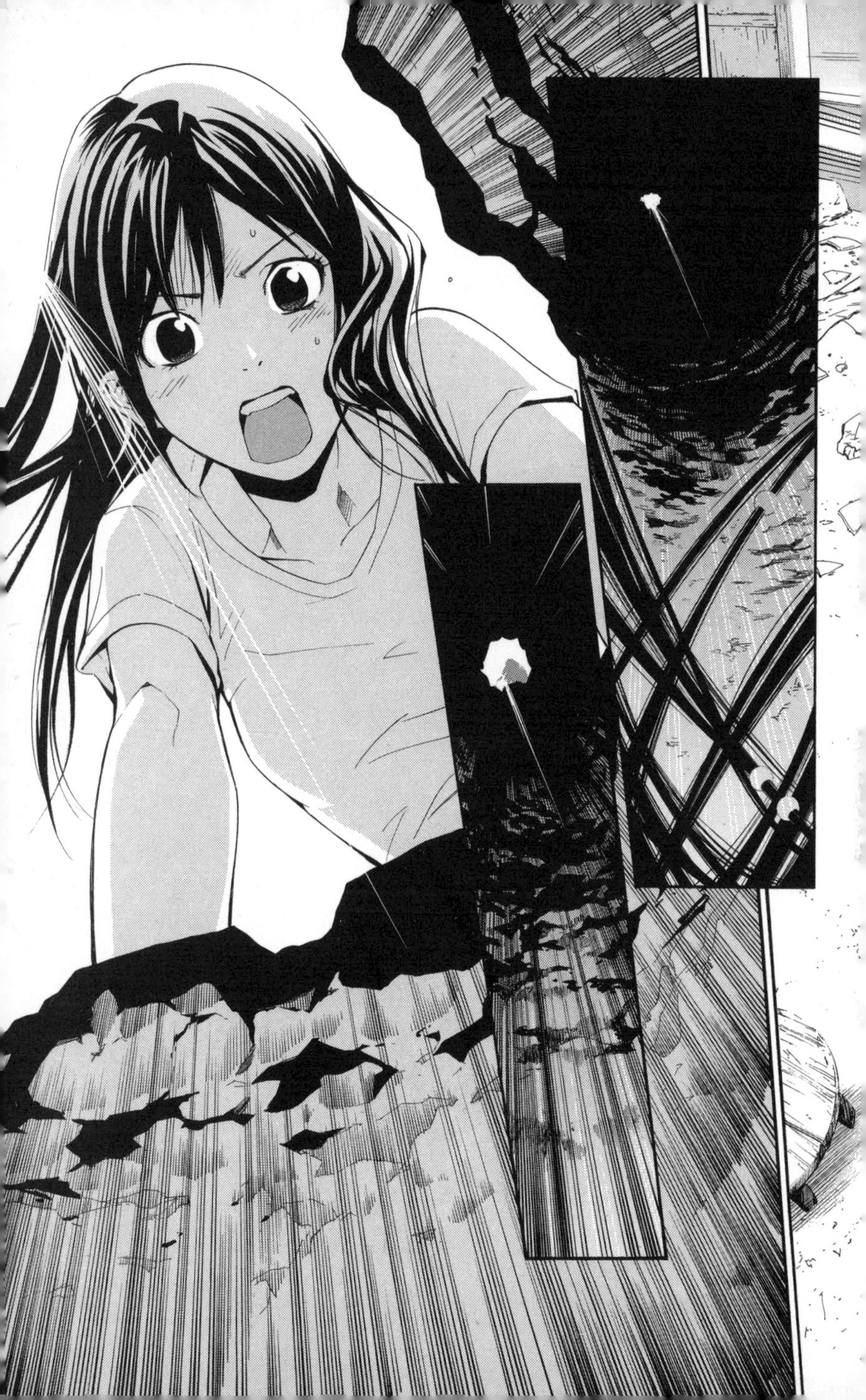

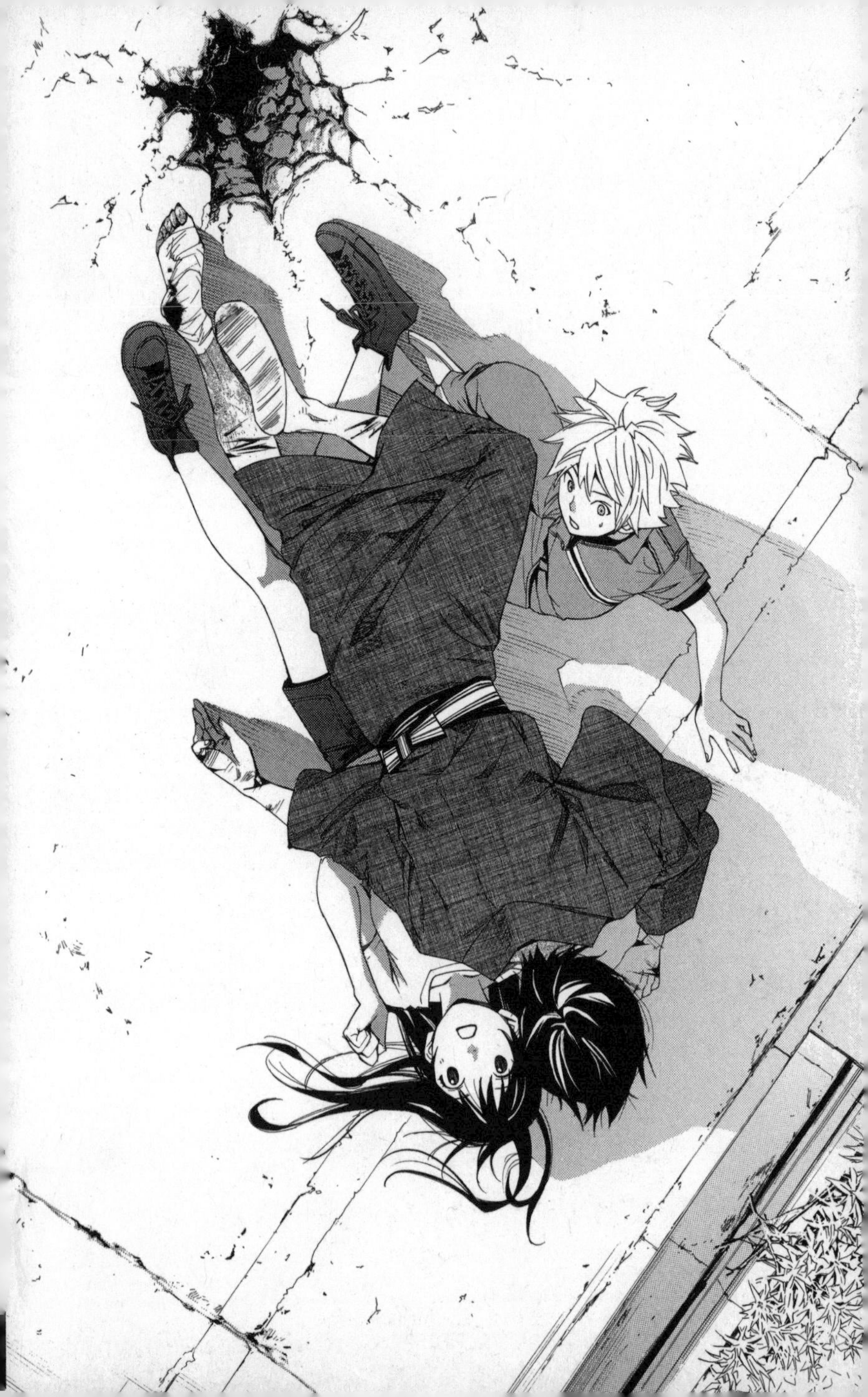

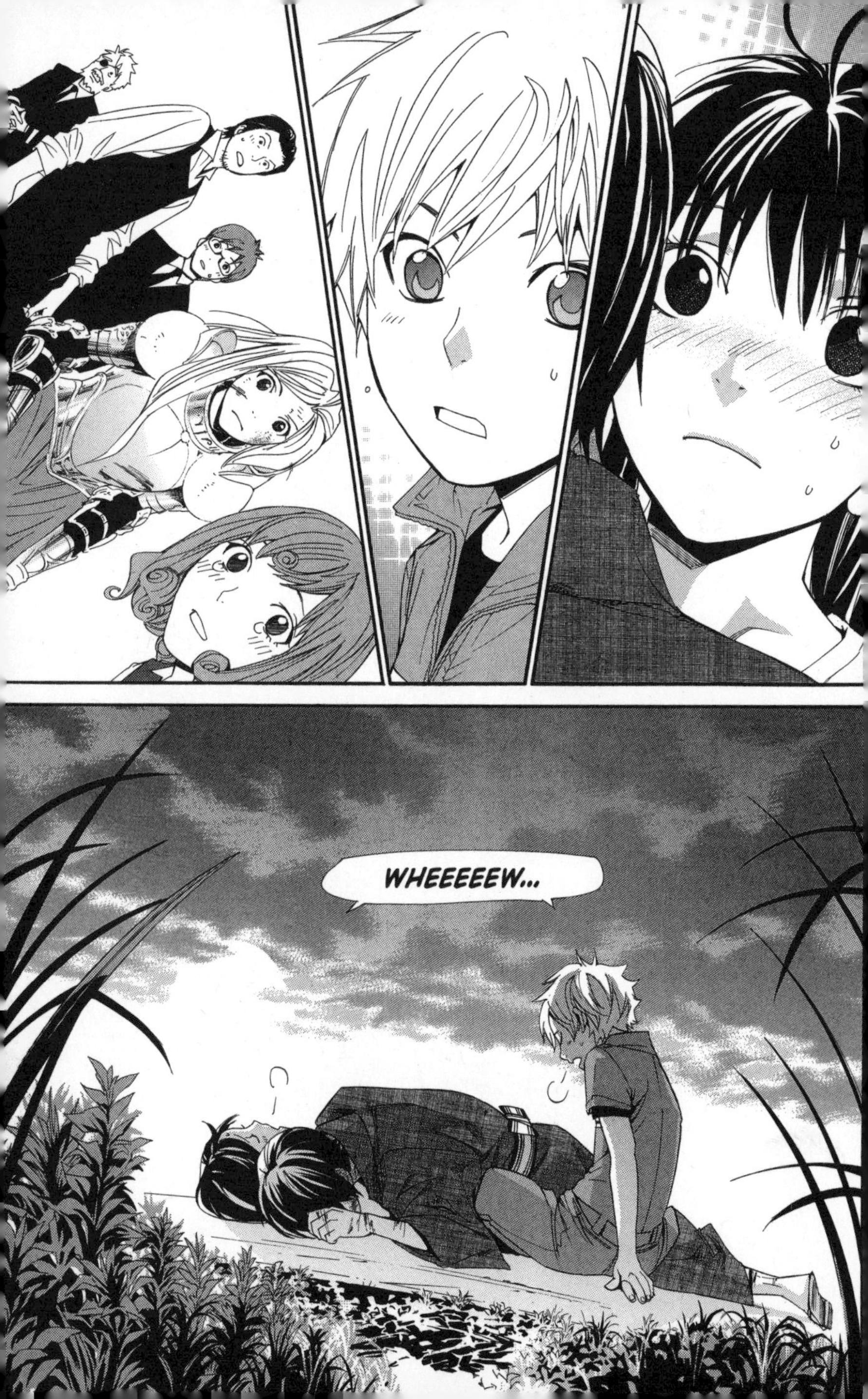
WHEEEEEW...

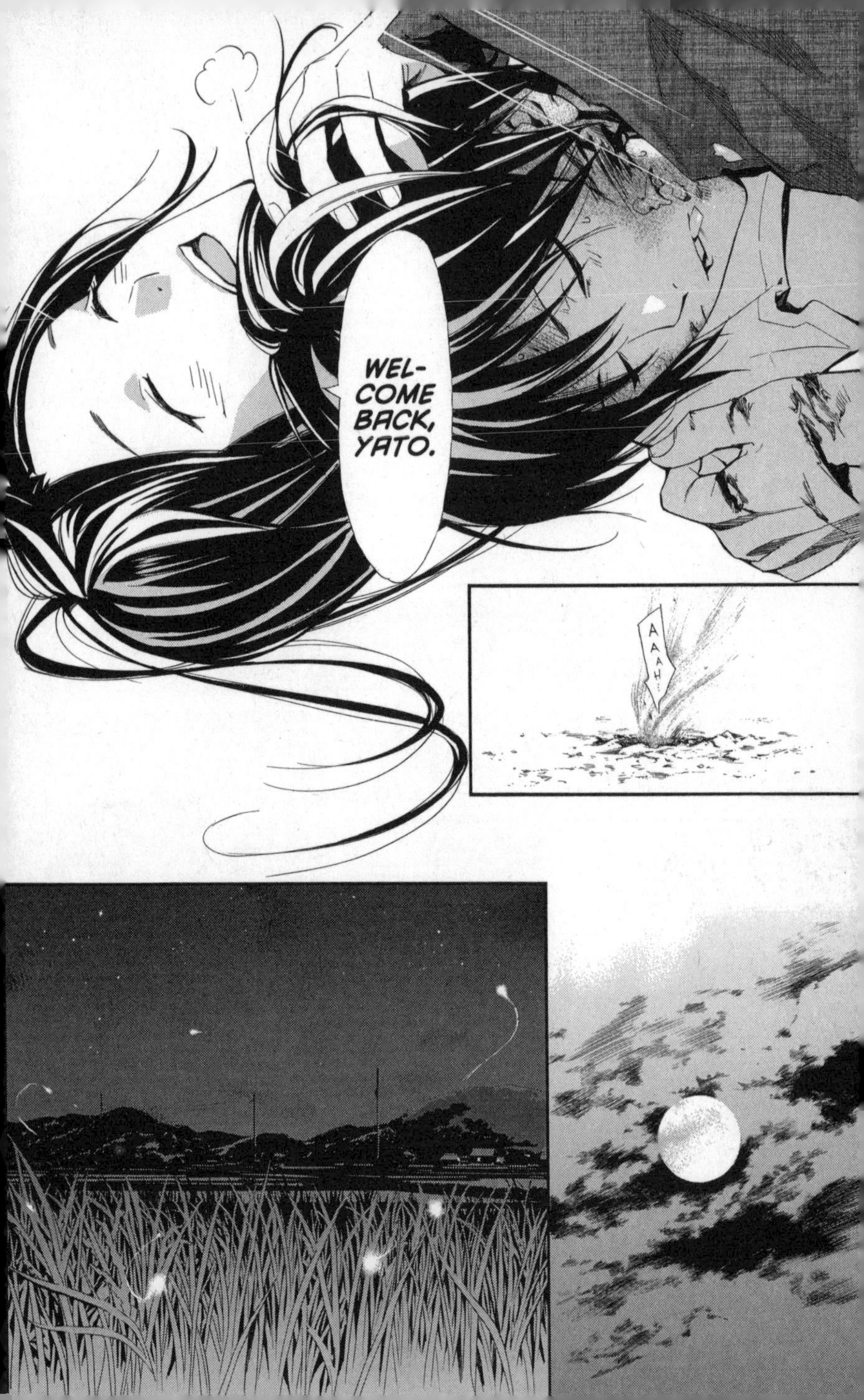
WEL-COME BACK, YATO.
AAAH...

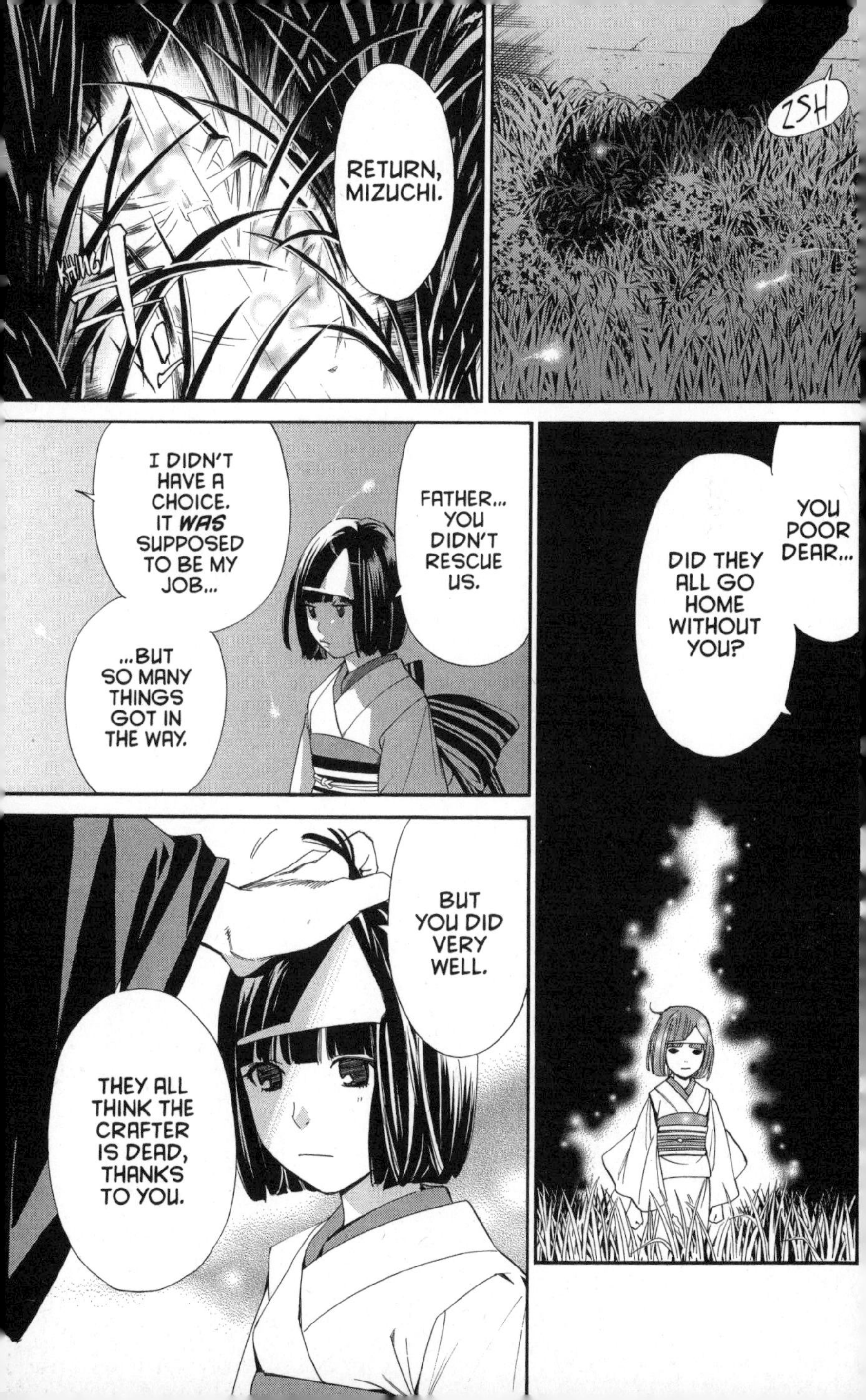
ZSH
KHING
RETURN, MIZUCHI.
YOU POOR DEAR...
DID THEY ALL GO HOME WITHOUT YOU?
FATHER... YOU DIDN'T RESCUE US.
I DIDN'T HAVE A CHOICE. IT ***WAS*** SUPPOSED TO BE MY JOB...
...BUT SO MANY THINGS GOT IN THE WAY.
BUT YOU DID VERY WELL.
THEY ALL THINK THE CRAFTER IS DEAD, THANKS TO YOU.

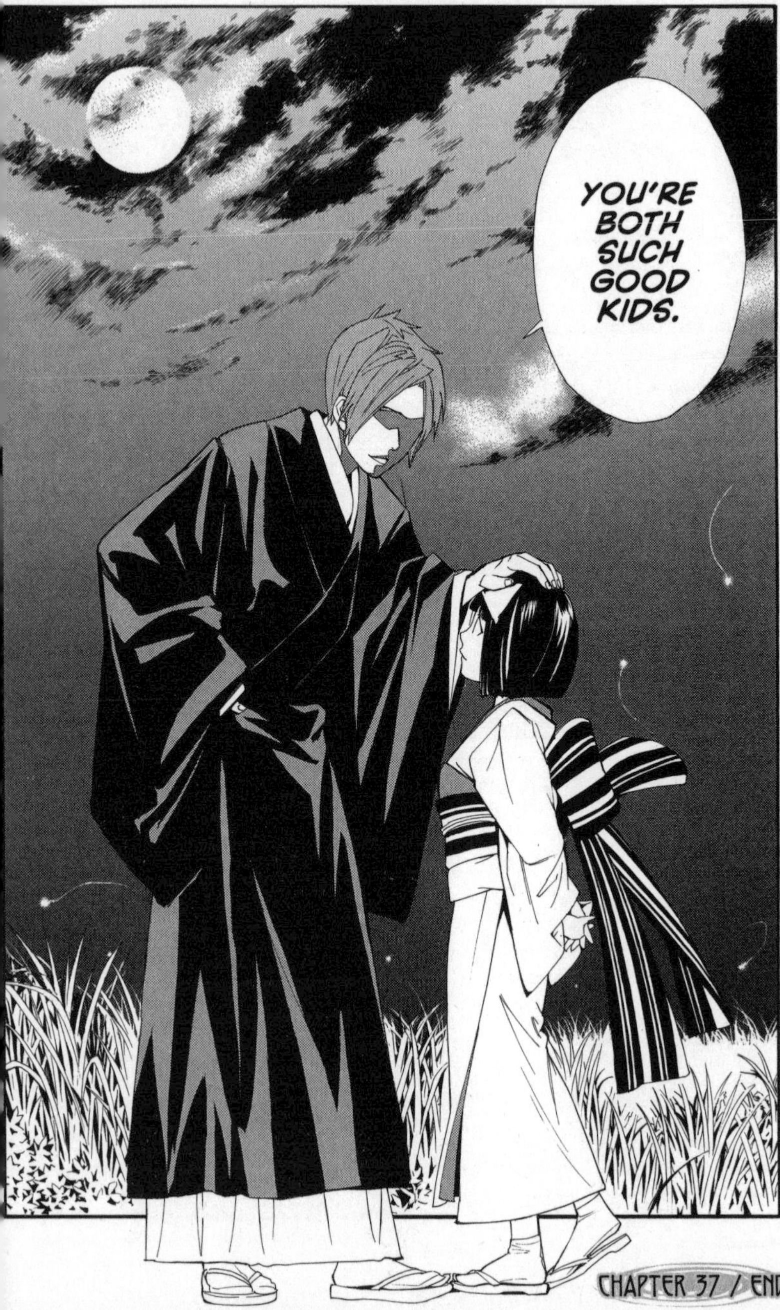
YOU'RE BOTH SUCH GOOD KIDS.
CHAPTER 37 / END

野

[illegible]

神

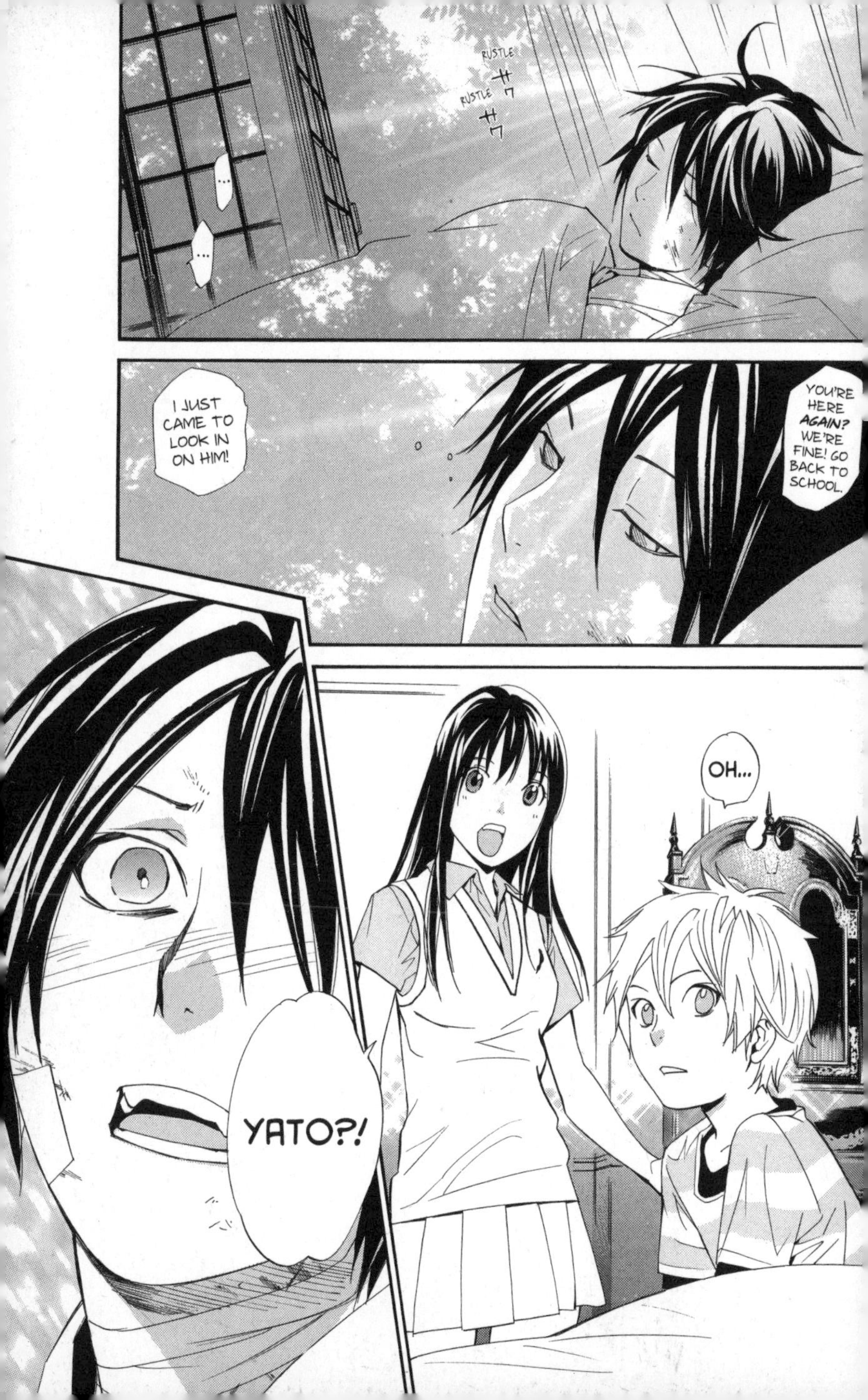
RUSTLE
RUSTLE
...
...
YOU'RE HERE AGAIN? WE'RE FINE! GO BACK TO SCHOOL.
I JUST CAME TO LOOK IN ON HIM!
OH...
YATO?!

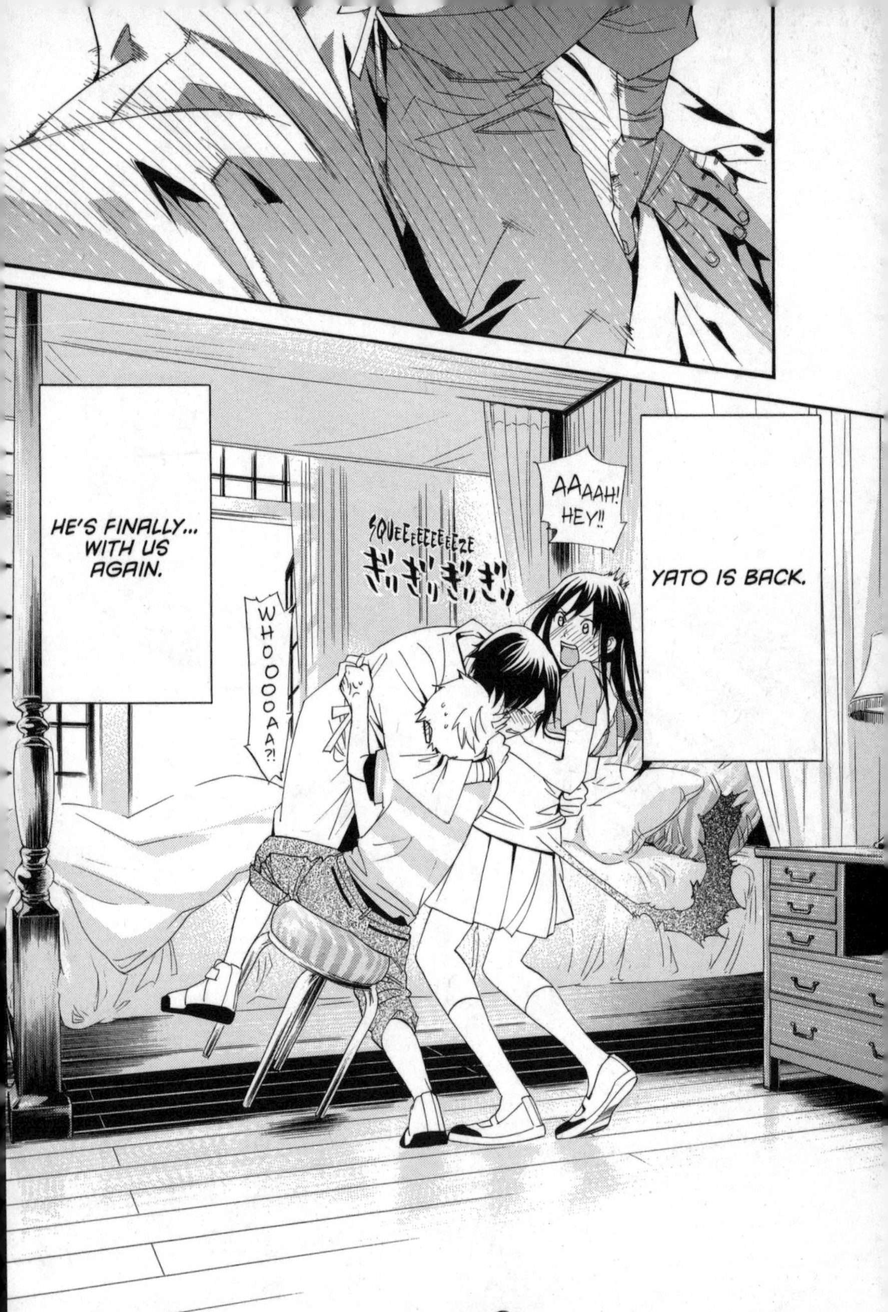
YATO IS BACK.
AAAAH! HEY!!
SQUEEEEEEEEEEZE
WHOOOOOAA?!
HE'S FINALLY... WITH US AGAIN.

CHAPTER 38: BECAUSE I PROMISED

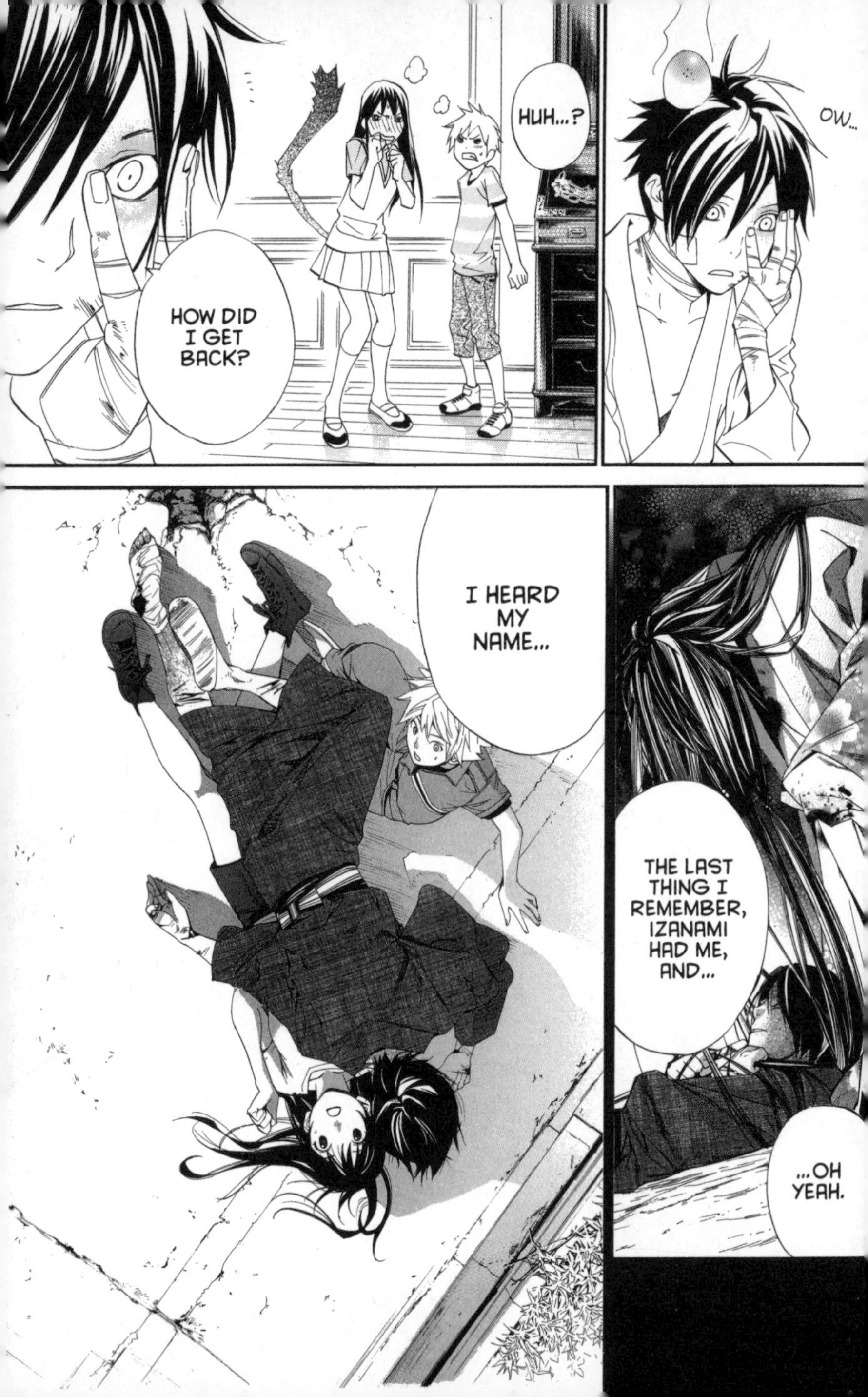
OW...
HUH...?
HOW DID I GET BACK?
THE LAST THING I REMEMBER, IZANAMI HAD ME, AND...
...OH YEAH.
I HEARD MY NAME...

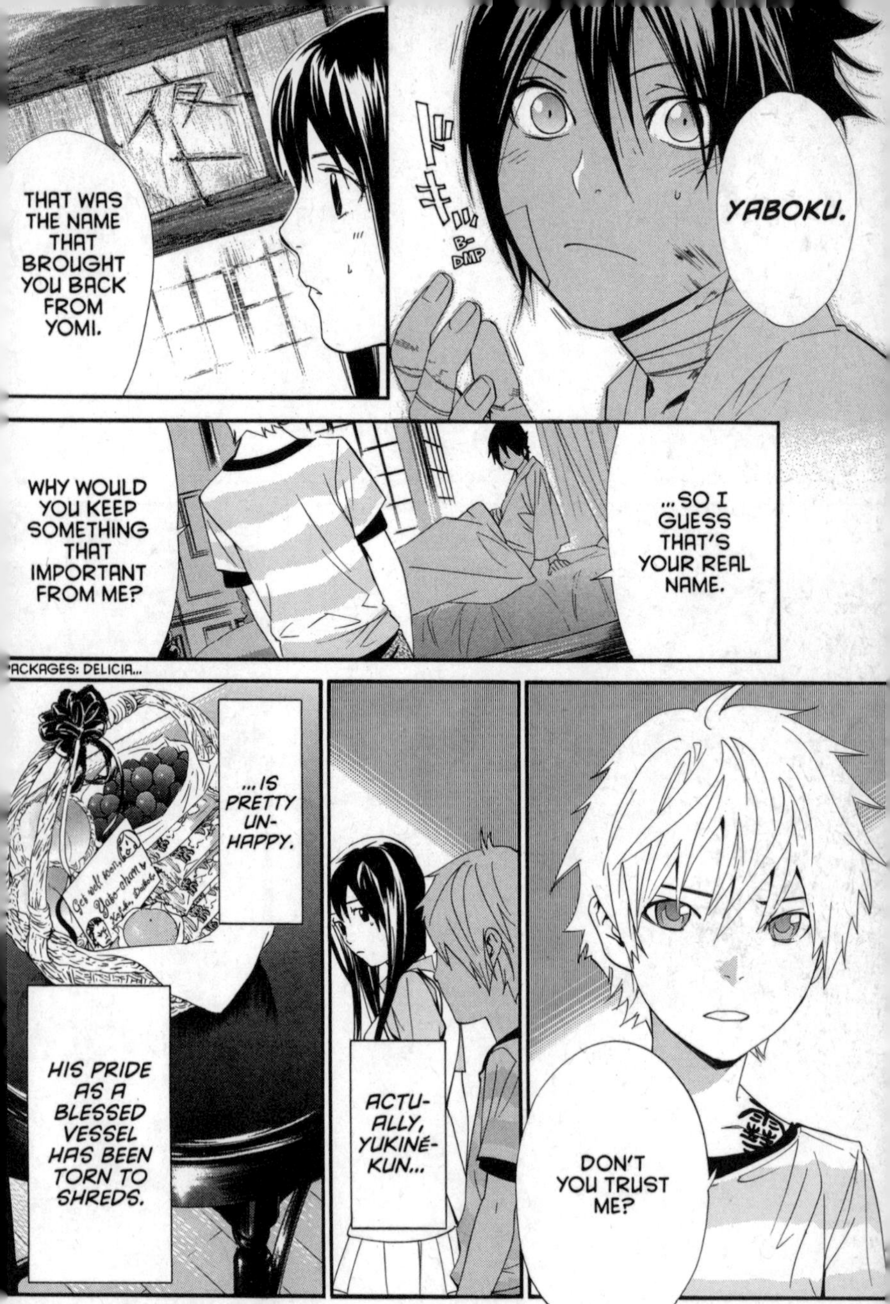
YABOKU.
B-DMP
THAT WAS THE NAME THAT BROUGHT YOU BACK FROM YOMI.
...SO I GUESS THAT'S YOUR REAL NAME.
WHY WOULD YOU KEEP SOMETHING THAT IMPORTANT FROM ME?
PACKAGES: DELICIA...
DON'T YOU TRUST ME?
ACTU-ALLY, YUKINÉ-KUN...
...IS PRETTY UN-HAPPY.
HIS PRIDE AS A BLESSED VESSEL HAS BEEN TORN TO SHREDS.

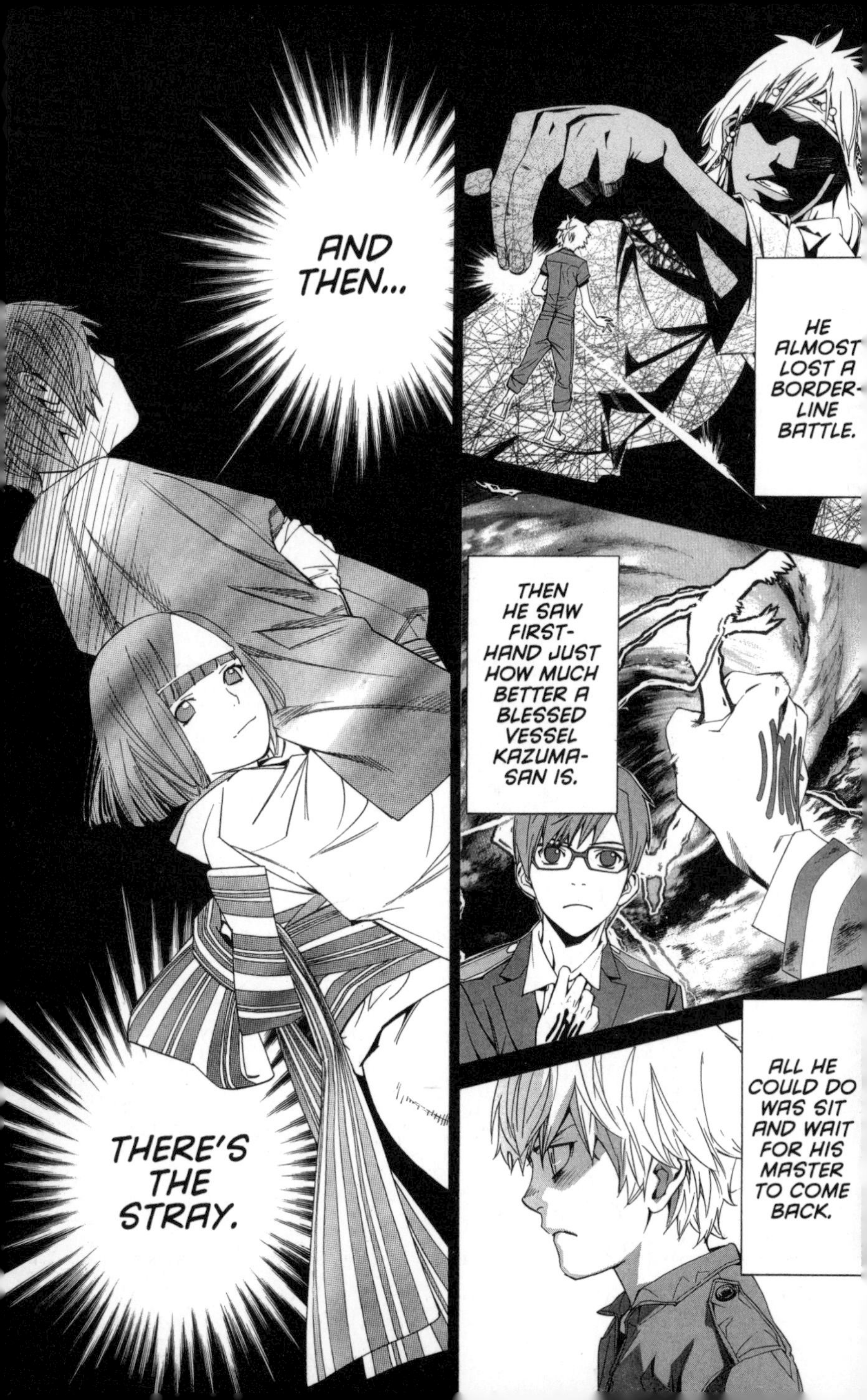
HE ALMOST LOST A BORDER-LINE BATTLE.
THEN HE SAW FIRST-HAND JUST HOW MUCH BETTER A BLESSED VESSEL KAZUMA-SAN IS.
ALL HE COULD DO WAS SIT AND WAIT FOR HIS MASTER TO COME BACK.
AND THEN...
THERE'S THE STRAY.

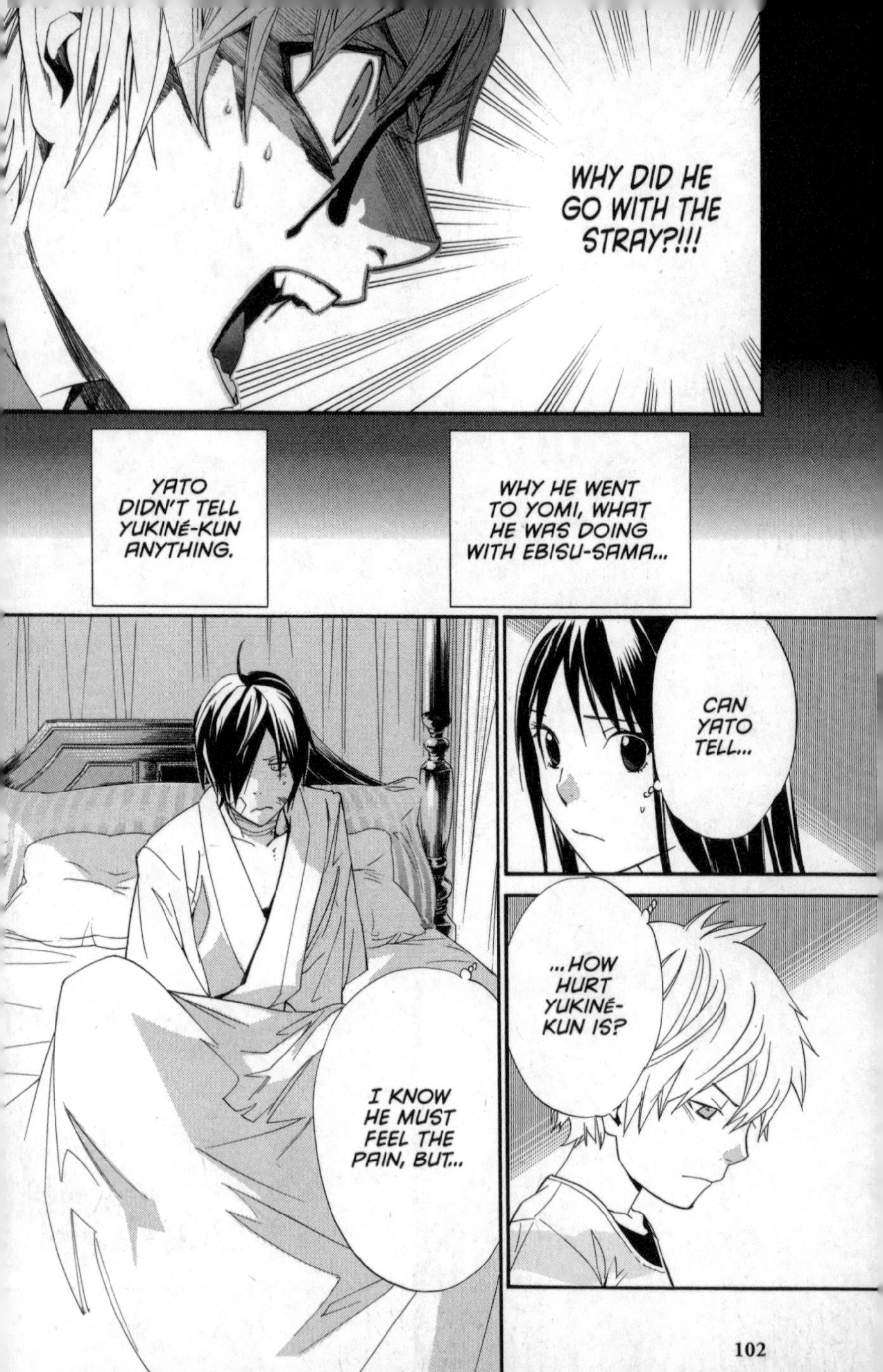
WHY DID HE GO WITH THE STRAY?!!!
WHY HE WENT TO YOMI, WHAT HE WAS DOING WITH EBISU-SAMA...
YATO DIDN'T TELL YUKINÉ-KUN ANYTHING.
CAN YATO TELL...
...HOW HURT YUKINÉ-KUN IS?
I KNOW HE MUST FEEL THE PAIN, BUT...

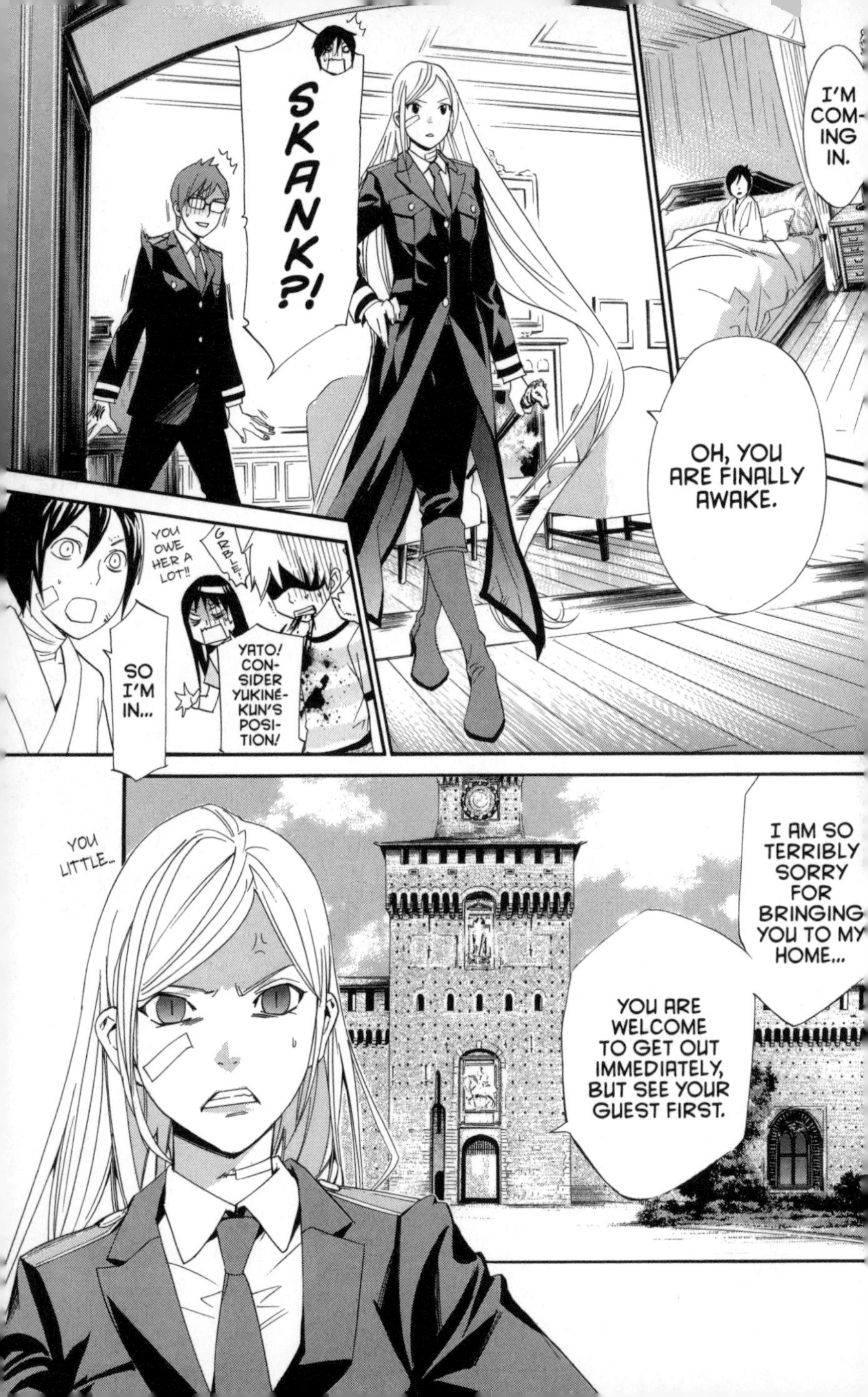
I'M COMING IN.
OH, YOU ARE FINALLY AWAKE.
SKANK?!
SO I'M IN...
YATO! CONSIDER YUKINÉ-KUN'S POSITION!
GRBLE!
YOU OWE HER A LOT!!
I AM SO TERRIBLY SORRY FOR BRINGING YOU TO MY HOME...
YOU ARE WELCOME TO GET OUT IMMEDIATELY, BUT SEE YOUR GUEST FIRST.
YOU LITTLE...

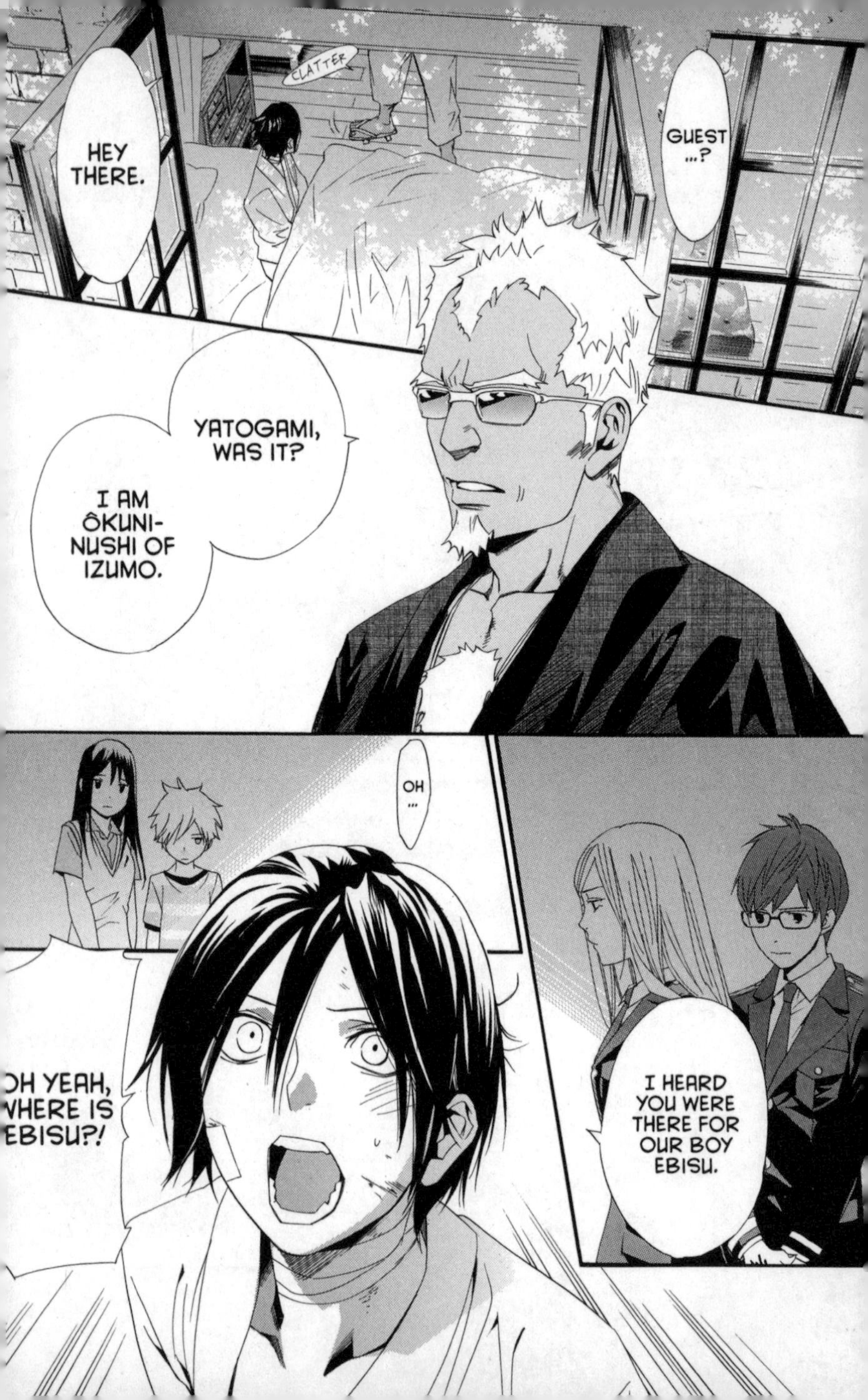
GUEST ...?
CLATTER
HEY THERE.
YATOGAMI, WAS IT?
I AM ÔKUNI-NUSHI OF IZUMO.
I HEARD YOU WERE THERE FOR OUR BOY EBISU.
OH ...
OH YEAH, WHERE IS EBISU?!

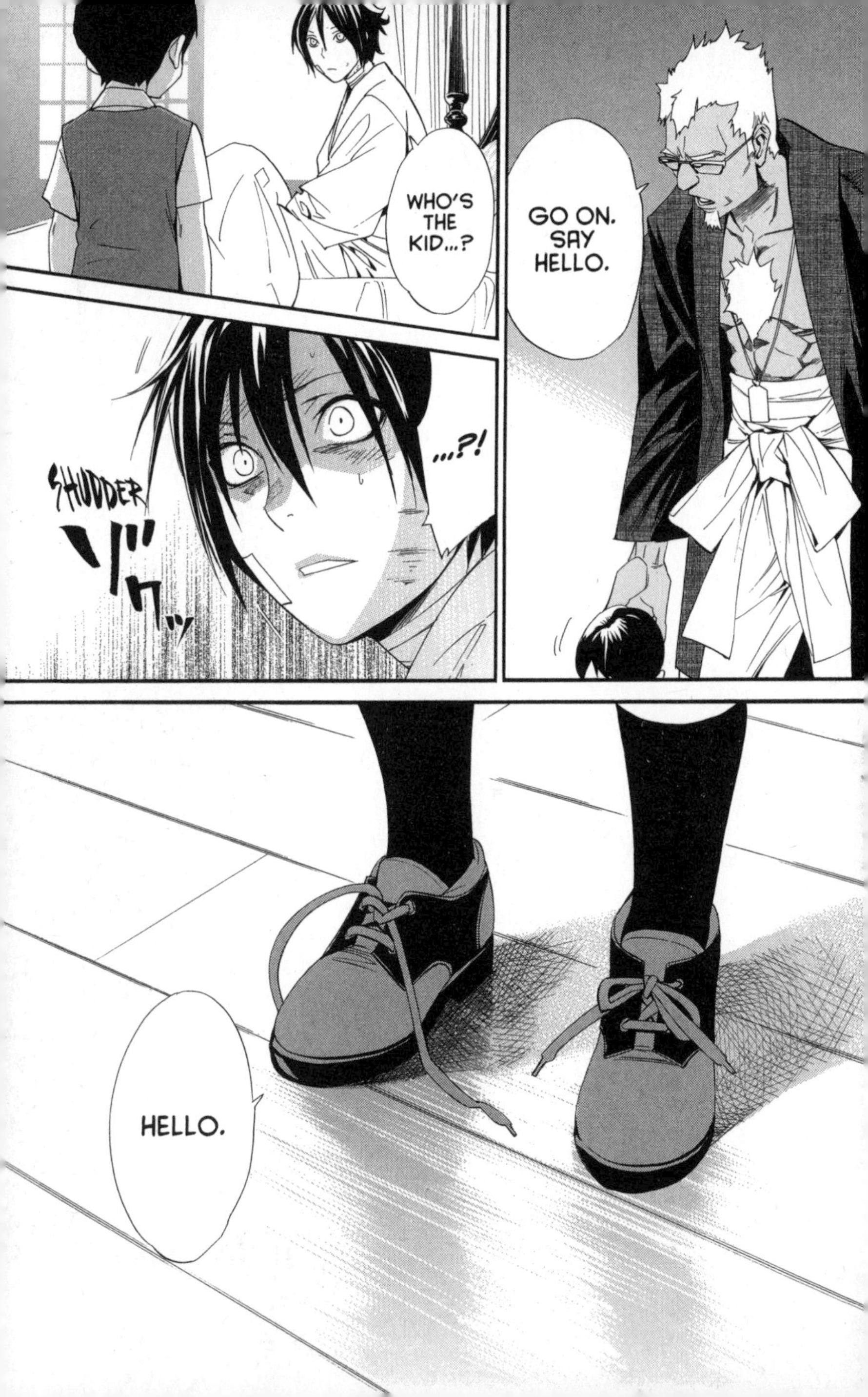
GO ON. SAY HELLO.
WHO'S THE KID...?
...?!
SHUDDER
ゾクッ
HELLO.

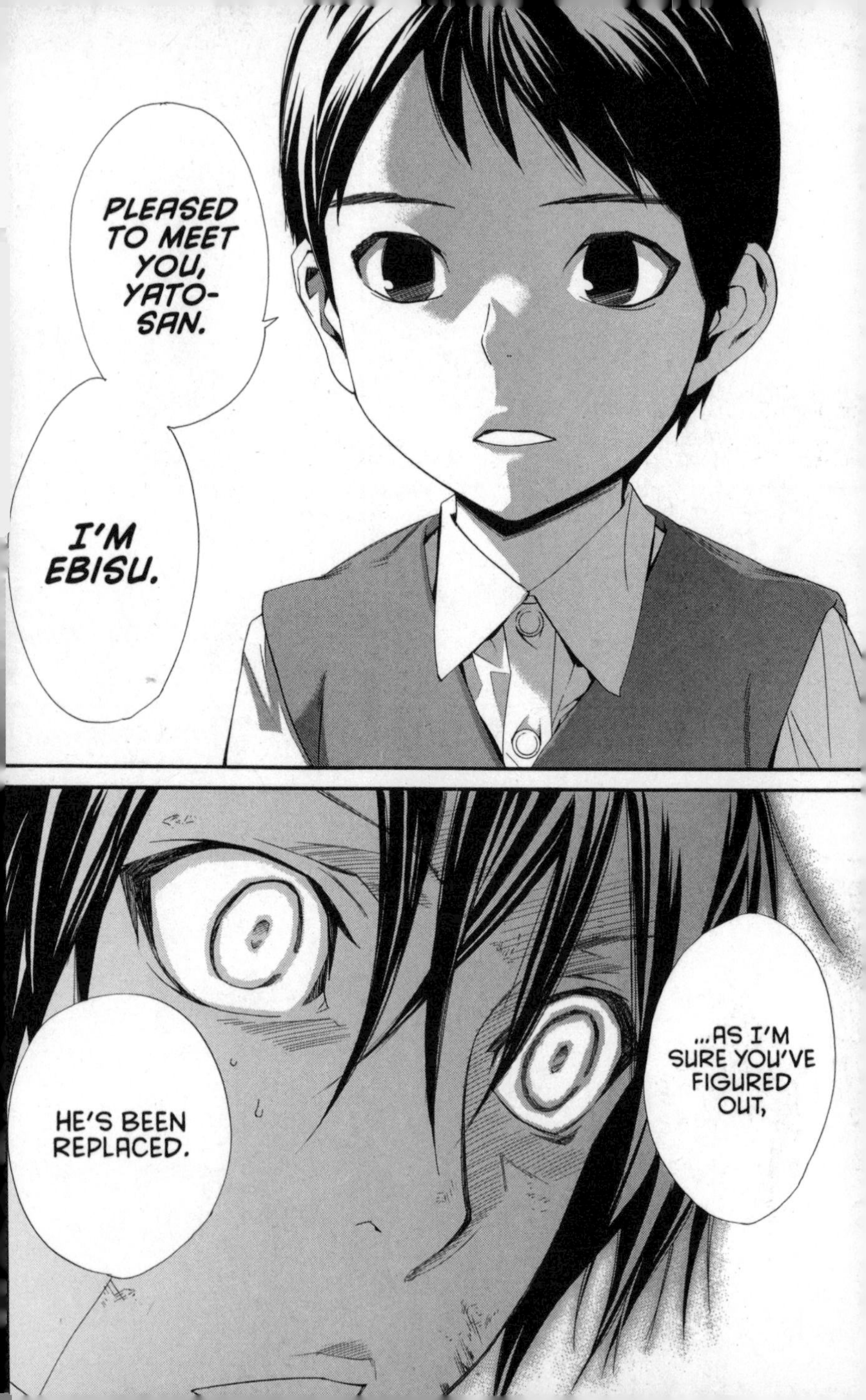
PLEASED TO MEET YOU, YATO-SAN.
I'M EBISU.
...AS I'M SURE YOU'VE FIGURED OUT,
HE'S BEEN REPLACED.

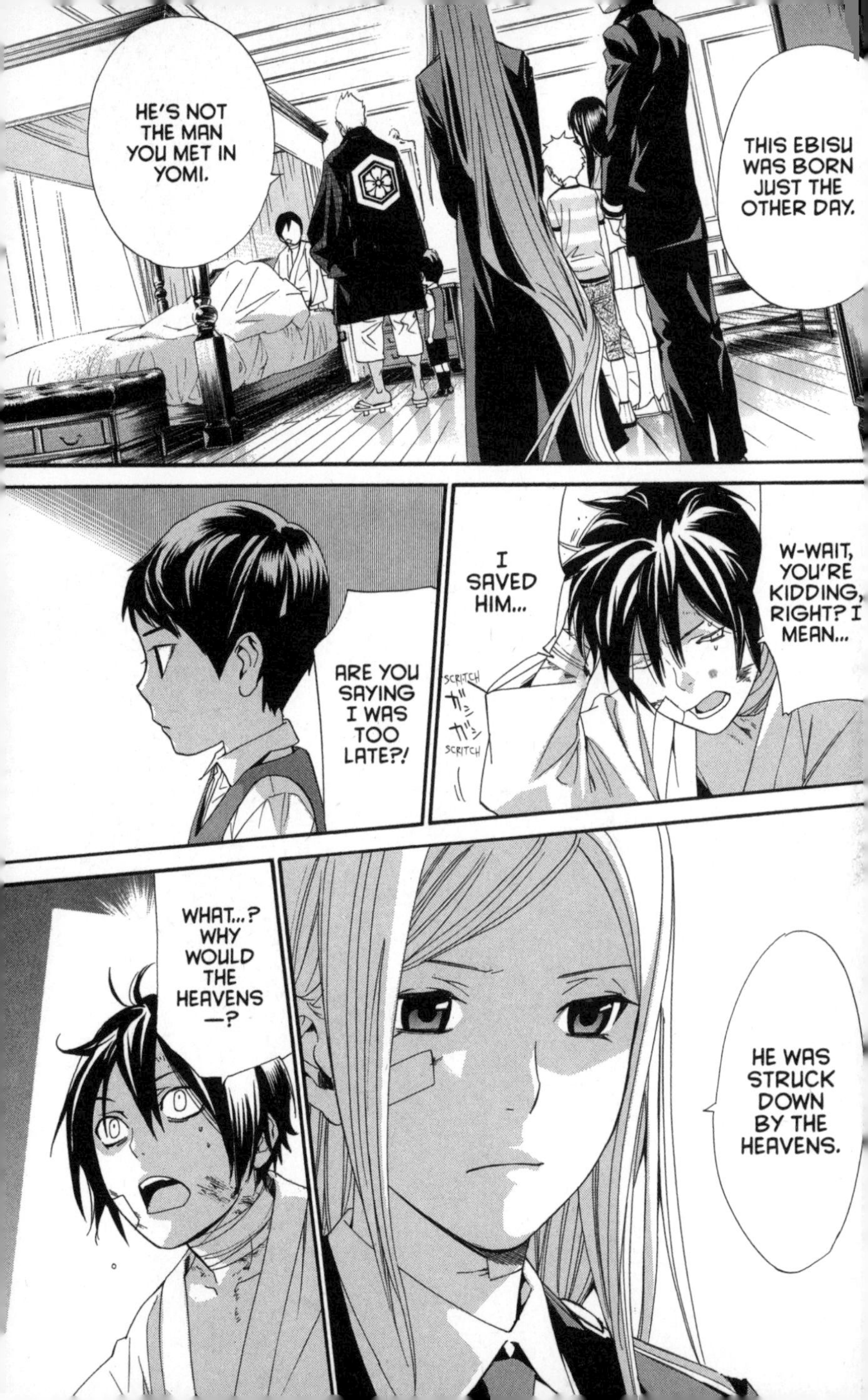
THIS EBISU WAS BORN JUST THE OTHER DAY.
HE'S NOT THE MAN YOU MET IN YOMI.
W-WAIT, YOU'RE KIDDING, RIGHT? I MEAN...
I SAVED HIM...
SCRITCH
ガシ
ガシ
SCRITCH
ARE YOU SAYING I WAS TOO LATE?!
HE WAS STRUCK DOWN BY THE HEAVENS.
WHAT...? WHY WOULD THE HEAVENS—?

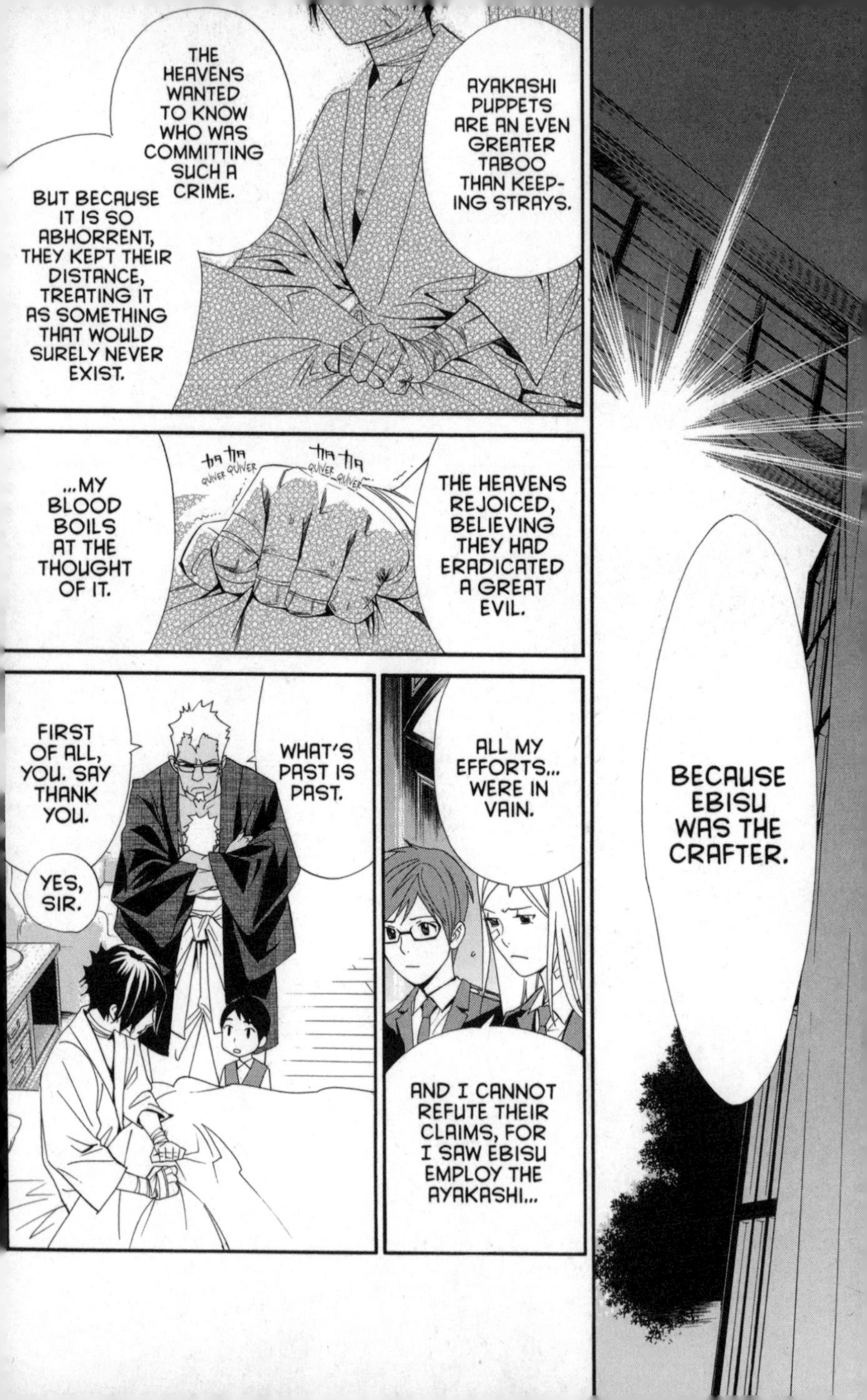
BECAUSE EBISU WAS THE CRAFTER.
AYAKASHI PUPPETS ARE AN EVEN GREATER TABOO THAN KEEP-ING STRAYS.
THE HEAVENS WANTED TO KNOW WHO WAS COMMITTING SUCH A CRIME.
BUT BECAUSE IT IS SO ABHORRENT, THEY KEPT THEIR DISTANCE, TREATING IT AS SOMETHING THAT WOULD SURELY NEVER EXIST.
THE HEAVENS REJOICED, BELIEVING THEY HAD ERADICATED A GREAT EVIL.
QUIVER QUIVER
QUIVER QUIVER
...MY BLOOD BOILS AT THE THOUGHT OF IT.
ALL MY EFFORTS... WERE IN VAIN.
AND I CANNOT REFUTE THEIR CLAIMS, FOR I SAW EBISU EMPLOY THE AYAKASHI...
WHAT'S PAST IS PAST.
FIRST OF ALL, YOU. SAY THANK YOU.
YES, SIR.

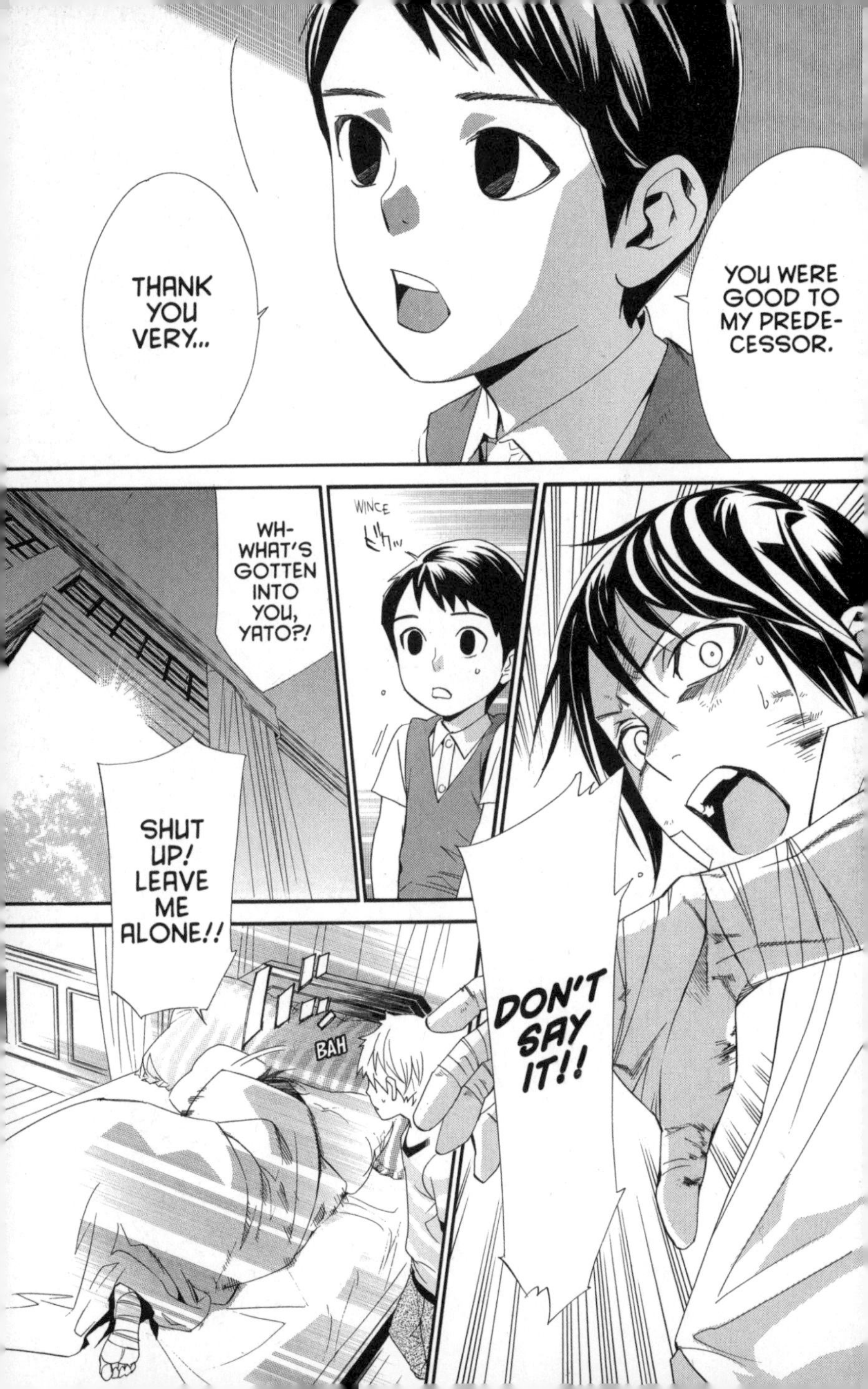

YOU WERE GOOD TO MY PREDE-CESSOR.
THANK YOU VERY...
DON'T SAY IT!!
WINCE
WH- WHAT'S GOTTEN INTO YOU, YATO?!
SHUT UP! LEAVE ME ALONE!!
BAH

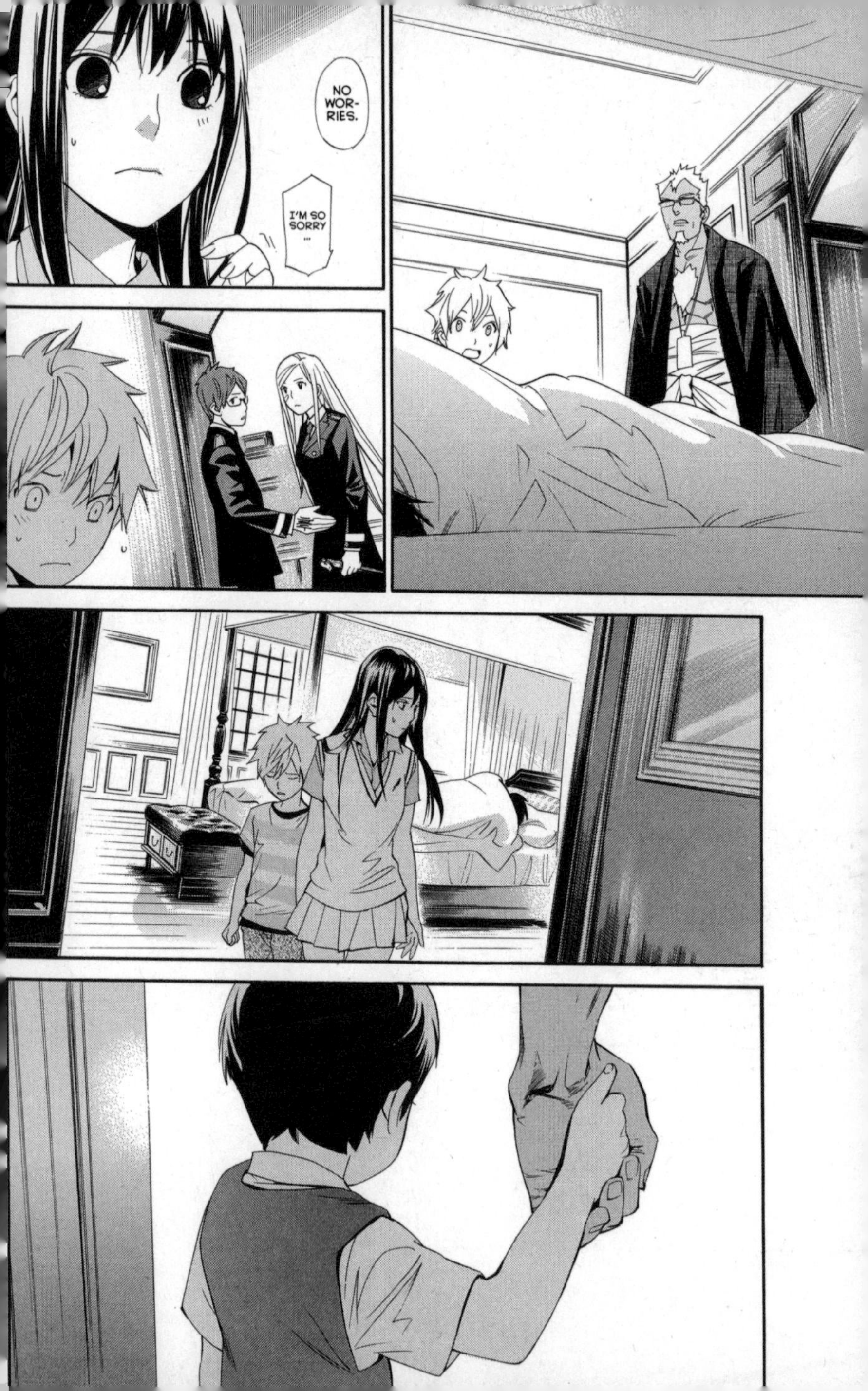
NO WOR-RIES.
I'M SO SORRY ...

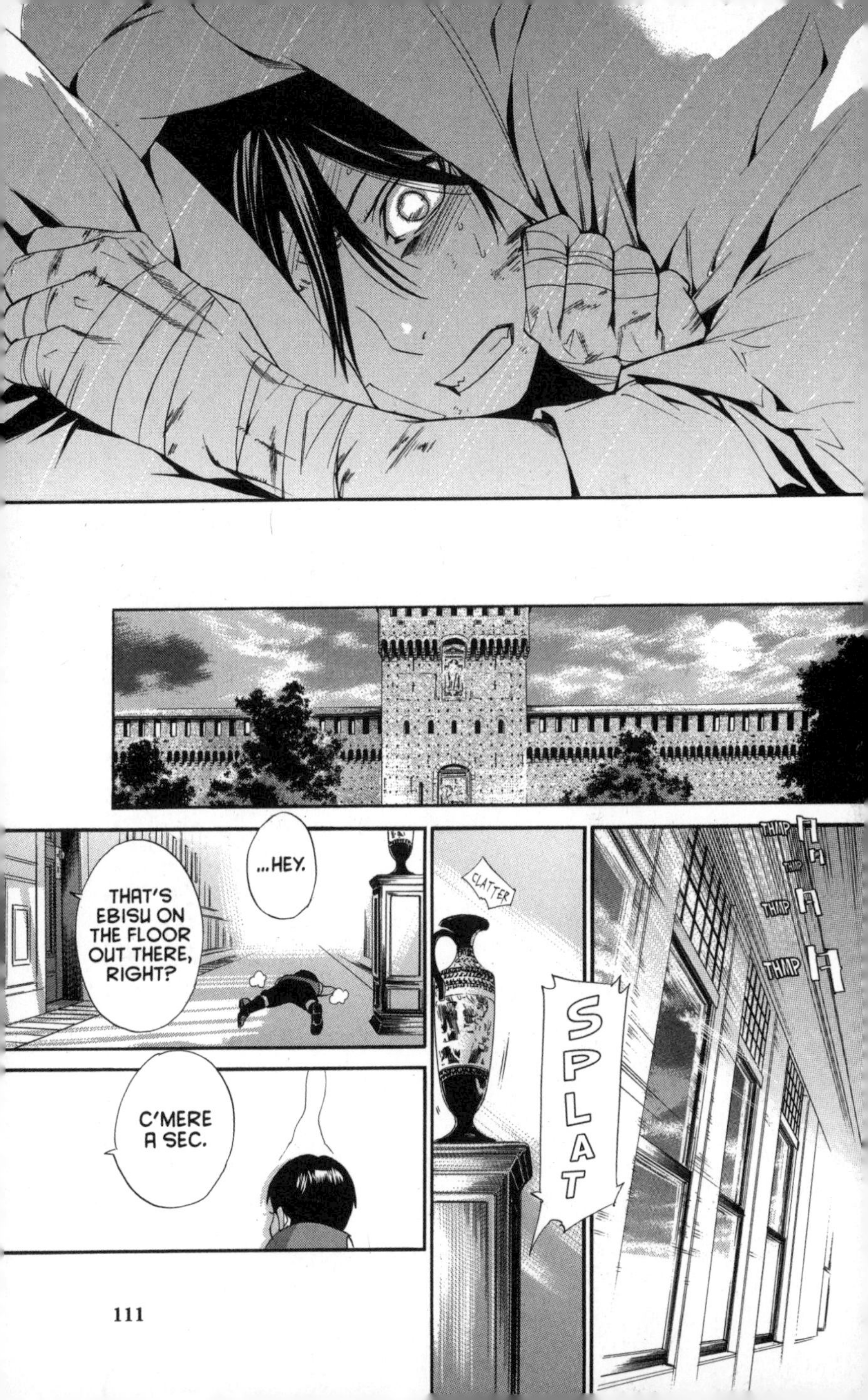
THMP
THMP
THMP
THMP
CLATTER
SPLAT
...HEY.
THAT'S EBISU ON THE FLOOR OUT THERE, RIGHT?
C'MERE A SEC.

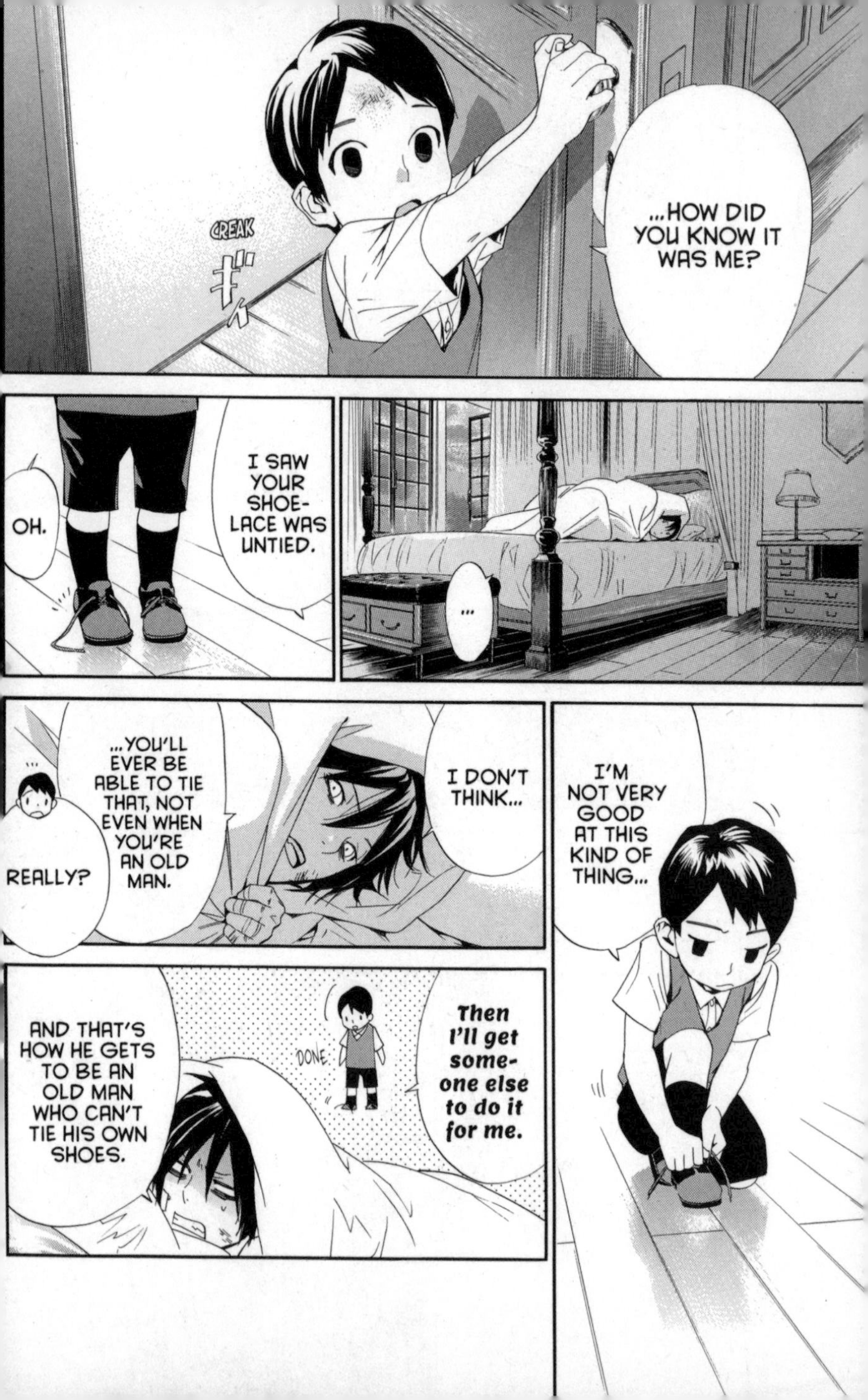
...HOW DID YOU KNOW IT WAS ME?
CREAK
ギィ
...
I SAW YOUR SHOE-LACE WAS UNTIED.
OH.
I'M NOT VERY GOOD AT THIS KIND OF THING...
I DON'T THINK...
...YOU'LL EVER BE ABLE TO TIE THAT, NOT EVEN WHEN YOU'RE AN OLD MAN.
...
REALLY?
Then I'll get some-one else to do it for me.
DONE
AND THAT'S HOW HE GETS TO BE AN OLD MAN WHO CAN'T TIE HIS OWN SHOES.

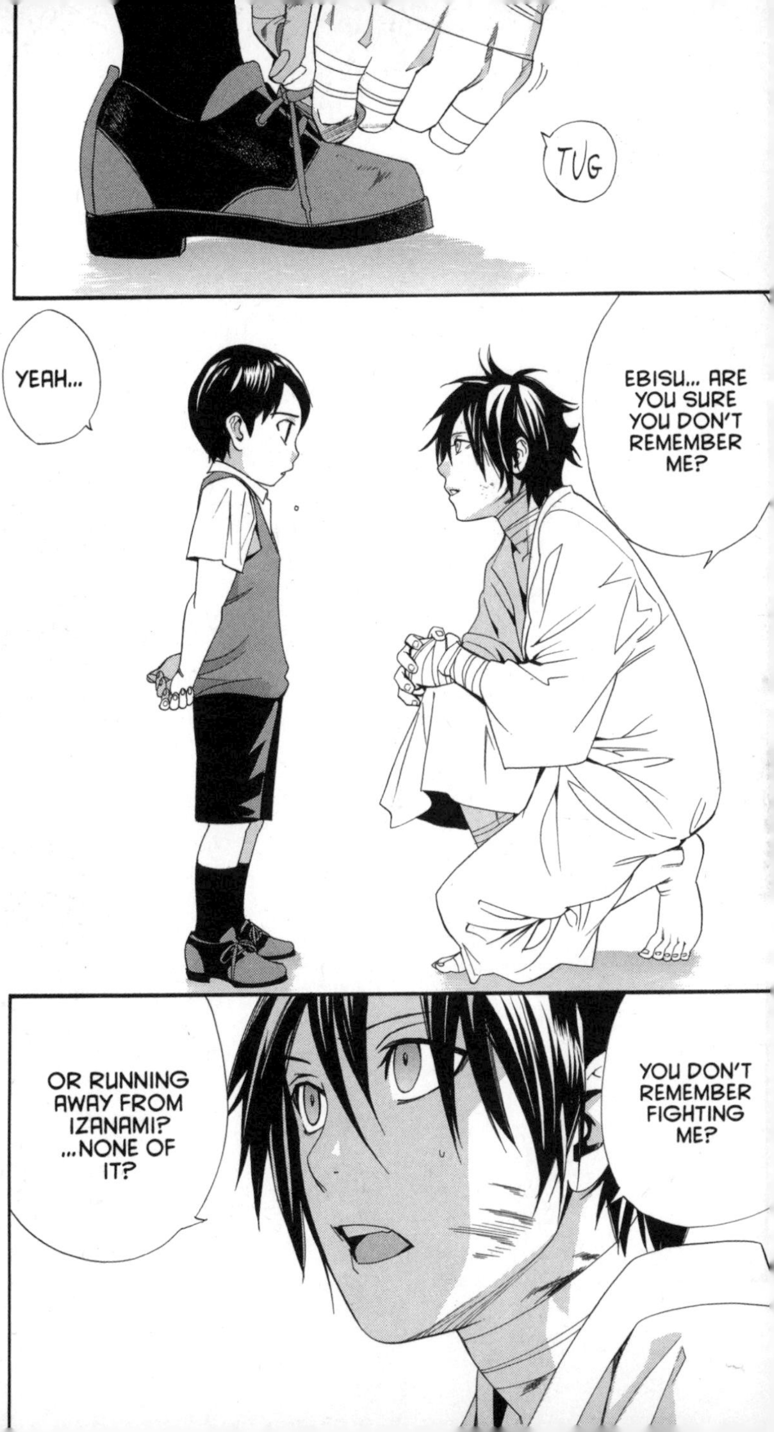
TUG
EBISU... ARE YOU SURE YOU DON'T REMEMBER ME?
YEAH...
YOU DON'T REMEMBER FIGHTING ME?
OR RUNNING AWAY FROM IZANAMI? ...NONE OF IT?

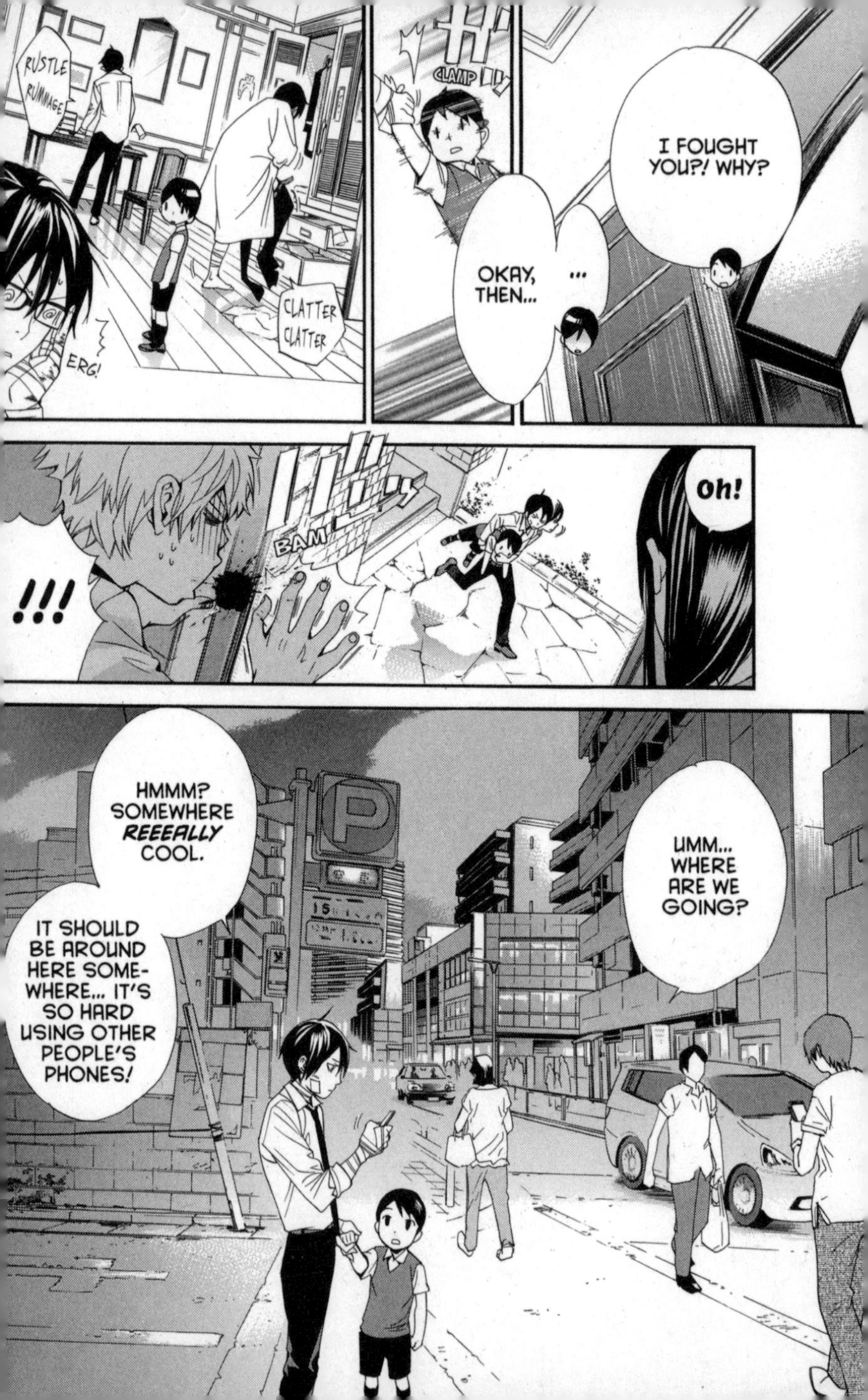
I FOUGHT YOU?! WHY?
...
CLAMP
OKAY, THEN...
RUSTLE RUMMAGE
CLATTER CLATTER
ERG!
Oh!
BAM
!!!
UMM... WHERE ARE WE GOING?
HMMM? SOMEWHERE ***REEEALLY*** COOL.
IT SHOULD BE AROUND HERE SOME-WHERE... IT'S SO HARD USING OTHER PEOPLE'S PHONES!

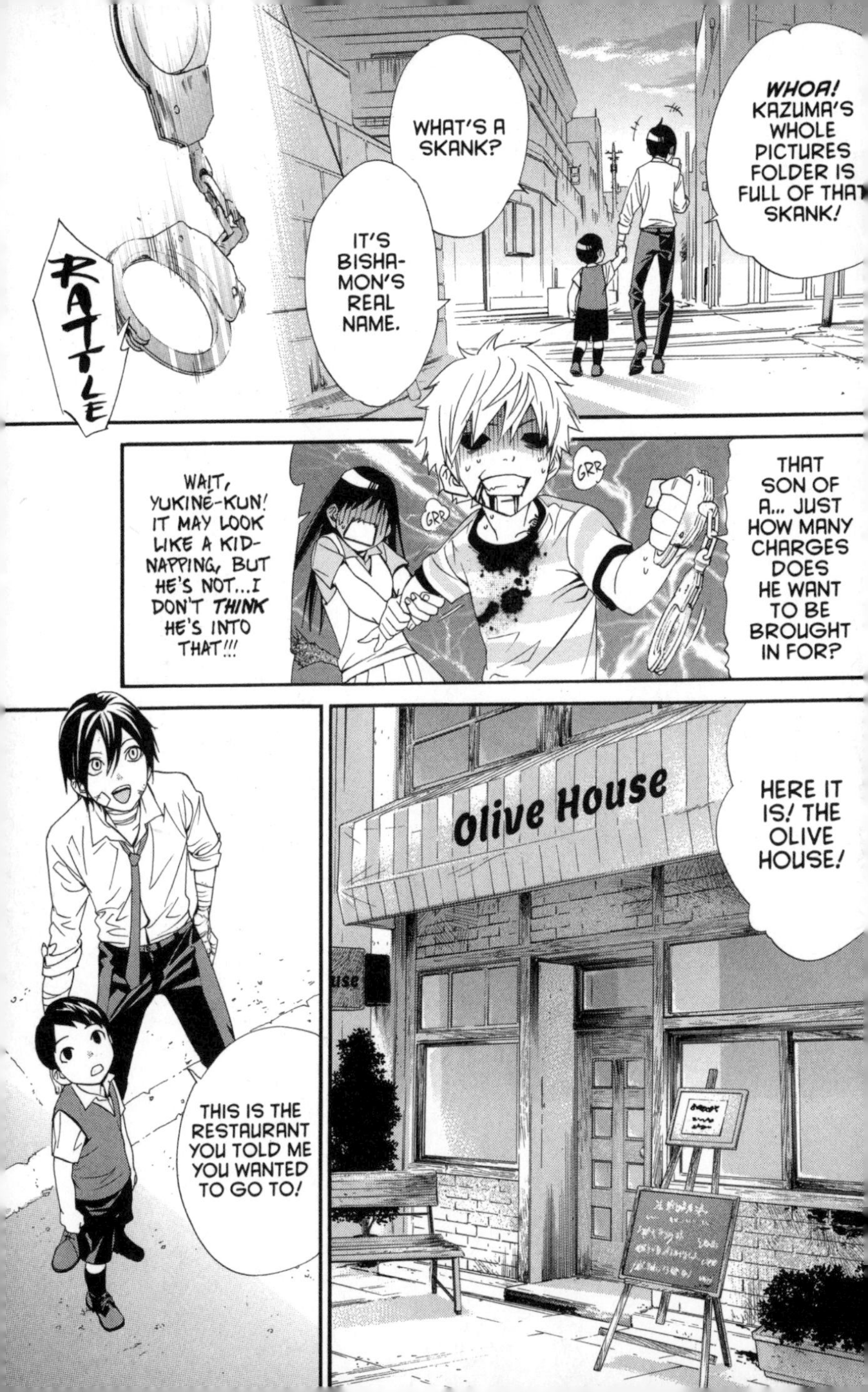
WHOA! KAZUMA'S WHOLE PICTURES FOLDER IS FULL OF THAT SKANK!
WHAT'S A SKANK?
IT'S BISHA-MON'S REAL NAME.
RATTLE
THAT SON OF A... JUST HOW MANY CHARGES DOES HE WANT TO BE BROUGHT IN FOR?
GRR
GRR
WAIT, YUKINÉ-KUN! IT MAY LOOK LIKE A KID-NAPPING, BUT HE'S NOT...I DON'T THINK HE'S INTO THAT!!!
HERE IT IS! THE OLIVE HOUSE!
Olive House
THIS IS THE RESTAURANT YOU TOLD ME YOU WANTED TO GO TO!

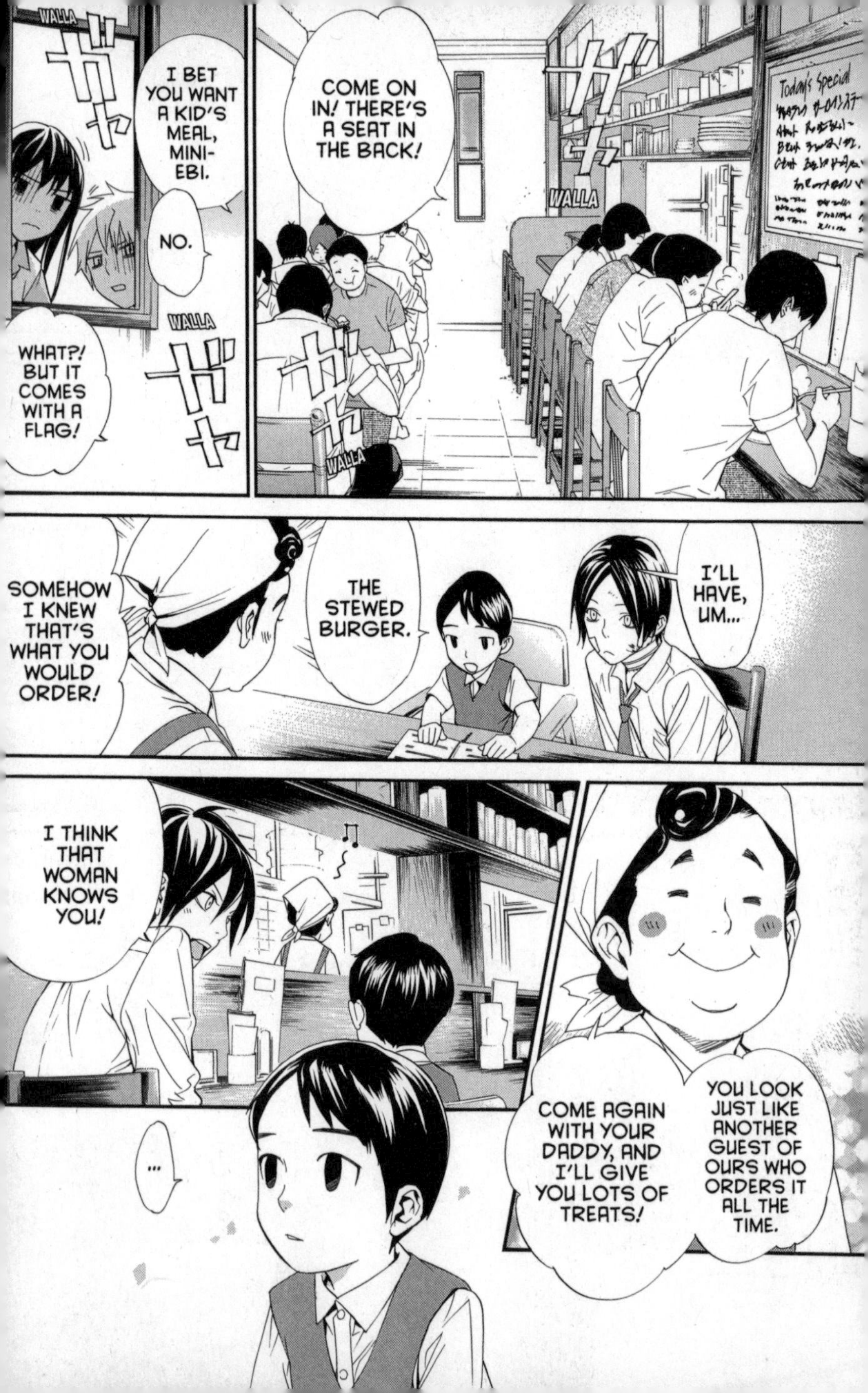

Today's Special
WALLA
WALLA
COME ON IN! THERE'S A SEAT IN THE BACK!
WALLA
I BET YOU WANT A KID'S MEAL, MINI-EBI.
NO.
WHAT?! BUT IT COMES WITH A FLAG!
WALLA
I'LL HAVE, UM...
THE STEWED BURGER.
SOMEHOW I KNEW THAT'S WHAT YOU WOULD ORDER!
YOU LOOK JUST LIKE ANOTHER GUEST OF OURS WHO ORDERS IT ALL THE TIME.
COME AGAIN WITH YOUR DADDY, AND I'LL GIVE YOU LOTS OF TREATS!
I THINK THAT WOMAN KNOWS YOU!
...

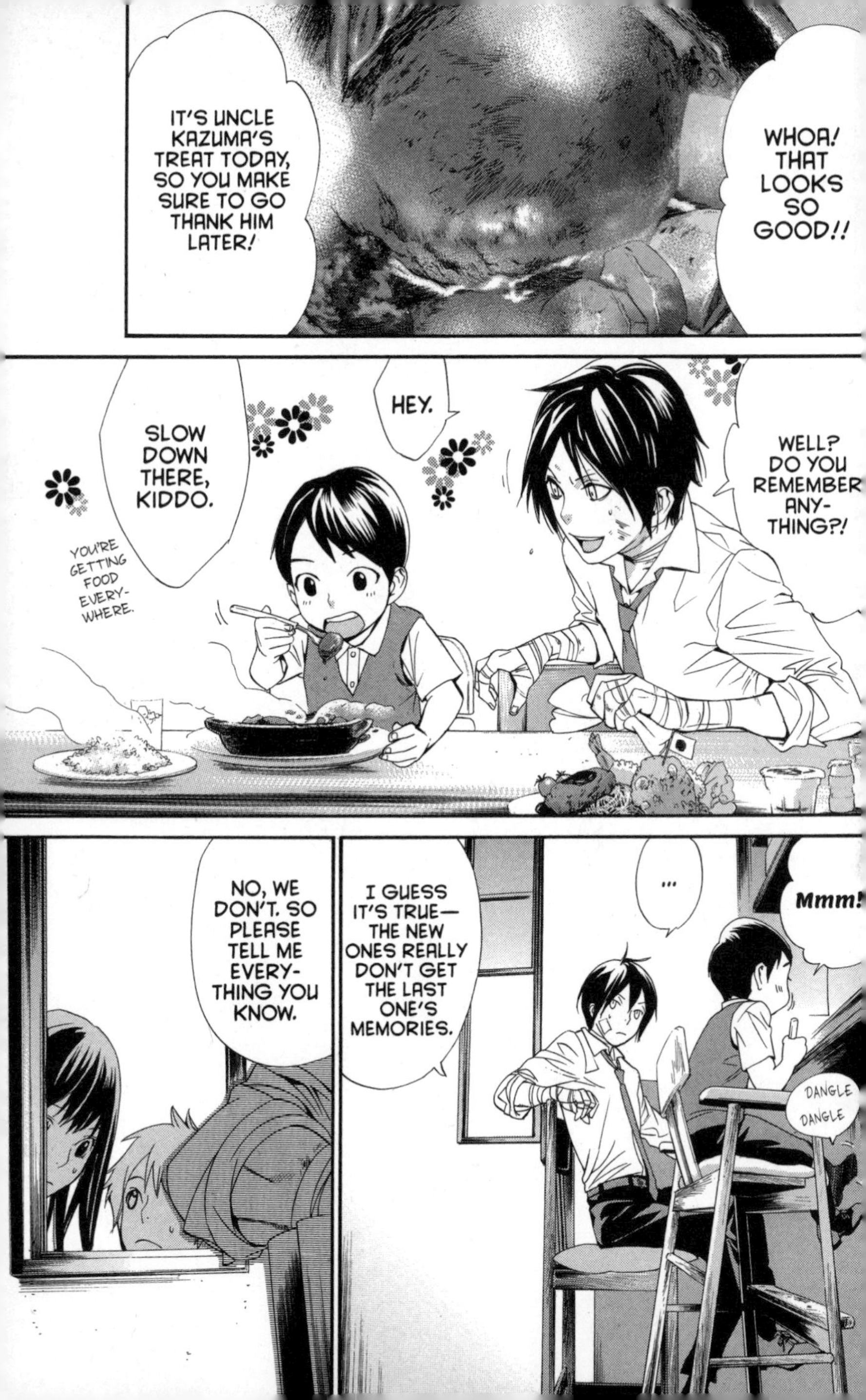
WHOA! THAT LOOKS SO GOOD!!
IT'S UNCLE KAZUMA'S TREAT TODAY, SO YOU MAKE SURE TO GO THANK HIM LATER!
WELL? DO YOU REMEMBER ANY-THING?!
HEY.
SLOW DOWN THERE, KIDDO.
YOU'RE GETTING FOOD EVERY-WHERE.
Mmm!
...
I GUESS IT'S TRUE— THE NEW ONES REALLY DON'T GET THE LAST ONE'S MEMORIES.
DANGLE DANGLE
NO, WE DON'T. SO PLEASE TELL ME EVERY-THING YOU KNOW.

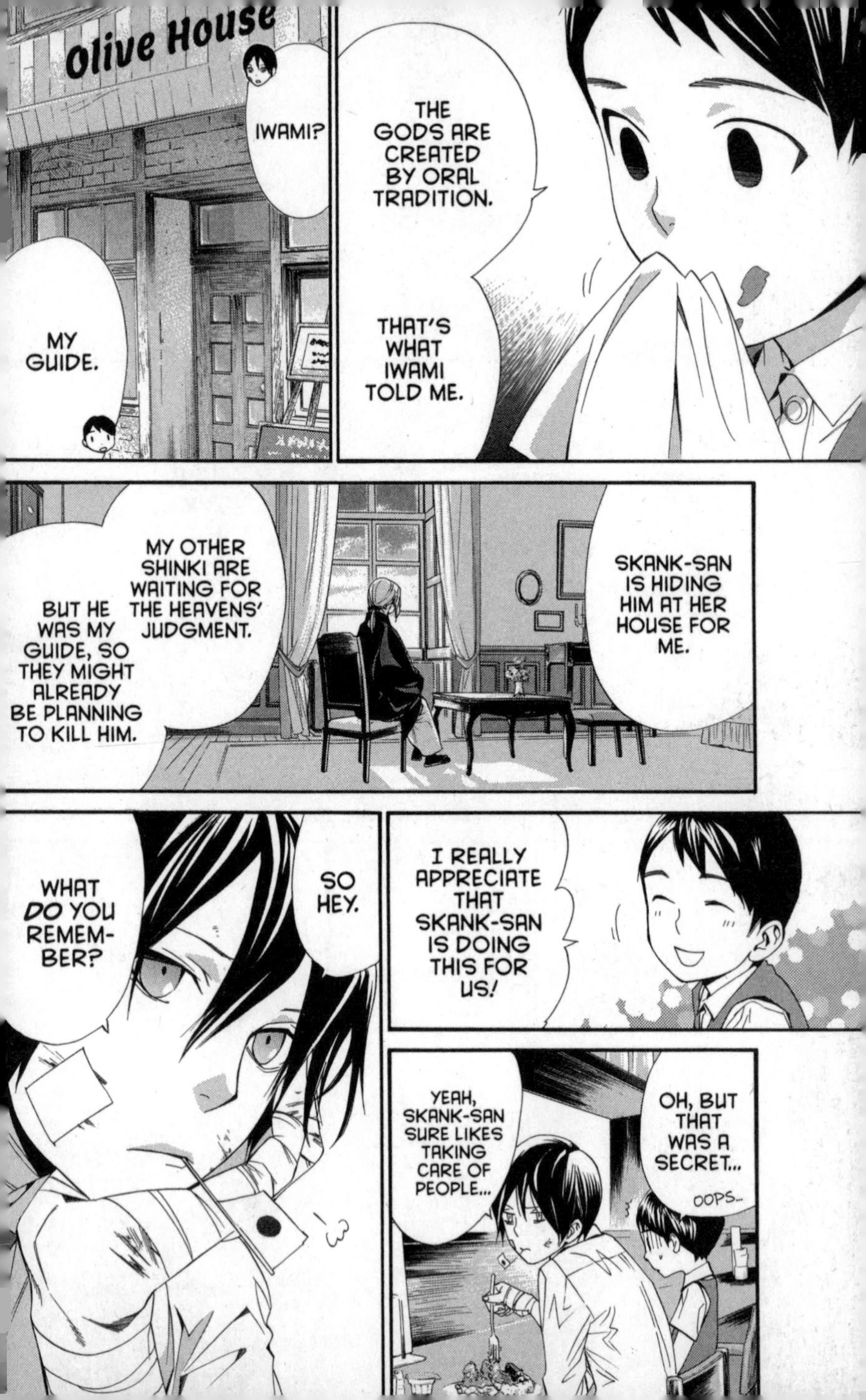
THE GODS ARE CREATED BY ORAL TRADITION.
THAT'S WHAT IWAMI TOLD ME.
Olive House
IWAMI?
MY GUIDE.
SKANK-SAN IS HIDING HIM AT HER HOUSE FOR ME.
MY OTHER SHINKI ARE WAITING FOR THE HEAVENS' JUDGMENT.
BUT HE WAS MY GUIDE, SO THEY MIGHT ALREADY BE PLANNING TO KILL HIM.
I REALLY APPRECIATE THAT SKANK-SAN IS DOING THIS FOR US!
OH, BUT THAT WAS A SECRET...
OOPS...
YEAH, SKANK-SAN SURE LIKES TAKING CARE OF PEOPLE...
SO HEY.
WHAT *DO* YOU REMEMBER?

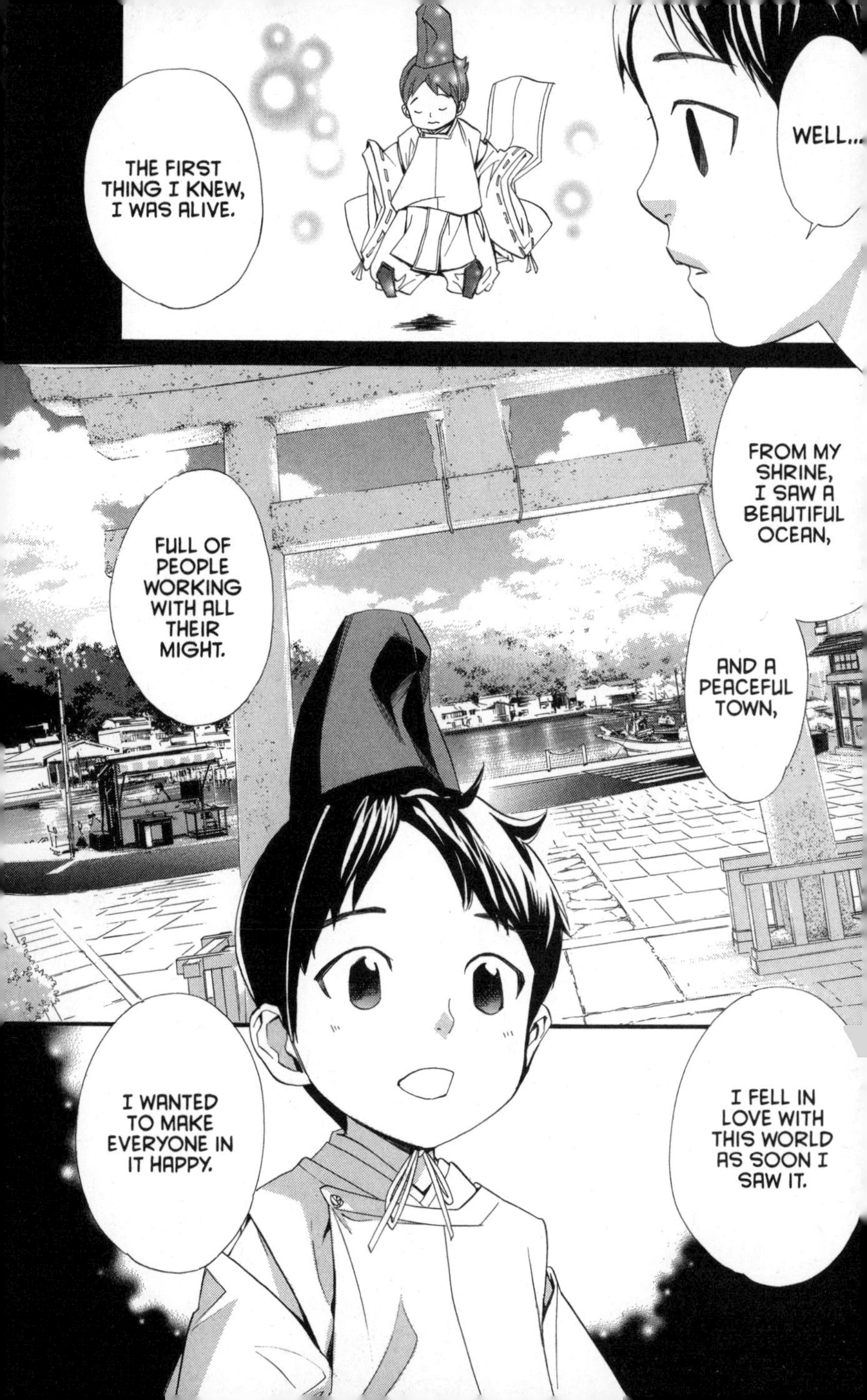
WELL...
THE FIRST THING I KNEW, I WAS ALIVE.
FROM MY SHRINE, I SAW A BEAUTIFUL OCEAN,
AND A PEACEFUL TOWN,
FULL OF PEOPLE WORKING WITH ALL THEIR MIGHT.
I FELL IN LOVE WITH THIS WORLD AS SOON I SAW IT.
I WANTED TO MAKE EVERYONE IN IT HAPPY.

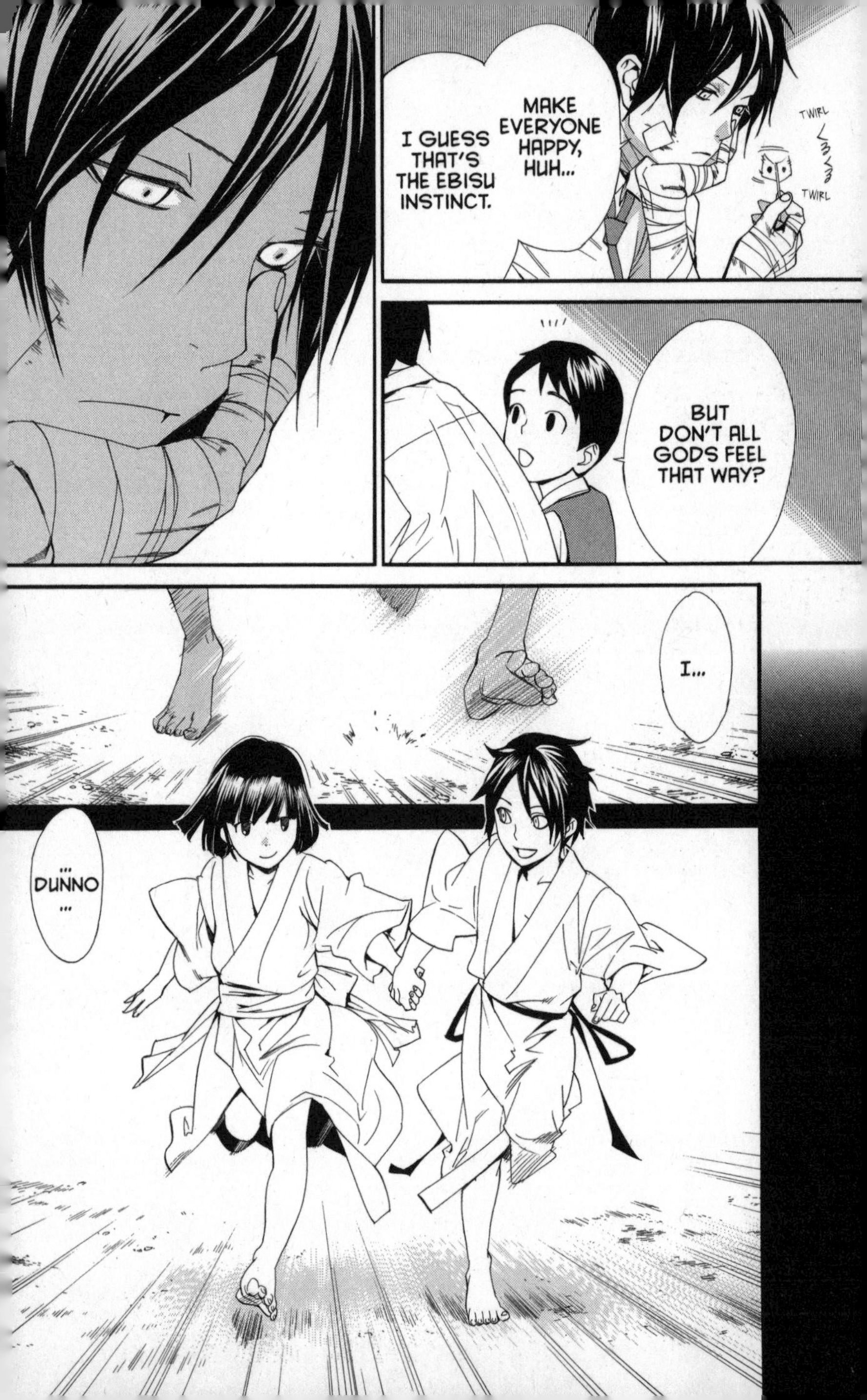

TWIRL TWIRL
MAKE EVERYONE HAPPY, HUH...
I GUESS THAT'S THE EBISU INSTINCT.
BUT DON'T ALL GODS FEEL THAT WAY?
I...
...DUNNO...

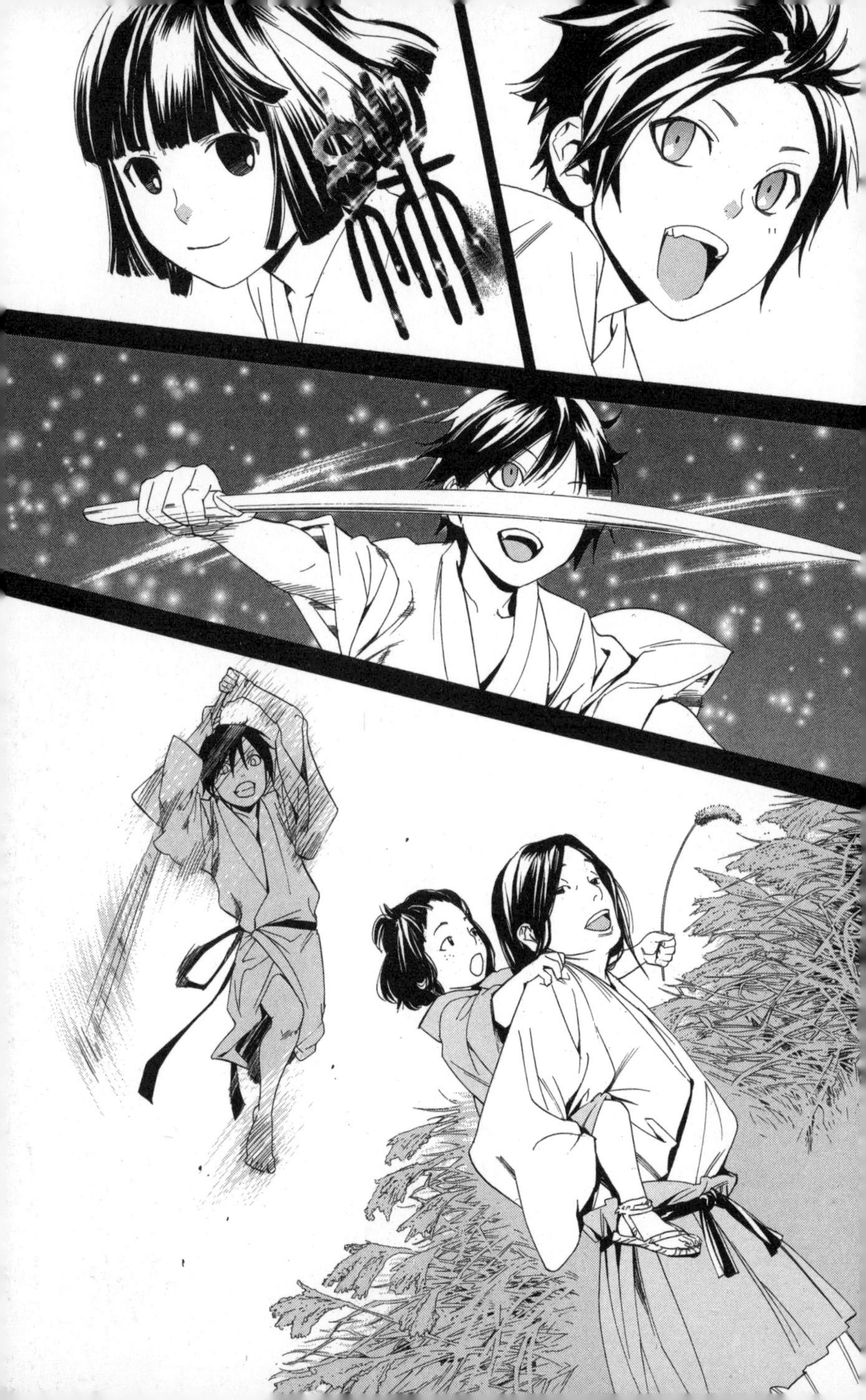

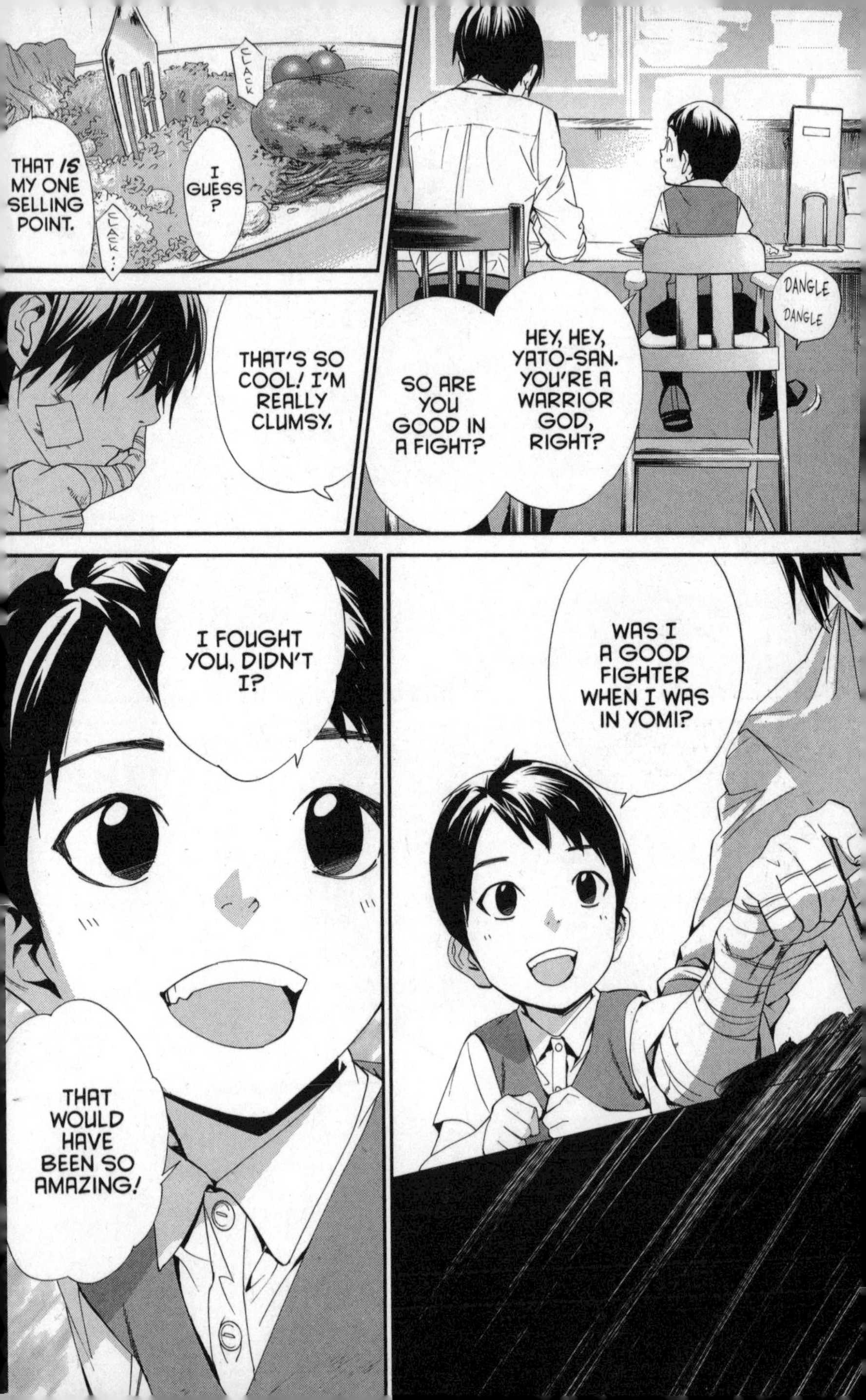
HEY, HEY, YATO-SAN. YOU'RE A WARRIOR GOD, RIGHT?
SO ARE YOU GOOD IN A FIGHT?
DANGLE DANGLE
CLACK
I GUESS?
THAT *IS* MY ONE SELLING POINT.
CLACK...
THAT'S SO COOL! I'M REALLY CLUMSY.
WAS I A GOOD FIGHTER WHEN I WAS IN YOMI?
I FOUGHT YOU, DIDN'T I?
THAT WOULD HAVE BEEN SO AMAZING!

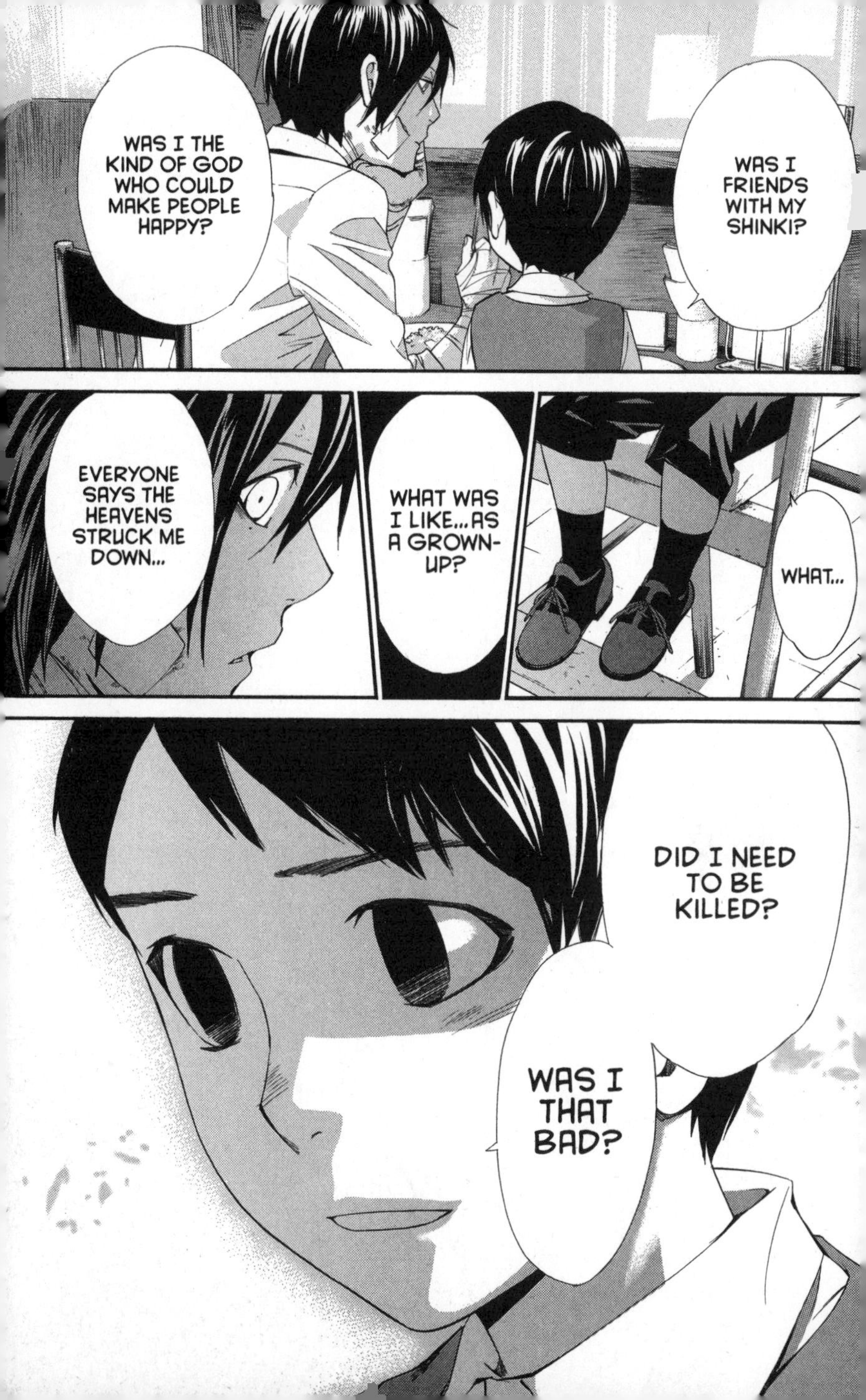
WAS I FRIENDS WITH MY SHINKI?
WAS I THE KIND OF GOD WHO COULD MAKE PEOPLE HAPPY?
WHAT...
WHAT WAS I LIKE...AS A GROWN-UP?
EVERYONE SAYS THE HEAVENS STRUCK ME DOWN...
DID I NEED TO BE KILLED?
WAS I THAT BAD?

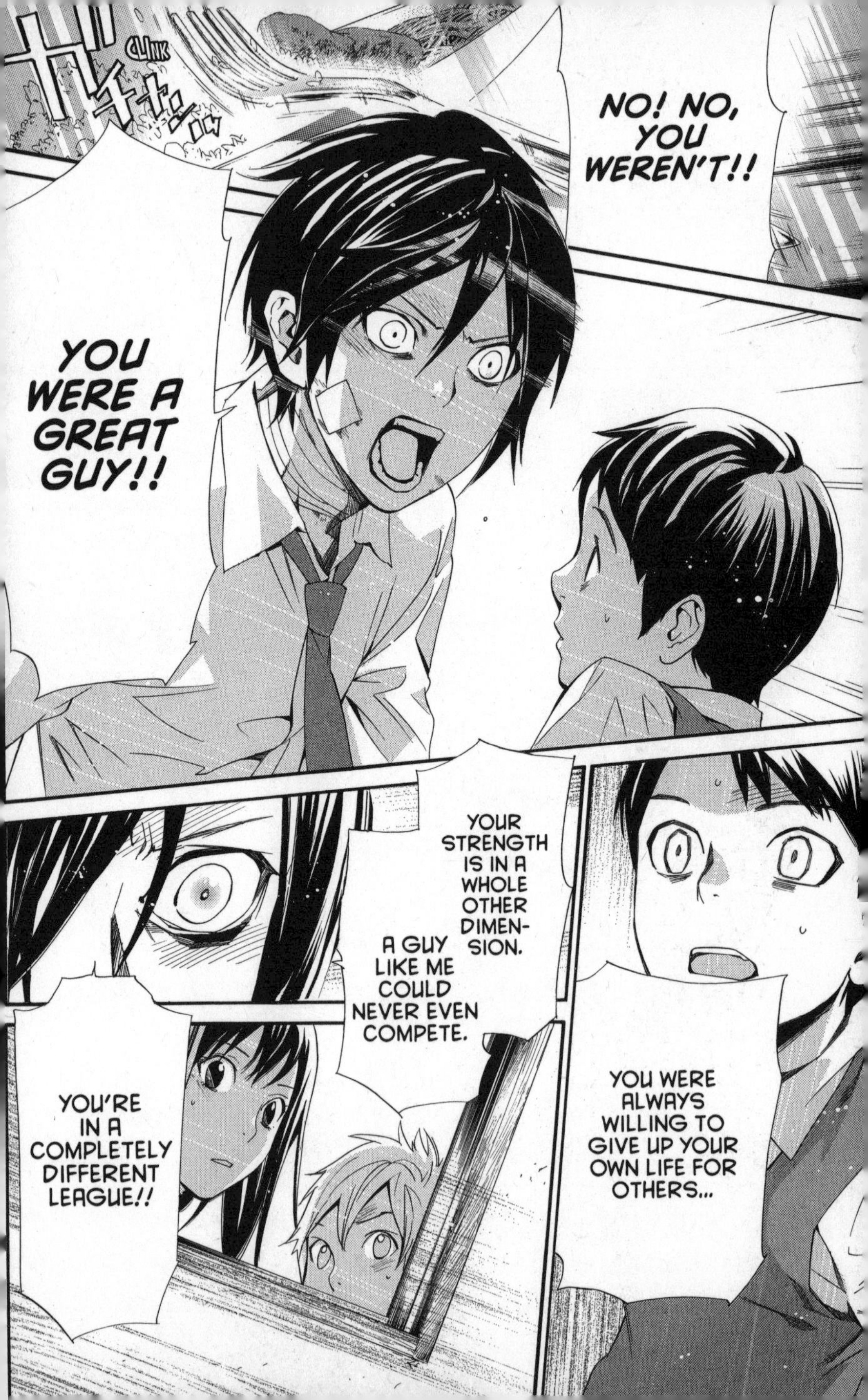
CLINK
NO! NO, YOU WEREN'T!!
YOU WERE A GREAT GUY!!
YOU WERE ALWAYS WILLING TO GIVE UP YOUR OWN LIFE FOR OTHERS...
YOUR STRENGTH IS IN A WHOLE OTHER DIMENSION.
A GUY LIKE ME COULD NEVER EVEN COMPETE.
YOU'RE IN A COMPLETELY DIFFERENT LEAGUE!!

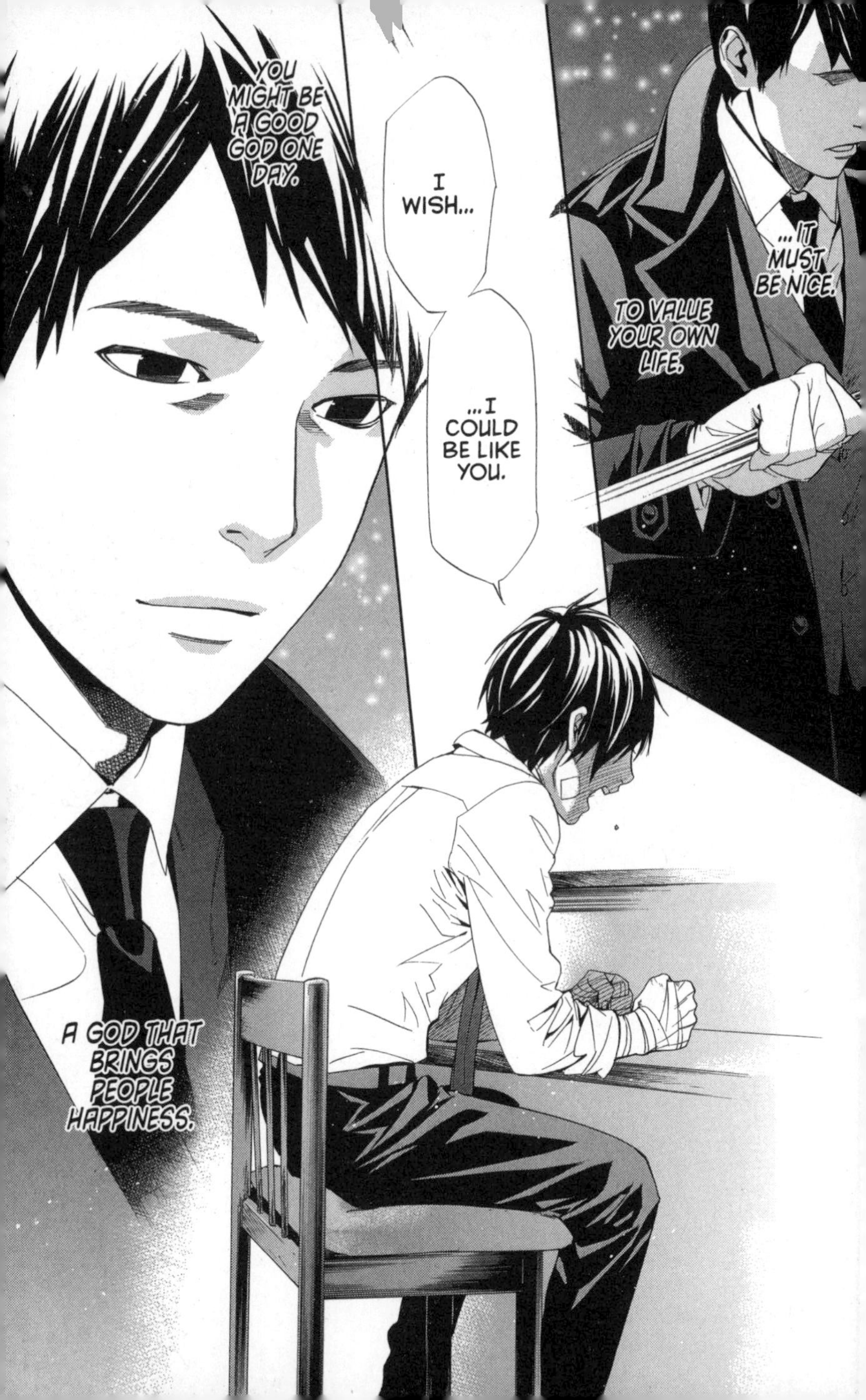
...IT MUST BE NICE.
TO VALUE YOUR OWN LIFE.
I WISH...
...I COULD BE LIKE YOU.
YOU MIGHT BE A GOOD GOD ONE DAY.
A GOD THAT BRINGS PEOPLE HAPPINESS.

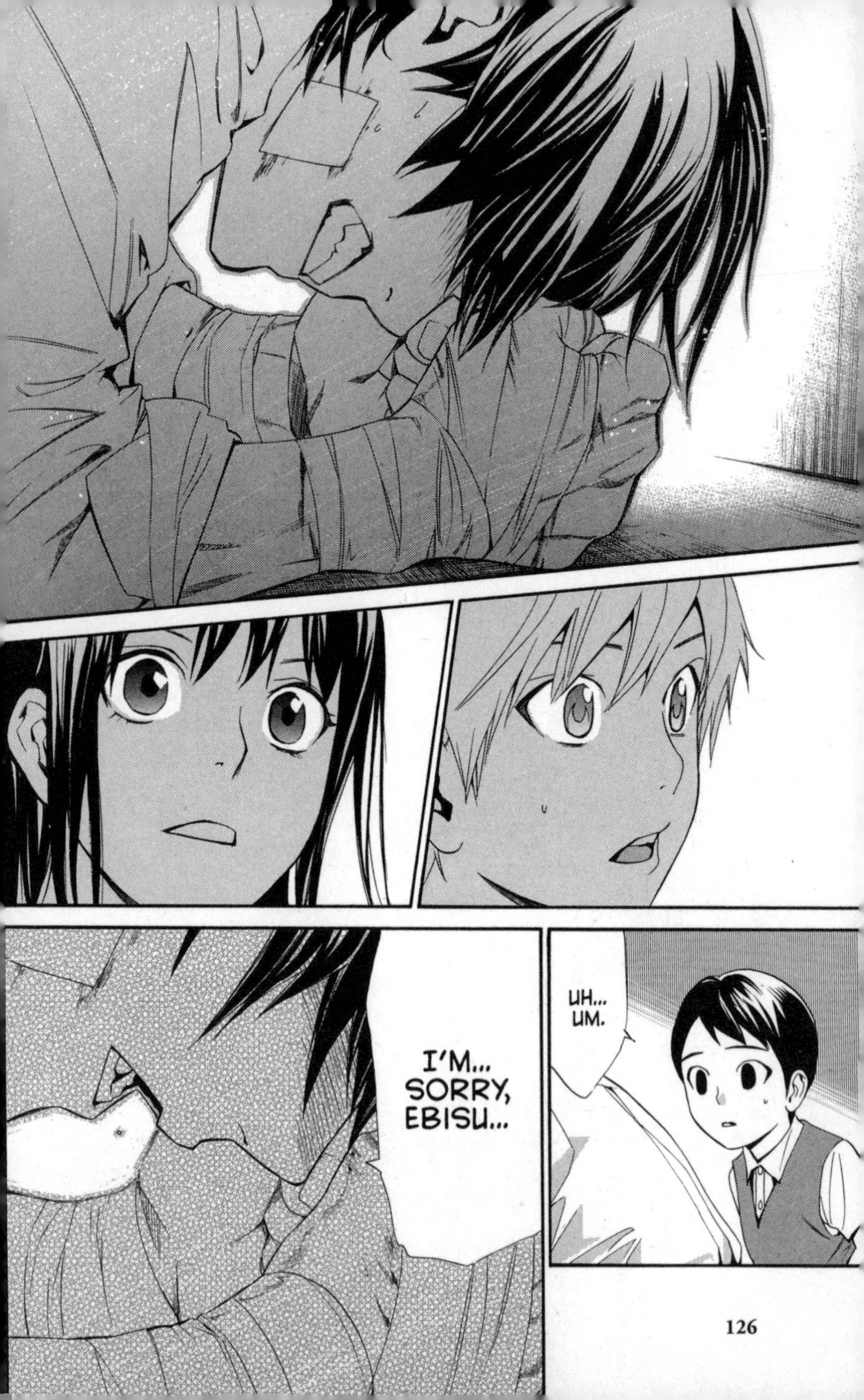
UH... UM.
I'M... SORRY, EBISU...

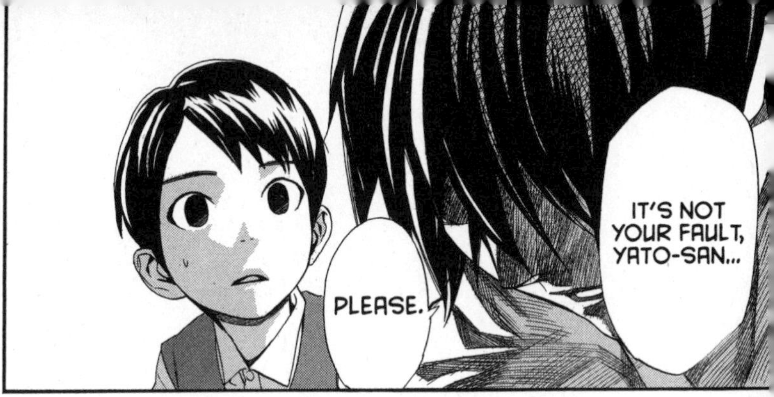
IT'S NOT YOUR FAULT, YATO-SAN...
PLEASE.

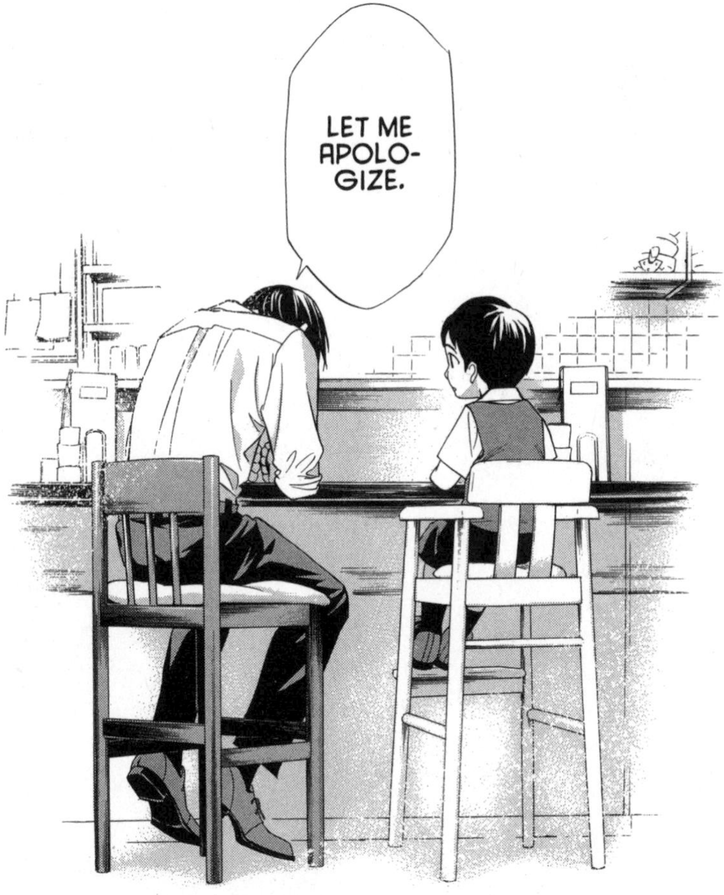
LET ME APOLO-GIZE.

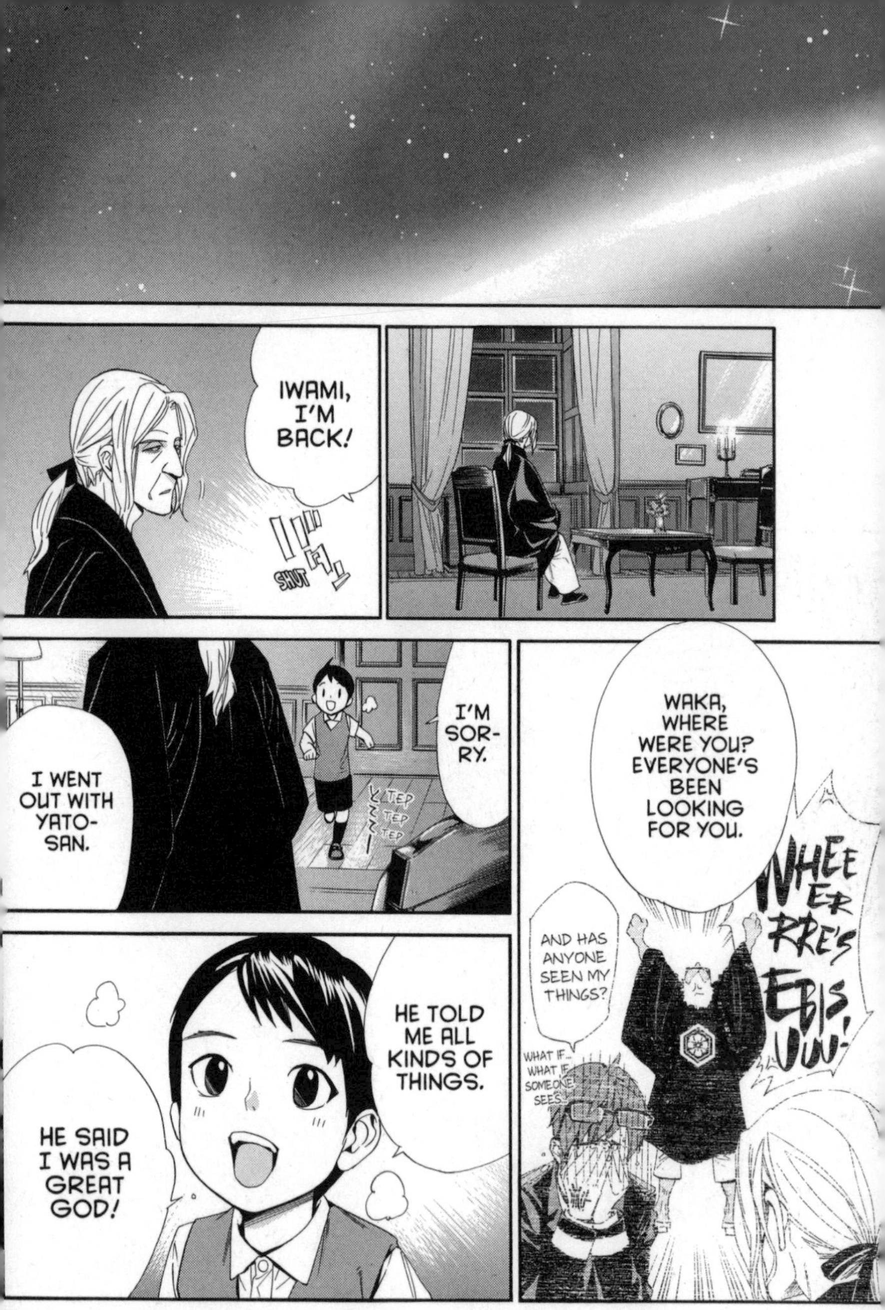
IWAMI, I'M BACK!
SHUT
WAKA, WHERE WERE YOU? EVERYONE'S BEEN LOOKING FOR YOU.
WHEE ERRRE'S EBIS, UUU!
AND HAS ANYONE SEEN MY THINGS?
WHAT IF... WHAT IF SOMEONE SEES...
I'M SOR-RY.
TEP TEP TEP
I WENT OUT WITH YATO-SAN.
HE TOLD ME ALL KINDS OF THINGS.
HE SAID I WAS A GREAT GOD!

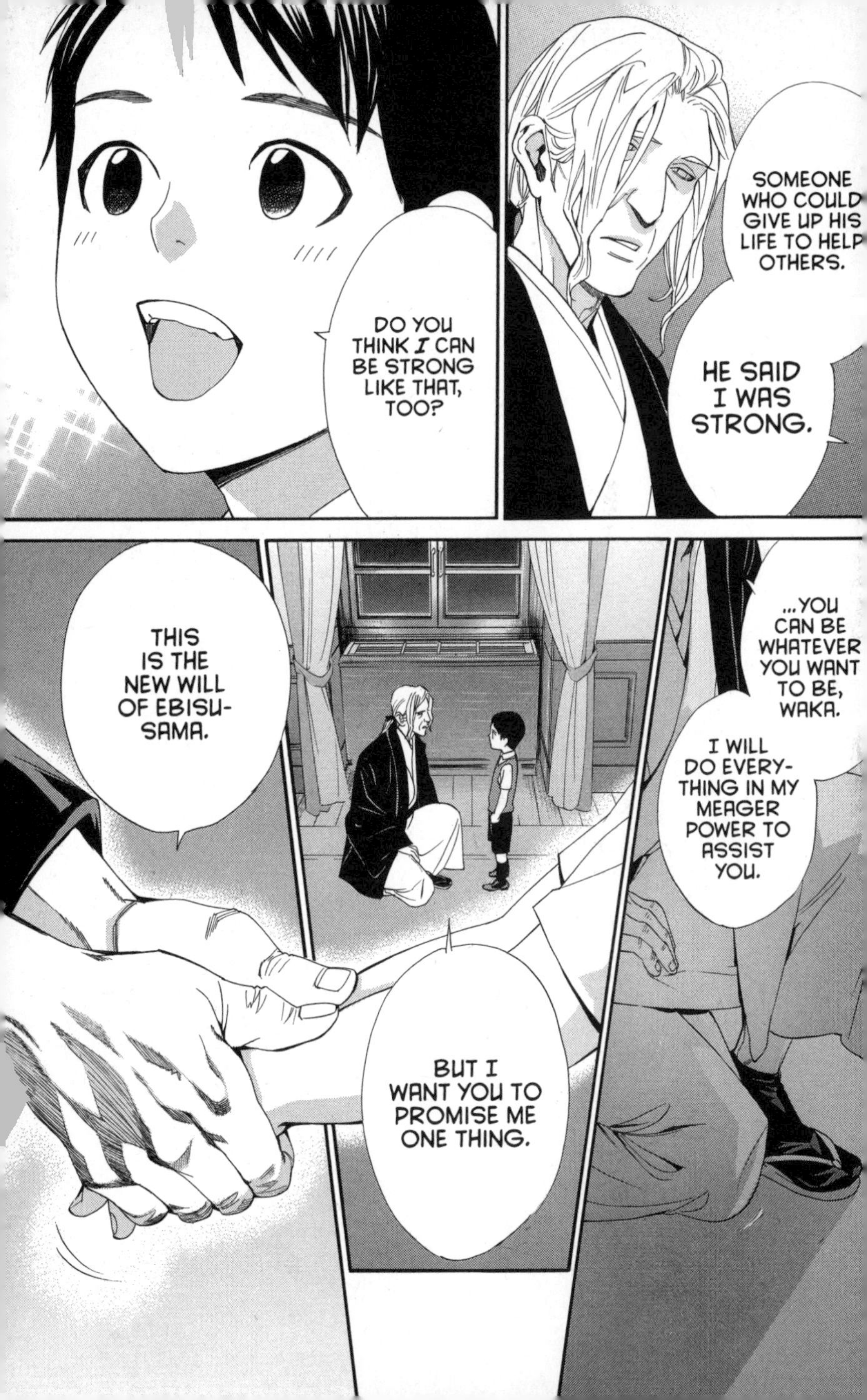
SOMEONE WHO COULD GIVE UP HIS LIFE TO HELP OTHERS.
HE SAID I WAS STRONG.
DO YOU THINK *I* CAN BE STRONG LIKE THAT, TOO?
...YOU CAN BE WHATEVER YOU WANT TO BE, WAKA.
I WILL DO EVERY-THING IN MY MEAGER POWER TO ASSIST YOU.
BUT I WANT YOU TO PROMISE ME ONE THING.
THIS IS THE NEW WILL OF EBISU-SAMA.

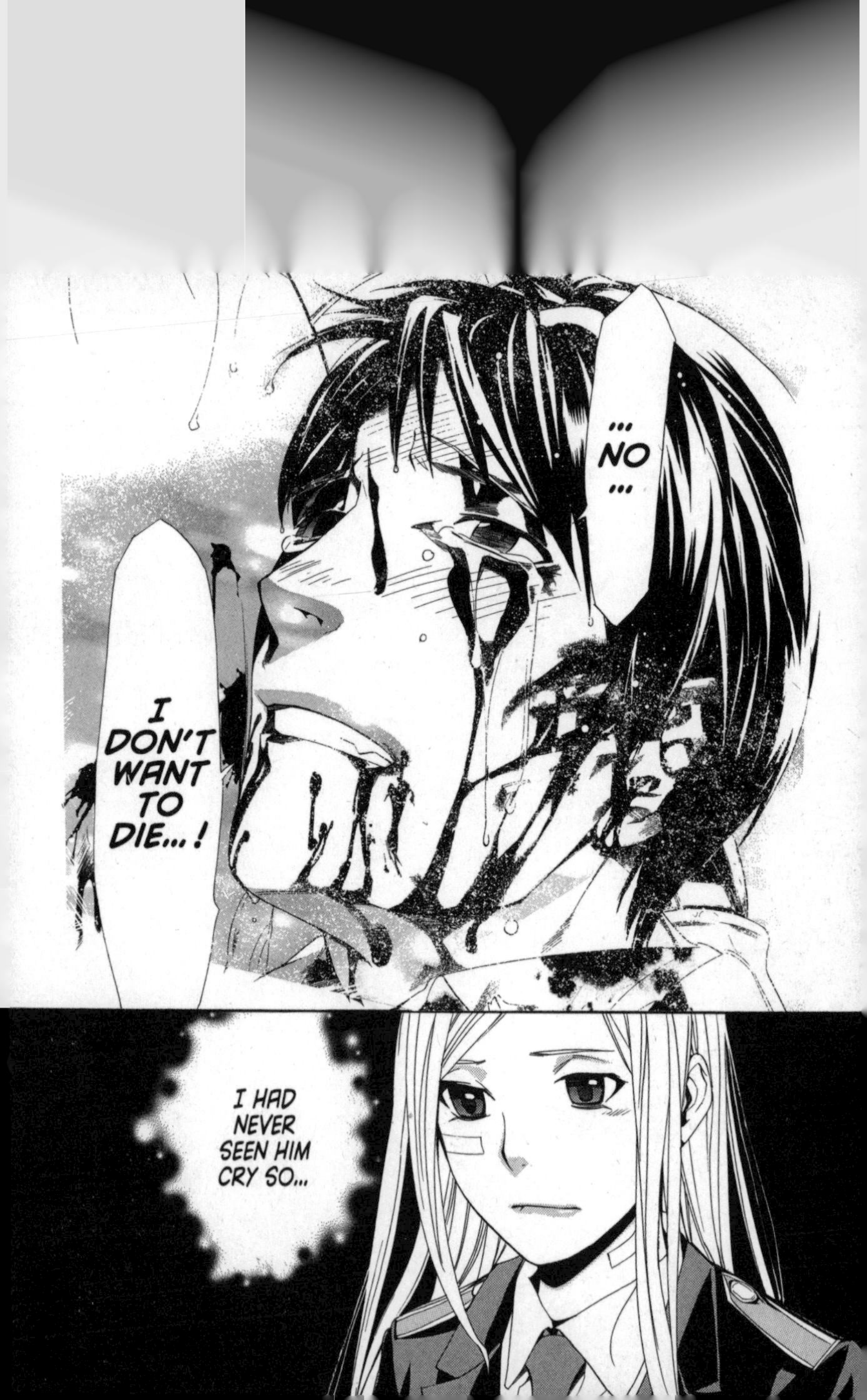
...NO...
I DON'T WANT TO DIE...!
I HAD NEVER SEEN HIM CRY SO...

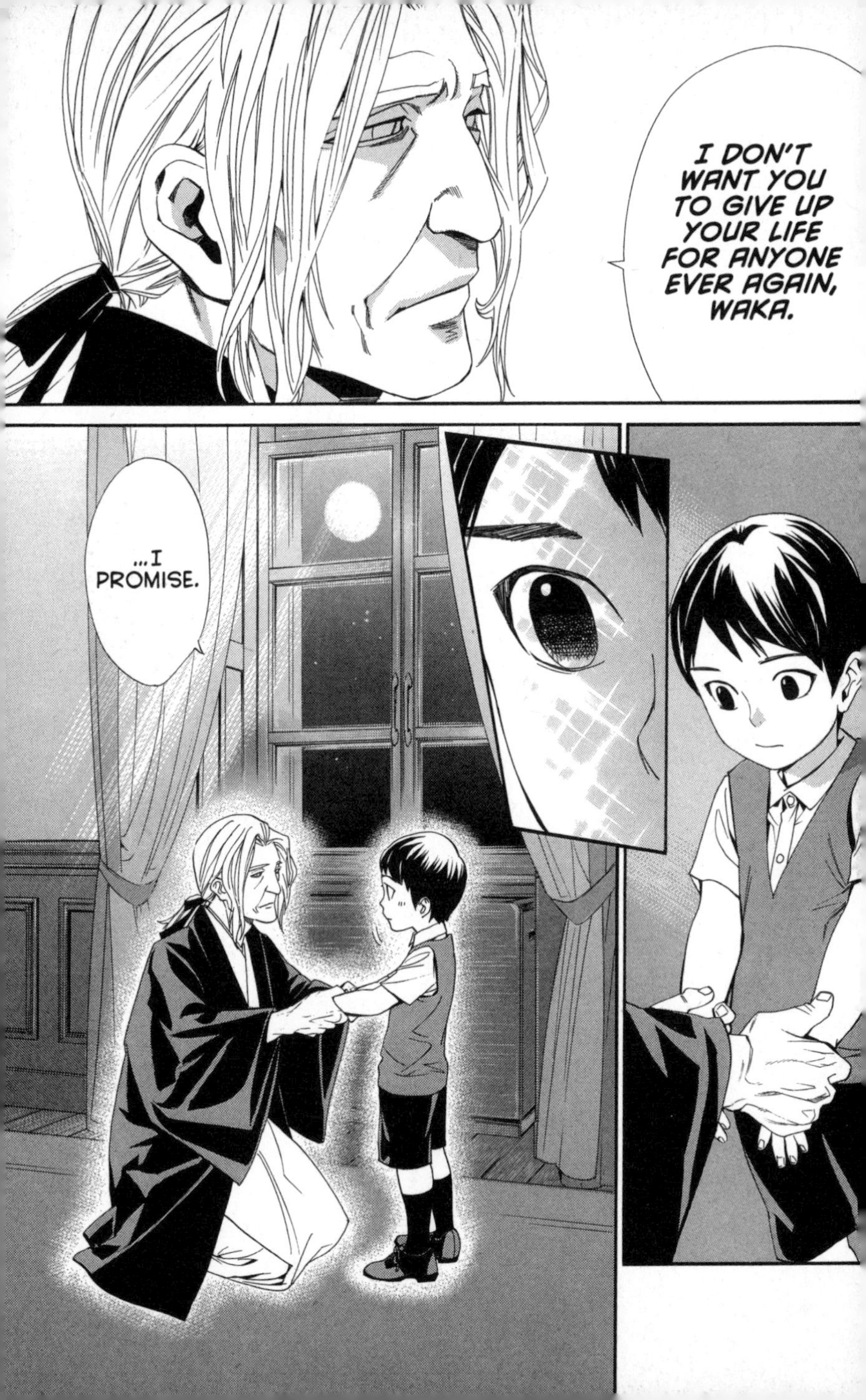
I DON'T WANT YOU TO GIVE UP YOUR LIFE FOR ANYONE EVER AGAIN, WAKA.
...I PROMISE.

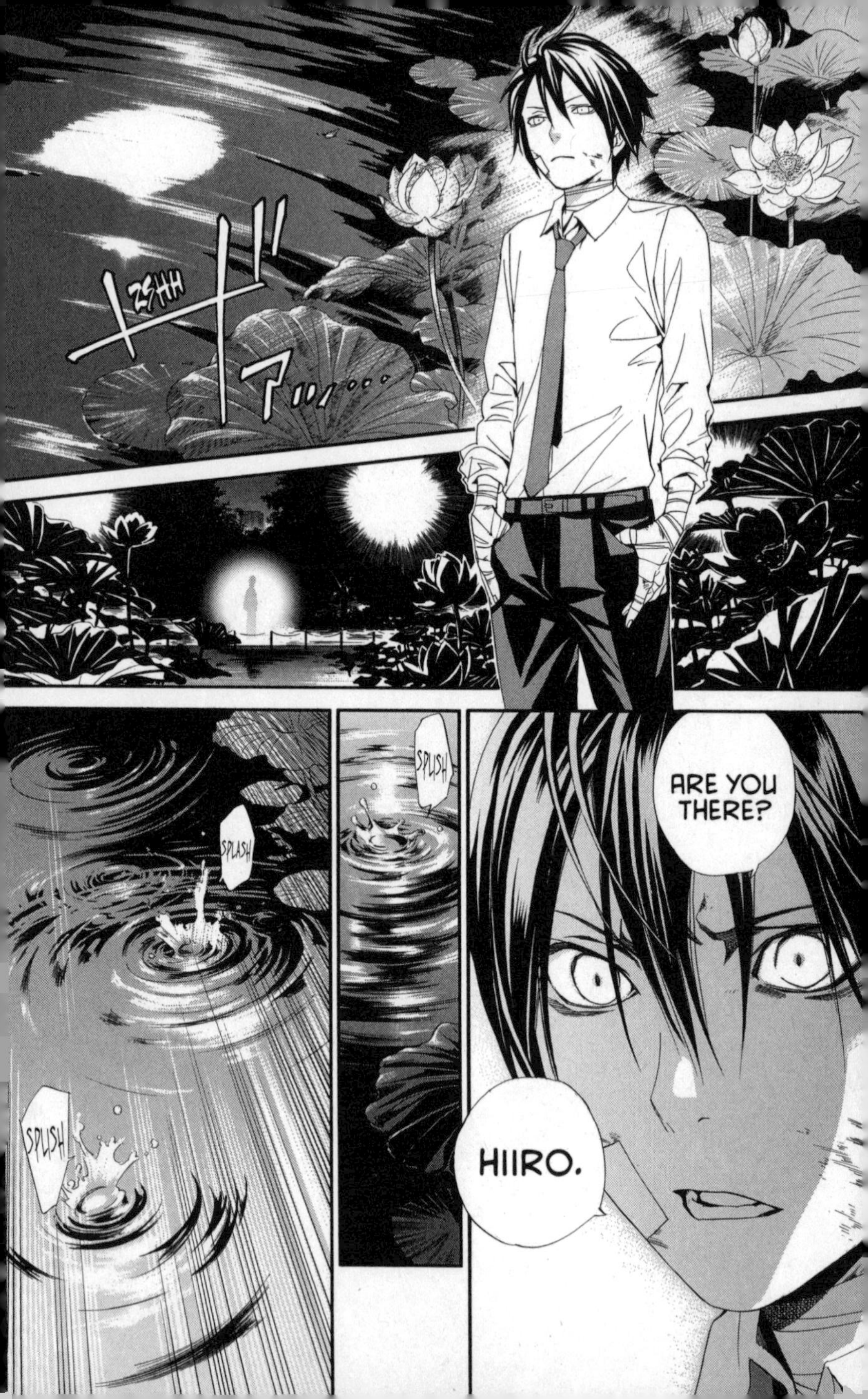
ZSHH
ARE YOU THERE?
HIIRO.
SPLASH
SPLASH
SPLASH

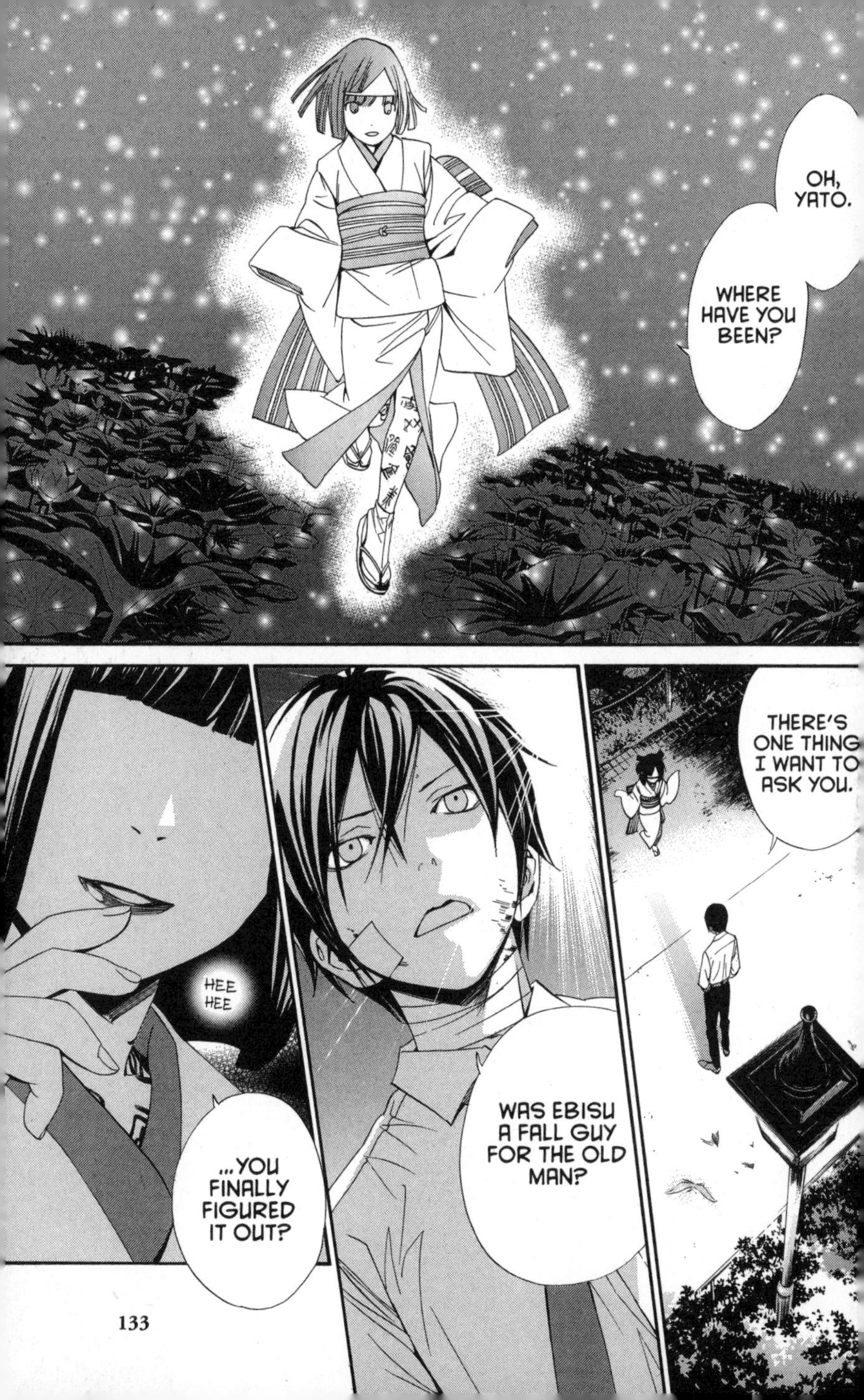
OH, YATO.
WHERE HAVE YOU BEEN?
THERE'S ONE THING I WANT TO ASK YOU.
WAS EBISU A FALL GUY FOR THE OLD MAN?
HEE HEE
...YOU FINALLY FIGURED IT OUT?

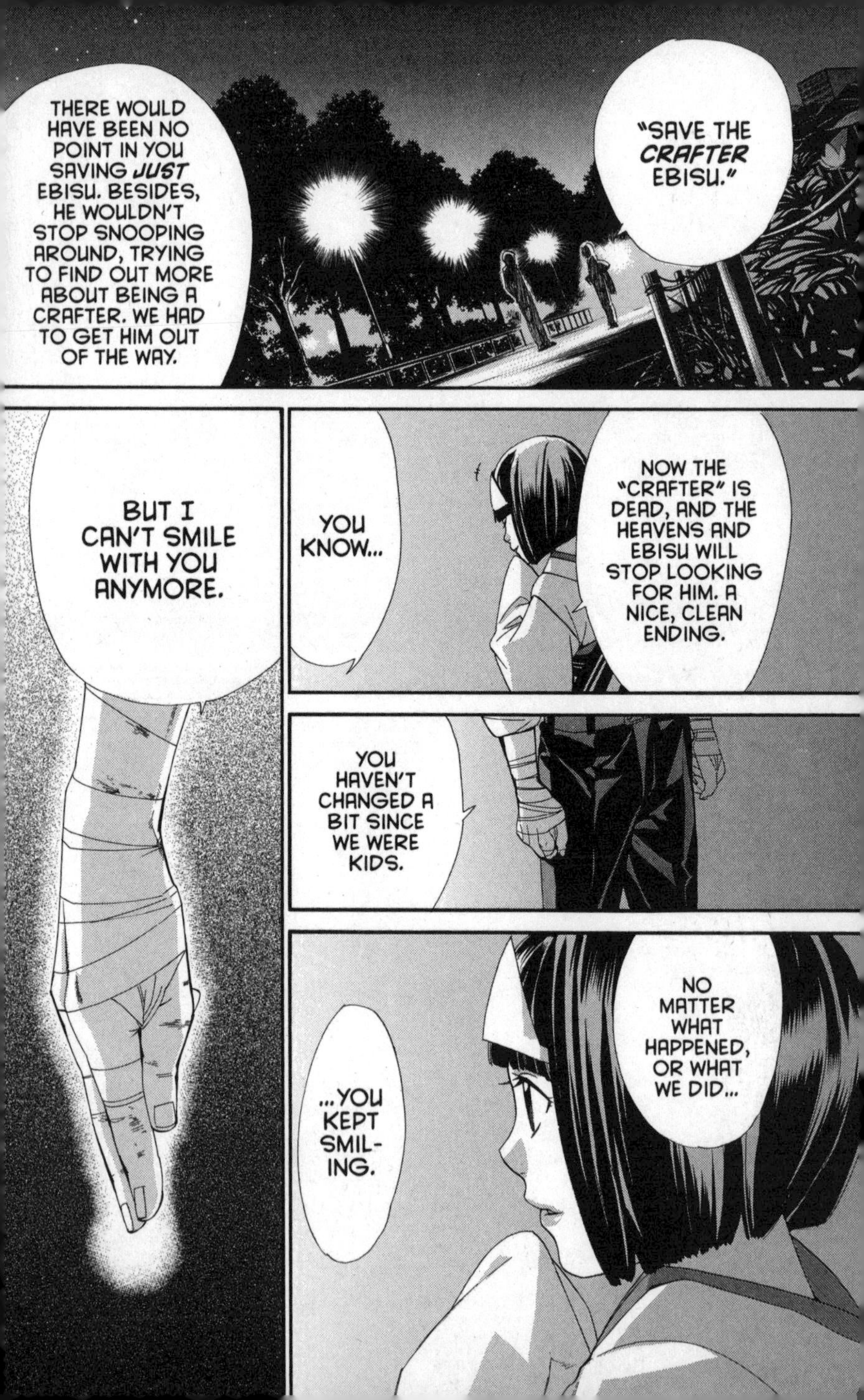
"SAVE THE CRAFTER EBISU."
THERE WOULD HAVE BEEN NO POINT IN YOU SAVING JUST EBISU. BESIDES, HE WOULDN'T STOP SNOOPING AROUND, TRYING TO FIND OUT MORE ABOUT BEING A CRAFTER. WE HAD TO GET HIM OUT OF THE WAY.
NOW THE "CRAFTER" IS DEAD, AND THE HEAVENS AND EBISU WILL STOP LOOKING FOR HIM. A NICE, CLEAN ENDING.
YOU KNOW...
YOU HAVEN'T CHANGED A BIT SINCE WE WERE KIDS.
NO MATTER WHAT HAPPENED, OR WHAT WE DID...
...YOU KEPT SMIL-ING.
BUT I CAN'T SMILE WITH YOU ANYMORE.

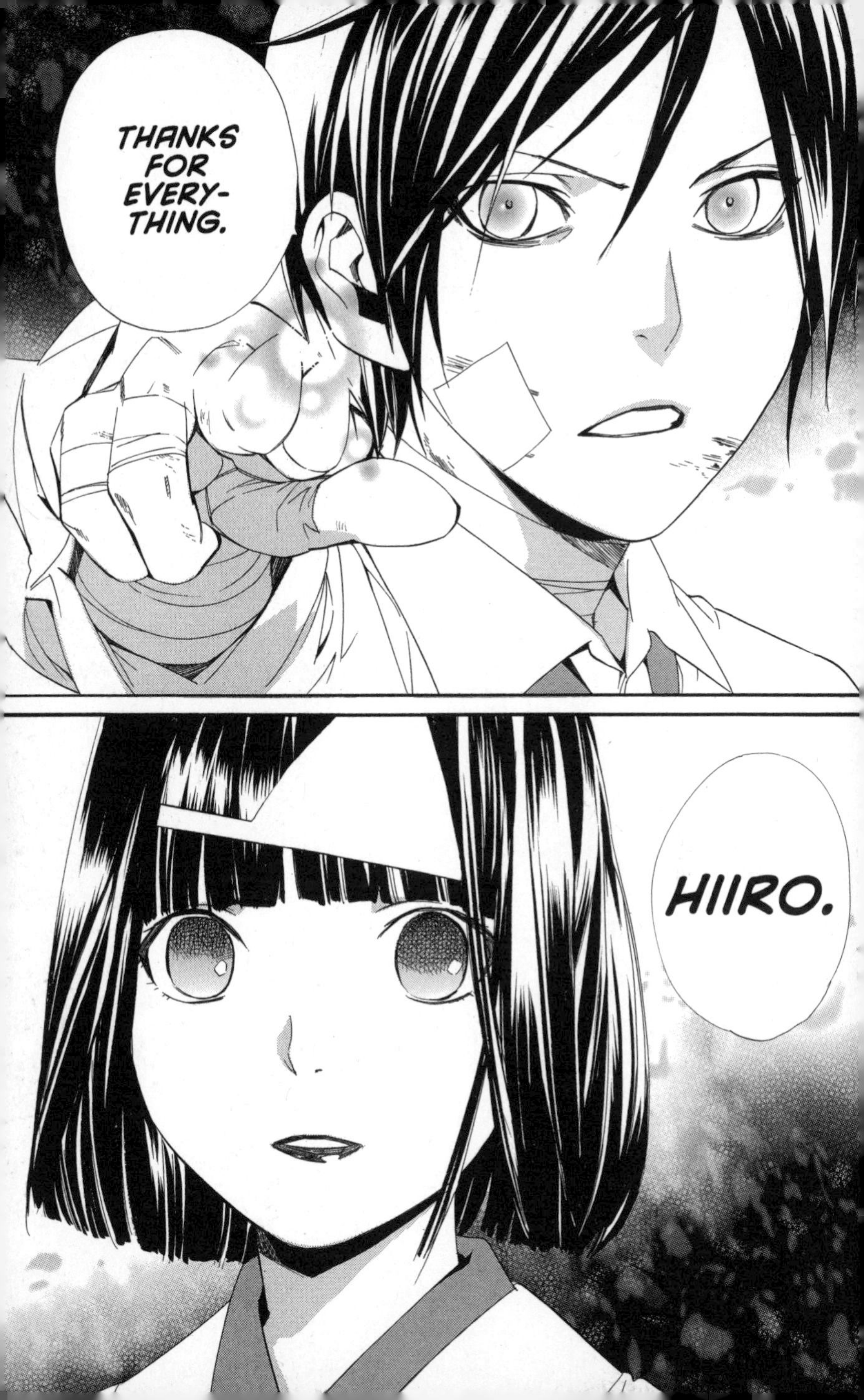
THANKS FOR EVERY-THING.
HIIRO.

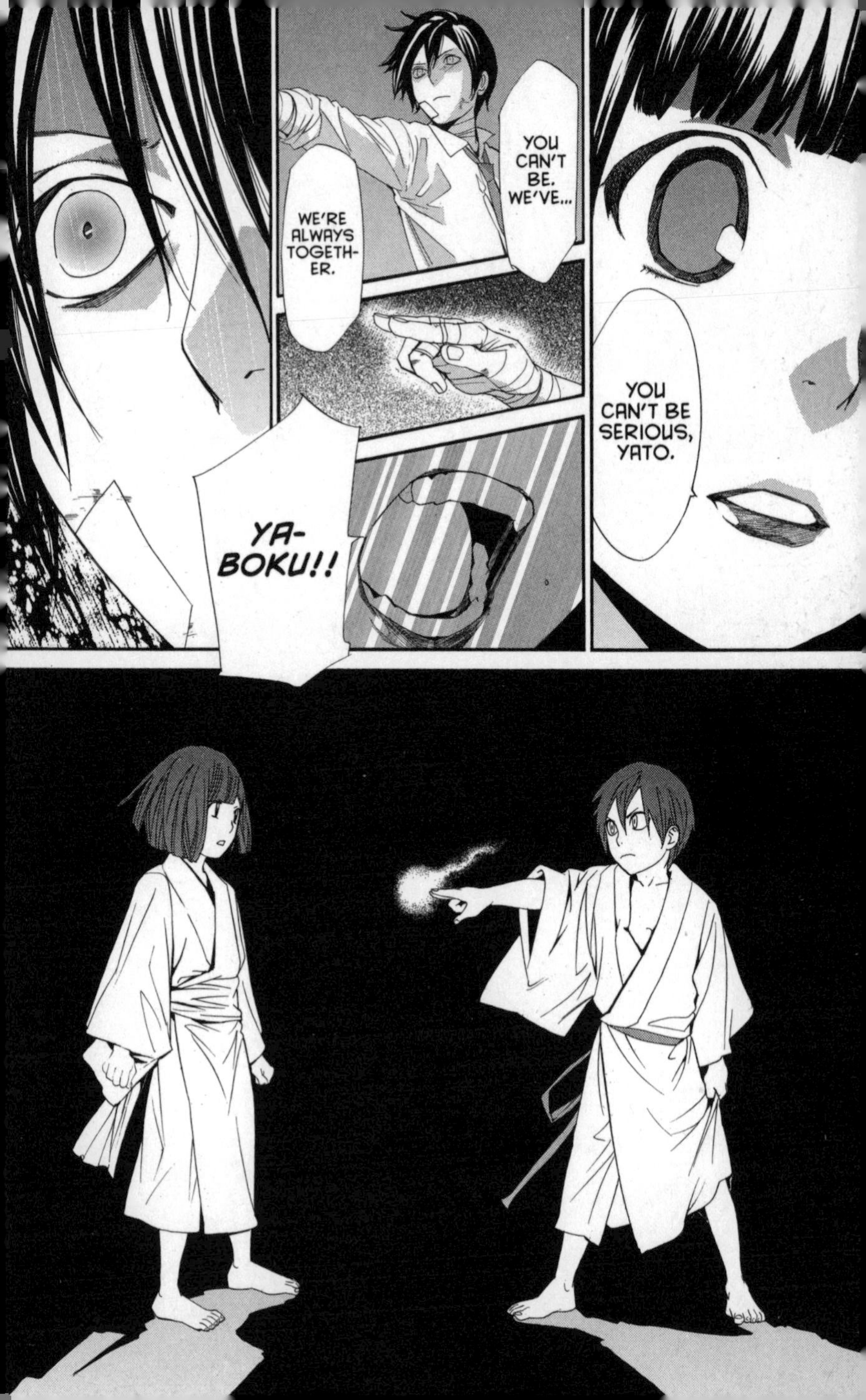
YOU CAN'T BE SERIOUS, YATO.
YOU CAN'T BE. WE'VE...
WE'RE ALWAYS TOGETHER.
YA-BOKU!!

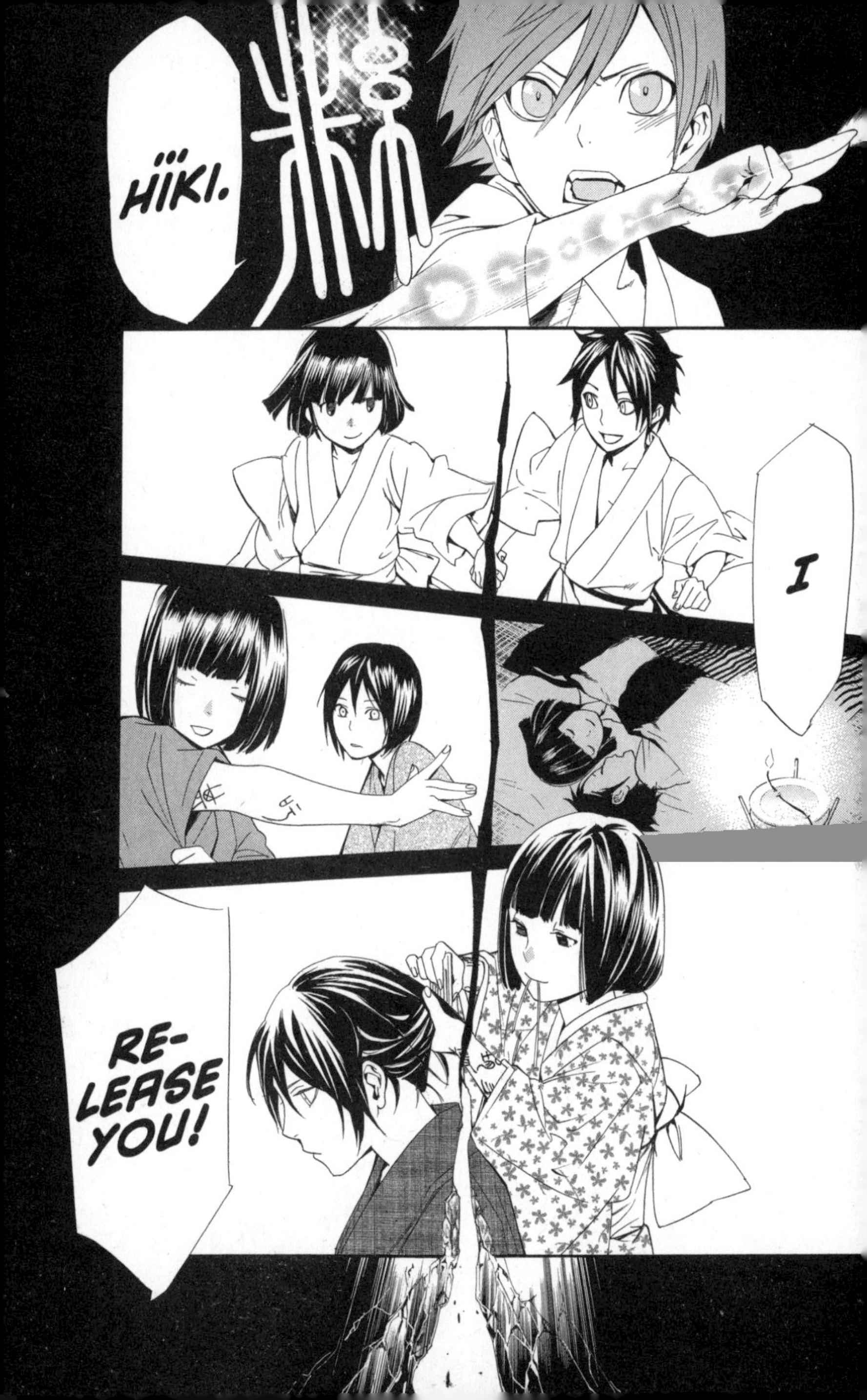
...HIKI.
I
RE-
LEASE
YOU!

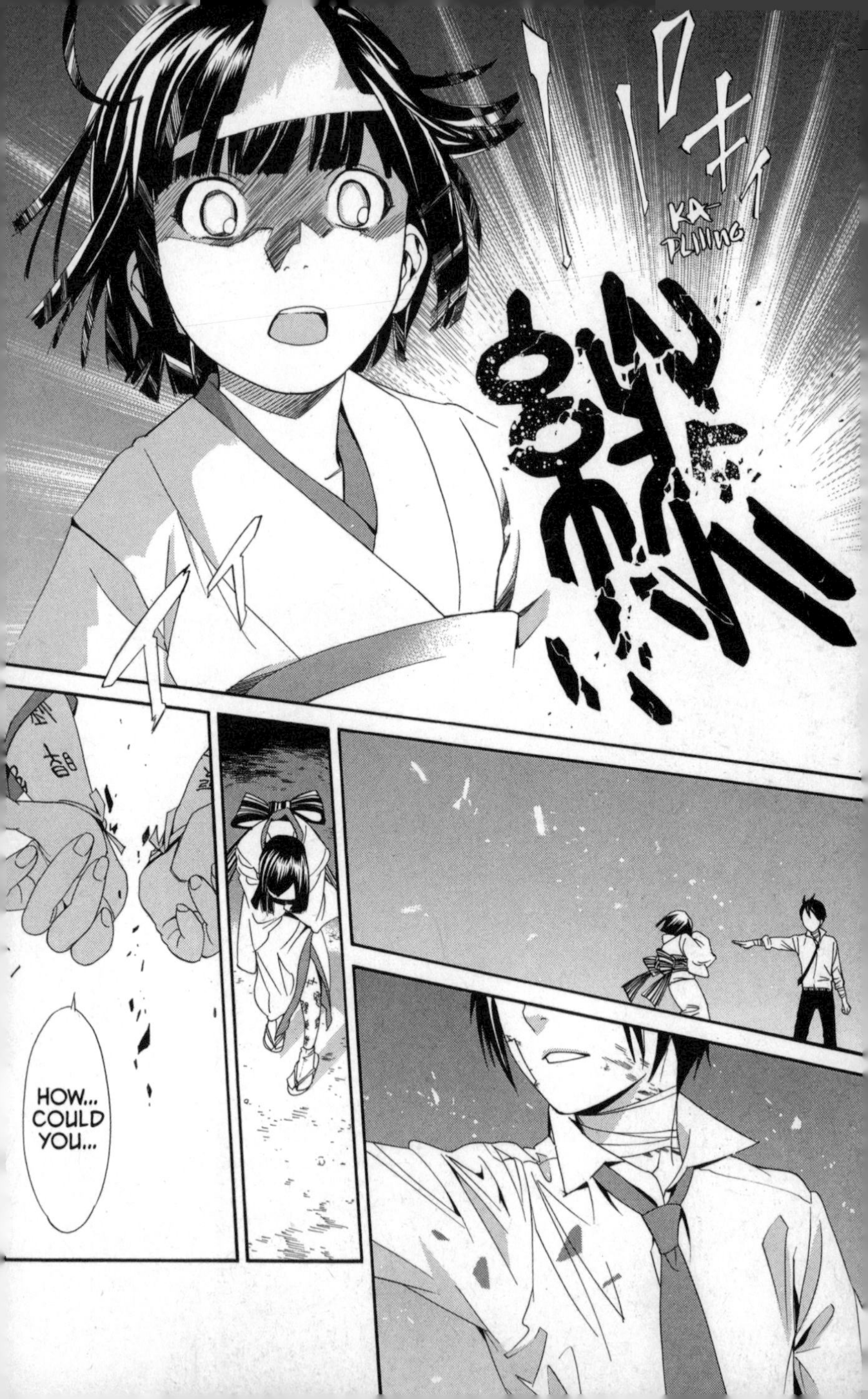
KA-PLIIING
HOW... COULD YOU...

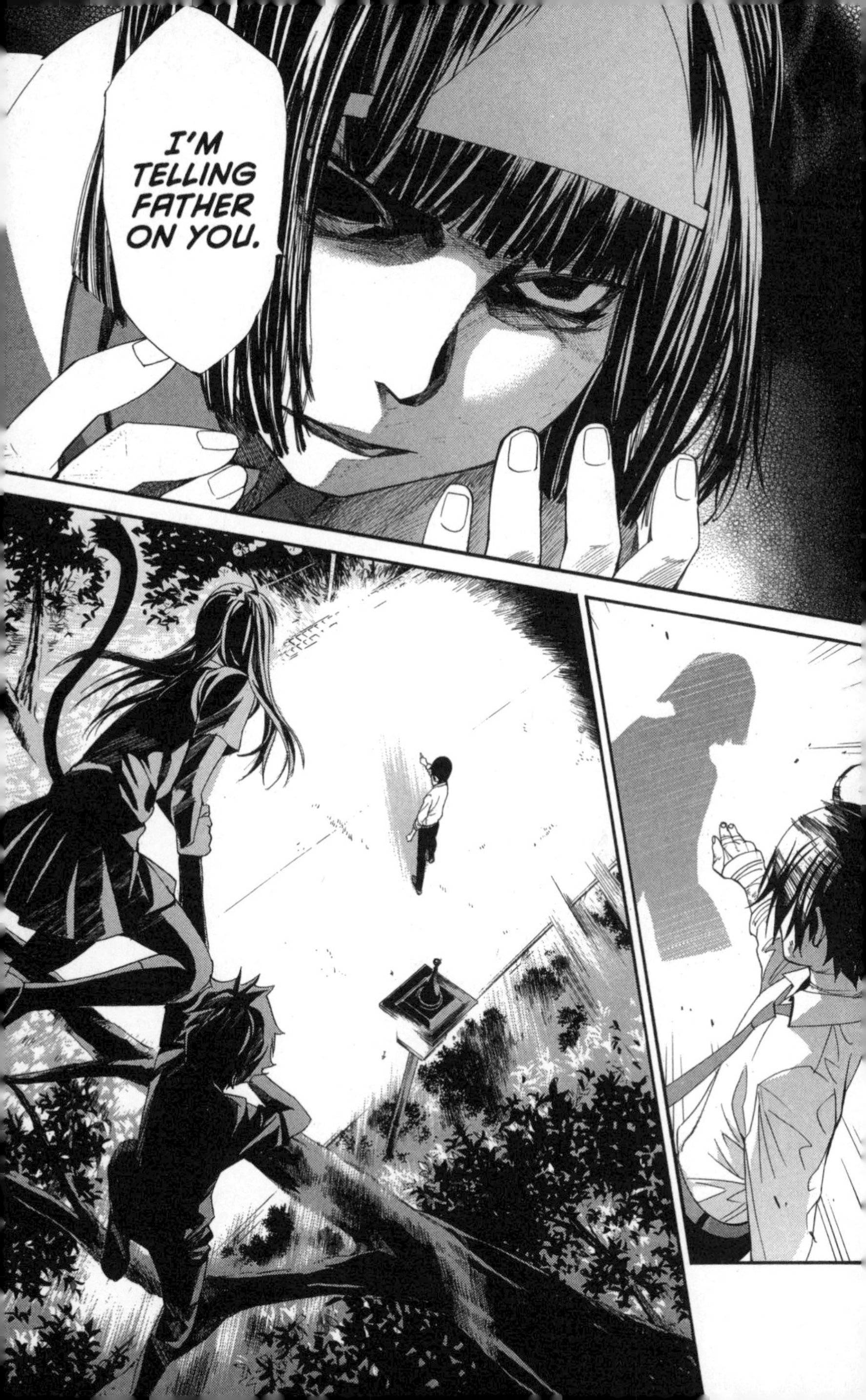
I'M TELLING FATHER ON YOU.

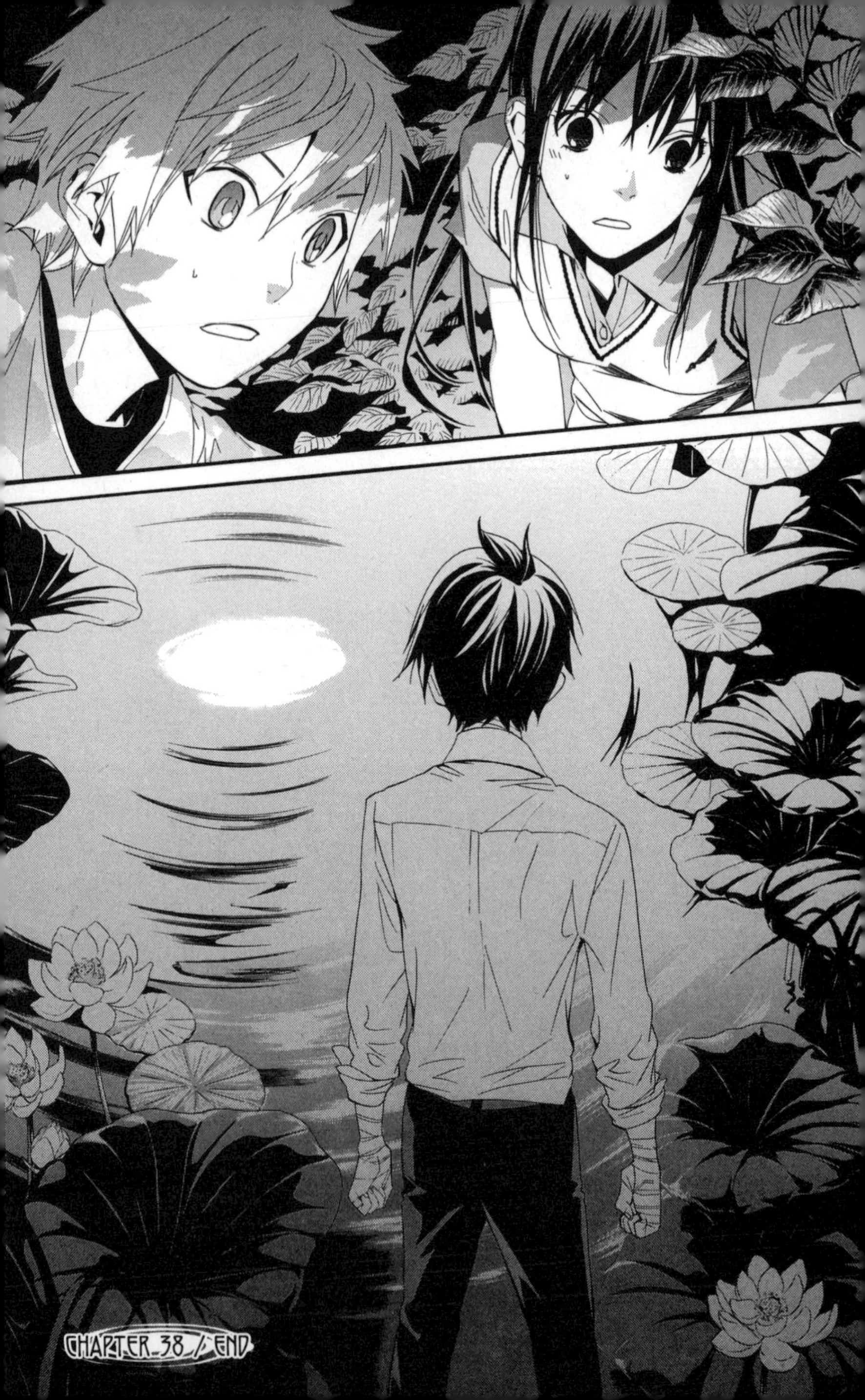
CHAPTER 38 / END

野

頁

神

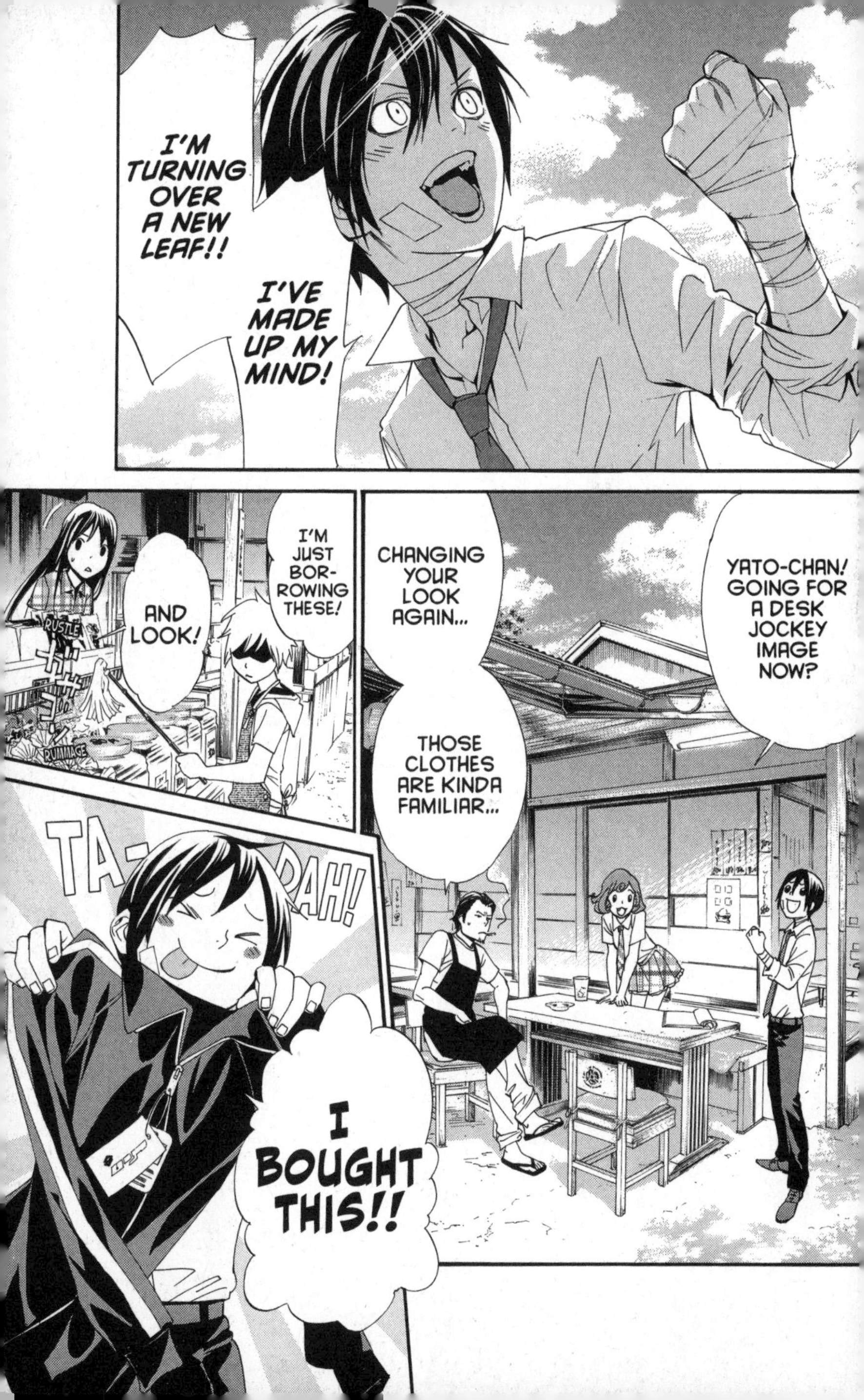
I'M TURNING OVER A NEW LEAF!!
I'VE MADE UP MY MIND!
YATO-CHAN! GOING FOR A DESK JOCKEY IMAGE NOW?
CHANGING YOUR LOOK AGAIN...
THOSE CLOTHES ARE KINDA FAMILIAR...
I'M JUST BOR-ROWING THESE!
RUSTLE
AND LOOK!
RUMMAGE
TA-
DAH!
I BOUGHT THIS!!

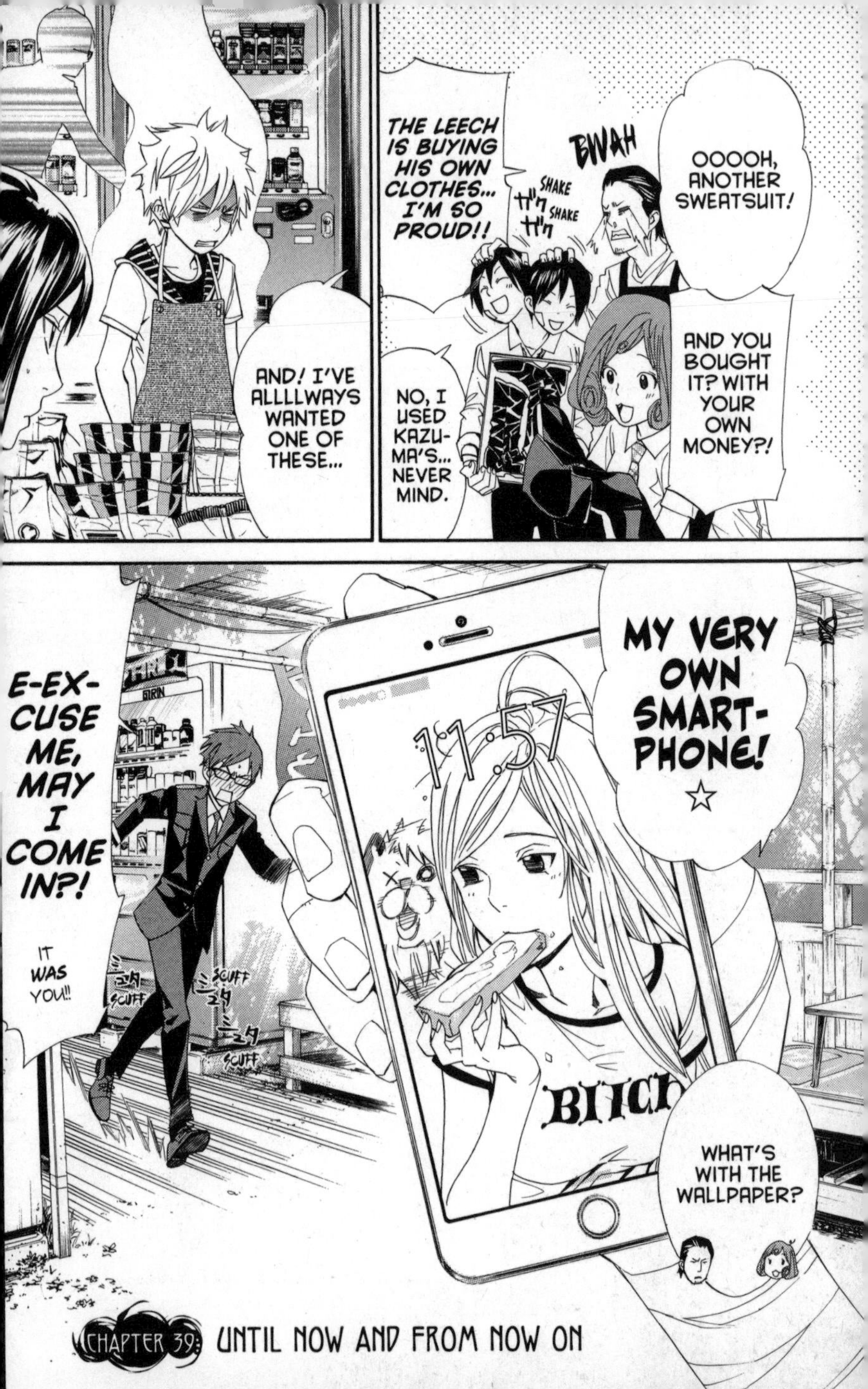
OOOOH, ANOTHER SWEATSUIT!
BWAH
THE LEECH IS BUYING HIS OWN CLOTHES... I'M SO PROUD!!
SHAKE SHAKE
AND YOU BOUGHT IT? WITH YOUR OWN MONEY?!
NO, I USED KAZUMA'S... NEVER MIND.
AND! I'VE ALLLLWAYS WANTED ONE OF THESE...
MY VERY OWN SMARTPHONE! ☆
WHAT'S WITH THE WALLPAPER?
BITCH
E-EXCUSE ME, MAY I COME IN?!
SCUFF SCUFF SCUFF
IT WAS YOU!!

CHAPTER 39: UNTIL NOW AND FROM NOW ON

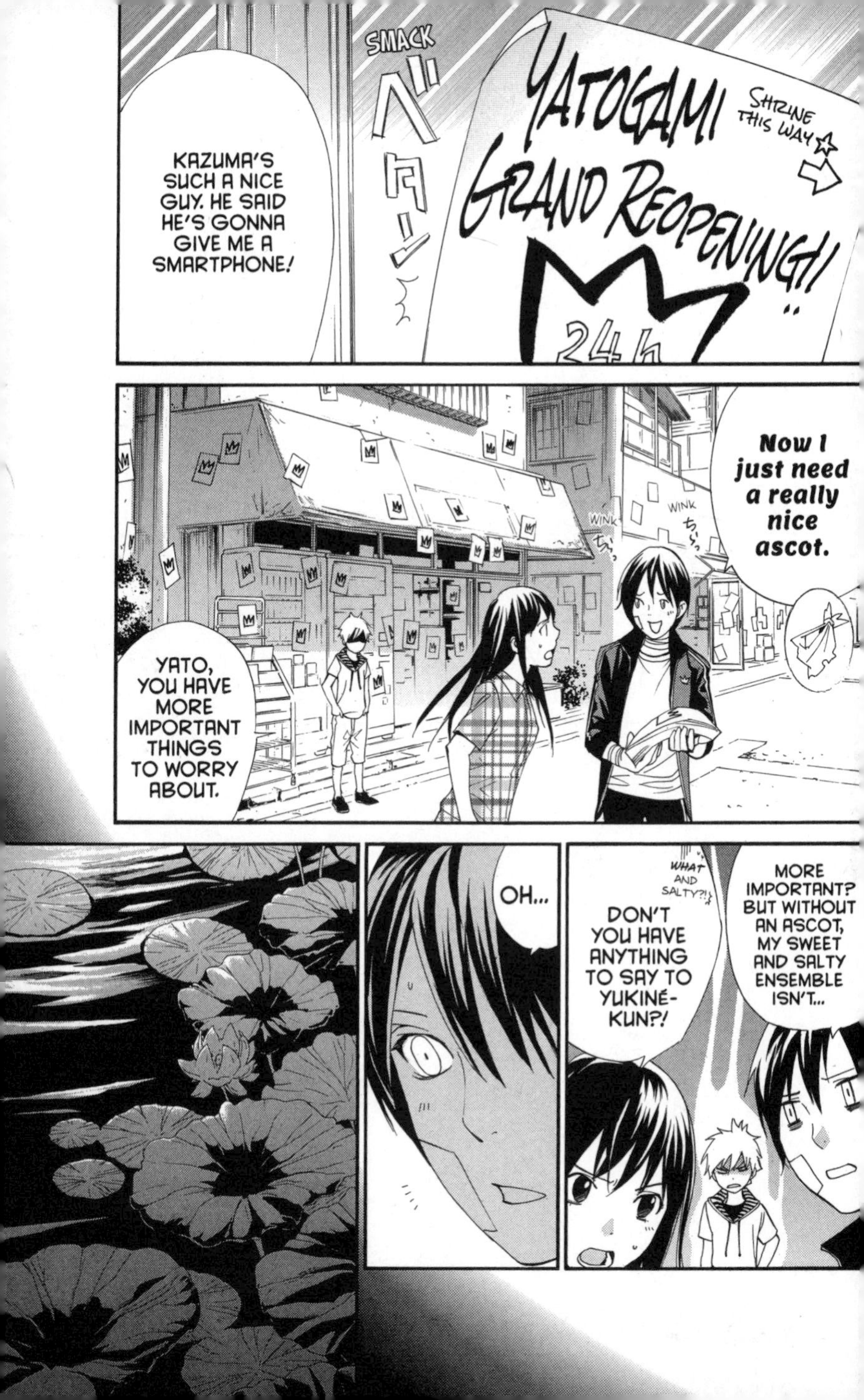
YATOGAMI GRAND REOPENING!!
24h
SHRINE THIS WAY☆
SMACK
KAZUMA'S SUCH A NICE GUY. HE SAID HE'S GONNA GIVE ME A SMARTPHONE!
Now I just need a really nice ascot.
WINK
WINK
YATO, YOU HAVE MORE IMPORTANT THINGS TO WORRY ABOUT.
MORE IMPORTANT? BUT WITHOUT AN ASCOT, MY SWEET AND SALTY ENSEMBLE ISN'T...
WHAT AND SALTY?!
DON'T YOU HAVE ANYTHING TO SAY TO YUKINÉ-KUN?!
OH...

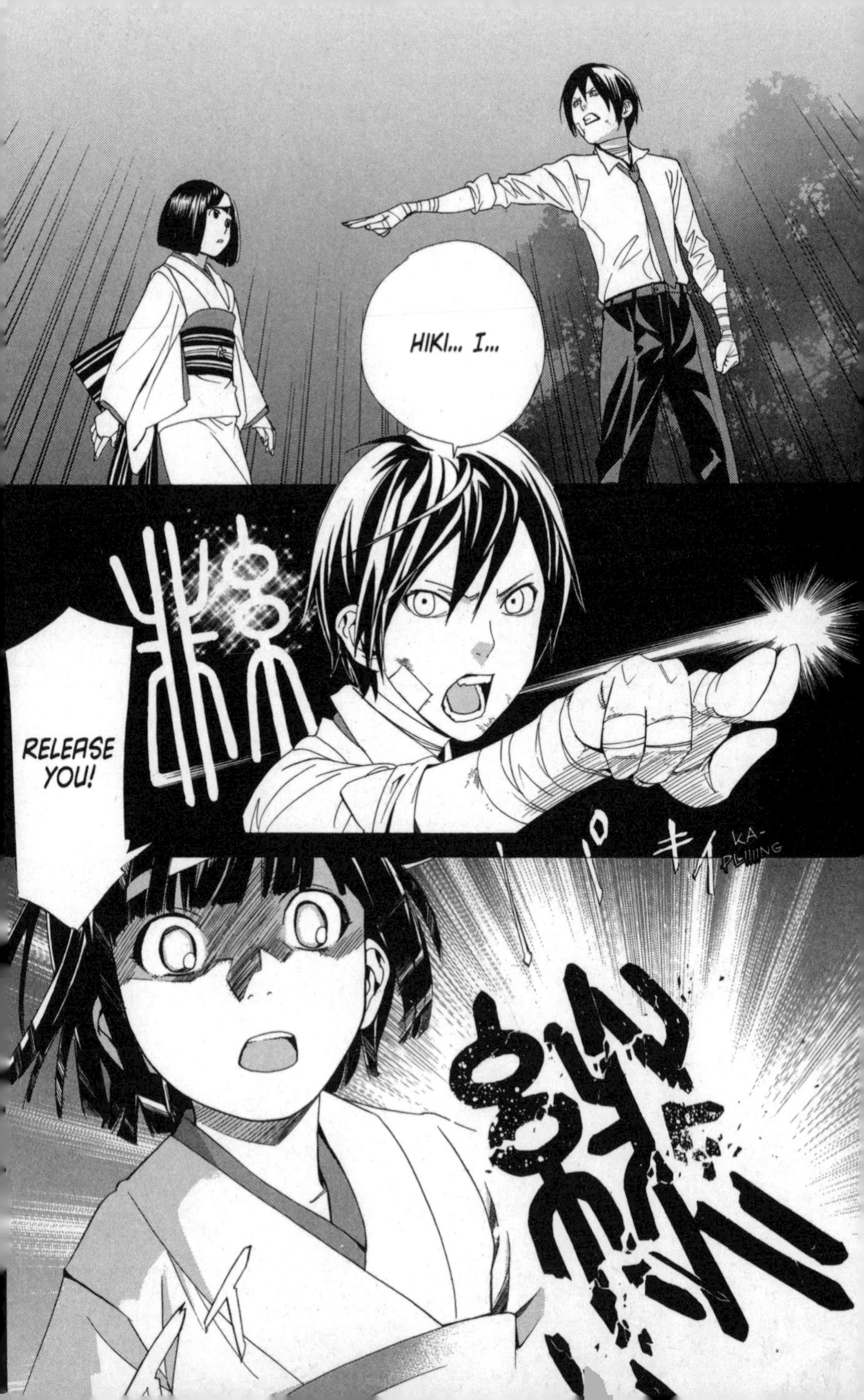
HIKI... I...
RELEASE YOU!
KA-PLIIIING

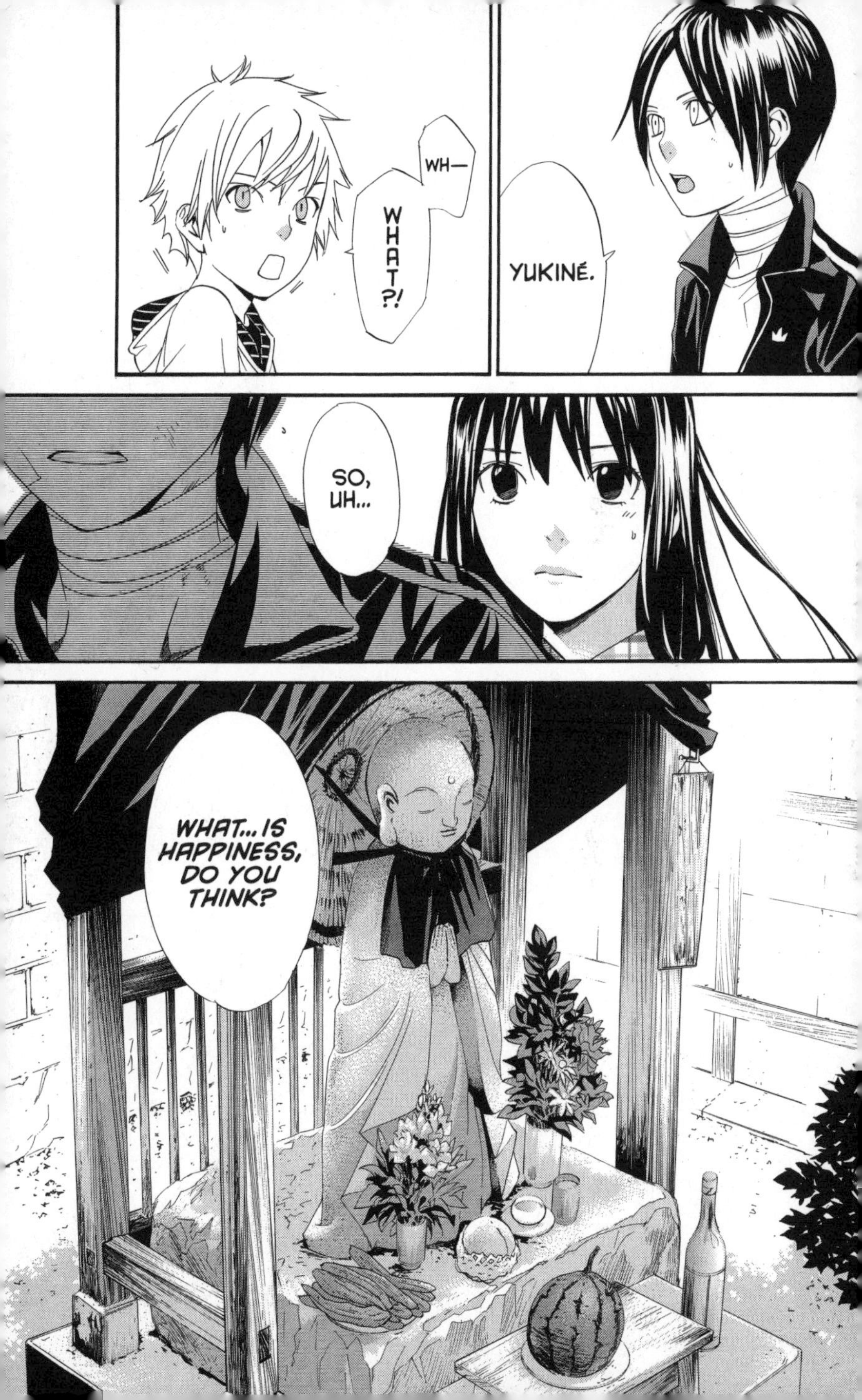
YUKINÉ.
WH—
WHAT?!
SO, UH...
WHAT... IS HAPPINESS, DO YOU THINK?

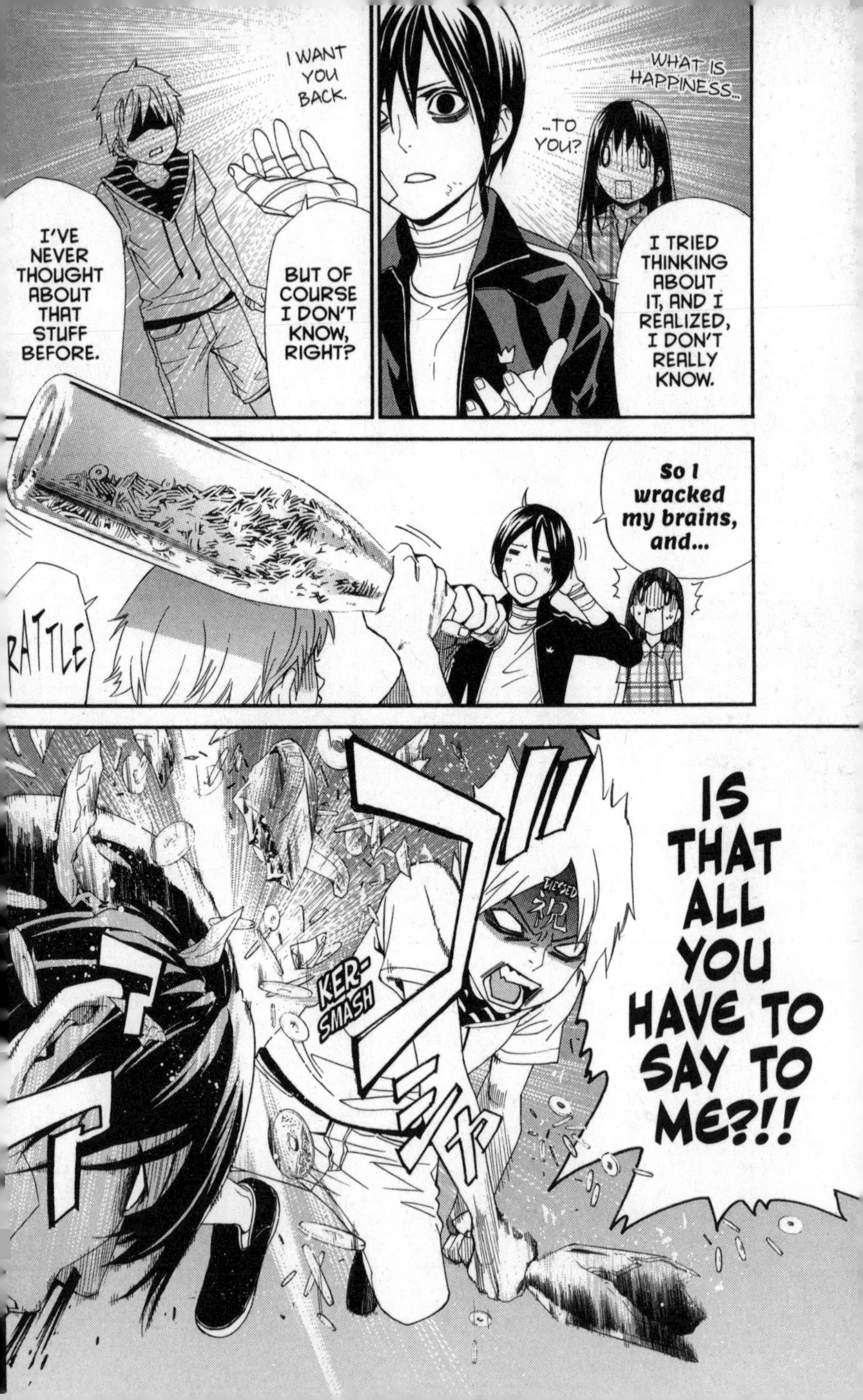
WHAT IS HAPPINESS...
...TO YOU?
I TRIED THINKING ABOUT IT, AND I REALIZED, I DON'T REALLY KNOW.
I WANT YOU BACK.
BUT OF COURSE I DON'T KNOW, RIGHT?
I'VE NEVER THOUGHT ABOUT THAT STUFF BEFORE.
So I wracked my brains, and...
RATTLE
IS THAT ALL YOU HAVE TO SAY TO ME?!!
KER-SMASH

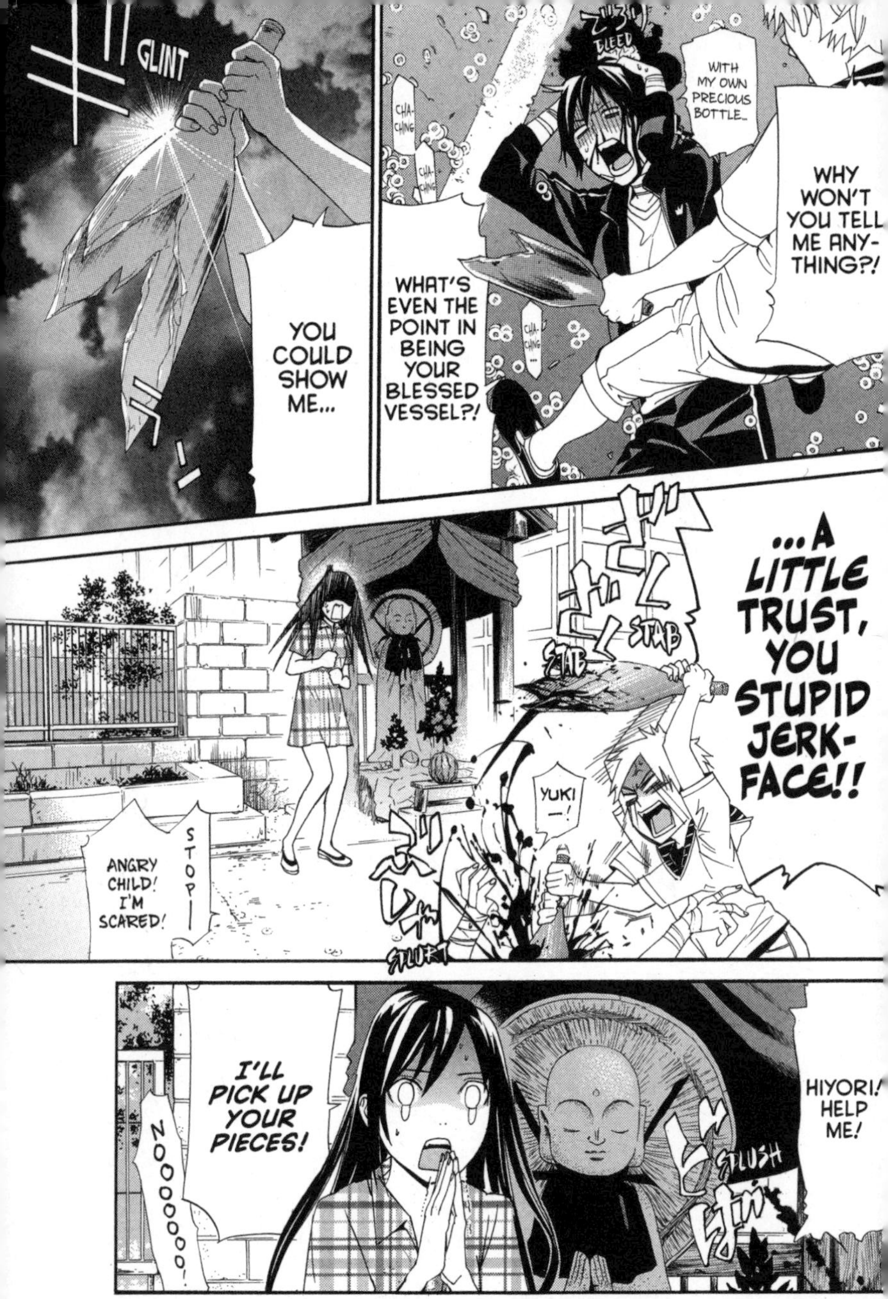
BLEED
WITH MY OWN PRECIOUS BOTTLE...
WHY WON'T YOU TELL ME ANYTHING?!
CHA-CHING
CHA-CHING
CHA-CHING...
WHAT'S EVEN THE POINT IN BEING YOUR BLESSED VESSEL?!
GLINT
YOU COULD SHOW ME...
...A LITTLE TRUST, YOU STUPID JERK-FACE!!
STAB
STAB
YUKI—!
SPLURT
STOP—
ANGRY CHILD! I'M SCARED!
HIYORI! HELP ME!
SPLUSH
I'LL PICK UP YOUR PIECES!
NOOOOOOO!

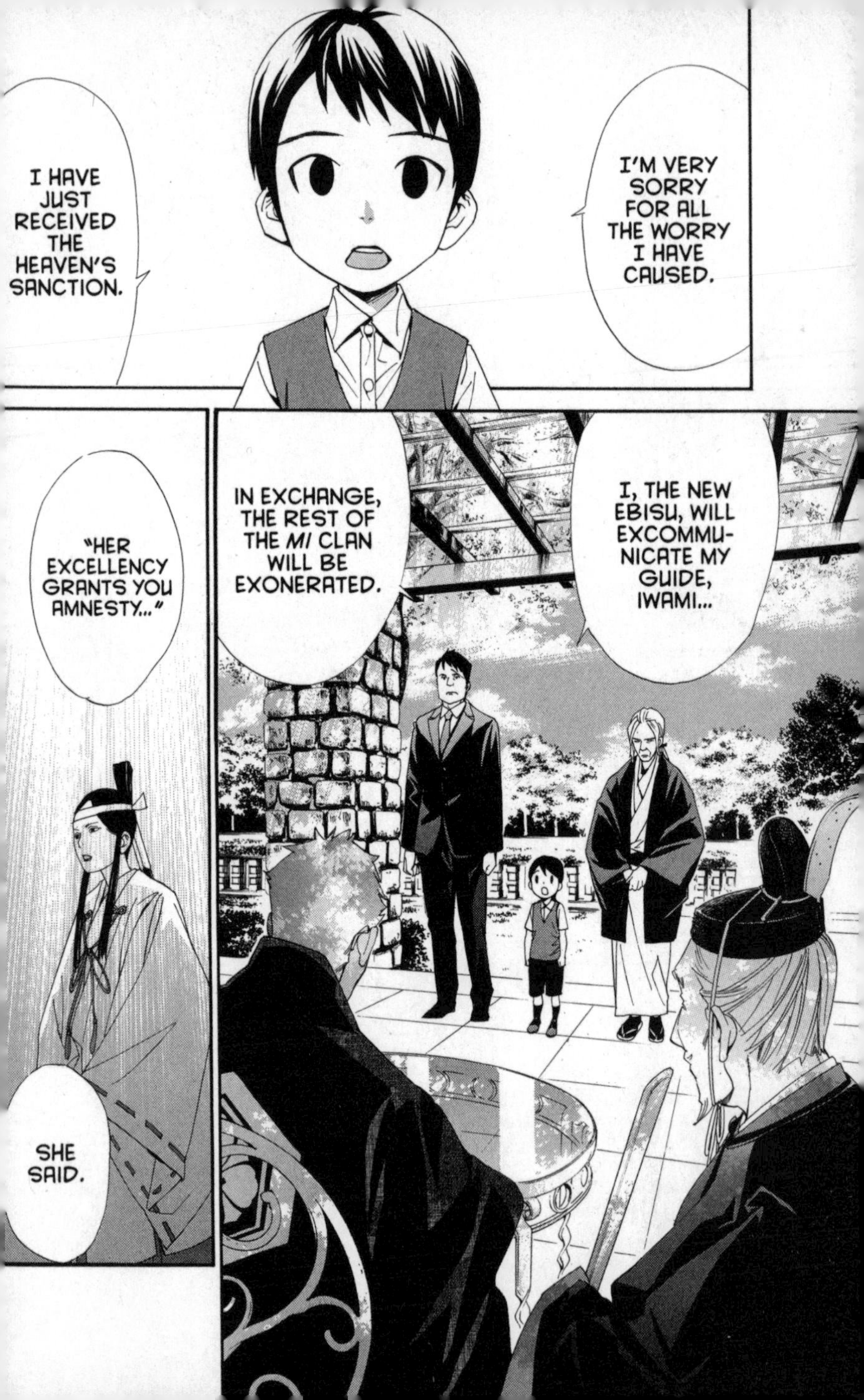
I'M VERY SORRY FOR ALL THE WORRY I HAVE CAUSED.
I HAVE JUST RECEIVED THE HEAVEN'S SANCTION.
I, THE NEW EBISU, WILL EXCOMMU-NICATE MY GUIDE, IWAMI...
IN EXCHANGE, THE REST OF THE *MI* CLAN WILL BE EXONERATED.
"HER EXCELLENCY GRANTS YOU AMNESTY..."
SHE SAID.

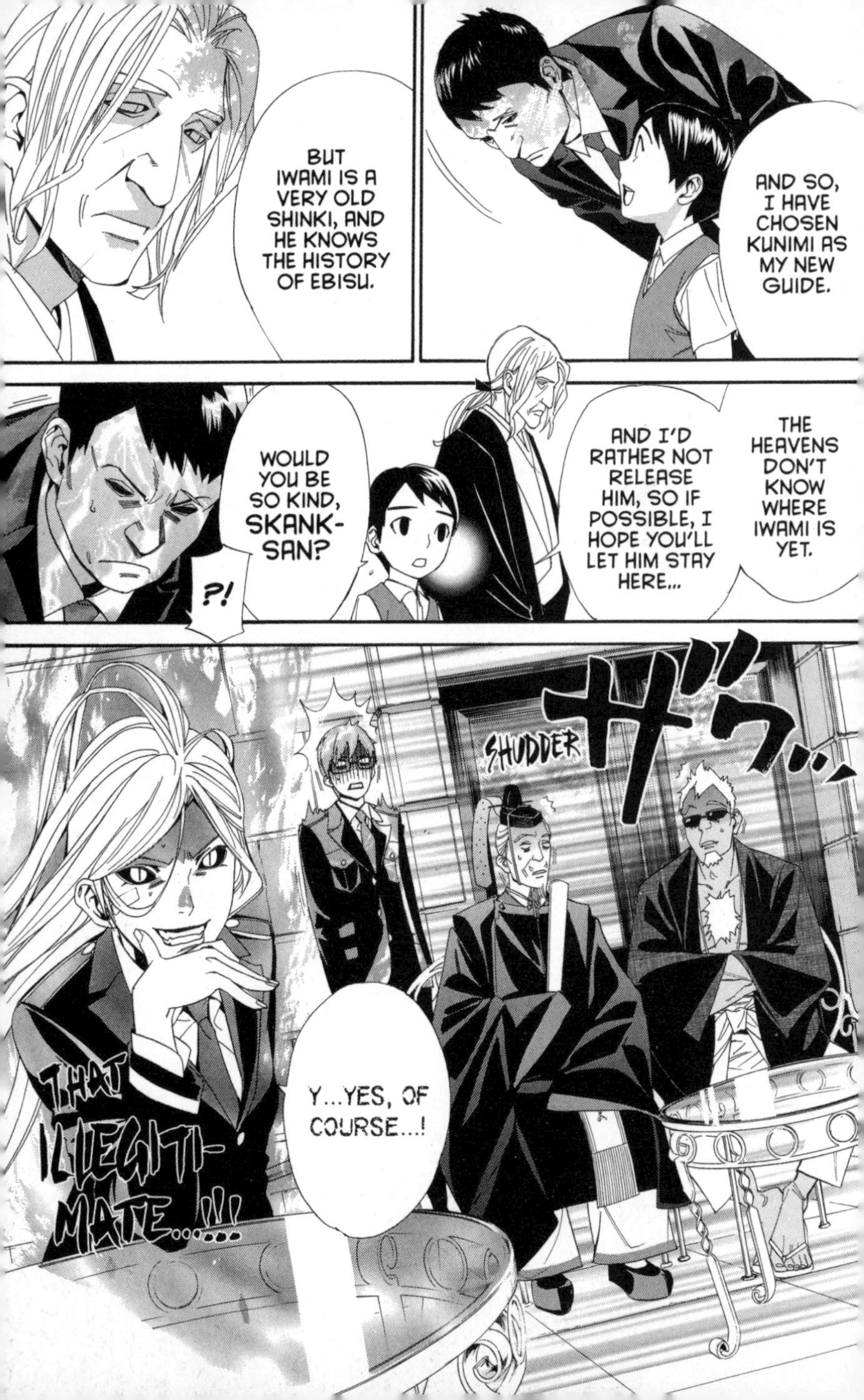
AND SO, I HAVE CHOSEN KUNIMI AS MY NEW GUIDE.
BUT IWAMI IS A VERY OLD SHINKI, AND HE KNOWS THE HISTORY OF EBISU.
THE HEAVENS DON'T KNOW WHERE IWAMI IS YET.
AND I'D RATHER NOT RELEASE HIM, SO IF POSSIBLE, I HOPE YOU'LL LET HIM STAY HERE...
WOULD YOU BE SO KIND, SKANK-SAN?
?!
SHUDDER
Y...YES, OF COURSE...!
THAT ILLEGITI-MATE...!!!

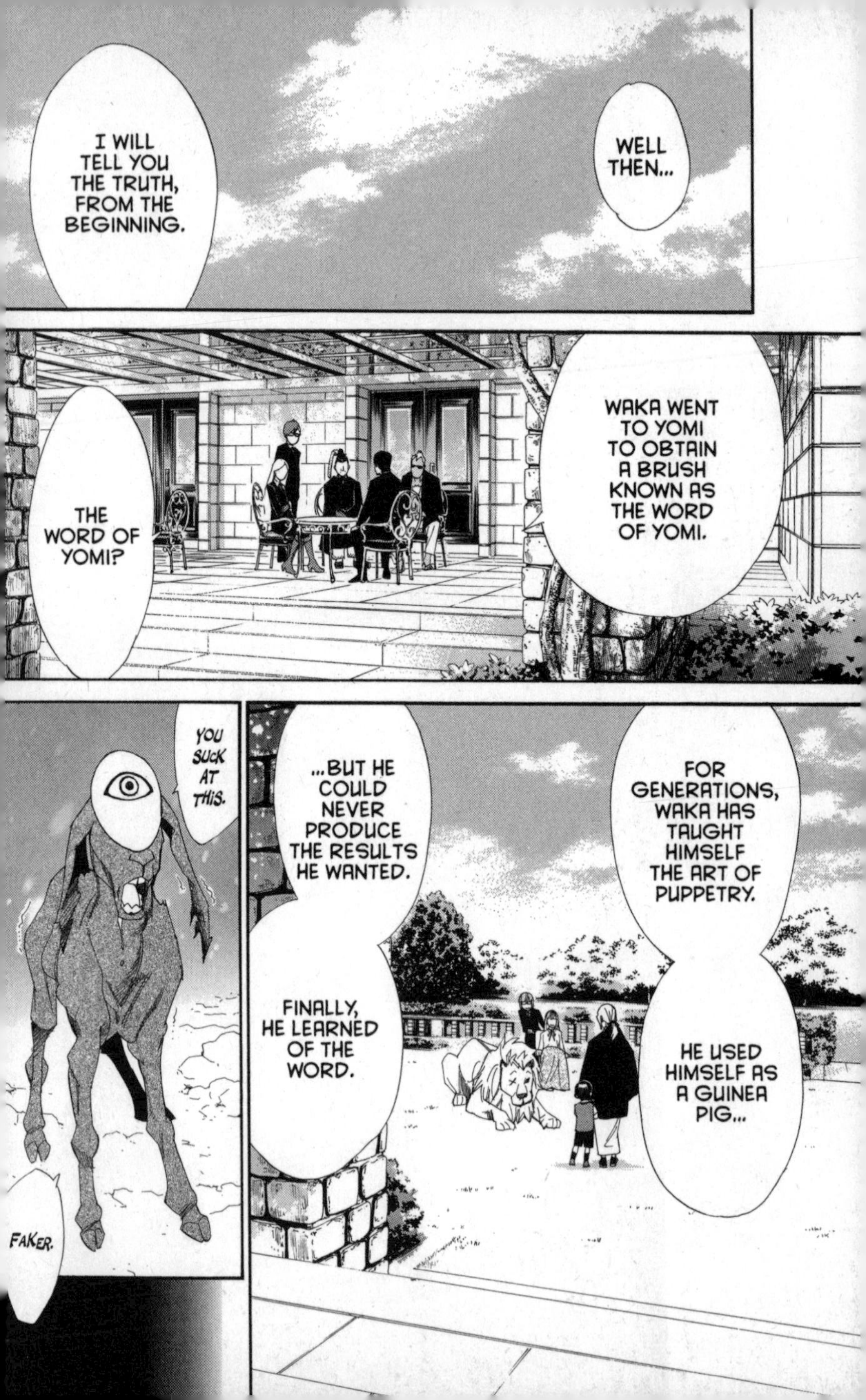
WELL THEN...
I WILL TELL YOU THE TRUTH, FROM THE BEGINNING.
WAKA WENT TO YOMI TO OBTAIN A BRUSH KNOWN AS THE WORD OF YOMI.
THE WORD OF YOMI?
FOR GENERATIONS, WAKA HAS TAUGHT HIMSELF THE ART OF PUPPETRY.
HE USED HIMSELF AS A GUINEA PIG...
...BUT HE COULD NEVER PRODUCE THE RESULTS HE WANTED.
FINALLY, HE LEARNED OF THE WORD.
YOU SUCK AT THIS.
FAKER.

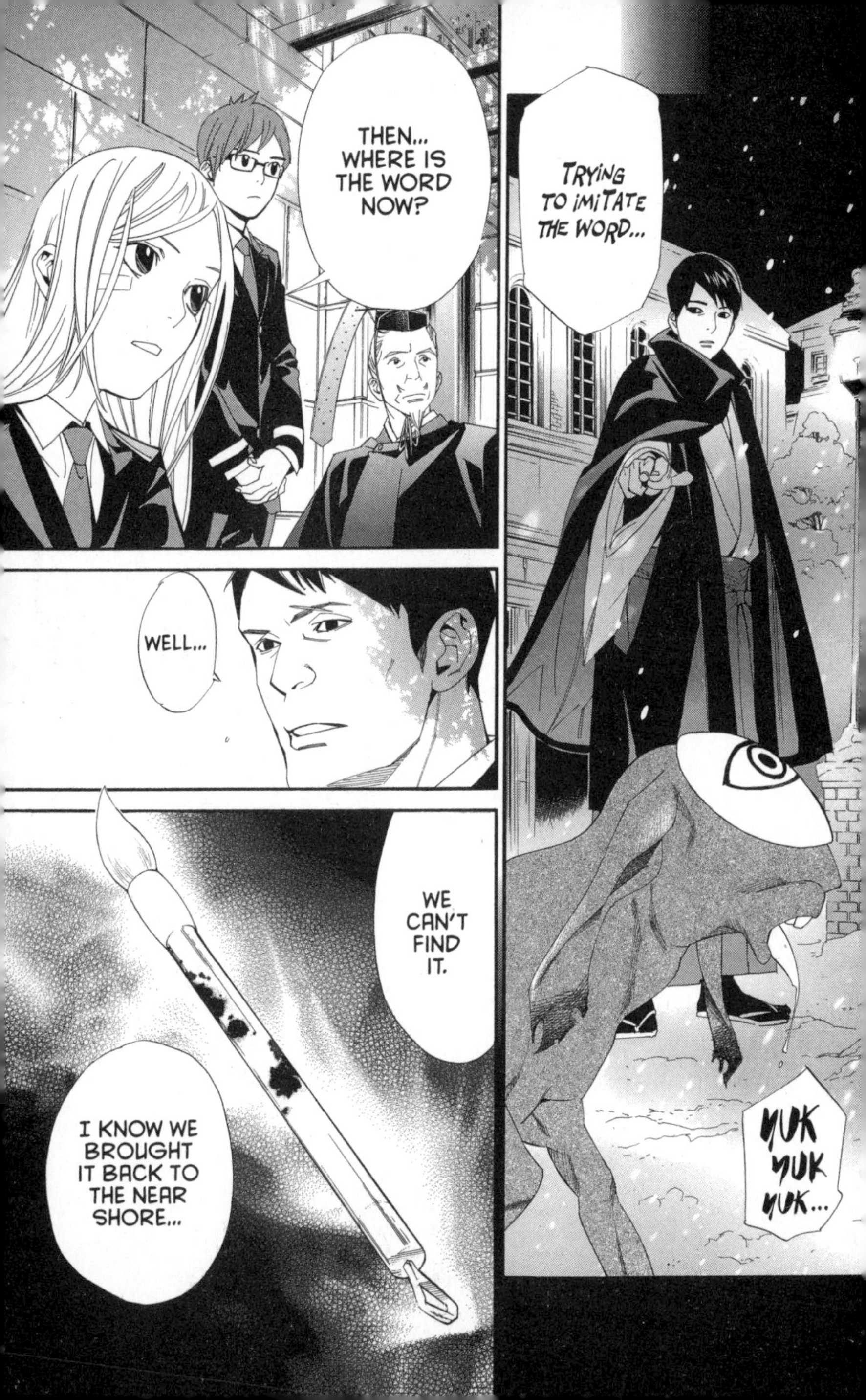
TRYING TO IMITATE THE WORD...
YUK YUK YUK...
THEN... WHERE IS THE WORD NOW?
WELL...
WE CAN'T FIND IT.
I KNOW WE BROUGHT IT BACK TO THE NEAR SHORE...

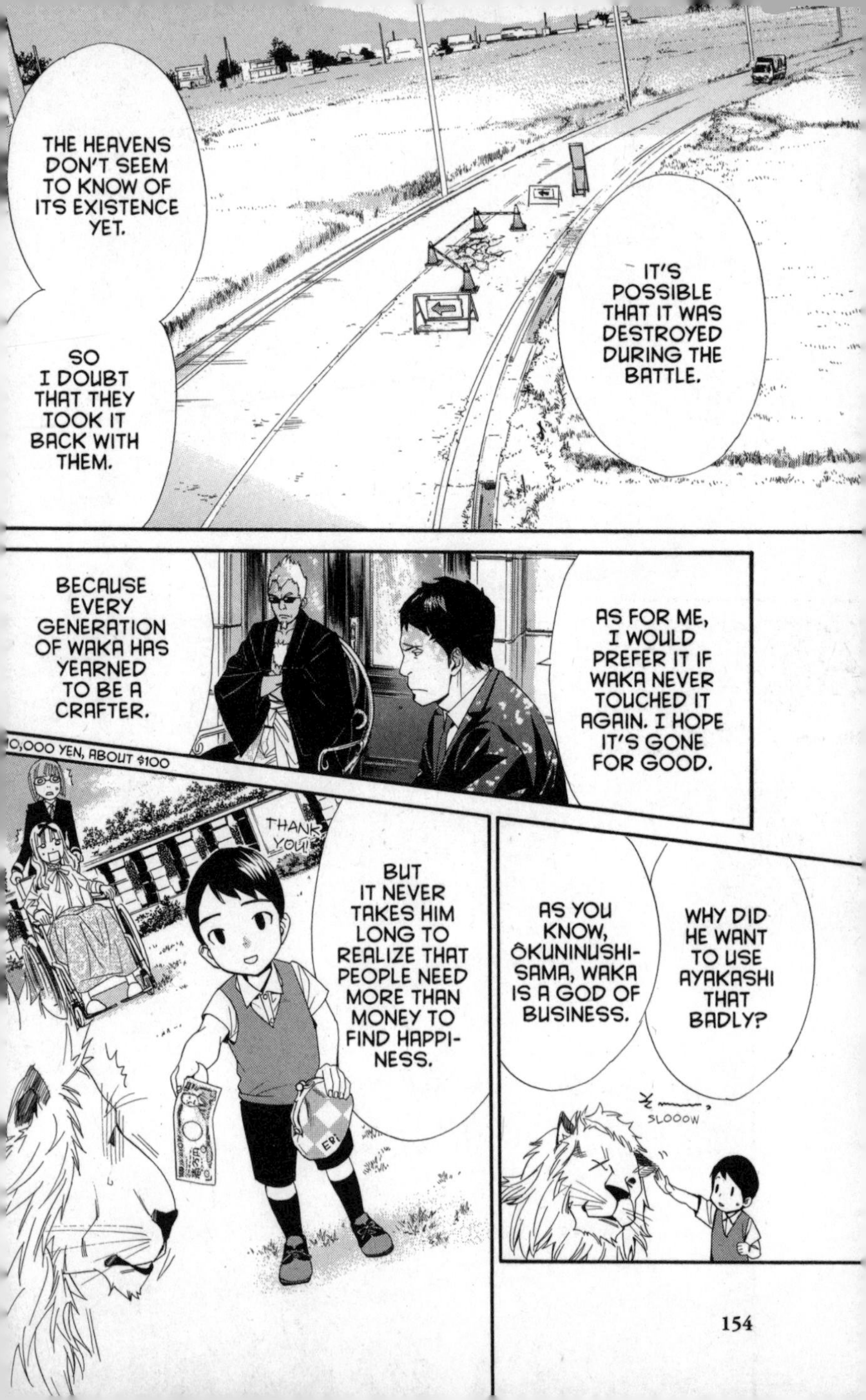
IT'S POSSIBLE THAT IT WAS DESTROYED DURING THE BATTLE.
THE HEAVENS DON'T SEEM TO KNOW OF ITS EXISTENCE YET.
SO I DOUBT THAT THEY TOOK IT BACK WITH THEM.
AS FOR ME, I WOULD PREFER IT IF WAKA NEVER TOUCHED IT AGAIN. I HOPE IT'S GONE FOR GOOD.
BECAUSE EVERY GENERATION OF WAKA HAS YEARNED TO BE A CRAFTER.
WHY DID HE WANT TO USE AYAKASHI THAT BADLY?
AS YOU KNOW, ÔKUNINUSHI-SAMA, WAKA IS A GOD OF BUSINESS.
SLOOOW
BUT IT NEVER TAKES HIM LONG TO REALIZE THAT PEOPLE NEED MORE THAN MONEY TO FIND HAPPI-NESS.
THANK YOU!
10,000 YEN, ABOUT $100

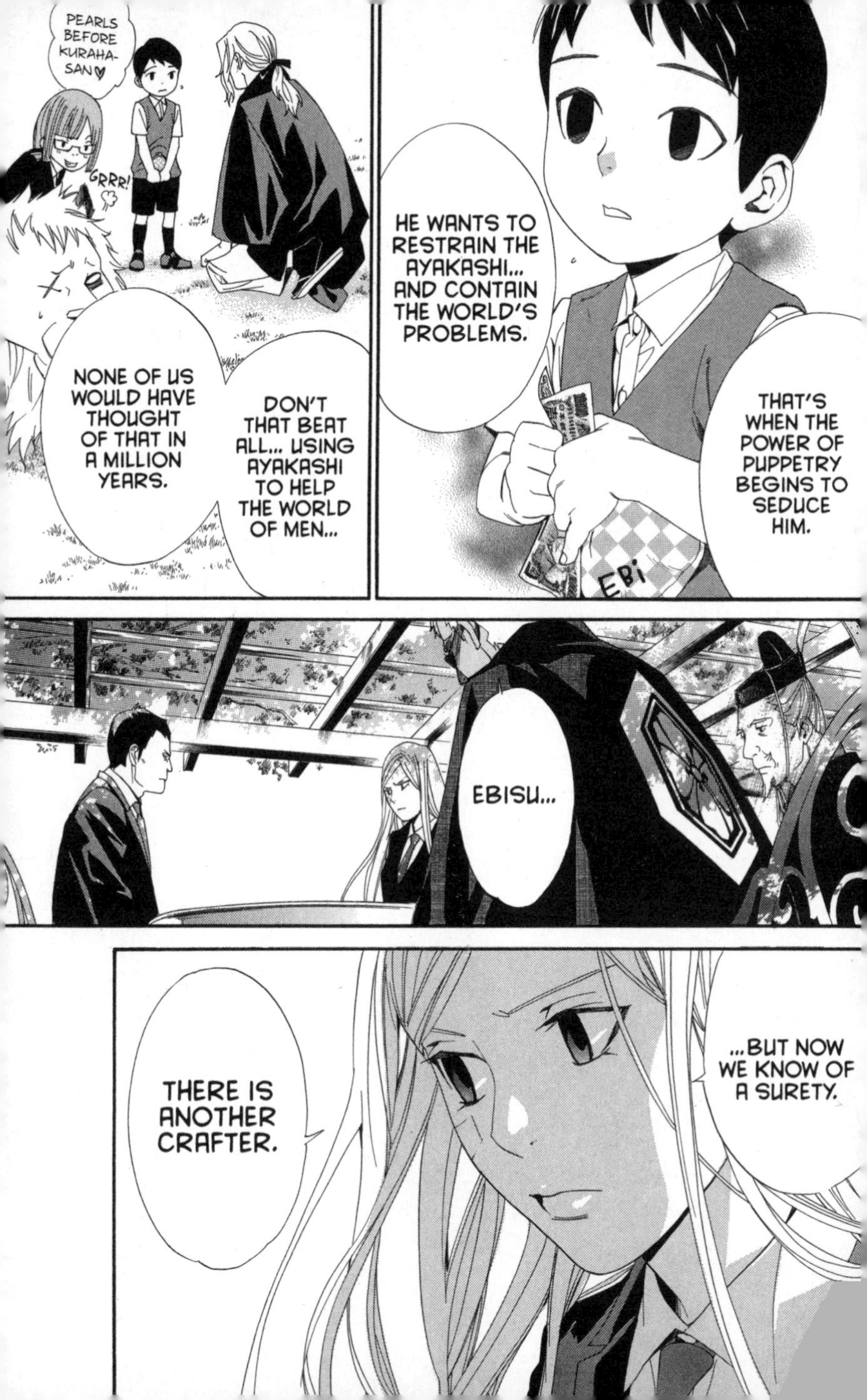
HE WANTS TO RESTRAIN THE AYAKASHI... AND CONTAIN THE WORLD'S PROBLEMS.
THAT'S WHEN THE POWER OF PUPPETRY BEGINS TO SEDUCE HIM.
EBi
PEARLS BEFORE KURAHA-SAN♥
GRRR!
DON'T THAT BEAT ALL... USING AYAKASHI TO HELP THE WORLD OF MEN...
NONE OF US WOULD HAVE THOUGHT OF THAT IN A MILLION YEARS.
EBISU...
...BUT NOW WE KNOW OF A SURETY.
THERE IS ANOTHER CRAFTER.

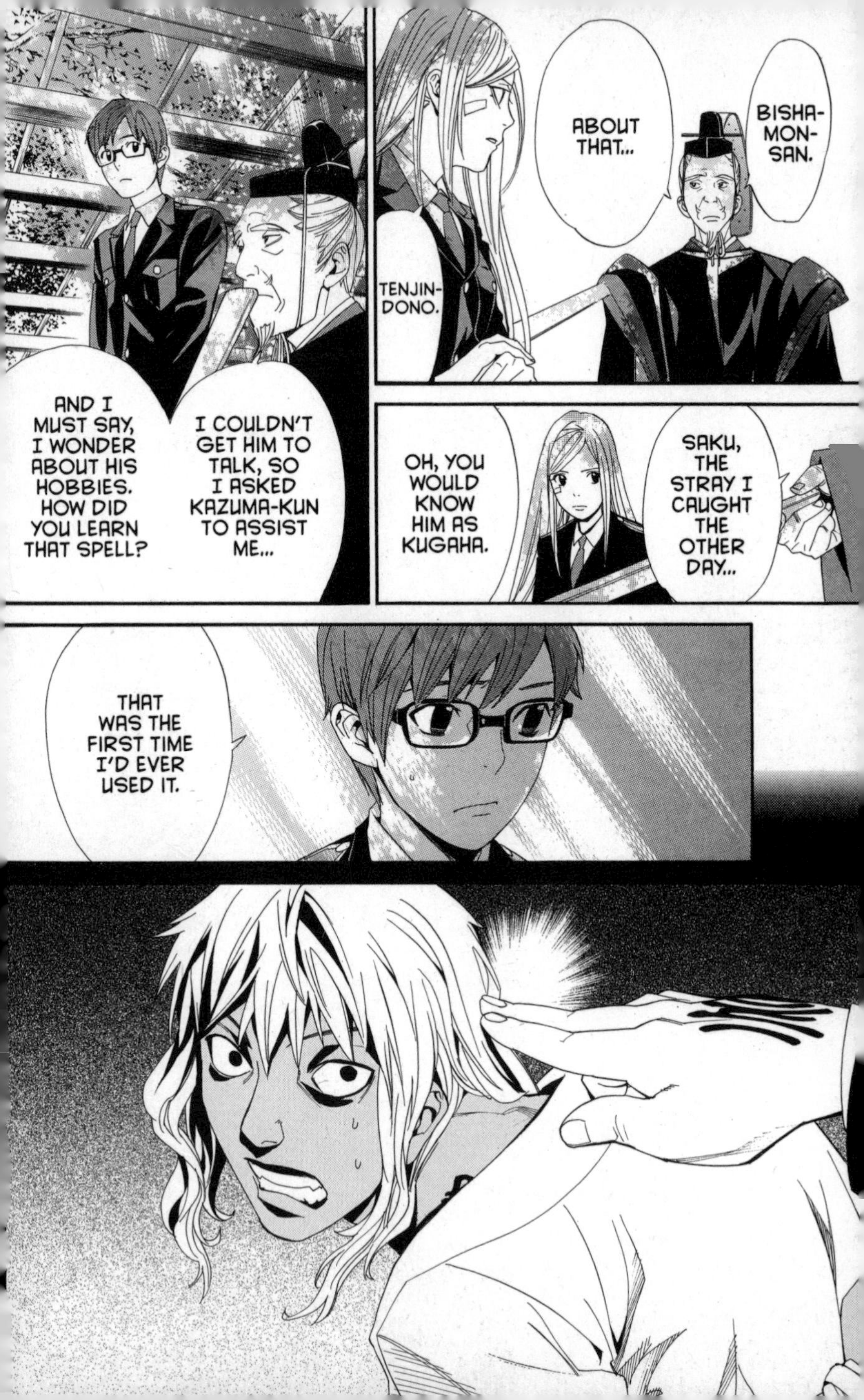
BISHA-MON-SAN.
ABOUT THAT...
TENJIN-DONO.
SAKU, THE STRAY I CAUGHT THE OTHER DAY...
OH, YOU WOULD KNOW HIM AS KUGAHA.
I COULDN'T GET HIM TO TALK, SO I ASKED KAZUMA-KUN TO ASSIST ME...
AND I MUST SAY, I WONDER ABOUT HIS HOBBIES. HOW DID YOU LEARN THAT SPELL?
THAT WAS THE FIRST TIME I'D EVER USED IT.

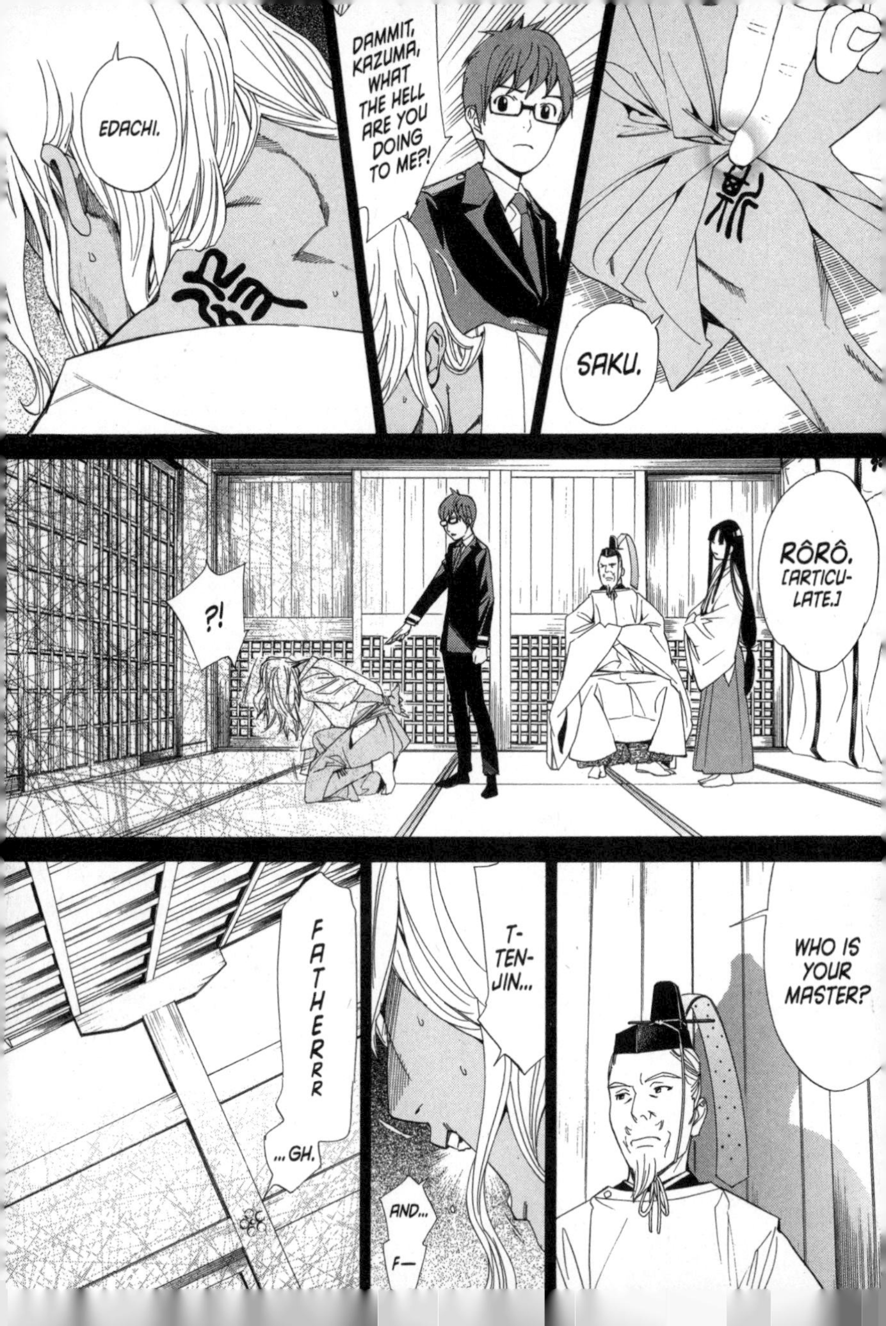
SAKU.
DAMMIT, KAZUMA, WHAT THE HELL ARE YOU DOING TO ME?!
EDACHI.
RÔRÔ. [ARTICULATE.]
?!
WHO IS YOUR MASTER?
T-TEN-JIN...
AND...
F—
FATHERRR
...GH.

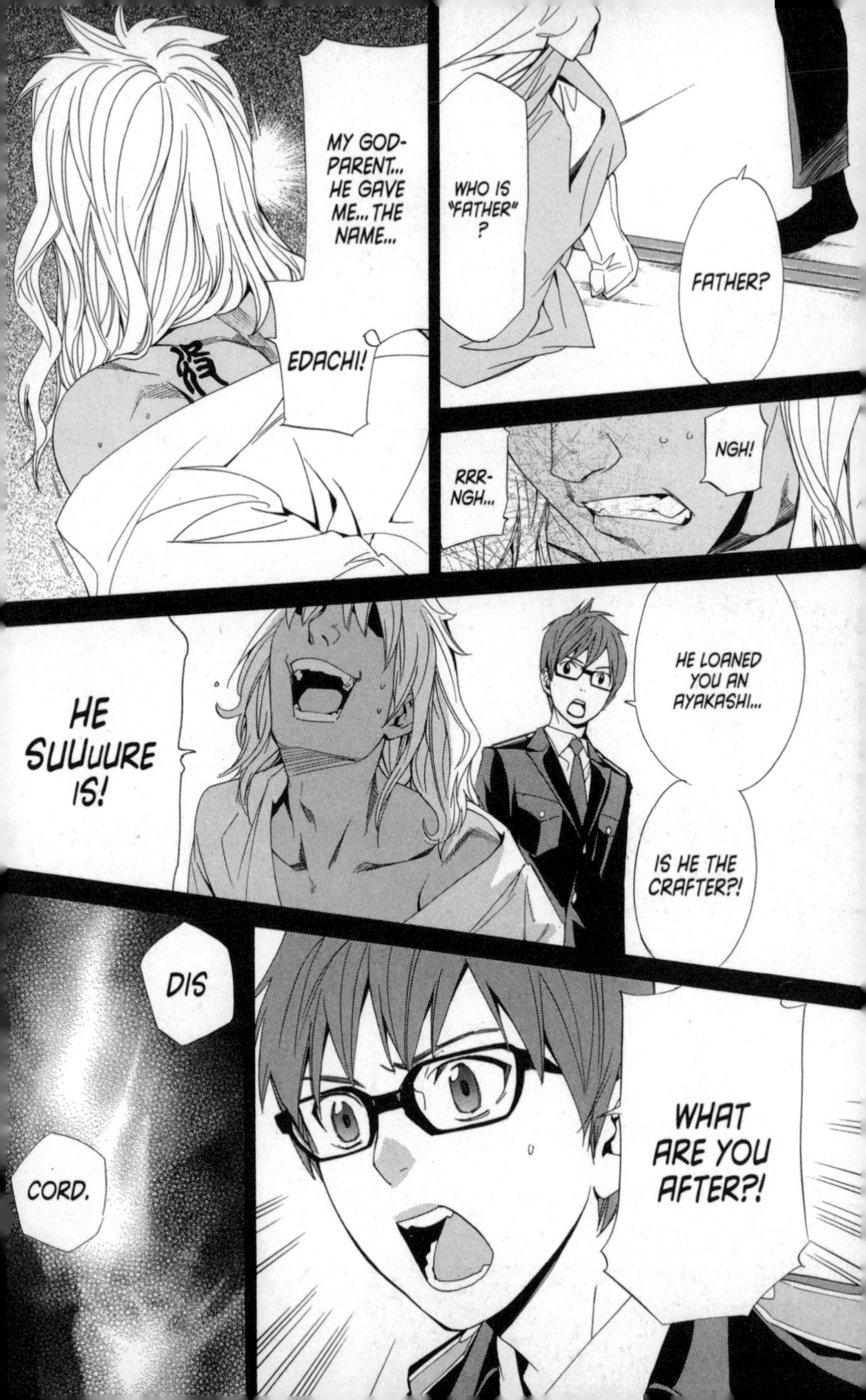
FATHER?
WHO IS "FATHER" ?
NGH!
RRR-NGH...
MY GOD-PARENT... HE GAVE ME... THE NAME...
EDACHI!
HE LOANED YOU AN AYAKASHI...
IS HE THE CRAFTER?!
HE SUUuURE IS!
WHAT ARE YOU AFTER?!
DIS
CORD.

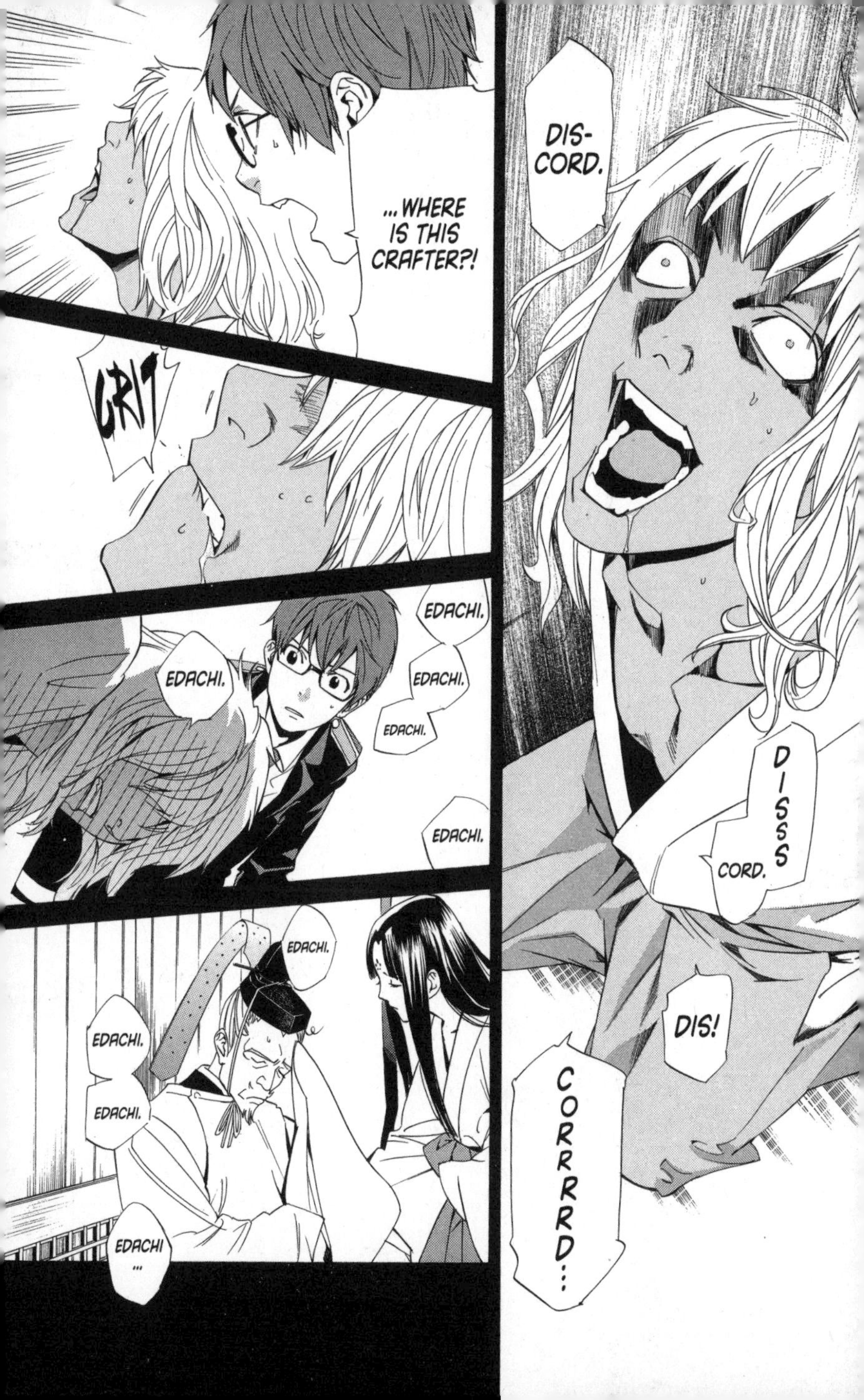
DIS-
CORD.
DISSS
CORD.
DIS!
CORRRRD...
...WHERE IS THIS CRAFTER?!
GRIT
EDACHI.
EDACHI.
EDACHI.
EDACHI.
EDACHI.
EDACHI.
EDACHI.
EDACHI.
EDACHI ...

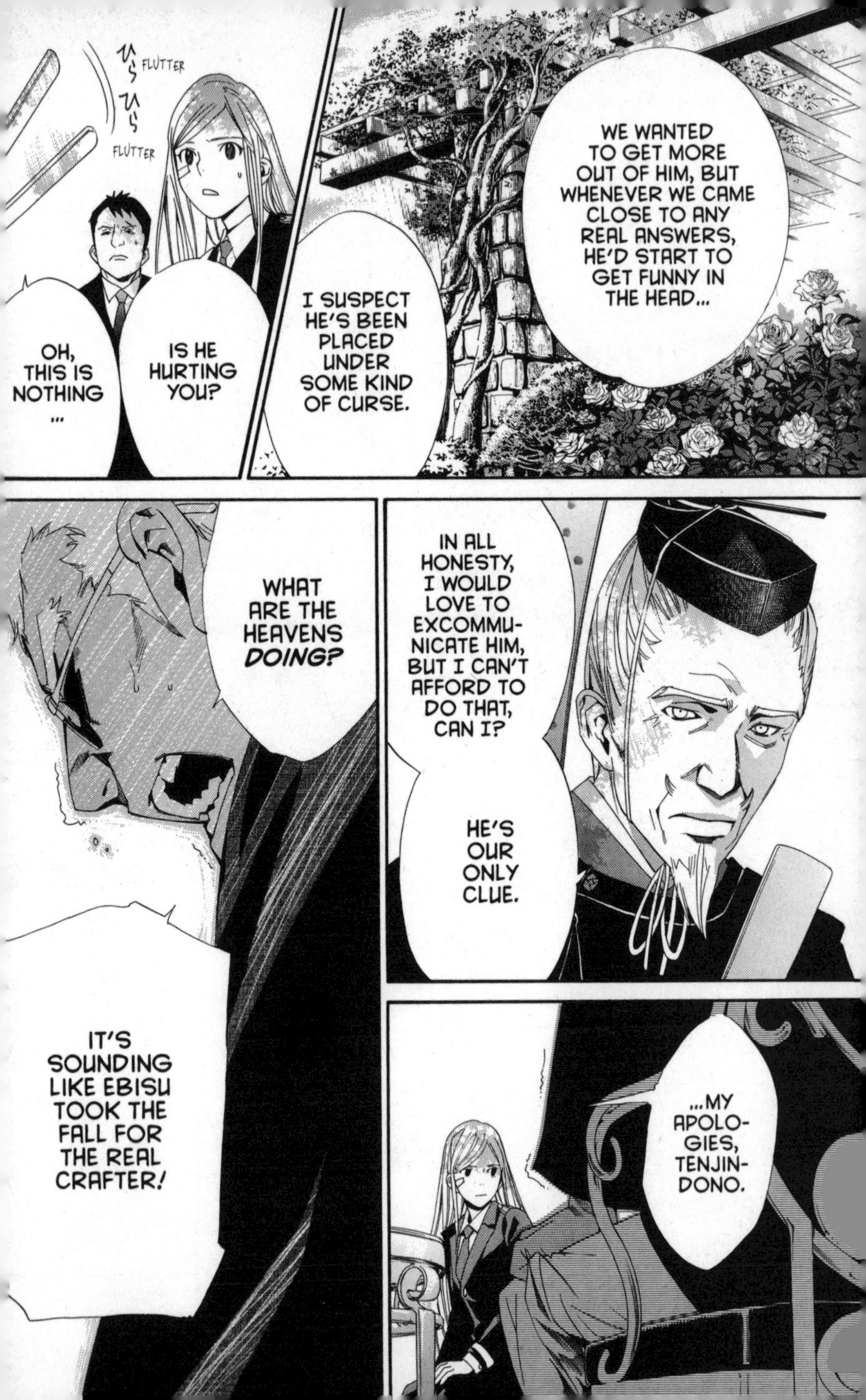
WE WANTED TO GET MORE OUT OF HIM, BUT WHENEVER WE CAME CLOSE TO ANY REAL ANSWERS, HE'D START TO GET FUNNY IN THE HEAD...
I SUSPECT HE'S BEEN PLACED UNDER SOME KIND OF CURSE.
ひら FLUTTER
ひら FLUTTER
IS HE HURTING YOU?
OH, THIS IS NOTHING...
IN ALL HONESTY, I WOULD LOVE TO EXCOMMUNICATE HIM, BUT I CAN'T AFFORD TO DO THAT, CAN I?
HE'S OUR ONLY CLUE.
...MY APOLOGIES, TENJIN-DONO.
WHAT ARE THE HEAVENS *DOING?*
IT'S SOUNDING LIKE EBISU TOOK THE FALL FOR THE REAL CRAFTER!

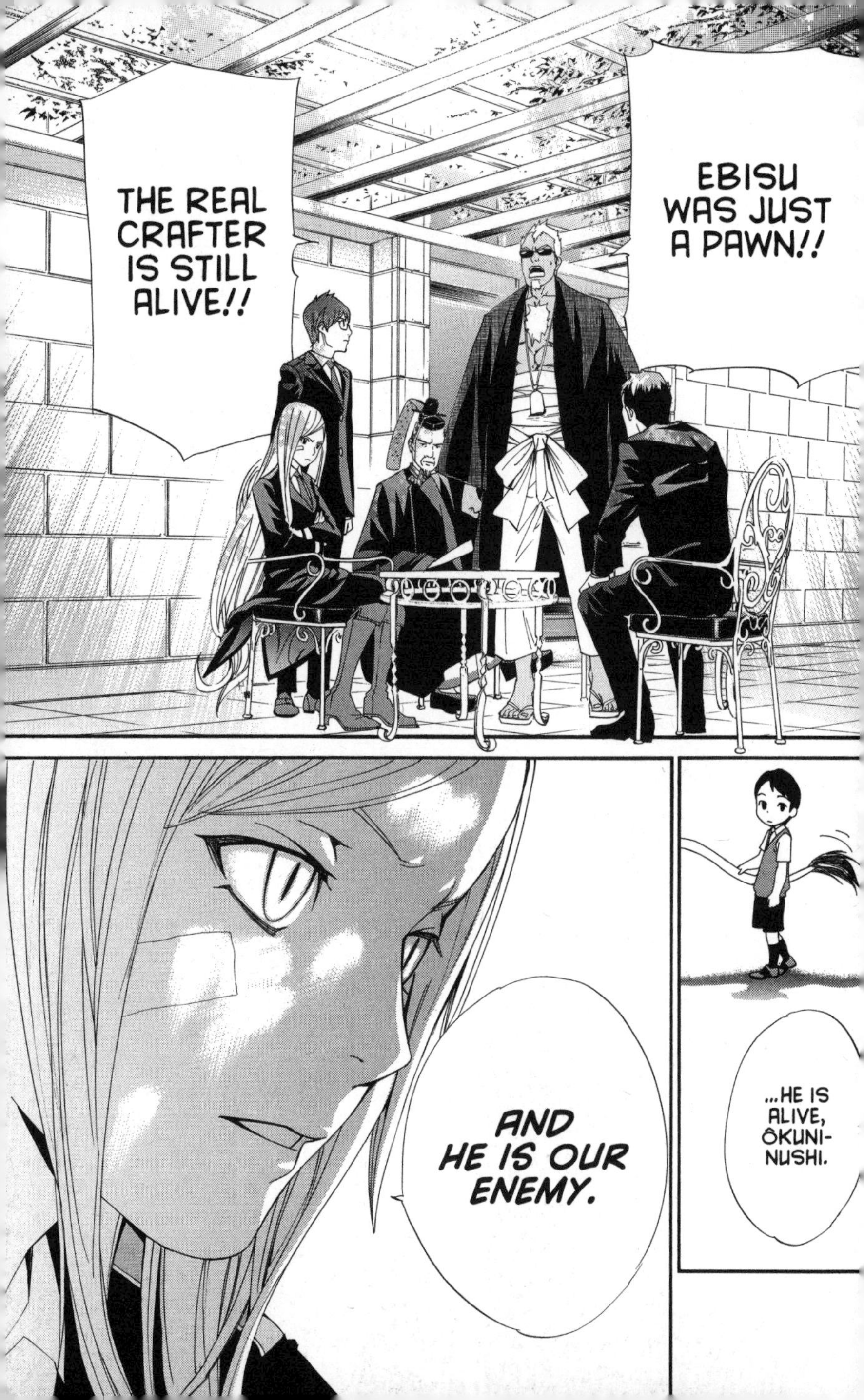
EBISU WAS JUST A PAWN!!
THE REAL CRAFTER IS STILL ALIVE!!
...HE IS ALIVE, ŌKUNI-NUSHI.
AND HE IS OUR ENEMY.

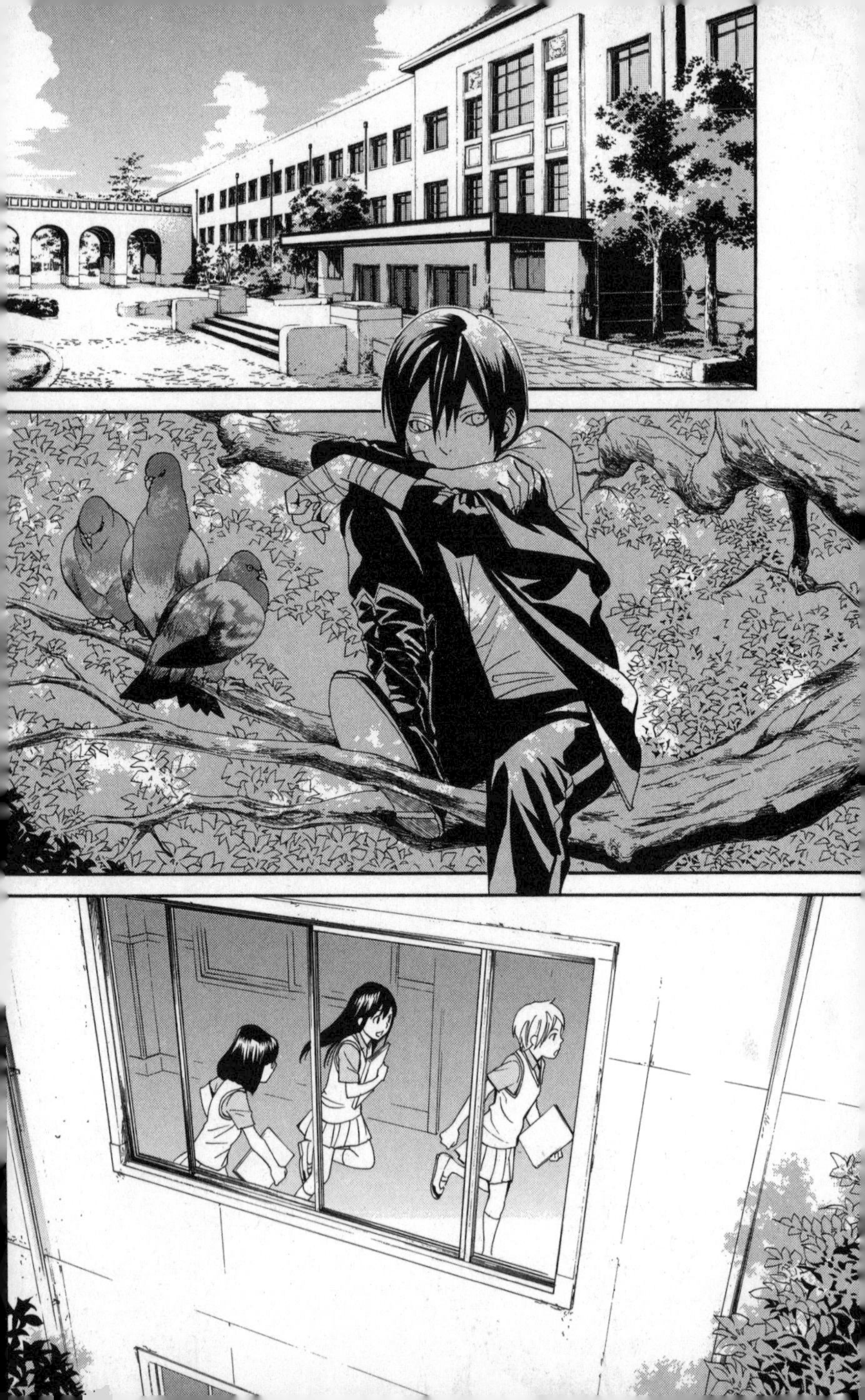

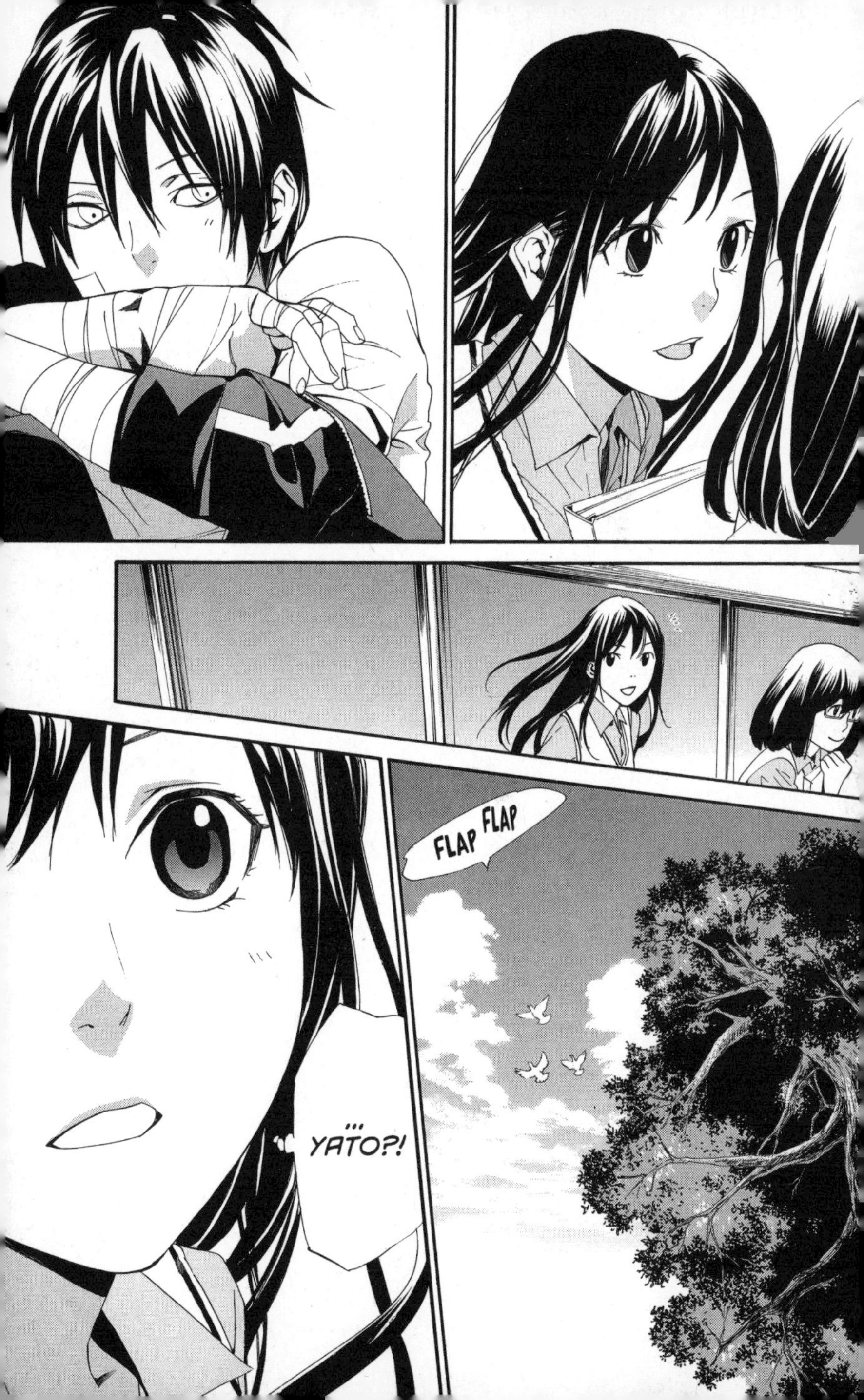
FLAP FLAP
...YATO?!

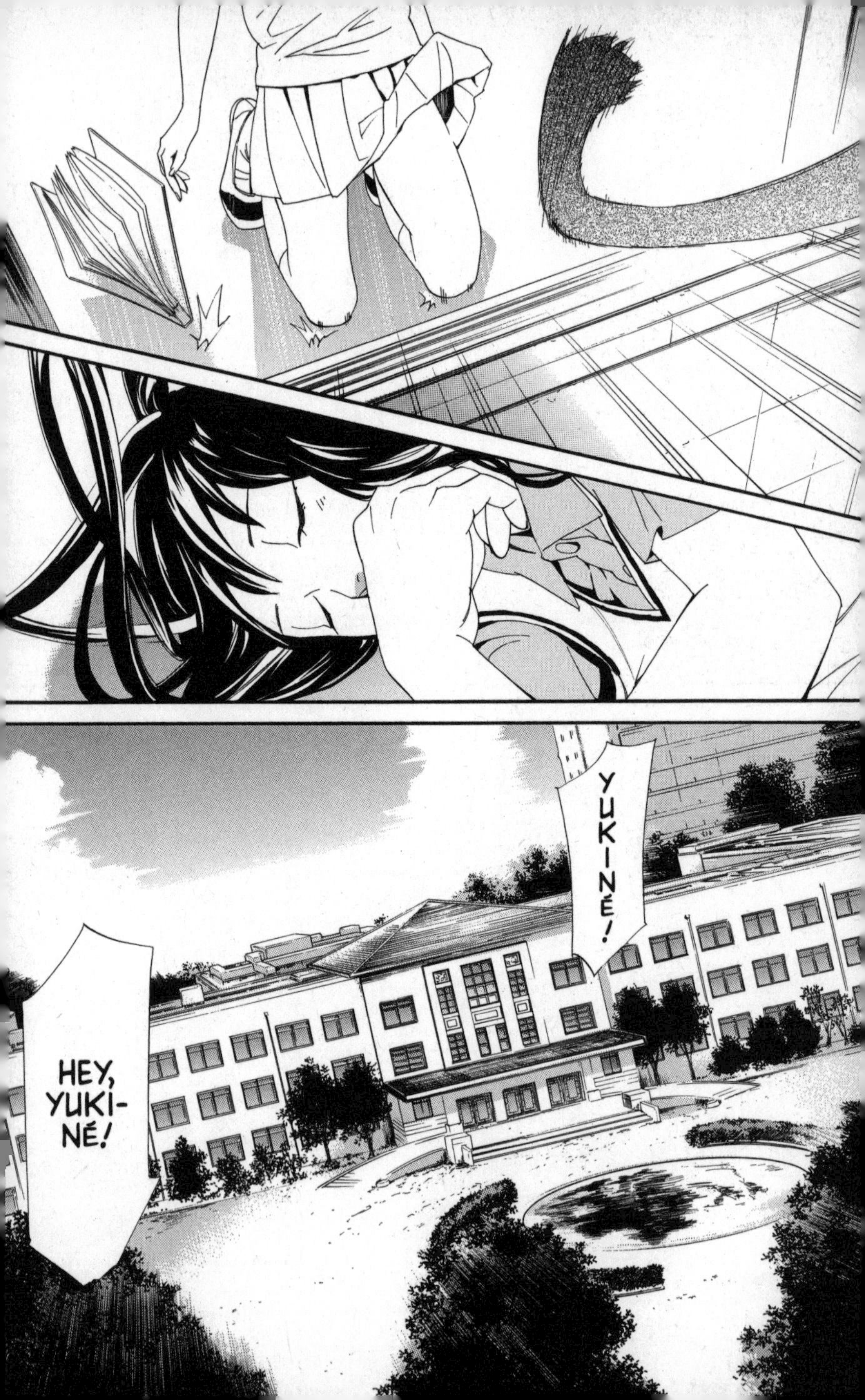
YUKINÉ!
HEY, YUKI-NÉ!

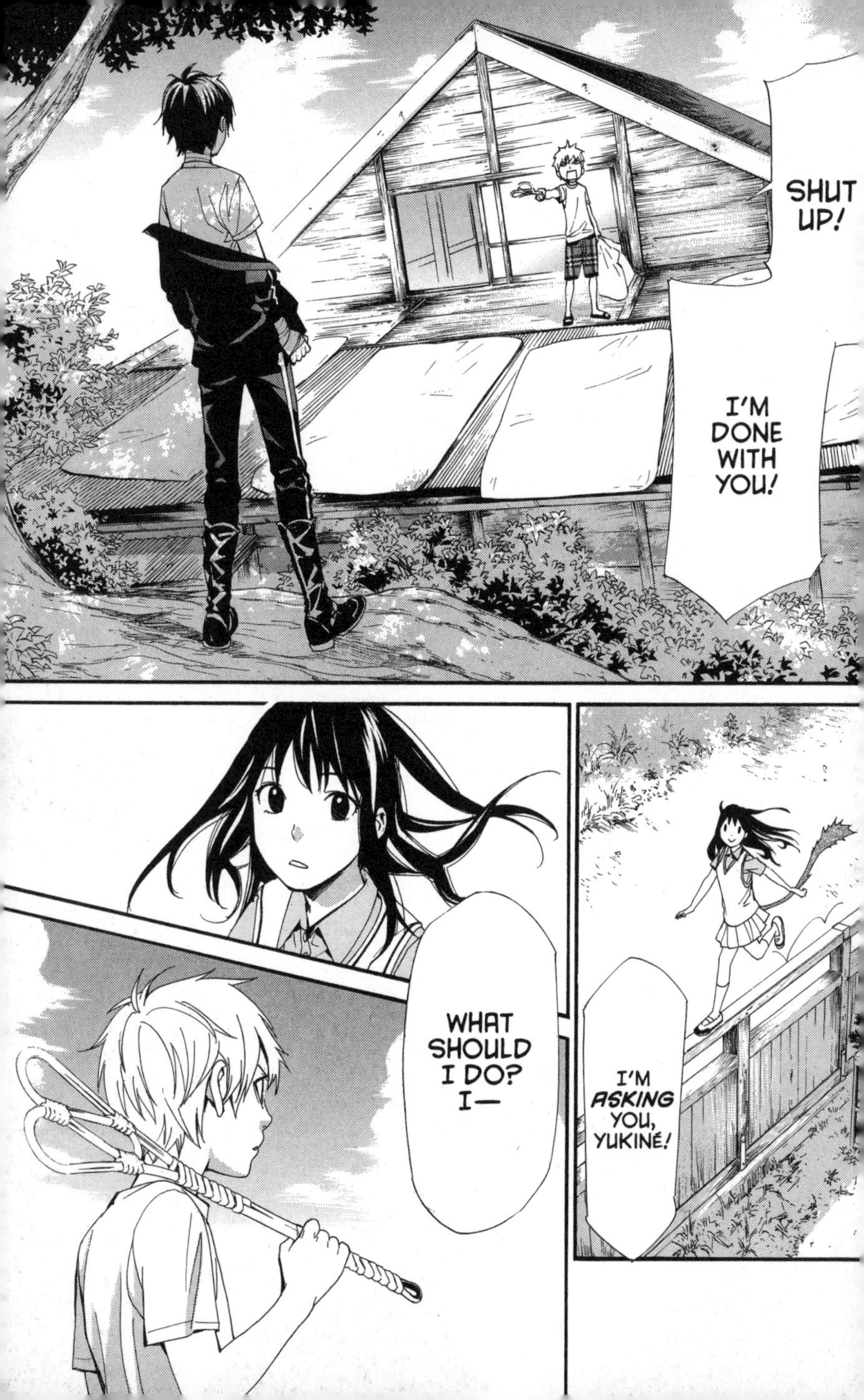
SHUT UP!
I'M DONE WITH YOU!
I'M *ASKING* YOU, YUKINE!
WHAT SHOULD I DO? I—

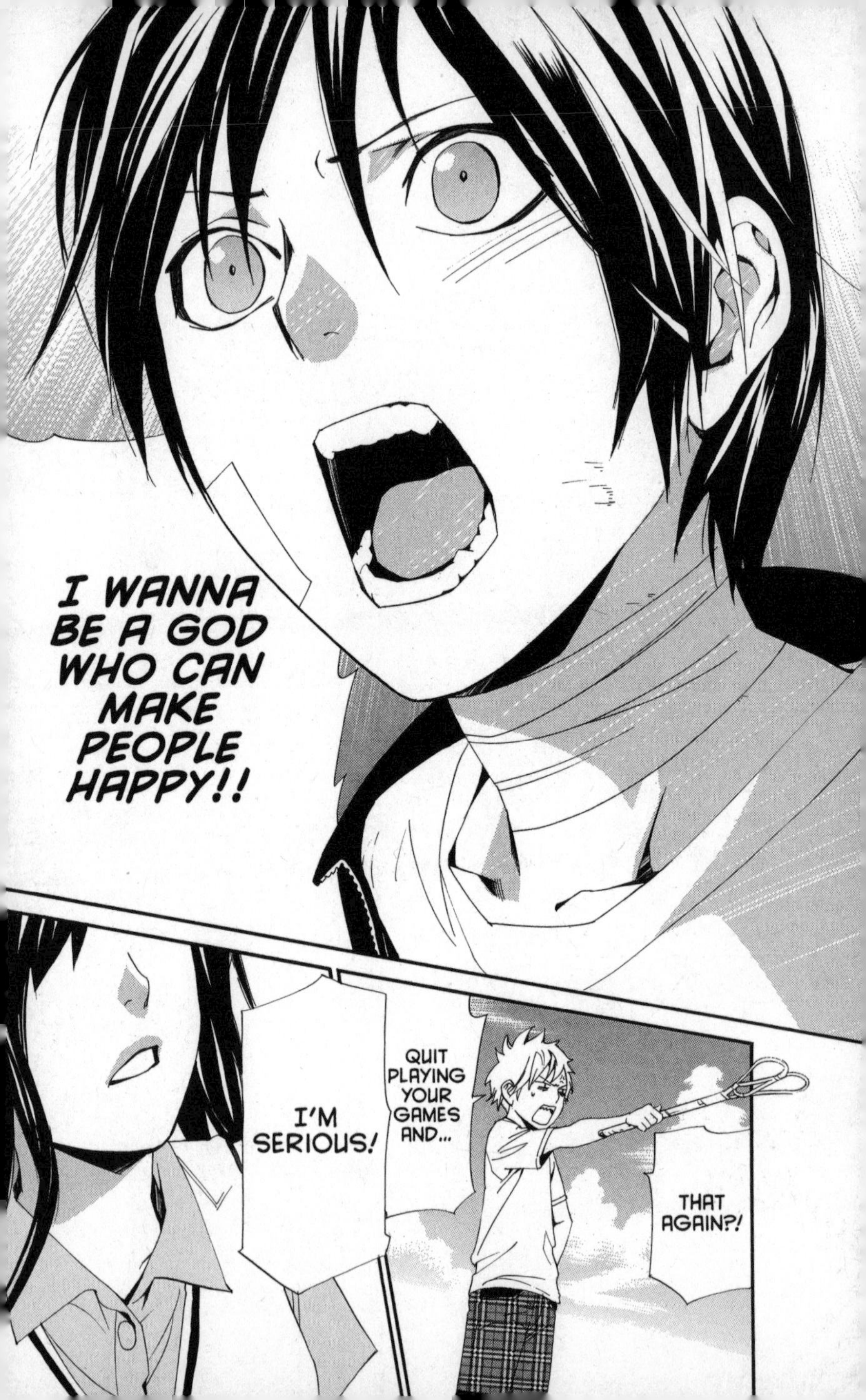
I WANNA BE A GOD WHO CAN MAKE PEOPLE HAPPY!!
QUIT PLAYING YOUR GAMES AND...
THAT AGAIN?!
I'M SERIOUS!

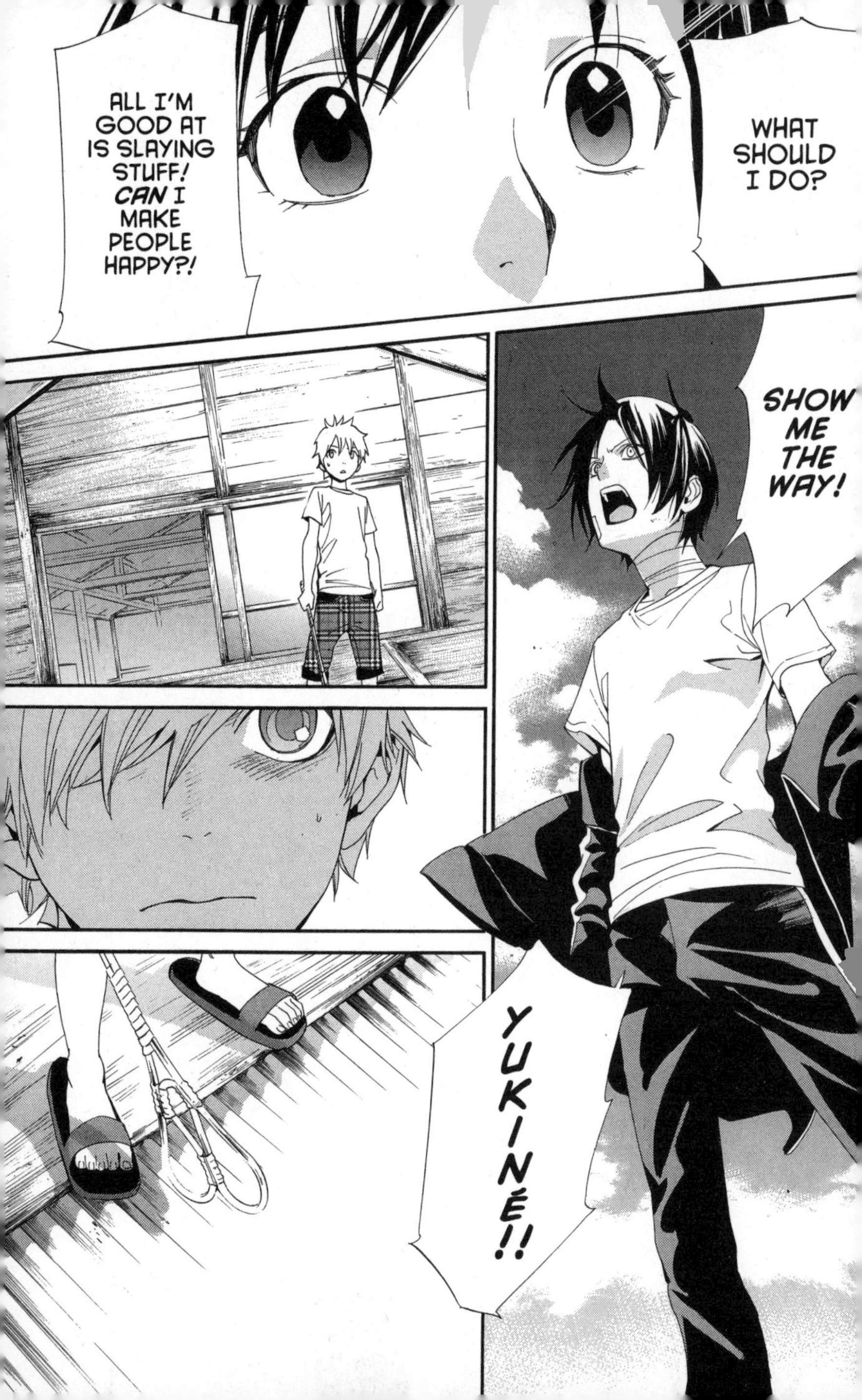
WHAT SHOULD I DO?
ALL I'M GOOD AT IS SLAYING STUFF! *CAN* I MAKE PEOPLE HAPPY?!
SHOW ME THE WAY!
YUKINÉ!!

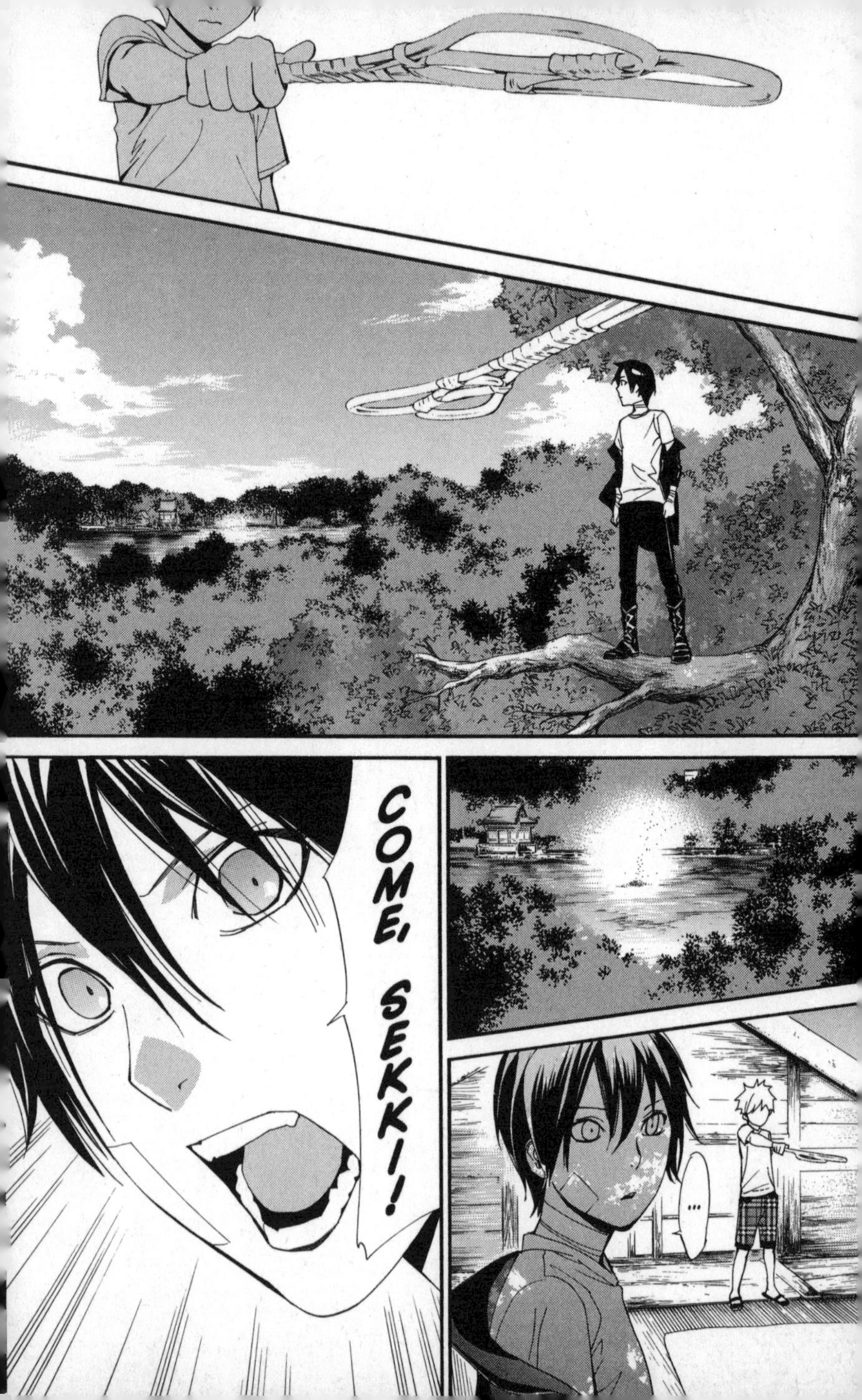
COME, SEKKI!!
...

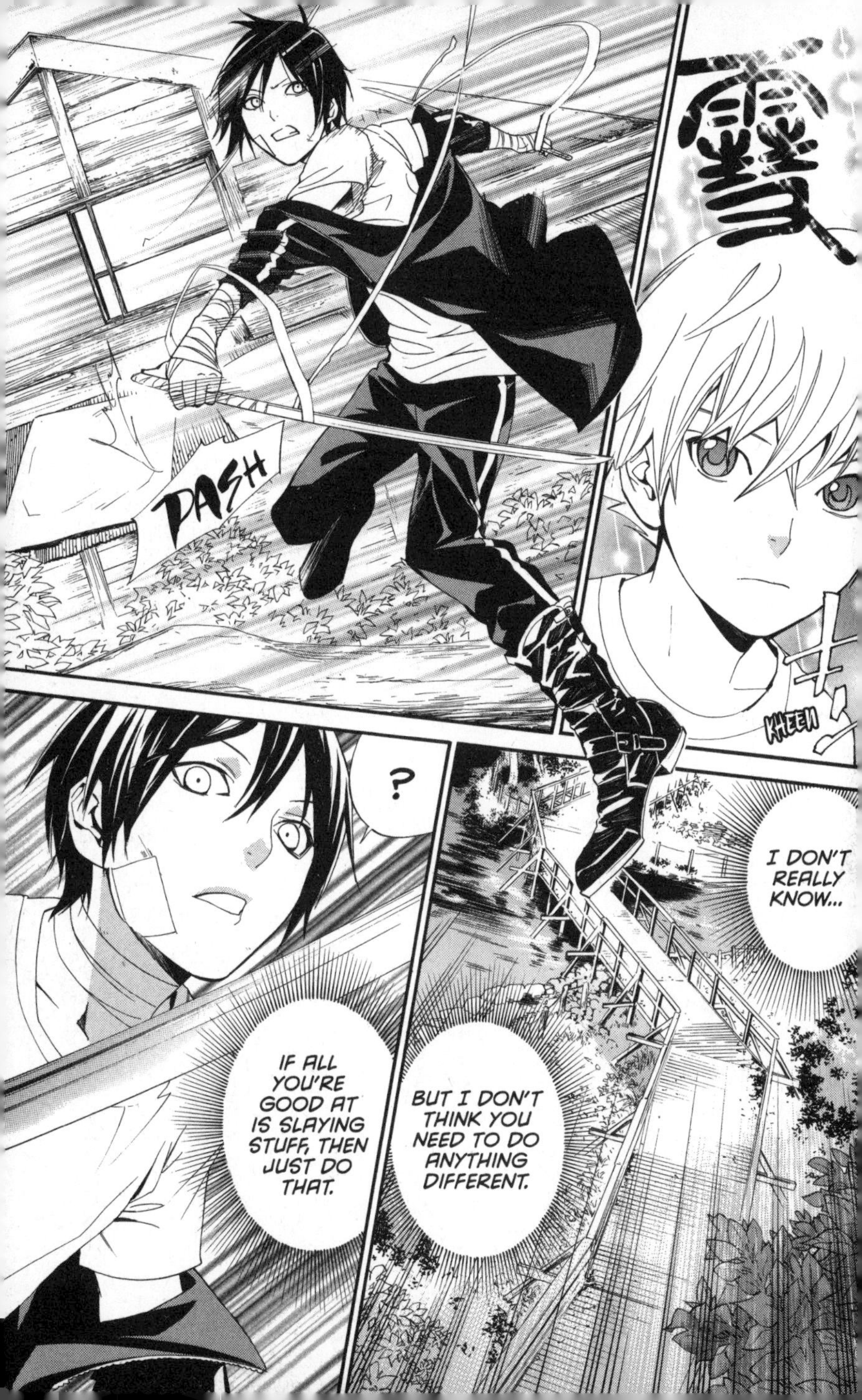
KHEEN
DASH
I DON'T REALLY KNOW...
BUT I DON'T THINK YOU NEED TO DO ANYTHING DIFFERENT.
?
IF ALL YOU'RE GOOD AT IS SLAYING STUFF, THEN JUST DO THAT.

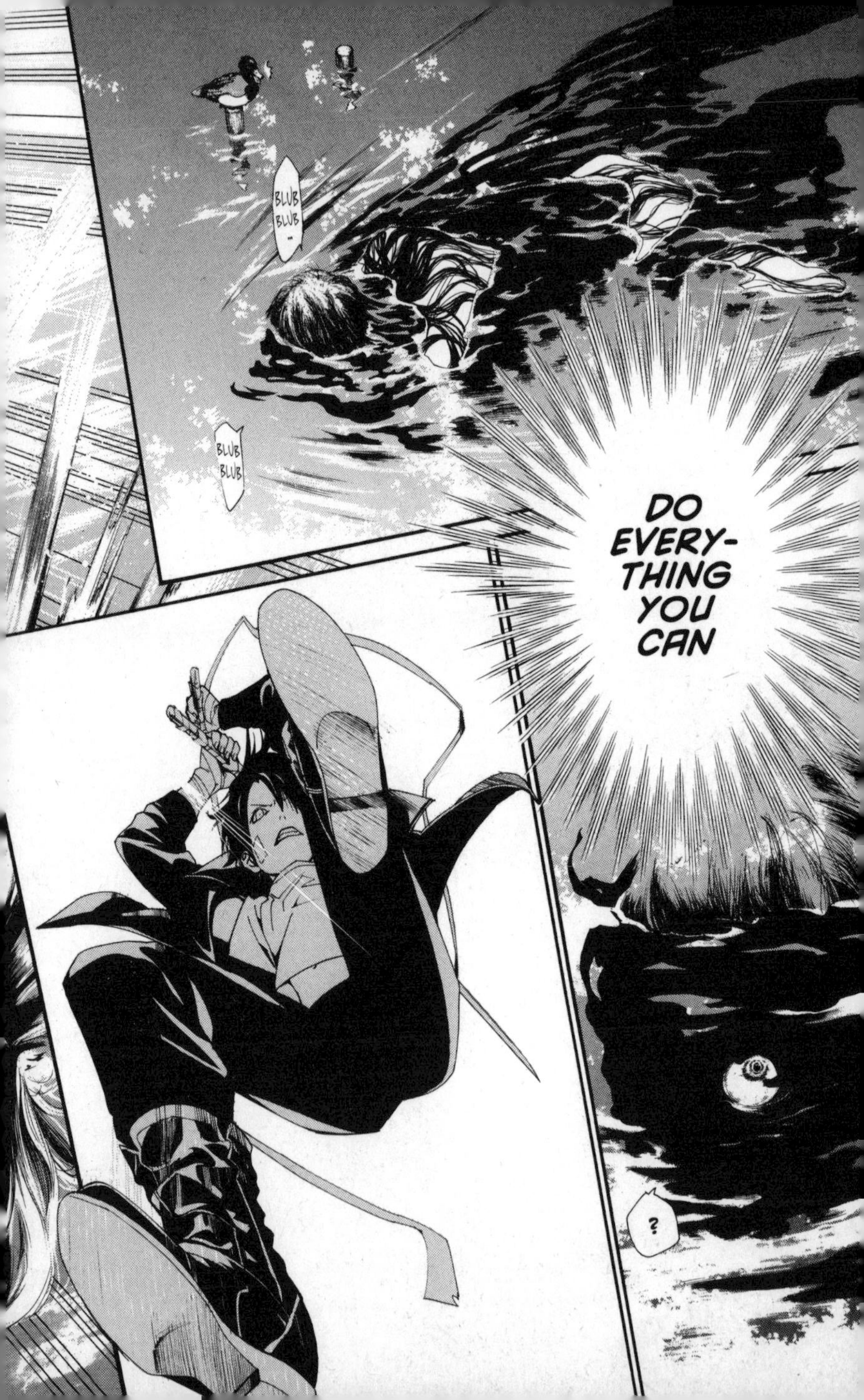
BLUB BLUB ...
BLUB BLUB
DO EVERY-THING YOU CAN
?

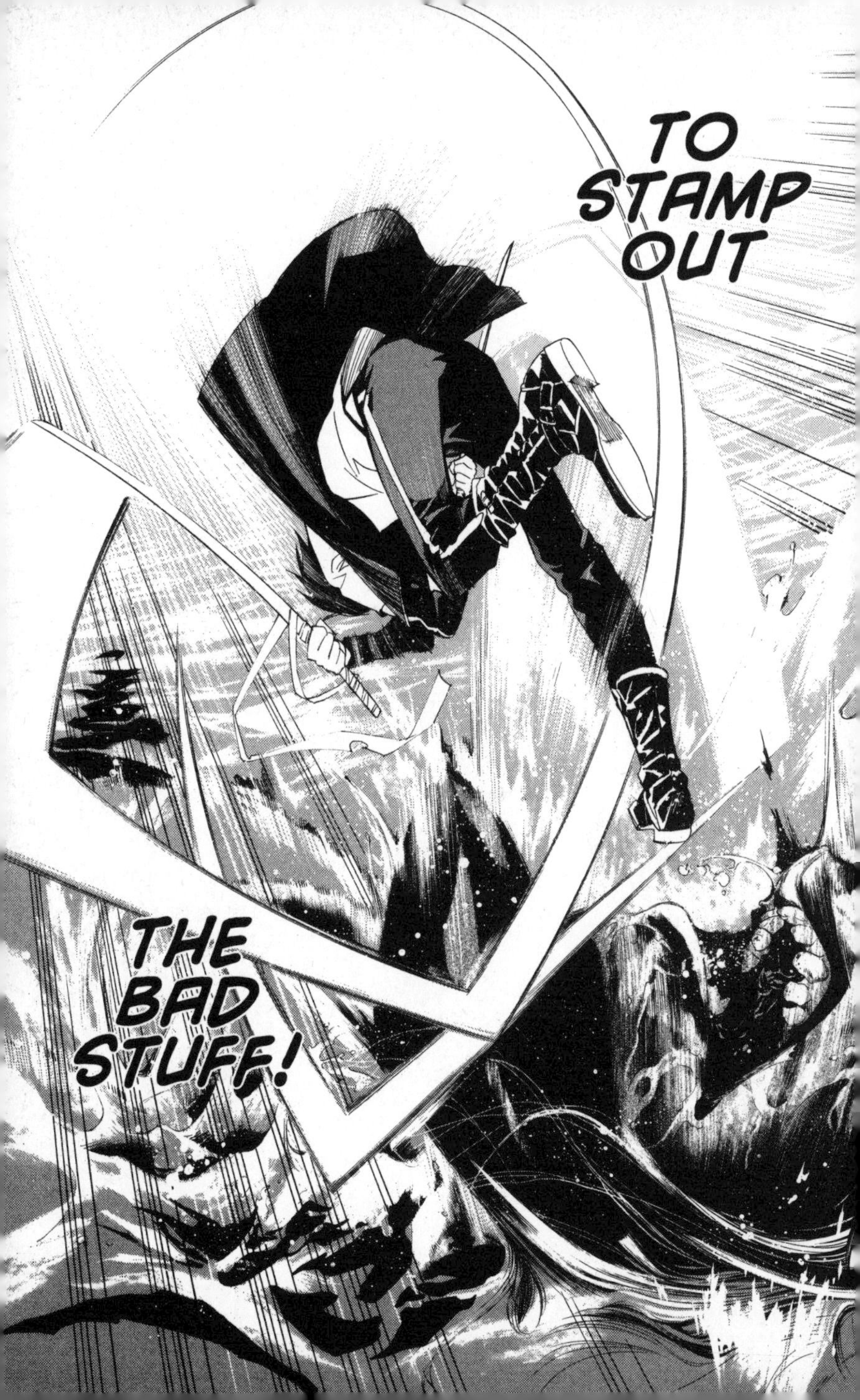
TO STAMP OUT
THE BAD STUFF!

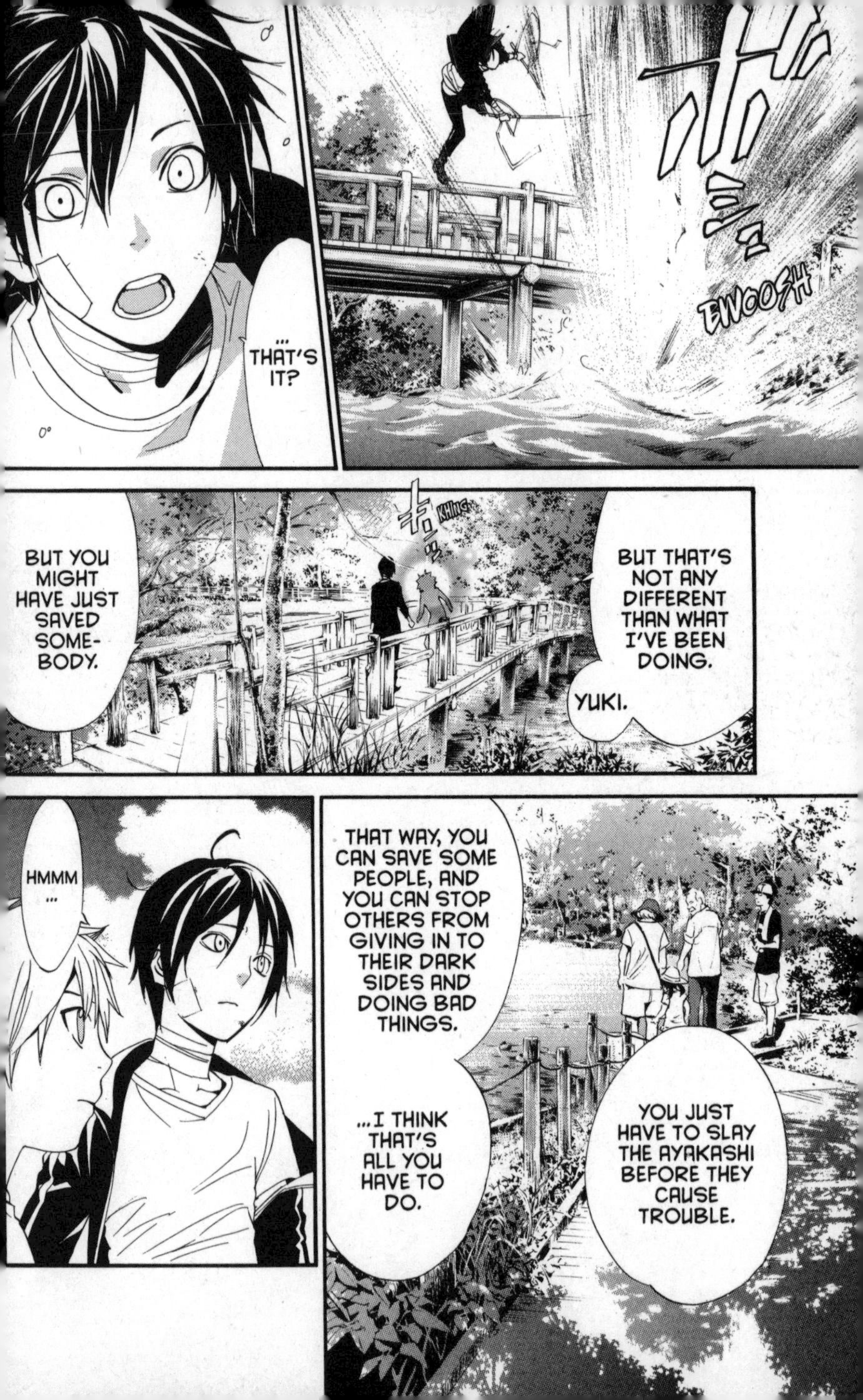
BWOOSH
... THAT'S IT?
BUT THAT'S NOT ANY DIFFERENT THAN WHAT I'VE BEEN DOING.
YUKI.
KHING
BUT YOU MIGHT HAVE JUST SAVED SOME-BODY.
YOU JUST HAVE TO SLAY THE AYAKASHI BEFORE THEY CAUSE TROUBLE.
THAT WAY, YOU CAN SAVE SOME PEOPLE, AND YOU CAN STOP OTHERS FROM GIVING IN TO THEIR DARK SIDES AND DOING BAD THINGS.
...I THINK THAT'S ALL YOU HAVE TO DO.
HMMM ...

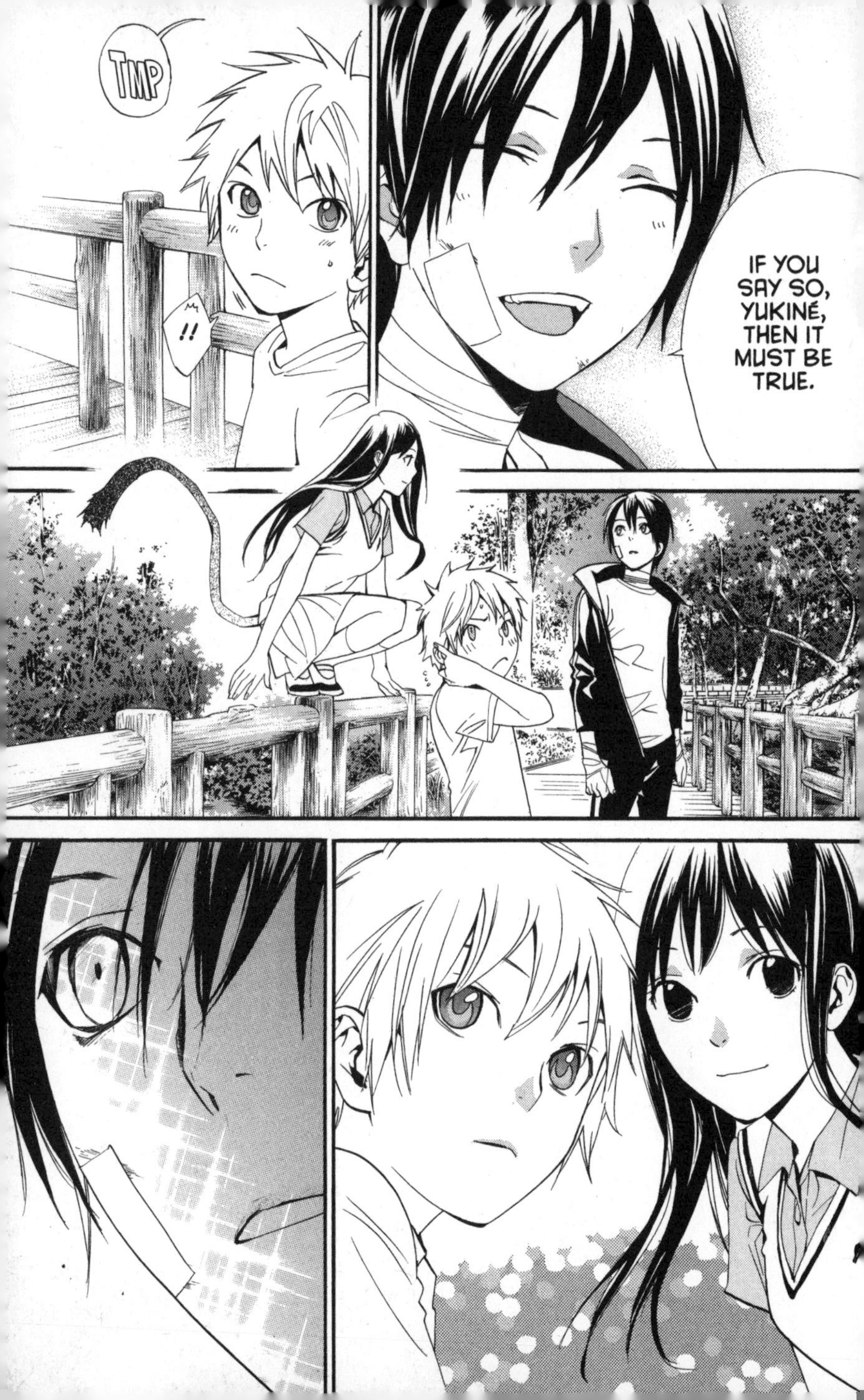
IF YOU SAY SO, YUKINÉ, THEN IT MUST BE TRUE.
TMP
!!

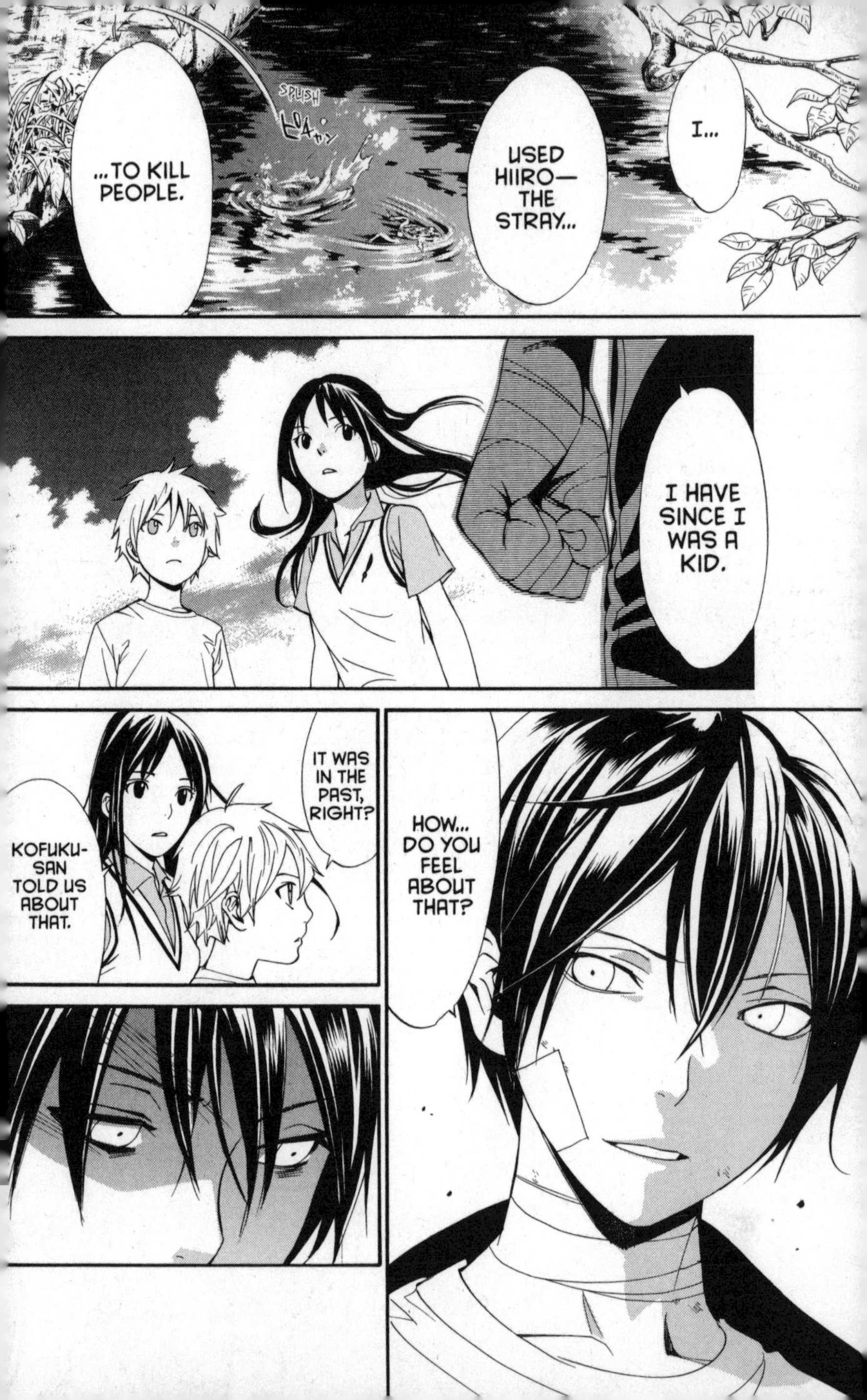
I...
USED HIIRO—THE STRAY...
SPLISH
...TO KILL PEOPLE.
I HAVE SINCE I WAS A KID.
HOW... DO YOU FEEL ABOUT THAT?
IT WAS IN THE PAST, RIGHT?
KOFUKU-SAN TOLD US ABOUT THAT.

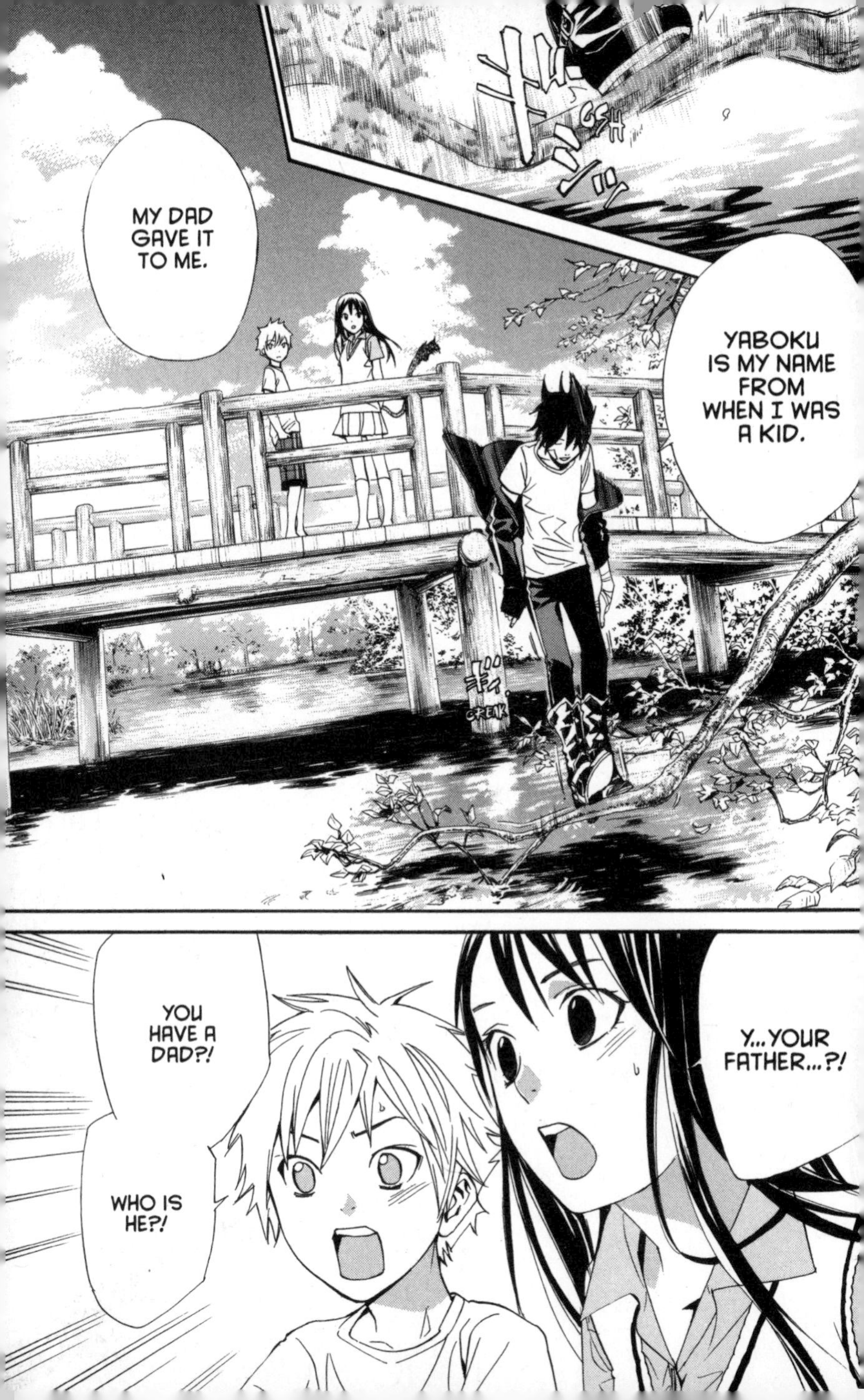
GSH
YABOKU IS MY NAME FROM WHEN I WAS A KID.
MY DAD GAVE IT TO ME.
CREAK
Y...YOUR FATHER...?!
YOU HAVE A DAD?!
WHO IS HE?!

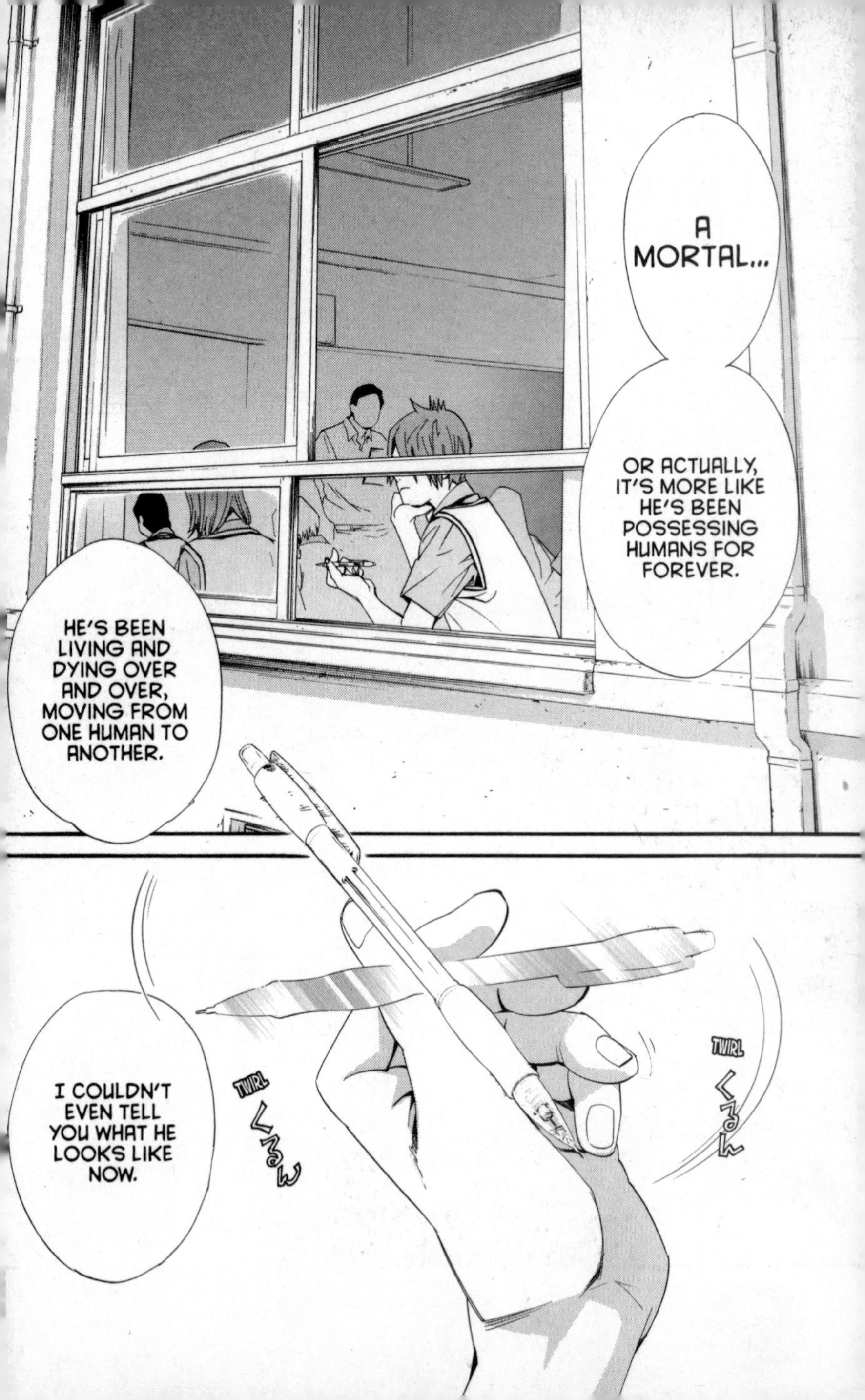
A MORTAL...
OR ACTUALLY, IT'S MORE LIKE HE'S BEEN POSSESSING HUMANS FOR FOREVER.
HE'S BEEN LIVING AND DYING OVER AND OVER, MOVING FROM ONE HUMAN TO ANOTHER.
TWIRL
くるん
TWIRL
くるん
I COULDN'T EVEN TELL YOU WHAT HE LOOKS LIKE NOW.

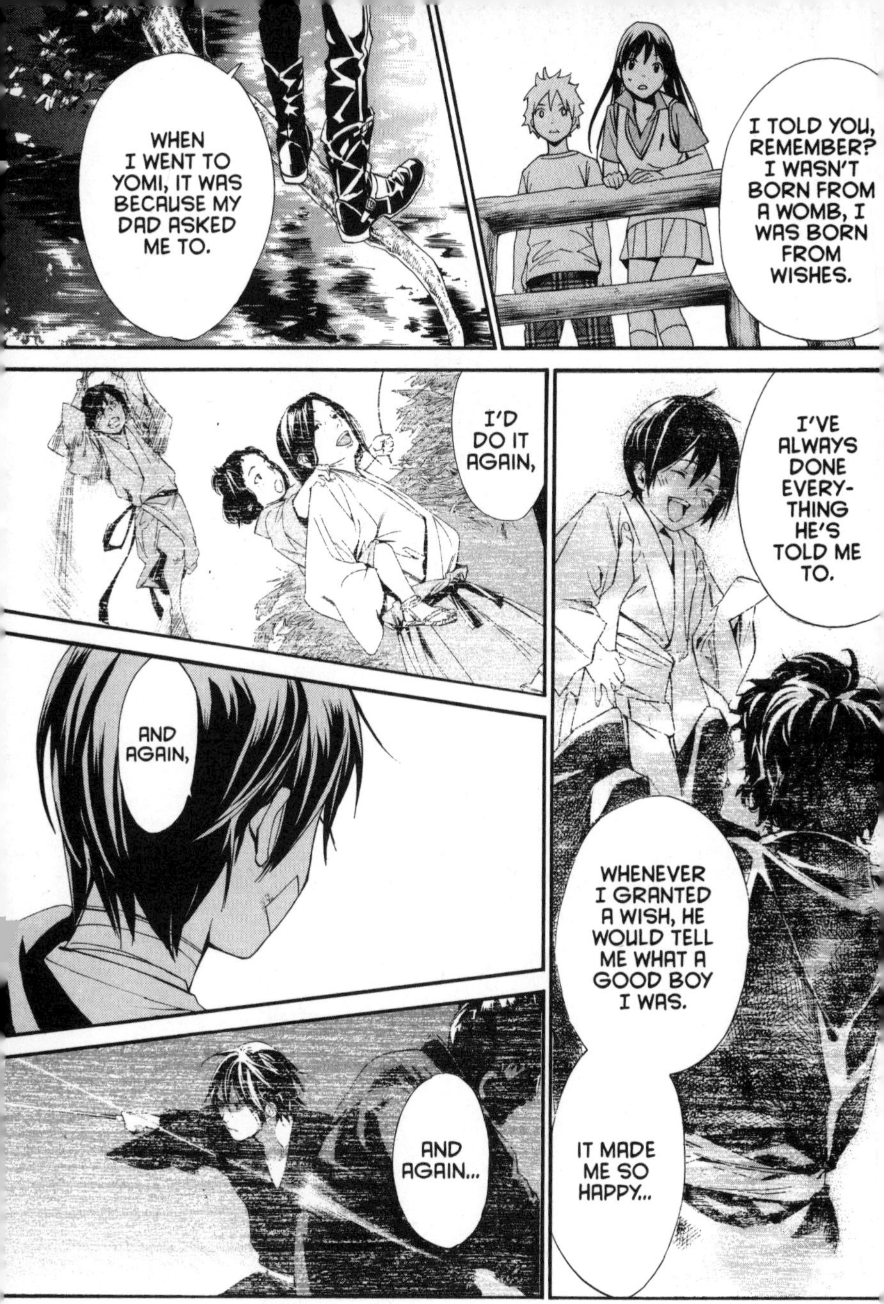
I TOLD YOU, REMEMBER? I WASN'T BORN FROM A WOMB, I WAS BORN FROM WISHES.
WHEN I WENT TO YOMI, IT WAS BECAUSE MY DAD ASKED ME TO.
I'VE ALWAYS DONE EVERY-THING HE'S TOLD ME TO.
WHENEVER I GRANTED A WISH, HE WOULD TELL ME WHAT A GOOD BOY I WAS.
IT MADE ME SO HAPPY...
I'D DO IT AGAIN,
AND AGAIN,
AND AGAIN...

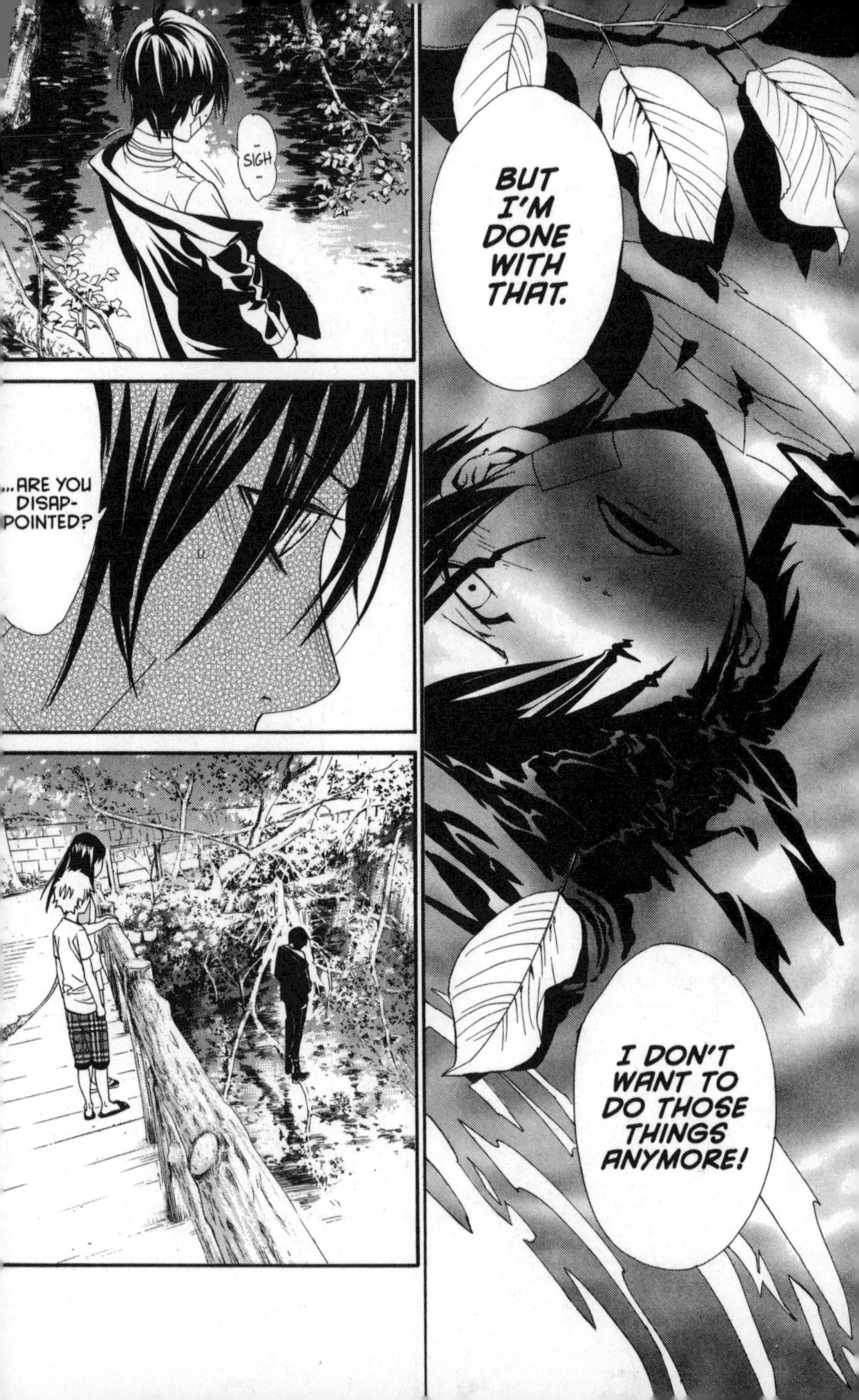
BUT I'M DONE WITH THAT.
I DON'T WANT TO DO THOSE THINGS ANYMORE!
...SIGH...
...ARE YOU DISAPPOINTED?

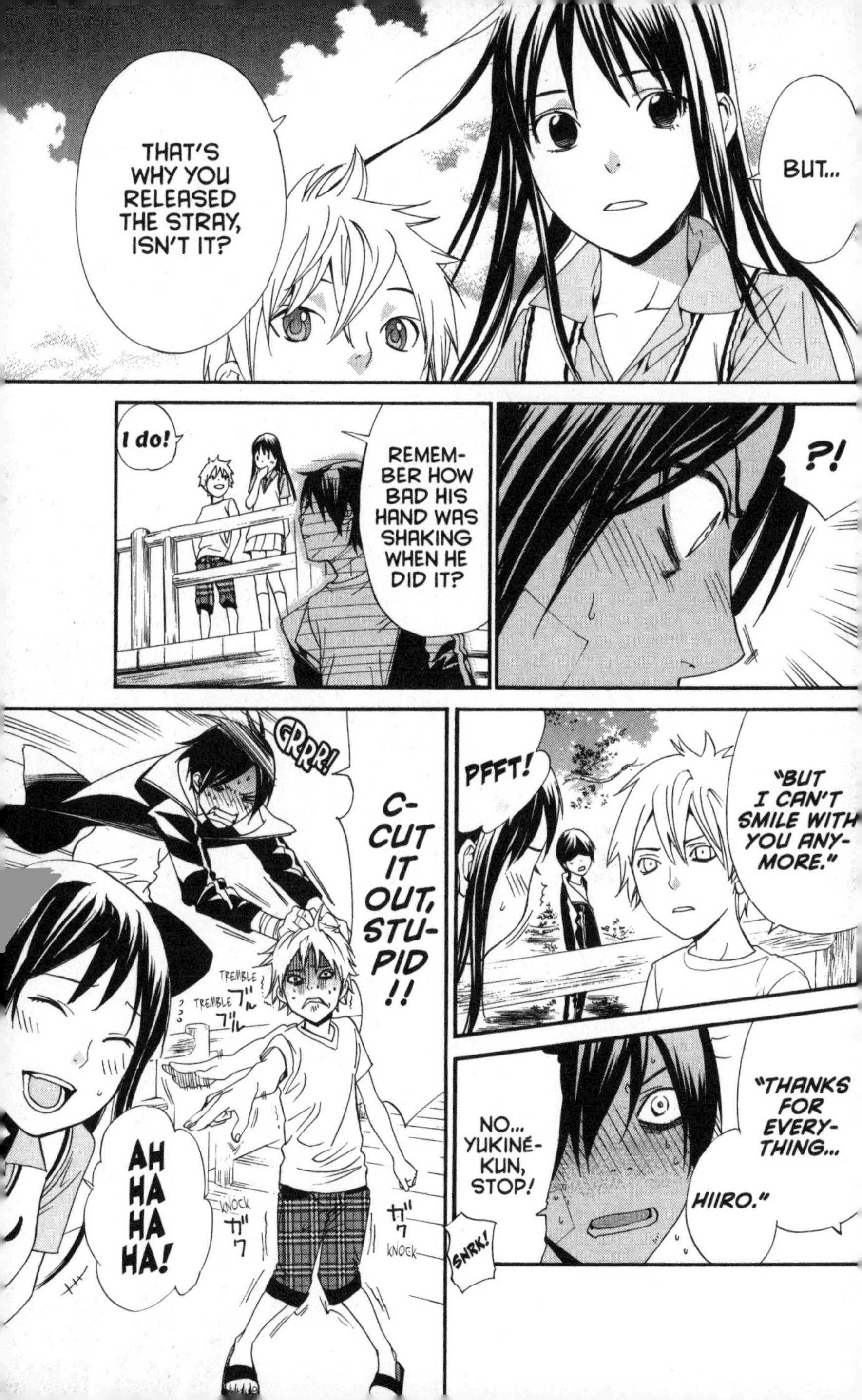
BUT...
THAT'S WHY YOU RELEASED THE STRAY, ISN'T IT?
?!
REMEMBER HOW BAD HIS HAND WAS SHAKING WHEN HE DID IT?
I do!
"BUT I CAN'T SMILE WITH YOU ANYMORE."
PFFT!
"THANKS FOR EVERYTHING...
HIIRO."
NO... YUKINÉ-KUN, STOP!
SNRK!
GRRR!
C-CUT IT OUT, STUPID!!
TREMBLE ブル
TREMBLE ブル
AH HA HA HA HA!
KNOCK ガク
ガク KNOCK

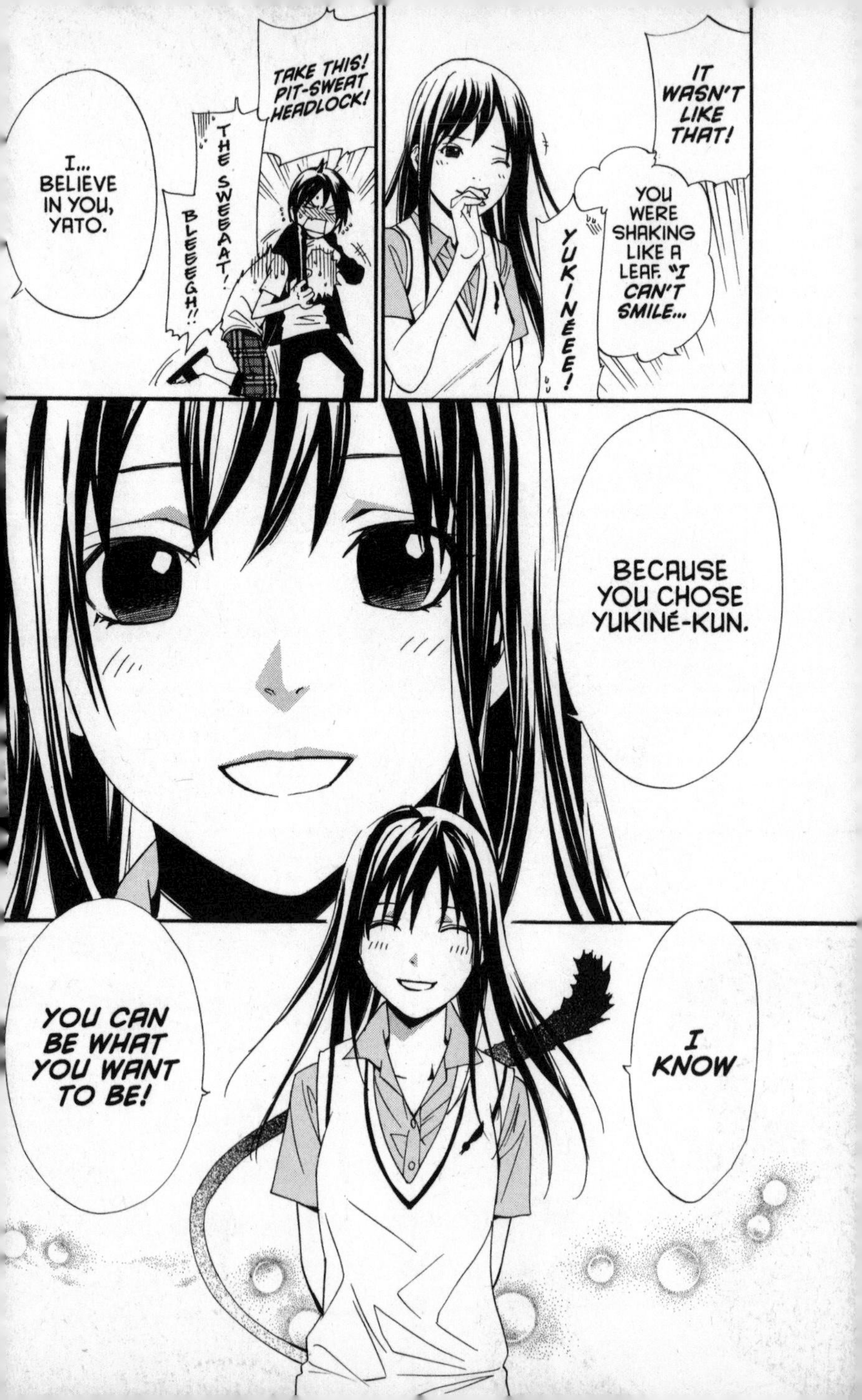
IT WASN'T LIKE THAT!
YOU WERE SHAKING LIKE A LEAF. "I CAN'T SMILE...
YUKINÉEEE!
TAKE THIS! PIT-SWEAT HEADLOCK!
THE SWEEAAT!
BLEEEGH!!
I... BELIEVE IN YOU, YATO.
BECAUSE YOU CHOSE YUKINÉ-KUN.
I KNOW
YOU CAN BE WHAT YOU WANT TO BE!

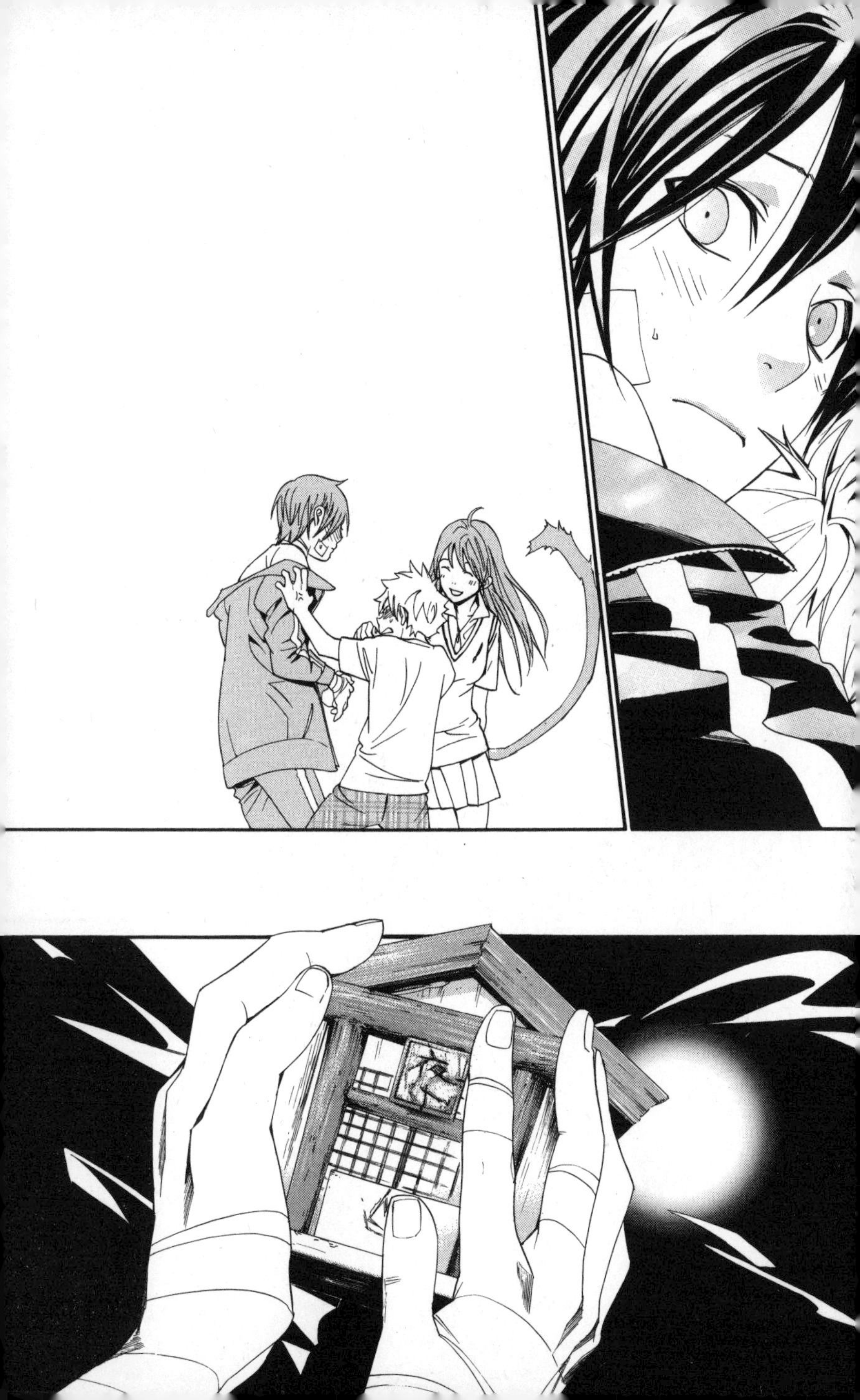

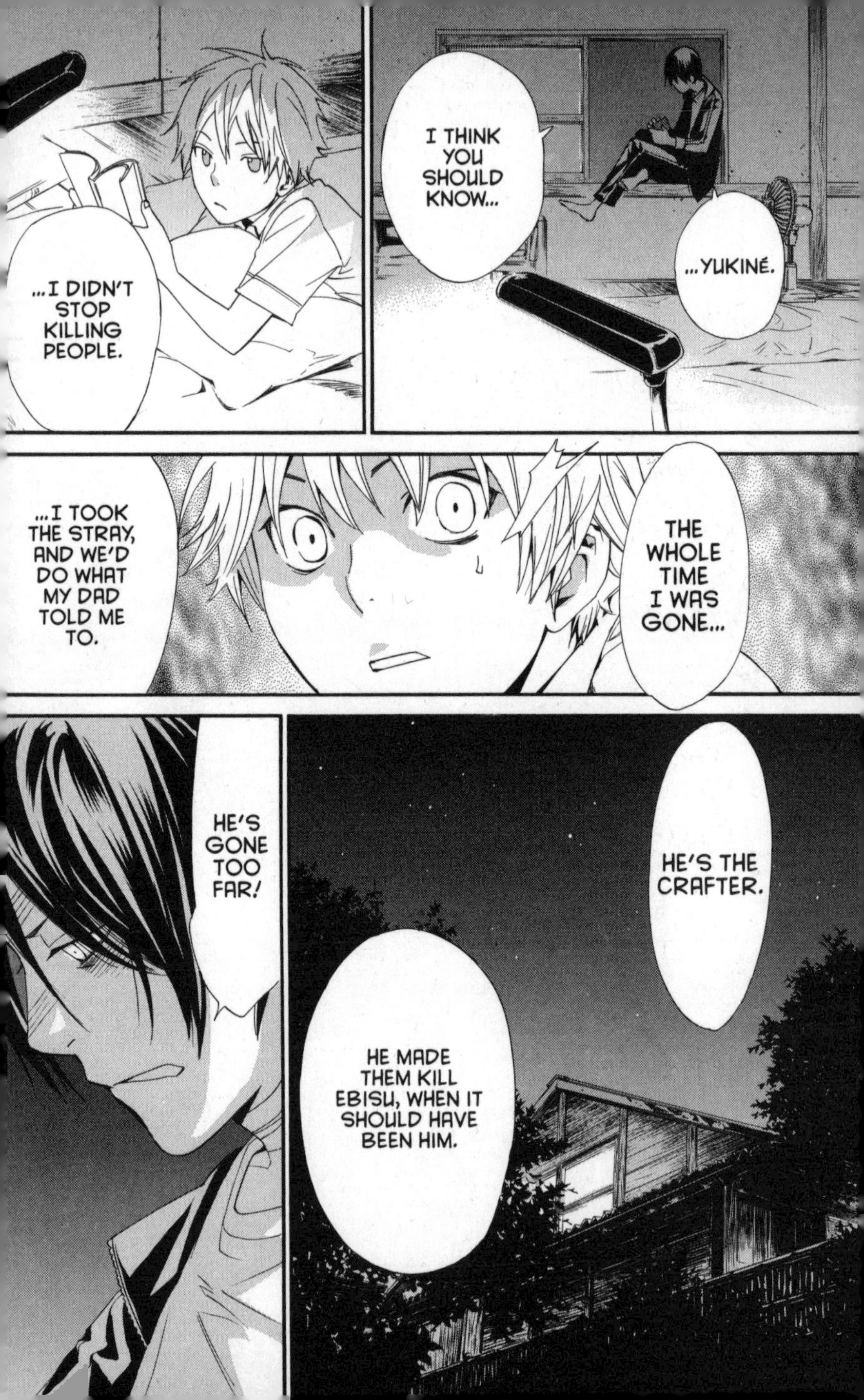
I THINK YOU SHOULD KNOW...
...YUKINÉ.
...I DIDN'T STOP KILLING PEOPLE.
THE WHOLE TIME I WAS GONE...
...I TOOK THE STRAY, AND WE'D DO WHAT MY DAD TOLD ME TO.
HE'S THE CRAFTER.
HE MADE THEM KILL EBISU, WHEN IT SHOULD HAVE BEEN HIM.
HE'S GONE TOO FAR!

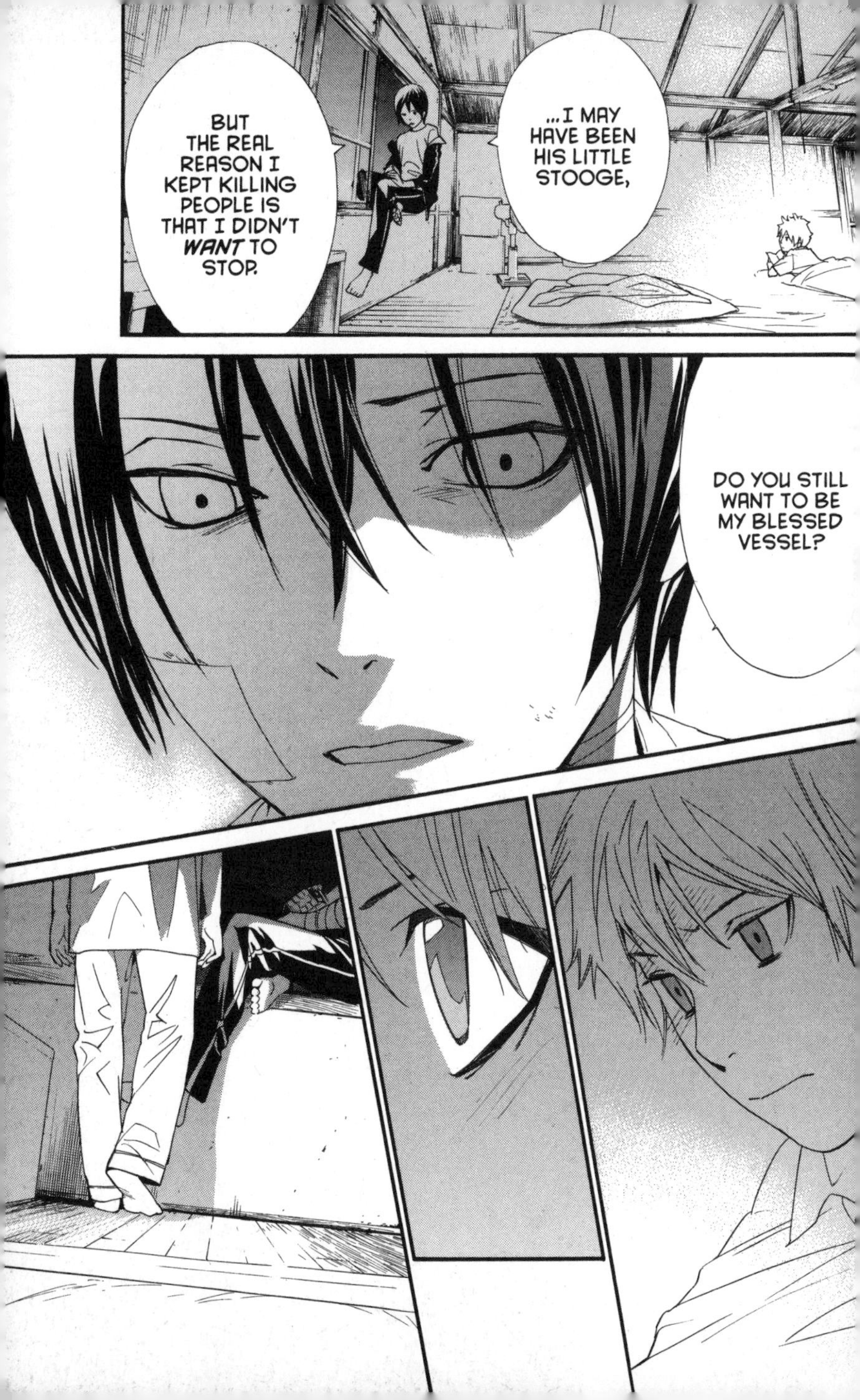
...I MAY HAVE BEEN HIS LITTLE STOOGE,
BUT THE REAL REASON I KEPT KILLING PEOPLE IS THAT I DIDN'T *WANT* TO STOP.
DO YOU STILL WANT TO BE MY BLESSED VESSEL?

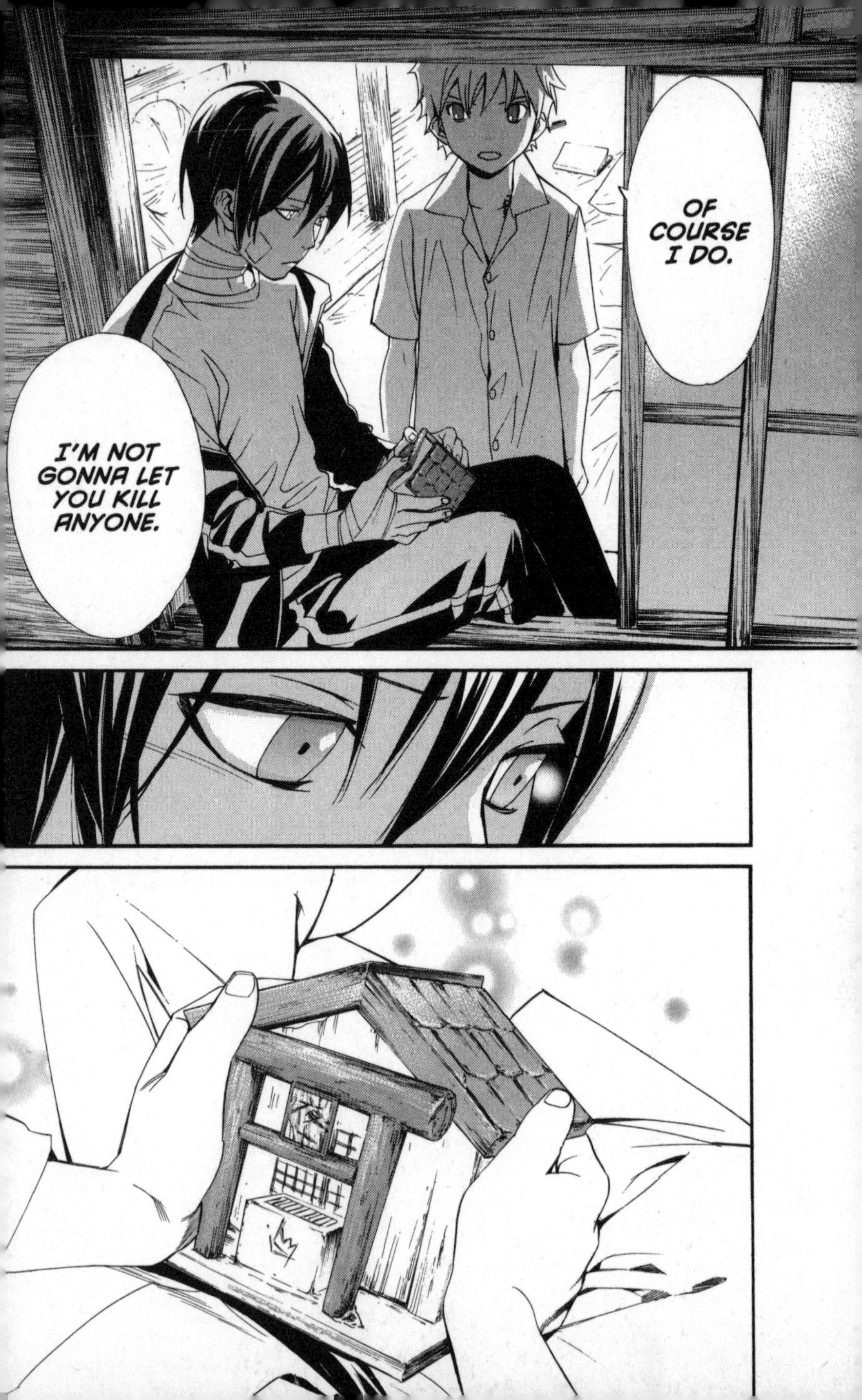
OF COURSE I DO.
I'M NOT GONNA LET YOU KILL ANYONE.

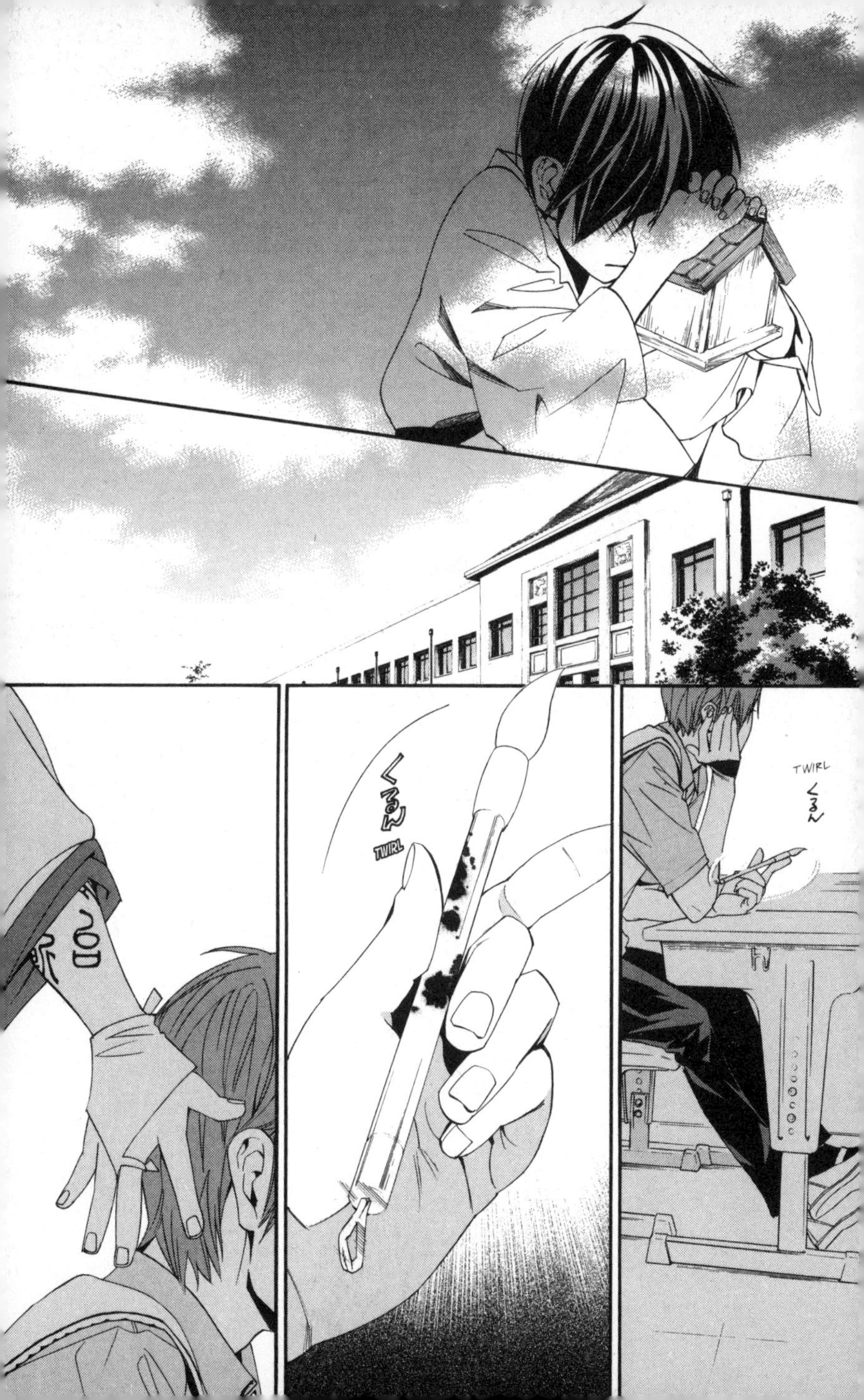
TWIRL
くるん
くるん
TWIRL

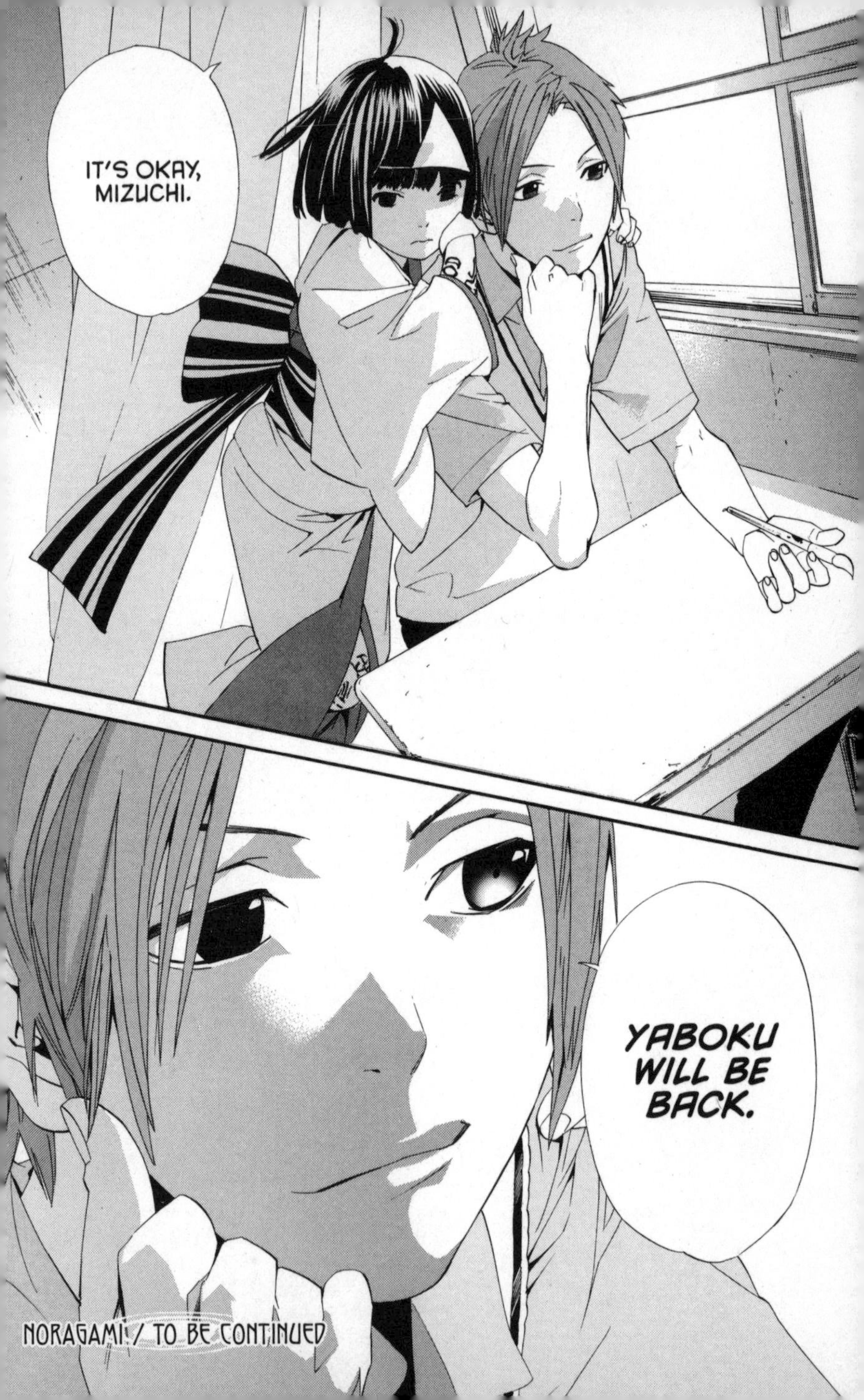
IT'S OKAY, MIZUCHI.
YABOKU WILL BE BACK.
NORAGAMI / TO BE CONTINUED

野

兌

神

ATROCIOUS MANGA

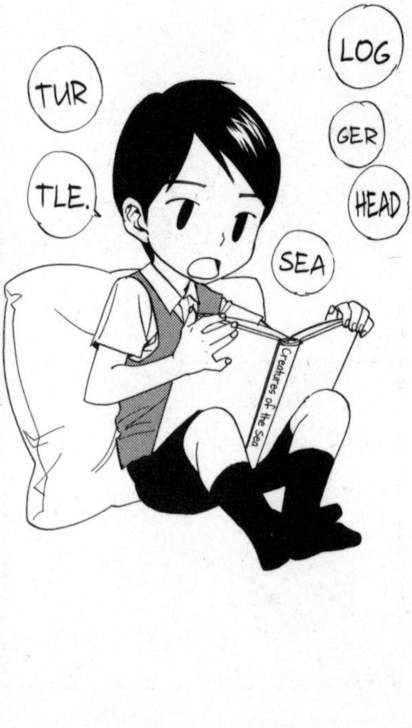
LOG
GER
HEAD
SEA
TUR
TLE.
Creatures of the Sea

LEARNING HOW TO READ

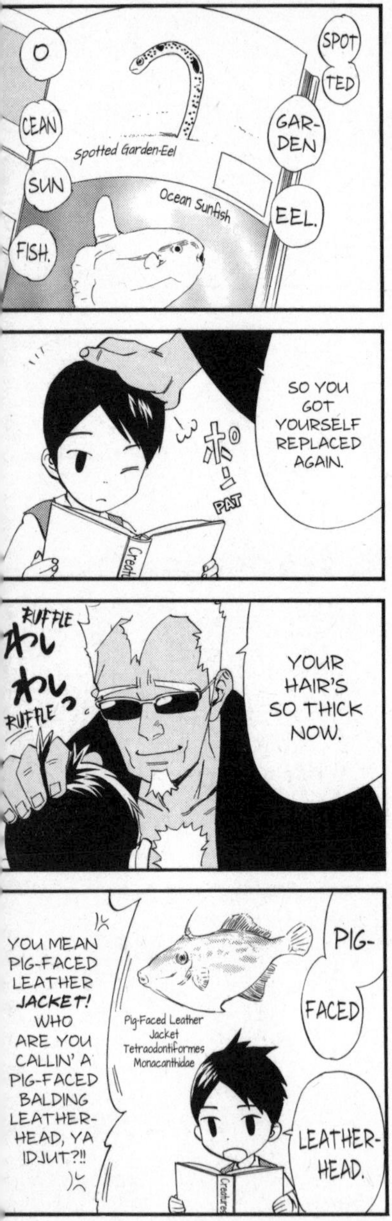
SPOT
TED
GAR-
DEN
EEL.
Spotted Garden-Eel
Ocean Sunfish
O
CEAN
SUN
FISH.
SO YOU GOT YOURSELF REPLACED AGAIN.
ポン
PAT
Creatures
YOUR HAIR'S SO THICK NOW.
わしわしっ
RUFFLE
RUFFLE
PIG-
FACED
LEATHER-HEAD.
Pig-Faced Leather Jacket Tetraodontiformes Monacanthidae
Creatures
YOU MEAN PIG-FACED LEATHER JACKET! WHO ARE YOU CALLIN' A PIG-FACED BALDING LEATHER-HEAD, YA IDJUT?!!

YUP, THAT HAPPENS WITH LIONS

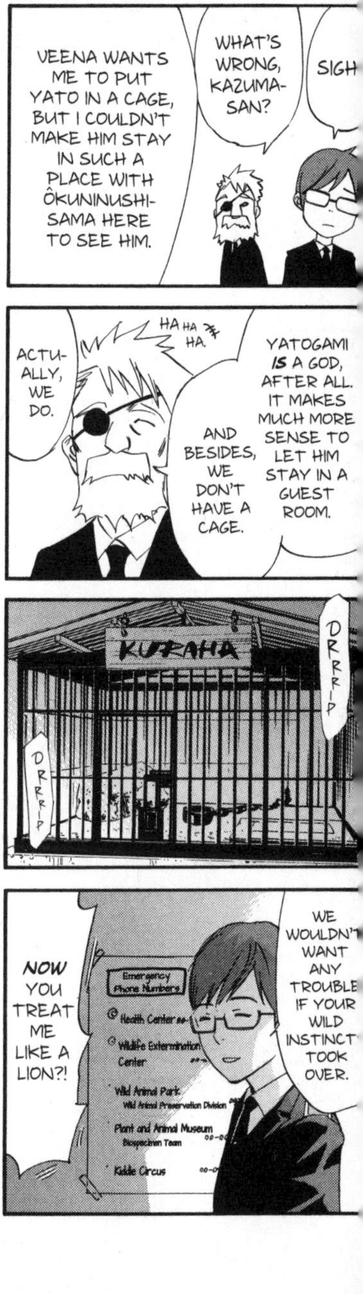
SIGH
WHAT'S WRONG, KAZUMA-SAN?
VEENA WANTS ME TO PUT YATO IN A CAGE, BUT I COULDN'T MAKE HIM STAY IN SUCH A PLACE WITH ÔKUNINUSHI-SAMA HERE TO SEE HIM.
YATOGAMI **IS** A GOD, AFTER ALL. IT MAKES MUCH MORE SENSE TO LET HIM STAY IN A GUEST ROOM.
AND BESIDES, WE DON'T HAVE A CAGE.
HA HA HA.
ACTUALLY, WE DO.
DRRRIP
KURAHA
DRRRIP
WE WOULDN'T WANT ANY TROUBLE IF YOUR WILD INSTINCT TOOK OVER.
Emergency Phone Numbers
Health Center
Wildlife Extermination Center
Wild Animal Park
Wild Animal Preservation Division
Plant and Animal Museum
Biospecimen Team
Kiddie Circus
NOW YOU TREAT ME LIKE A LION?!

YUP, THAT HAPPENS WITH CATS

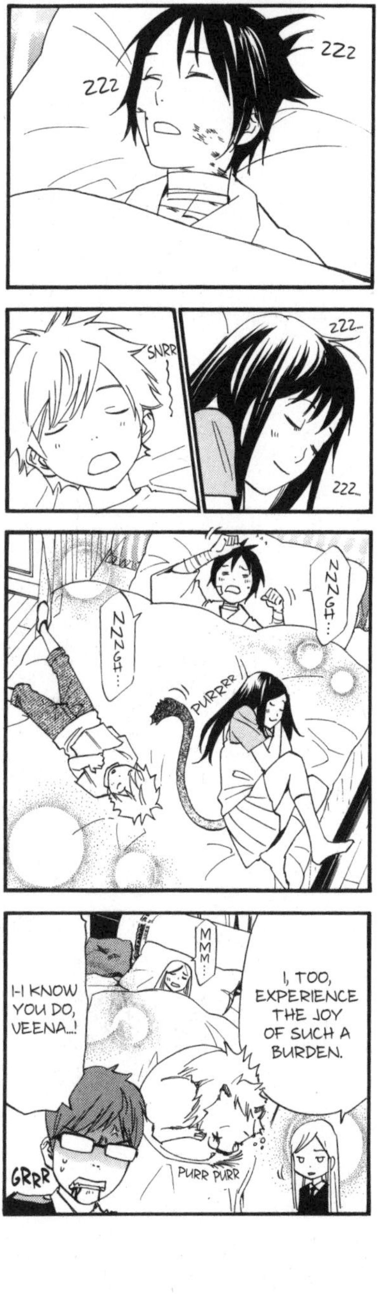
ZZZ
ZZZ
ZZZ...
ZZZ...
SNRR
NNNGH...
NNNGH...
PURRRR
I, TOO, EXPERIENCE THE JOY OF SUCH A BURDEN.
MMM...
I-I KNOW YOU DO, VEENA...!
PURR PURR
GRRR

BIG DADDY

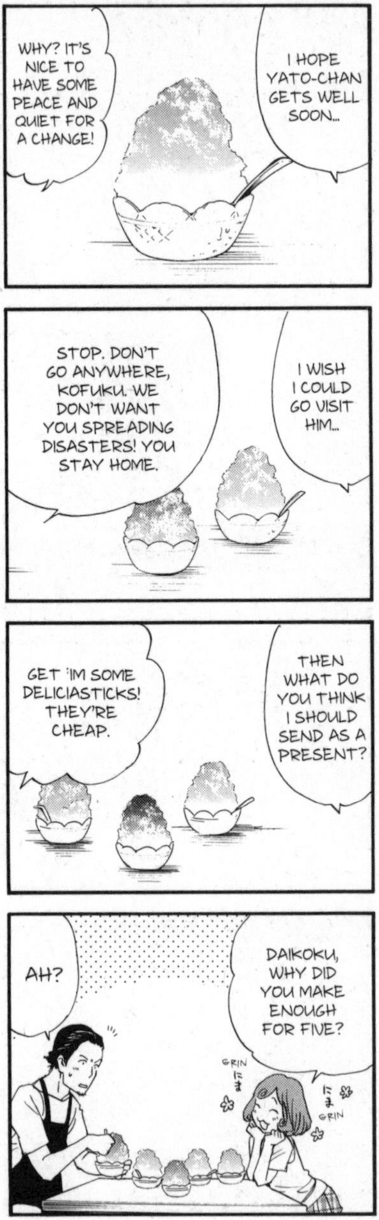
I HOPE YATO-CHAN GETS WELL SOON...
WHY? IT'S NICE TO HAVE SOME PEACE AND QUIET FOR A CHANGE!
I WISH I COULD GO VISIT HIM...
STOP. DON'T GO ANYWHERE, KOFUKU. WE DON'T WANT YOU SPREADING DISASTERS! YOU STAY HOME.
THEN WHAT DO YOU THINK I SHOULD SEND AS A PRESENT?
GET 'IM SOME DELICIASTICKS! THEY'RE CHEAP.
DAIKOKU, WHY DID YOU MAKE ENOUGH FOR FIVE?
GRIN にま
GRIN にま
AH?

LEARNING GROWNUP WORDS

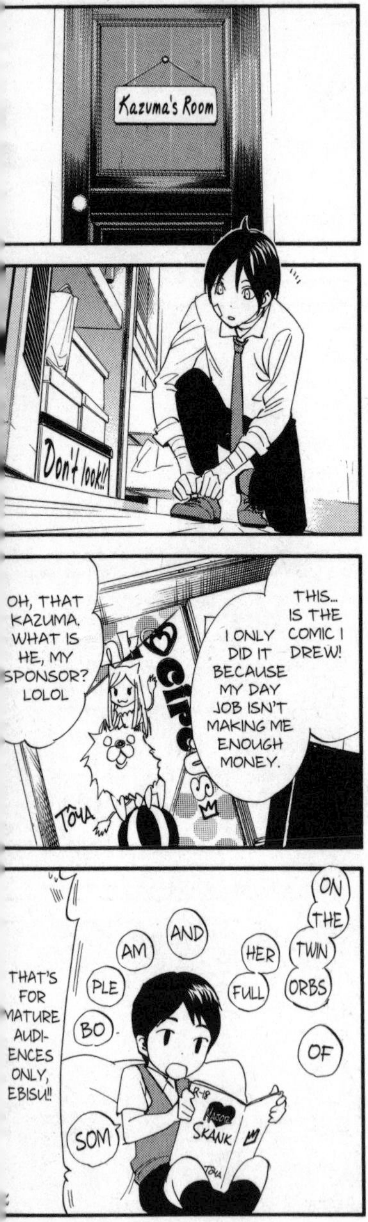
Kazuma's Room
Don't look!!
THIS... IS THE COMIC I DREW!
I ONLY DID IT BECAUSE MY DAY JOB ISN'T MAKING ME ENOUGH MONEY.
OH, THAT KAZUMA. WHAT IS HE, MY SPONSOR? LOLOL
TÔYA
ON
THE
TWIN
ORBS
OF
HER
FULL
AND
AM
PLE
BO
SOM
R-18
MAJOR SKANK
TÔYA
THAT'S FOR MATURE AUDIENCES ONLY, EBISU!!

MYSTERIOUS OBJECT

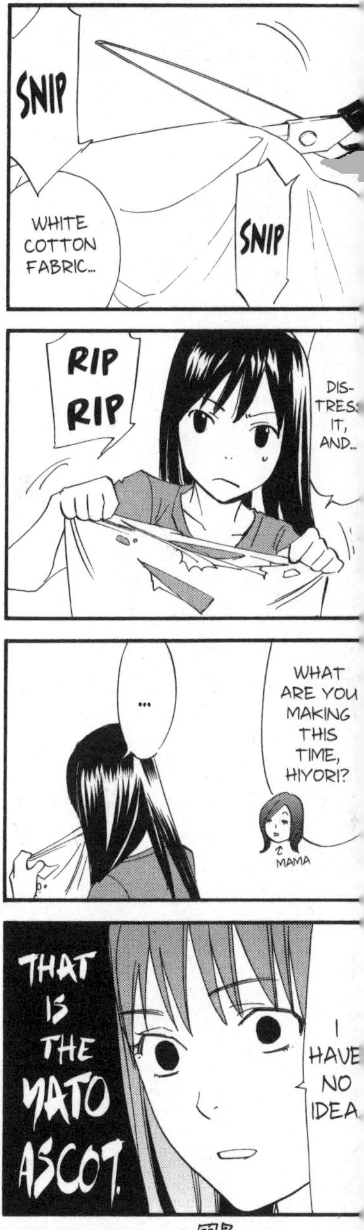
SNIP
SNIP
WHITE COTTON FABRIC...
DIS-TRES IT, AND...
RIP RIP
WHAT ARE YOU MAKING THIS TIME, HIYORI?
MAMA
...
I HAVE NO IDEA.
THAT IS THE YATO ASCOT.

COME TO THINK OF IT...

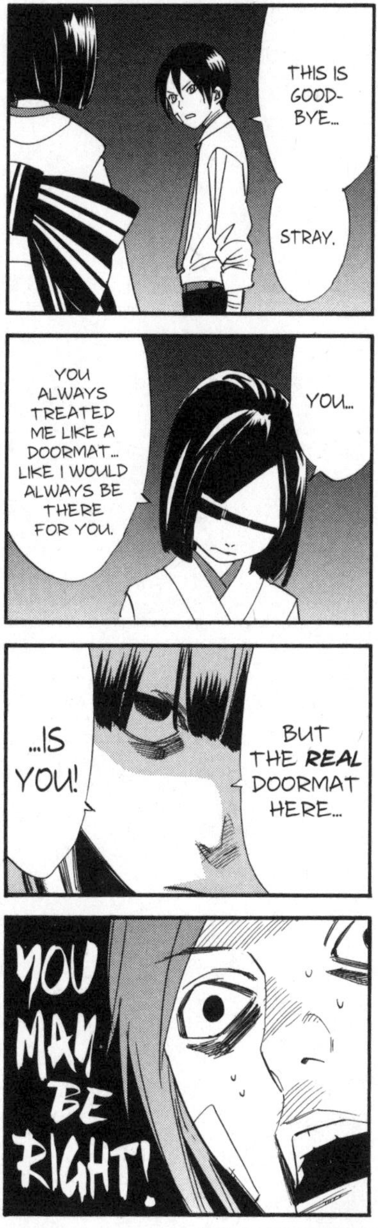
THIS IS GOOD-BYE...
STRAY.
YOU...
YOU ALWAYS TREATED ME LIKE A DOORMAT... LIKE I WOULD ALWAYS BE THERE FOR YOU.
BUT THE **REAL** DOORMAT HERE...
...IS YOU!
YOU MAY BE RIGHT!

THANK YOU TO EVERYONE WHO READ THIS FAR!

TRANSLATION NOTES

Japanese is a tricky language for most Westerners, and translation is often more art than science. For your edification and reading pleasure, here are notes on some of the places where we could have gone in a different direction in our translation of the work, or where a Japanese cultural reference is used.

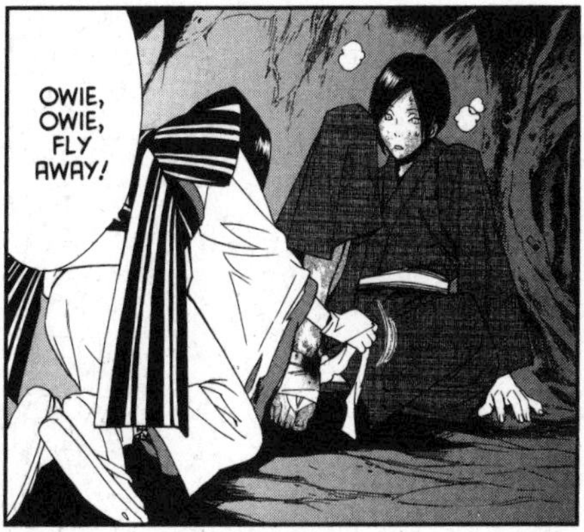
OWIE, OWIE, FLY AWAY!

Owie, owie, fly away, page 26
To make someone feel better when they have a boo-boo, it's common to put one's hands over the injury and make a gesture to indicate tossing the pain away. This is a placebo usually used by mothers on their minorly injured children, much like "kissing it better."

Soul summoning, page 74
Kofuku is referring to an old tradition called *tamayobi* or *tamayobai* (literally, "soul summoning"). Death was seen as something that could be reversed, and so the bereaved would attempt to call the deceased's soul back to the world of the living. The attempt was made by either climbing to the roof or looking down a well, then shouting the departed's name.

Incidentally, the modern Japanese word for "revive" or "come back to life" is *yomigaeru*—literally, "to return from Yomi."

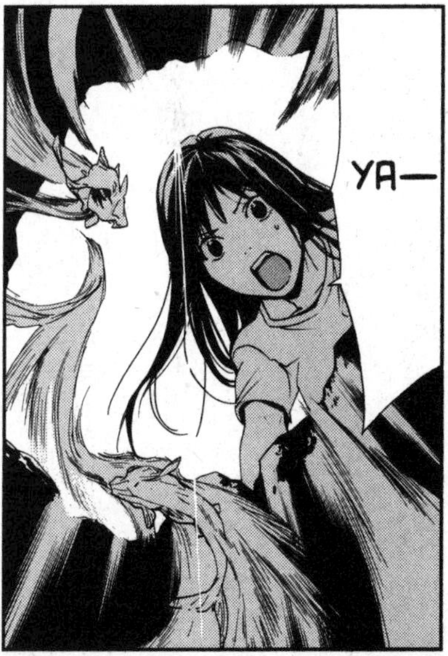
YA—

Yaboku, page 88

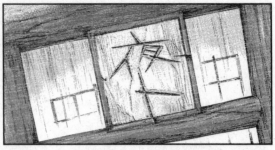

Hiyori's sudden inspiration may seem random at first, but in fact, the series has told us from the very beginning what Yato's real name is. His name is written in Japanese, as seen on his shrine, like this: 夜卜. Up until now, Yato has been letting his friends and potential followers think that it was the Chinese character "*ya* (night)" and the *katakana* character "*to*." The reader may remember that *kana* (as in *katakana*) can mean "borrowed name," in other words telling us that Yato is not his real name. The reader may also remember that there is a word for the Chinese characters that also means "true name," *mana*. In other words, in Yato's real name, what looks like a *katakana* character pronounced *to* is actually a Chinese character, which is not ever pronounced *to*, but rather has the sound reading (*on-yomi*) of *boku*. Fortunately for Yato and his friends, Hiyori has a strong knowledge of *kanji*.

For the curious, the name Yaboku means "night diviner."

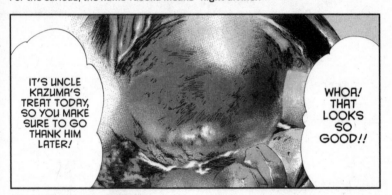

WHOA! THAT LOOKS SO GOOD!!
IT'S UNCLE KAZUMA'S TREAT TODAY, SO YOU MAKE SURE TO GO THANK HIM LATER!

Uncle Kazuma, page 117

The Japanese word for "uncle" is *oji-san*, which is also a general term of address for any middle-aged man. But in fact, Yato did not really imply that Kazuma looks old—he called him Kazuma-*oniisan*, which means "Big Brother Kazuma." The reason Yato made it a point to give Kazuma any sort of title is to establish a close-knit relationship, perhaps a familial one, between Kazuma and Mini-Ebisu, either to encourage Ebisu to spend more, or possibly to get himself out of trouble when Kazuma inevitably finds out that Yato stole his stuff. Who could say no to adorable little Ebi? (It doesn't hurt that Ebisu is an old friend of Bishamon's.)

The translators opted to use "Uncle" instead of "Brother," because the English use of the word "uncle" usually doesn't come with age restrictions, and "uncle" is used more commonly as a friendly nickname for a respected male figure.

Pearls before Kuraha-san, page 155

In English, there is a saying, "pearls before swine," which means "giving something valuable to someone who won't ever appreciate it." The Japanese version of the saying translates to "*koban* before kitties." A *koban* is a valuable gold coin used as currency in the Edo era. Once again, Kuraha is being treated like a lowly housecat, and one who doesn't understand the value of money.

BUT IT NEVER TAKES HIM LONG TO REALIZE THAT PEOPLE NEED MORE THAN MONEY TO FIND HAPPINESS.

THANK YOU!

EDACHI.

Edachi, page 157

The name Edachi is represented by the character 役 (*yaku*), which means "service." But the word *edachi* refers to laborers or soldiers who were drafted into compulsory service by the Imperial Court. As for what this says about Edachi's relationship to the crafter, that has yet to be revealed.

Pig-Faced Leather Jacket, page 188

The translators would like to apologize for misrepresenting the fish presented in this comic. Fish experts may notice that this is actually a black scraper, from the same family of fish as the pig-faced leather jacket, but due to the translators' inability to come up with insults related to Ôkuninushi's face and hairline based on the name black scraper, we hoped the black scraper wouldn't mind posing as its cousin. The black scraper's Japanese name is *umazurahagi*. With a simple mispronunciation (*umazurahage*), the name can mean "horse-faced baldy." Ôkuninushi takes the insult a step further, and asks, "Who are you saying has a horse face and M-pattern baldness?"

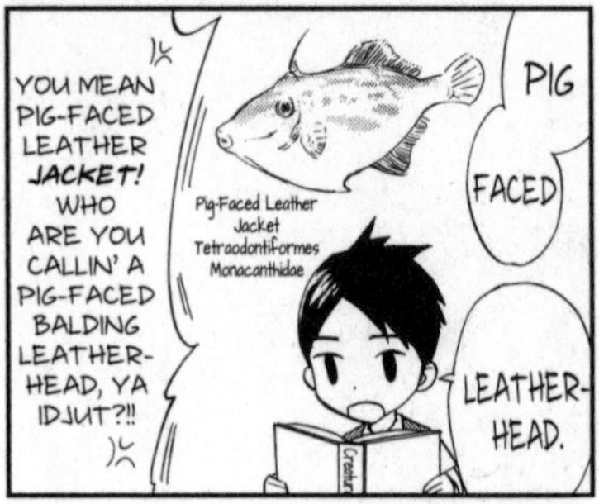
PIG
FACED
LEATHER-HEAD.
Pig-Faced Leather Jacket Tetraodontiformes Monacanthidae
YOU MEAN PIG-FACED LEATHER JACKET! WHO ARE YOU CALLIN' A PIG-FACED BALDING LEATHER-HEAD, YA IDJUT?!!

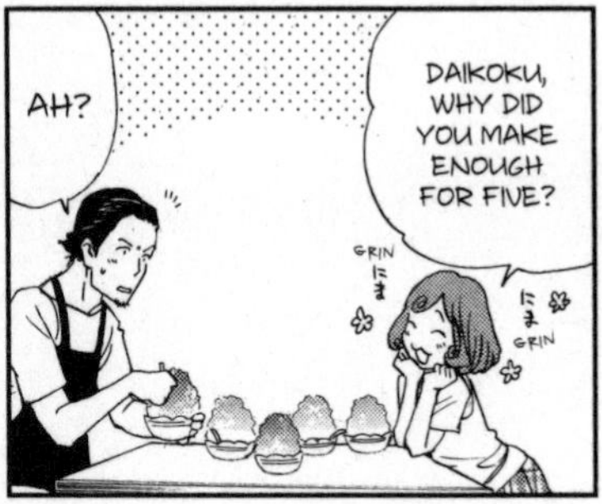
DAIKOKU, WHY DID YOU MAKE ENOUGH FOR FIVE?
GRIN
GRIN
AH?

Big Daddy, page 190

While Daikoku is a large man who acts very fatherly, it may also be interesting to note that *Big Daddy* is part of the name of a Japanese reality TV show about a man with eight children.

The Yato Ascot, page 191

The translators felt the readers might appreciate a little bit of clarification on the lack of clarity about Yato's "ascot." The Japanese term used is *yurufuwa*, which means "loose and airy" and is usually used to refer to hairstyles, so while Yato uses the word proudly, it's still up to his friends to figure out what in the world he means by it.

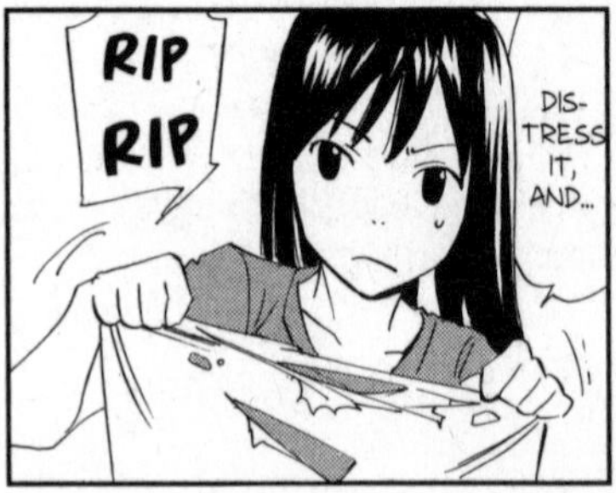
DIS-TRESS IT, AND...
RIP
RIP

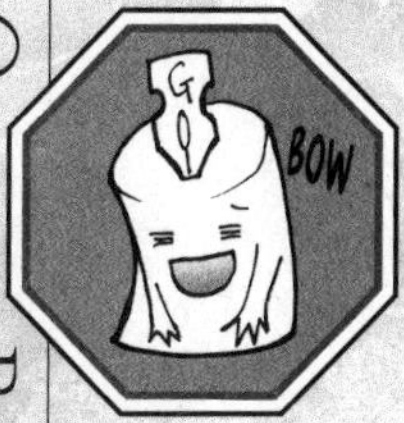
BOW

Before I knew it, I'd reached my goal of ten volumes. It's thanks to all of you that the series has made it this far. I appreciate all of the fan letters and gifts you've sent me; I carefully store them and put some of them up to look at. I can't even say how much support they give me... Thank you so, so much!
Now I'm starting to cry...
The words really sink in...
I'll keep working hard to create a work that will always have some place in your memories!

Adachitoka

DON'T MISS THE MOST ACCLAIMED ACTION MANGA OF 2013!

Gripping doesn't begin to describe Vinland Saga. stars."
—ICv2

Deeply engrossing… If you have any interest at l in Vikings, the Medieval period, or pirates, this not a series you want to miss."
—Anime News Network

"The art is gorgeous, a combination of beautiful cartooning and realistic backgrounds. Yukimura is also a master of pacing, both in frenetic battle scenes and charged emotional moments."
—Faith Erin Hicks, *Friends With Boys*

"For those who love Berserk, you'll love this too… Worth the long wait."
—A Case Suitable for Treatment

"It will be impossible to stop watching this story unfold."
—Japan Media Arts Awards jury

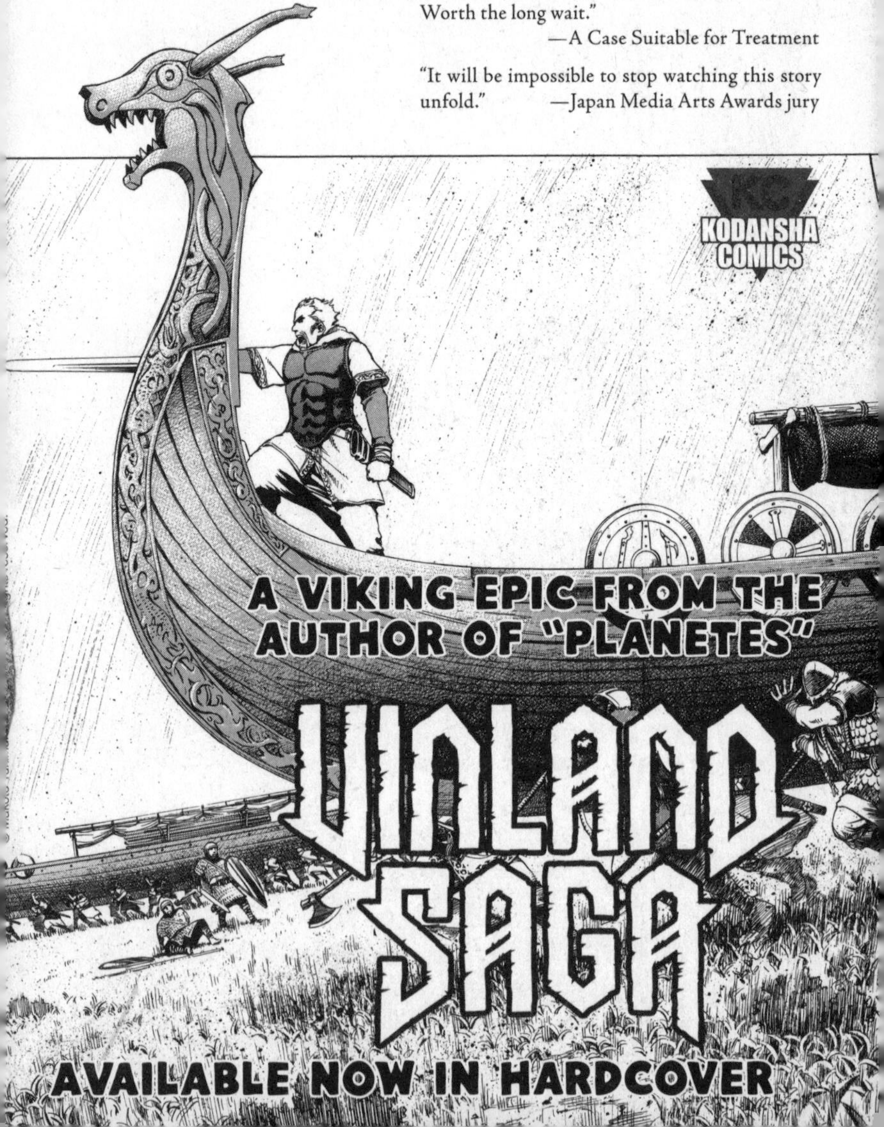

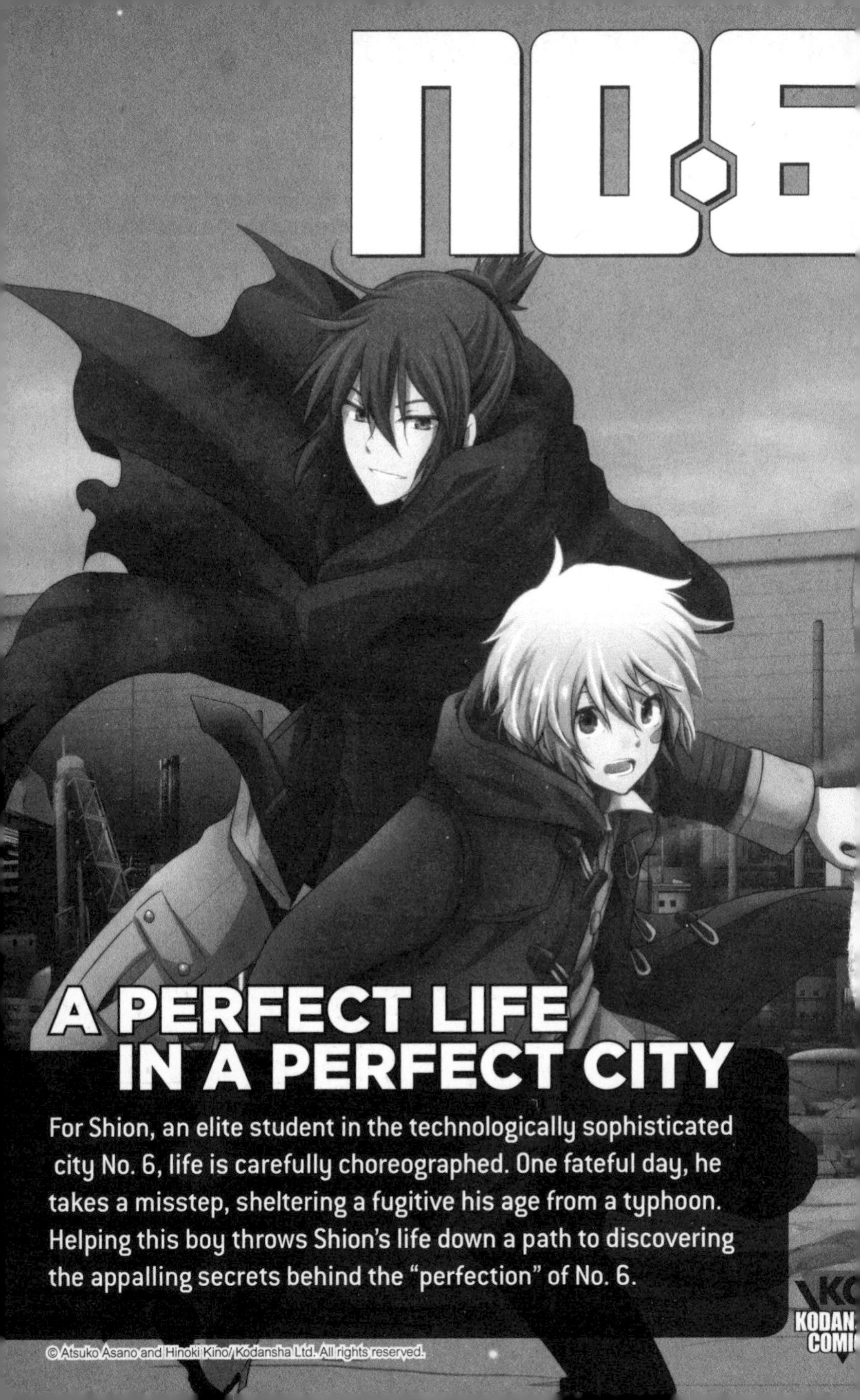
NO.6
A PERFECT LIFE
IN A PERFECT CITY
For Shion, an elite student in the technologically sophisticated city No. 6, life is carefully choreographed. One fateful day, he takes a misstep, sheltering a fugitive his age from a typhoon. Helping this boy throws Shion's life down a path to discovering the appalling secrets behind the "perfection" of No. 6.
KODAN
COMI
© Atsuko Asano and Hinoki Kino/Kodansha Ltd. All rights reserved.

Noragami: Stray God volume 10 is a work of fiction. Names, characters, places, and incidents are the products of the author's imagination or are used fictitiously. Any resemblance to actual events, locales, or persons, living or dead, is entirely coincidental.

A Kodansha Comics Trade Paperback Original.

Noragami: Stray God volume 10 copyright © 2014 Adachitoka
English translation copyright © 2016 Adachitoka

All rights reserved.

Published in the United States by Kodansha Comics, an imprint of Kodansha USA Publishing, LLC, New York.

Publication rights for this English edition arranged through Kodansha Ltd., Tokyo.

First published in Japan in 2014 by Kodansha Ltd., Tokyo.

ISBN 978-1-63236-213-1

Printed in the United States of America.

www.kodanshacomics.com

9 8 7 6 5 4 3 2 1

Editor: Lauren Scanlan
Translator: Alethea Nibley & Athena Nibley
Lettering: Lys Blakeslee